The Java EE 6 Tutorial

Basic Concepts

Fourth Edition

The Java EE 6 Tutorial

Basic Concepts

Fourth Edition

Eric Jendrock, Ian Evans, Devika Gollapudi,
Kim Haase, Chinmayee Srivathsa

✦✦ Addison-Wesley

Upper Saddle River, NJ • Boston • Indianapolis • San Francisco
New York • Toronto • Montreal • London • Munich • Paris • Madrid
Capetown • Sydney • Tokyo • Singapore • Mexico City

Many of the designations used by manufacturers and sellers to distinguish their products are claimed as trademarks. Where those designations appear in this book, and the publisher was aware of a trademark claim, the designations have been printed with initial capital letters or in all capitals.

Oracle and Java are registered trademarks of Oracle and/or its affiliates. Other names may be trademarks of their respective owners.

The authors and publisher have taken care in the preparation of this book, but make no expressed or implied warranty of any kind and assume no responsibility for errors or omissions. No liability is assumed for incidental or consequential damages in connection with or arising out of the use of the information or programs contained herein.

This document is provided for information purposes only and the contents hereof are subject to change without notice. This document is not warranted to be error-free, nor subject to any other warranties or conditions, whether expressed orally or implied in law, including implied warranties and conditions of merchantability or fitness for a particular purpose. We specifically disclaim any liability with respect to this document and no contractual obligations are formed either directly or indirectly by this document. This document may not be reproduced or transmitted in any form or by any means, electronic or mechanical, for any purpose, without our prior written permission.

The publisher offers excellent discounts on this book when ordered in quantity for bulk purchases or special sales, which may include electronic versions and/or custom covers and content particular to your business, training goals, marketing focus, and branding interests. For more information, please contact

> U.S. Corporate and Government Sales
> (800) 382-3419
> corpsales@pearsontechgroup.com

For sales outside the United States, please contact

> International Sales
> international@pearsoned.com

Visit us on the Web: informit.com/ph

Library of Congress Cataloging-in-Publication Data

The Java EE 6 tutorial : basic concepts / Eric Jendrock ... [et al.]. --
4th ed.
   p.   cm.
 Includes index.
  ISBN 0-13-708185-5 (pbk. : alk. paper)
1.   Java (Computer program language) 2.   Application program interfaces
(Computer software) 3.   Application software—Development. 4.   Internet
programming.   I. Jendrock, Eric.
  QA76.73.J38J3652 2010
  006.7'6--dc22

                                    2010025759

ISBN-13: 978-013-708185-1
ISBN-10:   0-137-08185-5

Text printed in the United States on recycled paper at Edwards Brothers in Ann Arbor, Michigan.
First printing, August, 2010

Contents

Preface

This tutorial is a guide to developing enterprise applications for the Java Platform, Enterprise Edition 6 (Java EE 6) using GlassFish Server Open Source Edition.

Oracle GlassFish Server, a Java EE compatible application server, is based on GlassFish Server Open Source Edition, the leading open-source and open-community platform for building and deploying next-generation applications and services. GlassFish Server Open Source Edition, developed by the GlassFish project open-source community at https://glassfish.dev.java.net/, is the first compatible implementation of the Java EE 6 platform specification. This lightweight, flexible, and open-source application server enables organizations not only to leverage the new capabilities introduced within the Java EE 6 specification, but also to add to their existing capabilities through a faster and more streamlined development and deployment cycle. Oracle GlassFish Server, the product version, and GlassFish Server Open Source Edition, the open-source version, are hereafter referred to as GlassFish Server.

The following topics are addressed here:

- "Before You Read This Book" on page xxi
- "Oracle GlassFish Server Documentation Set" on page xxii
- "Related Documentation" on page xxiv
- "Symbol Conventions" on page xxiv
- "Typographic Conventions" on page xxv
- "Default Paths and File Names" on page xxv
- "Documentation, Support, and Training" on page xxvi
- "Searching Oracle Product Documentation" on page xxvii
- "Third-Party Web Site References" on page xxvii

Before You Read This Book

Before proceeding with this tutorial, you should have a good knowledge of the Java programming language. A good way to get to that point is to work through *The Java Tutorial, Fourth Edition*, Sharon Zakhour et al. (Addison-Wesley, 2006).

Oracle GlassFish Server Documentation Set

The GlassFish Server documentation set describes deployment planning and system installation. The Uniform Resource Locator (URL) for GlassFish Server documentation is http://docs.sun.com/coll/1343.13. For an introduction to GlassFish Server, refer to the books in the order in which they are listed in the following table.

TABLE P–1   Books in the GlassFish Server Documentation Set

Book Title	Description
Release Notes	Provides late-breaking information about the software and the documentation and includes a comprehensive, table-based summary of the supported hardware, operating system, Java Development Kit (JDK), and database drivers.
Quick Start Guide	Explains how to get started with the GlassFish Server product.
Installation Guide	Explains how to install the software and its components.
Upgrade Guide	Explains how to upgrade to the latest version of GlassFish Server. This guide also describes differences between adjacent product releases and configuration options that can result in incompatibility with the product specifications.
Administration Guide	Explains how to configure, monitor, and manage GlassFish Server subsystems and components from the command line by using the asadmin(1M) utility. Instructions for performing these tasks from the Administration Console are provided in the Administration Console online help.
Application Deployment Guide	Explains how to assemble and deploy applications to the GlassFish Server and provides information about deployment descriptors.
Your First Cup: An Introduction to the Java EE Platform	For beginning Java EE programmers, provides a short tutorial that explains the entire process for developing a simple enterprise application. The sample application is a web application that consists of a component that is based on the Enterprise JavaBeans specification, a JAX-RS web service, and a JavaServer Faces component for the web front end.
Application Development Guide	Explains how to create and implement Java Platform, Enterprise Edition (Java EE platform) applications that are intended to run on the GlassFish Server. These applications follow the open Java standards model for Java EE components and application programmer interfaces (APIs). This guide provides information about developer tools, security, and debugging.

TABLE P–1 Books in the GlassFish Server Documentation Set   *(Continued)*

Book Title	Description
Add-On Component Development Guide	Explains how to use published interfaces of GlassFish Server to develop add-on components for GlassFish Server. This document explains how to perform *only* those tasks that ensure that the add-on component is suitable for GlassFish Server.
Embedded Server Guide	Explains how to run applications in embedded GlassFish Server and to develop applications in which GlassFish Server is embedded.
Scripting Framework Guide	Explains how to develop scripting applications in such languages as Ruby on Rails and Groovy on Grails for deployment to GlassFish Server.
Troubleshooting Guide	Describes common problems that you might encounter when using GlassFish Server and explains how to solve them.
Error Message Reference	Describes error messages that you might encounter when using GlassFish Server.
Reference Manual	Provides reference information in man page format for GlassFish Server administration commands, utility commands, and related concepts.
Domain File Format Reference	Describes the format of the GlassFish Server configuration file, `domain.xml`.
Java EE 6 Tutorial	Explains how to use Java EE 6 platform technologies and APIs to develop Java EE applications.
Message Queue Release Notes	Describes new features, compatibility issues, and existing bugs for GlassFish Message Queue.
Message Queue Administration Guide	Explains how to set up and manage a Message Queue messaging system.
Message Queue Developer's Guide for JMX Clients	Describes the application programming interface in Message Queue for programmatically configuring and monitoring Message Queue resources in conformance with the Java Management Extensions (JMX).

Related Documentation

Javadoc tool reference documentation for packages that are provided with GlassFish Server is available as follows.

- The API specification for version 6 of Java EE is located at http://download.oracle.com/docs/cd/E17410_01/javaee/6/api/.

- The API specification for GlassFish Server 3.0.1, including Java EE 6 platform packages and nonplatform packages that are specific to the GlassFish Server product, is located at https://glassfish.dev.java.net/nonav/docs/v3/api/.

Additionally, the Java EE Specifications at http://www.oracle.com/technetwork/java/javaee/tech/index.html might be useful.

For information about creating enterprise applications in the NetBeans Integrated Development Environment (IDE), see http://www.netbeans.org/kb/.

For information about the Java DB database for use with the GlassFish Server, see http://www.oracle.com/technetwork/java/javadb/overview/index.html.

The GlassFish Samples project is a collection of sample applications that demonstrate a broad range of Java EE technologies. The GlassFish Samples are bundled with the Java EE Software Development Kit (SDK) and are also available from the GlassFish Samples project page at https://glassfish-samples.dev.java.net/.

Symbol Conventions

The following table explains symbols that might be used in this book.

TABLE P–2   Symbol Conventions

Symbol	Description	Example	Meaning
[ ]	Contains optional arguments and command options.	ls [-l]	The -l option is not required.
{ | }	Contains a set of choices for a required command option.	-d {y|n}	The -d option requires that you use either the y argument or the n argument.
${ }	Indicates a variable reference.	${com.sun.javaRoot}	References the value of the com.sun.javaRoot variable.
-	Joins simultaneous multiple keystrokes.	Control-A	Press the Control key while you press the A key.

TABLE P–2 Symbol Conventions   *(Continued)*

Symbol	Description	Example	Meaning
+	Joins consecutive multiple keystrokes.	Ctrl+A+N	Press the Control key, release it, and then press the subsequent keys.
→	Indicates menu item selection in a graphical user interface.	File → New → Templates	From the File menu, choose New. From the New submenu, choose Templates.

Typographic Conventions

The following table describes the typographic changes that are used in this book.

TABLE P–3 Typographic Conventions

Typeface	Meaning	Example
AaBbCc123	The names of commands, files, and directories, and onscreen computer output	Edit your `.login` file. Use `ls -a` to list all files. `machine_name% you have mail.`
AaBbCc123	What you type, contrasted with onscreen computer output	`machine_name%` **su** `Password:`
AaBbCc123	A placeholder to be replaced with a real name or value	The command to remove a file is `rm` *filename*.
AaBbCc123	Book titles, new terms, and terms to be emphasized (note that some emphasized items appear bold online)	Read Chapter 6 in the *User's Guide*. A *cache* is a copy that is stored locally. Do *not* save the file.

Default Paths and File Names

The following table describes the default paths and file names that are used in this book.

TABLE P–4 Default Paths and File Names

Placeholder	Description	Default Value
as-install	Represents the base installation directory for the GlassFish Server or the SDK of which the GlassFish Server is a part.	Installations on the Solaris operating system, Linux operating system, and Mac operating system: *user's-home-directory*/glassfishv3/glassfish Windows, all installations: *SystemDrive*:\glassfishv3\glassfish
as-install-parent	Represents the parent of the base installation directory for GlassFish Server.	Installations on the Solaris operating system, Linux operating system, and Mac operating system: *user's-home-directory*/glassfishv3 Windows, all installations: *SystemDrive*:\glassfishv3
tut-install	Represents the base installation directory for the *Java EE Tutorial* after you install the GlassFish Server or the SDK and run the Update Tool.	*as-install*/docs/javaee-tutorial
domain-root-dir	Represents the directory in which a domain is created by default.	*as-install*/domains/
domain-dir	Represents the directory in which a domain's configuration is stored. In configuration files, *domain-dir* is represented as follows: ${com.sun.aas.instanceRoot}	*domain-root-dir*/*domain-name*

Documentation, Support, and Training

The Oracle web site provides information about the following additional resources:

- Documentation (http://docs.sun.com/)
- Support (http://www.sun.com/support/)
- Training (http://education.oracle.com/)

Searching Oracle Product Documentation

Besides searching Oracle product documentation from the `http://docs.sun.com` web site, you can use a search engine by typing the following syntax in the search field:

search-term `site:docs.sun.com`

For example, to search for "broker," type the following:

`broker site:docs.sun.com`

To include other Oracle web sites in your search (for example, the Java Developer site on the Oracle Technology Network at `http://www.oracle.com/technetwork/java/index.html`), use `oracle.com` in place of `docs.sun.com` in the search field.

Third-Party Web Site References

Third-party URLs are referenced in this document and provide additional, related information.

Note – Oracle is not responsible for the availability of third-party web sites mentioned in this document. Oracle does not endorse and is not responsible or liable for any content, advertising, products, or other materials that are available on or through such sites or resources. Oracle will not be responsible or liable for any actual or alleged damage or loss caused or alleged to be caused by or in connection with use of or reliance on any such content, goods, or services that are available on or through such sites or resources.

Acknowledgments

The Java EE tutorial team would like to thank the Java EE specification leads: Roberto Chinnici, Bill Shannon, Kenneth Saks, Linda DeMichiel, Ed Burns, Roger Kitain, Ron Monzillo, Dhiru Pandey, Sankara Rao, Binod PG, Sivakumar Thyagarajan, Kin-Man Chung, Jan Luehe, Jitendra Kotamraju, Marc Hadley, Paul Sandoz, Gavin King, Emmanuel Bernard, Rod Johnson, Bob Lee, and Rajiv Mordani.

We would also like to thank the Java EE 6 SDK team, especially Carla Carlson, Snjezana Sevo-Zenzerovic, Adam Leftik, and John Clingan.

The JavaServer Faces technology and Facelets chapters benefited from the documentation reviews and example code contributions of Jim Driscoll and Ryan Lubke.

The EJB technology, Java Persistence API, and Criteria API chapters were written with extensive input from the EJB and Persistence teams, including Marina Vatkina and Mitesh Meswani.

We'd like to thank Pete Muir for his reviews of the CDI chapters and Tim Quinn for assistance with the application client container. Thanks also to the NetBeans engineering and documentation teams, particularly Petr Jiricka, John Jullion-Ceccarelli, and Troy Giunipero, for their help in enabling NetBeans IDE support for the code examples.

We would like to thank our manager, Alan Sommerer, for his support and steadying influence.

We also thank Dwayne Wolff for developing the illustrations and Jordan Douglas for updating them. Julie Bettis, our editor, contributed greatly to the readability and flow of the book. Sheila Cepero helped smooth our path in many ways. Steve Cogorno provided invaluable help with our tools.

Finally, we would like to express our profound appreciation to Greg Doench, John Fuller, Vicki Rowland, Evelyn Pyle, and the production team at Addison-Wesley for graciously seeing our large, complicated manuscript to publication.

Introduction

Part I introduces the platform, the tutorial, and the examples. This part contains the following chapters:

- Chapter 1, "Overview"
- Chapter 2, "Using the Tutorial Examples"

1

Overview

Developers today increasingly recognize the need for distributed, transactional, and portable applications that leverage the speed, security, and reliability of server-side technology. *Enterprise applications* provide the business logic for an enterprise. They are centrally managed and often interact with other enterprise software. In the world of information technology, enterprise applications must be designed, built, and produced for less money, with greater speed, and with fewer resources.

With the Java Platform, Enterprise Edition (Java EE), development of Java enterprise applications has never been easier or faster. The aim of the Java EE platform is to provide developers with a powerful set of APIs while shortening development time, reducing application complexity, and improving application performance.

The Java EE platform is developed through the Java Community Process (the JCP), which is responsible for all Java technologies. Expert groups, composed of interested parties, have created Java Specification Requests (JSRs) to define the various Java EE technologies. The work of the Java Community under the JCP program helps to ensure Java technology's standard of stability and cross-platform compatibility.

The Java EE platform uses a simplified programming model. XML deployment descriptors are optional. Instead, a developer can simply enter the information as an *annotation* directly into a Java source file, and the Java EE server will configure the component at deployment and runtime. These annotations are generally used to embed in a program data that would otherwise be furnished in a deployment descriptor. With annotations, you put the specification information in your code next to the program element affected.

In the Java EE platform, dependency injection can be applied to all resources that a component needs, effectively hiding the creation and lookup of resources from application code. Dependency injection can be used in EJB containers, web containers, and application clients. Dependency injection allows the Java EE container to automatically insert references to other required components or resources, using annotations.

This tutorial uses examples to describe the features available in the Java EE platform for developing enterprise applications. Whether you are a new or experienced Enterprise developer, you should find the examples and accompanying text a valuable and accessible knowledge base for creating your own solutions.

If you are new to Java EE enterprise application development, this chapter is a good place to start. Here you will review development basics, learn about the Java EE architecture and APIs, become acquainted with important terms and concepts, and find out how to approach Java EE application programming, assembly, and deployment.

The following topics are addressed here:

- "Java EE 6 Platform Highlights" on page 4
- "Java EE Application Model" on page 5
- "Distributed Multitiered Applications" on page 6
- "Java EE Containers" on page 13
- "Web Services Support" on page 15
- "Java EE Application Assembly and Deployment" on page 17
- "Packaging Applications" on page 17
- "Development Roles" on page 19
- "Java EE 6 APIs" on page 22
- "Java EE 6 APIs in the Java Platform, Standard Edition 6.0" on page 31
- "GlassFish Server Tools" on page 34

Java EE 6 Platform Highlights

The most important goal of the Java EE 6 platform is to simplify development by providing a common foundation for the various kinds of components in the Java EE platform. Developers benefit from productivity improvements with more annotations and less XML configuration, more Plain Old Java Objects (POJOs), and simplified packaging. The Java EE 6 platform includes the following new features:

- Profiles: configurations of the Java EE platform targeted at specific classes of applications. Specifically, the Java EE 6 platform introduces a lightweight Web Profile targeted at next-generation web applications, as well as a Full Profile that contains all Java EE technologies and provides the full power of the Java EE 6 platform for enterprise applications.

- New technologies, including the following:

    - Java API for RESTful Web Services (JAX-RS)

    - Managed Beans

    - Contexts and Dependency Injection for the Java EE Platform (JSR 299), informally known as CDI

- Dependency Injection for Java (JSR 330)
- Bean Validation (JSR 303)
- Java Authentication Service Provider Interface for Containers (JASPIC)
- New features for Enterprise JavaBeans (EJB) components (see "Enterprise JavaBeans Technology" on page 25 for details)
- New features for servlets (see "Java Servlet Technology" on page 26 for details)
- New features for JavaServer Faces components (see "JavaServer Faces Technology" on page 26 for details)

Java EE Application Model

The Java EE application model begins with the Java programming language and the Java virtual machine. The proven portability, security, and developer productivity they provide forms the basis of the application model. Java EE is designed to support applications that implement enterprise services for customers, employees, suppliers, partners, and others who make demands on or contributions to the enterprise. Such applications are inherently complex, potentially accessing data from a variety of sources and distributing applications to a variety of clients.

To better control and manage these applications, the business functions to support these various users are conducted in the middle tier. The middle tier represents an environment that is closely controlled by an enterprise's information technology department. The middle tier is typically run on dedicated server hardware and has access to the full services of the enterprise.

The Java EE application model defines an architecture for implementing services as multitier applications that deliver the scalability, accessibility, and manageability needed by enterprise-level applications. This model partitions the work needed to implement a multitier service into the following parts:

- The business and presentation logic to be implemented by the developer
- The standard system services provided by the Java EE platform

The developer can rely on the platform to provide solutions for the hard systems-level problems of developing a multitier service.

Distributed Multitiered Applications

The Java EE platform uses a distributed multitiered application model for enterprise applications. Application logic is divided into components according to function, and the application components that make up a Java EE application are installed on various machines, depending on the tier in the multitiered Java EE environment to which the application component belongs.

Figure 1–1 shows two multitiered Java EE applications divided into the tiers described in the following list. The Java EE application parts shown in Figure 1–1 are presented in "Java EE Components" on page 8.

- Client-tier components run on the client machine.
- Web-tier components run on the Java EE server.
- Business-tier components run on the Java EE server.
- Enterprise information system (EIS)-tier software runs on the EIS server.

Although a Java EE application can consist of the three or four tiers shown in Figure 1–1, Java EE multitiered applications are generally considered to be three-tiered applications because they are distributed over three locations: client machines, the Java EE server machine, and the database or legacy machines at the back end. Three-tiered applications that run in this way extend the standard two-tiered client-and-server model by placing a multithreaded application server between the client application and back-end storage.

FIGURE 1–1 Multitiered Applications

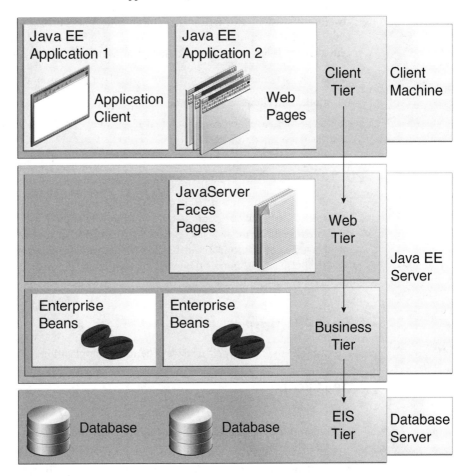

Security

Although other enterprise application models require platform-specific security measures in each application, the Java EE security environment enables security constraints to be defined at deployment time. The Java EE platform makes applications portable to a wide variety of security implementations by shielding application developers from the complexity of implementing security features.

The Java EE platform provides standard declarative access control rules that are defined by the developer and interpreted when the application is deployed on the server. Java EE also provides standard login mechanisms so application developers do not have to implement these mechanisms in their applications. The same application works in a variety of security environments without changing the source code.

Java EE Components

Java EE applications are made up of components. A *Java EE component* is a self-contained functional software unit that is assembled into a Java EE application with its related classes and files and that communicates with other components.

The Java EE specification defines the following Java EE components.

- Application clients and applets are components that run on the client.

- Java Servlet, JavaServer Faces, and JavaServer Pages (JSP) technology components are web components that run on the server.

- Enterprise JavaBeans (EJB) components (enterprise beans) are business components that run on the server.

Java EE components are written in the Java programming language and are compiled in the same way as any program in the language. The difference between Java EE components and "standard" Java classes is that Java EE components are assembled into a Java EE application, are verified to be well formed and in compliance with the Java EE specification, and are deployed to production, where they are run and managed by the Java EE server.

Java EE Clients

A Java EE client is usually either a web client or an application client.

Web Clients

A *web client* consists of two parts:

- Dynamic web pages containing various types of markup language (HTML, XML, and so on), which are generated by web components running in the web tier

- A web browser, which renders the pages received from the server

A web client is sometimes called a *thin client*. Thin clients usually do not query databases, execute complex business rules, or connect to legacy applications. When you use a thin client, such heavyweight operations are off-loaded to enterprise beans executing on the Java EE server, where they can leverage the security, speed, services, and reliability of Java EE server-side technologies.

Application Clients

An *application client* runs on a client machine and provides a way for users to handle tasks that require a richer user interface than can be provided by a markup language. An application client typically has a graphical user interface (GUI) created from the Swing or the Abstract Window Toolkit (AWT) API, but a command-line interface is certainly possible.

Application clients directly access enterprise beans running in the business tier. However, if application requirements warrant it, an application client can open an HTTP connection to establish communication with a servlet running in the web tier. Application clients written in languages other than Java can interact with Java EE servers, enabling the Java EE platform to interoperate with legacy systems, clients, and non-Java languages.

Applets

A web page received from the web tier can include an embedded applet. Written in the Java programming language, an *applet* is a small client application that executes in the Java virtual machine installed in the web browser. However, client systems will likely need the Java Plug-in and possibly a security policy file for the applet to successfully execute in the web browser.

Web components are the preferred API for creating a web client program, because no plug-ins or security policy files are needed on the client systems. Also, web components enable cleaner and more modular application design because they provide a way to separate applications programming from web page design. Personnel involved in web page design thus do not need to understand Java programming language syntax to do their jobs.

The JavaBeans Component Architecture

The server and client tiers might also include components based on the JavaBeans component architecture (JavaBeans components) to manage the data flow between the following:

- An application client or applet and components running on the Java EE server
- Server components and a database

JavaBeans components are not considered Java EE components by the Java EE specification.

JavaBeans components have properties and have get and set methods for accessing the properties. JavaBeans components used in this way are typically simple in design and implementation but should conform to the naming and design conventions outlined in the JavaBeans component architecture.

Java EE Server Communications

Figure 1–2 shows the various elements that can make up the client tier. The client communicates with the business tier running on the Java EE server either directly or, as in the case of a client running in a browser, by going through web pages or servlets running in the web tier.

FIGURE 1–2 Server Communication

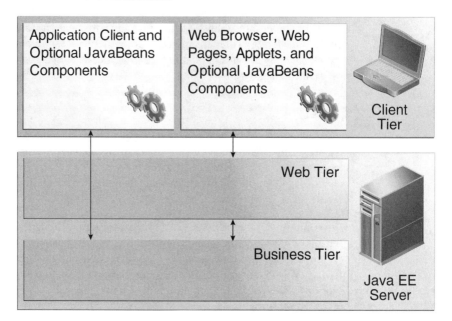

Web Components

Java EE web components are either servlets or web pages created using JavaServer Faces technology and/or JSP technology (JSP pages). *Servlets* are Java programming language classes that dynamically process requests and construct responses. *JSP pages* are text-based documents that execute as servlets but allow a more natural approach to creating static content. *JavaServer Faces technology* builds on servlets and JSP technology and provides a user interface component framework for web applications.

Static HTML pages and applets are bundled with web components during application assembly but are not considered web components by the Java EE specification. Server-side utility classes can also be bundled with web components and, like HTML pages, are not considered web components.

As shown in Figure 1–3, the web tier, like the client tier, might include a JavaBeans component to manage the user input and send that input to enterprise beans running in the business tier for processing.

FIGURE 1-3   Web Tier and Java EE Applications

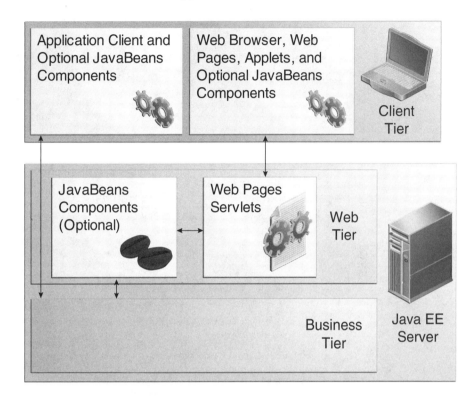

Business Components

Business code, which is logic that solves or meets the needs of a particular business domain, such as banking, retail, or finance, is handled by enterprise beans running in either the business tier or the web tier. Figure 1–4 shows how an enterprise bean receives data from client programs, processes it (if necessary), and sends it to the enterprise information system tier for storage. An enterprise bean also retrieves data from storage, processes it (if necessary), and sends it back to the client program.

FIGURE 1-4   Business and EIS Tiers

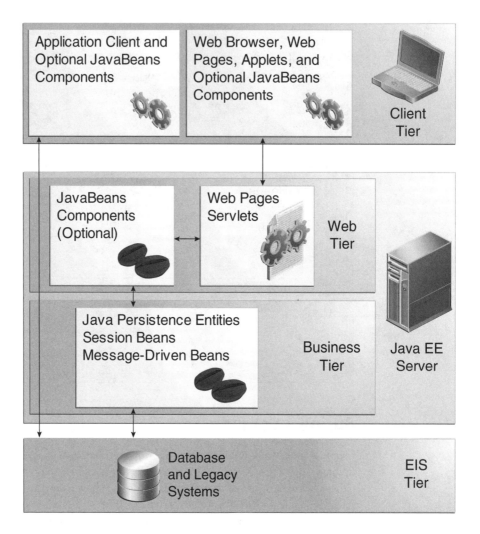

Enterprise Information System Tier

The enterprise information system tier handles EIS software and includes enterprise infrastructure systems, such as enterprise resource planning (ERP), mainframe transaction processing, database systems, and other legacy information systems. For example, Java EE application components might need access to enterprise information systems for database connectivity.

Java EE Containers

Normally, thin-client multitiered applications are hard to write because they involve many lines of intricate code to handle transaction and state management, multithreading, resource pooling, and other complex low-level details. The component-based and platform-independent Java EE architecture makes Java EE applications easy to write because business logic is organized into reusable components. In addition, the Java EE server provides underlying services in the form of a container for every component type. Because you do not have to develop these services yourself, you are free to concentrate on solving the business problem at hand.

Container Services

Containers are the interface between a component and the low-level platform-specific functionality that supports the component. Before it can be executed, a web, enterprise bean, or application client component must be assembled into a Java EE module and deployed into its container.

The assembly process involves specifying container settings for each component in the Java EE application and for the Java EE application itself. Container settings customize the underlying support provided by the Java EE server, including such services as security, transaction management, Java Naming and Directory Interface (JNDI) API lookups, and remote connectivity. Here are some of the highlights.

- The Java EE security model lets you configure a web component or enterprise bean so that system resources are accessed only by authorized users.

- The Java EE transaction model lets you specify relationships among methods that make up a single transaction so that all methods in one transaction are treated as a single unit.

- JNDI lookup services provide a unified interface to multiple naming and directory services in the enterprise so that application components can access these services.

- The Java EE remote connectivity model manages low-level communications between clients and enterprise beans. After an enterprise bean is created, a client invokes methods on it as if it were in the same virtual machine.

Because the Java EE architecture provides configurable services, application components within the same Java EE application can behave differently based on where they are deployed. For example, an enterprise bean can have security settings that allow it a certain level of access to database data in one production environment and another level of database access in another production environment.

The container also manages nonconfigurable services, such as enterprise bean and servlet lifecycles, database connection resource pooling, data persistence, and access to the Java EE platform APIs (see "Java EE 6 APIs" on page 22).

Container Types

The deployment process installs Java EE application components in the Java EE containers as illustrated in Figure 1–5.

FIGURE 1–5   Java EE Server and Containers

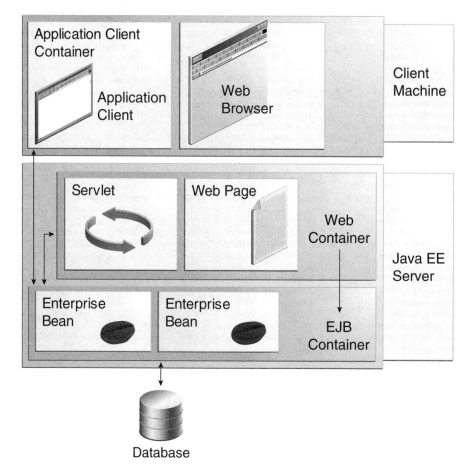

- **Java EE server**: The runtime portion of a Java EE product. A Java EE server provides EJB and web containers.
- **Enterprise JavaBeans (EJB) container**: Manages the execution of enterprise beans for Java EE applications. Enterprise beans and their container run on the Java EE server.

- **Web container**: Manages the execution of web pages, servlets, and some EJB components for Java EE applications. Web components and their container run on the Java EE server.

- **Application client container**: Manages the execution of application client components. Application clients and their container run on the client.

- **Applet container**: Manages the execution of applets. Consists of a web browser and Java Plug-in running on the client together.

Web Services Support

Web services are web-based enterprise applications that use open, XML-based standards and transport protocols to exchange data with calling clients. The Java EE platform provides the XML APIs and tools you need to quickly design, develop, test, and deploy web services and clients that fully interoperate with other web services and clients running on Java-based or non-Java-based platforms.

To write web services and clients with the Java EE XML APIs, all you do is pass parameter data to the method calls and process the data returned; for document-oriented web services, you send documents containing the service data back and forth. No low-level programming is needed, because the XML API implementations do the work of translating the application data to and from an XML-based data stream that is sent over the standardized XML-based transport protocols. These XML-based standards and protocols are introduced in the following sections.

The translation of data to a standardized XML-based data stream is what makes web services and clients written with the Java EE XML APIs fully interoperable. This does not necessarily mean that the data being transported includes XML tags, because the transported data can itself be plain text, XML data, or any kind of binary data, such as audio, video, maps, program files, computer-aided design (CAD) documents, and the like. The next section introduces XML and explains how parties doing business can use XML tags and schemas to exchange data in a meaningful way.

XML

Extensible Markup Language (XML) is a cross-platform, extensible, text-based standard for representing data. Parties that exchange XML data can create their own tags to describe the data, set up schemas to specify which tags can be used in a particular kind of XML document, and use XML style sheets to manage the display and handling of the data.

For example, a web service can use XML and a schema to produce price lists, and companies that receive the price lists and schema can have their own style sheets to handle the data in a way that best suits their needs. Here are examples.

- One company might put XML pricing information through a program to translate the XML to HTML so that it can post the price lists to its intranet.

- A partner company might put the XML pricing information through a tool to create a marketing presentation.

- Another company might read the XML pricing information into an application for processing.

SOAP Transport Protocol

Client requests and web service responses are transmitted as Simple Object Access Protocol (SOAP) messages over HTTP to enable a completely interoperable exchange between clients and web services, all running on different platforms and at various locations on the Internet. HTTP is a familiar request-and-response standard for sending messages over the Internet, and SOAP is an XML-based protocol that follows the HTTP request-and-response model.

The SOAP portion of a transported message does the following:

- Defines an XML-based envelope to describe what is in the message and explain how to process the message

- Includes XML-based encoding rules to express instances of application-defined data types within the message

- Defines an XML-based convention for representing the request to the remote service and the resulting response

WSDL Standard Format

The Web Services Description Language (WSDL) is a standardized XML format for describing network services. The description includes the name of the service, the location of the service, and ways to communicate with the service. WSDL service descriptions can be published on the Web. GlassFish Server provides a tool for generating the WSDL specification of a web service that uses remote procedure calls to communicate with clients.

Java EE Application Assembly and Deployment

A Java EE application is packaged into one or more standard units for deployment to any Java EE platform-compliant system. Each unit contains

- A functional component or components, such as an enterprise bean, web page, servlet, or applet
- An optional deployment descriptor that describes its content

Once a Java EE unit has been produced, it is ready to be deployed. Deployment typically involves using a platform's deployment tool to specify location-specific information, such as a list of local users who can access it and the name of the local database. Once deployed on a local platform, the application is ready to run.

Packaging Applications

A Java EE application is delivered in a Java Archive (JAR) file, a Web Archive (WAR) file, or an Enterprise Archive (EAR) file. A WAR or EAR file is a standard JAR (.jar) file with a .war or .ear extension. Using JAR, WAR, and EAR files and modules makes it possible to assemble a number of different Java EE applications using some of the same components. No extra coding is needed; it is only a matter of assembling (or packaging) various Java EE modules into Java EE JAR, WAR, or EAR files.

An EAR file (see Figure 1–6) contains Java EE modules and, optionally, deployment descriptors. A *deployment descriptor*, an XML document with an .xml extension, describes the deployment settings of an application, a module, or a component. Because deployment descriptor information is declarative, it can be changed without the need to modify the source code. At runtime, the Java EE server reads the deployment descriptor and acts upon the application, module, or component accordingly.

FIGURE 1–6   EAR File Structure

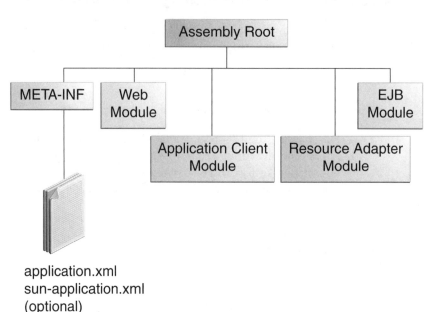

application.xml
sun-application.xml
(optional)

The two types of deployment descriptors are Java EE and runtime. A *Java EE deployment descriptor* is defined by a Java EE specification and can be used to configure deployment settings on any Java EE-compliant implementation. A *runtime deployment descriptor* is used to configure Java EE implementation-specific parameters. For example, the GlassFish Server runtime deployment descriptor contains such information as the context root of a web application, as well as GlassFish Server implementation-specific parameters, such as caching directives. The GlassFish Server runtime deployment descriptors are named sun-*moduleType*.xml and are located in the same META-INF directory as the Java EE deployment descriptor.

A *Java EE module* consists of one or more Java EE components for the same container type and, optionally, one component deployment descriptor of that type. An enterprise bean module deployment descriptor, for example, declares transaction attributes and security authorizations for an enterprise bean. A Java EE module can be deployed as a *stand-alone* module.

Java EE modules are of the following types:

- EJB modules, which contain class files for enterprise beans and an EJB deployment descriptor. EJB modules are packaged as JAR files with a `.jar` extension.

- Web modules, which contain servlet class files, web files, supporting class files, GIF and HTML files, and a web application deployment descriptor. Web modules are packaged as JAR files with a `.war` (web archive) extension.

- Application client modules, which contain class files and an application client deployment descriptor. Application client modules are packaged as JAR files with a `.jar` extension.

- Resource adapter modules, which contain all Java interfaces, classes, native libraries, and other documentation, along with the resource adapter deployment descriptor. Together, these implement the Connector architecture (see "Java EE Connector Architecture" on page 29) for a particular EIS. Resource adapter modules are packaged as JAR files with an `.rar` (resource adapter archive) extension.

Development Roles

Reusable modules make it possible to divide the application development and deployment process into distinct roles so that different people or companies can perform different parts of the process.

The first two roles, Java EE product provider and tool provider, involve purchasing and installing the Java EE product and tools. After software is purchased and installed, Java EE components can be developed by application component providers, assembled by application assemblers, and deployed by application deployers. In a large organization, each of these roles might be executed by different individuals or teams. This division of labor works because each of the earlier roles outputs a portable file that is the input for a subsequent role. For example, in the application component development phase, an enterprise bean software developer delivers EJB JAR files. In the application assembly role, another developer may combine these EJB JAR files into a Java EE application and save it in an EAR file. In the application deployment role, a system administrator at the customer site uses the EAR file to install the Java EE application into a Java EE server.

The different roles are not always executed by different people. If you work for a small company, for example, or if you are prototyping a sample application, you might perform the tasks in every phase.

Java EE Product Provider

The Java EE product provider is the company that designs and makes available for purchase the Java EE platform APIs and other features defined in the Java EE specification. Product providers are typically application server vendors that implement the Java EE platform according to the Java EE 6 Platform specification.

Tool Provider

The tool provider is the company or person who creates development, assembly, and packaging tools used by component providers, assemblers, and deployers.

Application Component Provider

The application component provider is the company or person who creates web components, enterprise beans, applets, or application clients for use in Java EE applications.

Enterprise Bean Developer

An enterprise bean developer performs the following tasks to deliver an EJB JAR file that contains one or more enterprise beans:

- Writes and compiles the source code
- Specifies the deployment descriptor (optional)
- Packages the .class files and deployment descriptor into the EJB JAR file

Web Component Developer

A web component developer performs the following tasks to deliver a WAR file containing one or more web components:

- Writes and compiles servlet source code

- Writes JavaServer Faces, JSP, and HTML files

- Specifies the deployment descriptor (optional)

- Packages the .class, .jsp, and .html files and deployment descriptor into the WAR file

Application Client Developer

An application client developer performs the following tasks to deliver a JAR file containing the application client:

- Writes and compiles the source code
- Specifies the deployment descriptor for the client (optional)
- Packages the `.class` files and deployment descriptor into the JAR file

Application Assembler

The application assembler is the company or person who receives application modules from component providers and may assemble them into a Java EE application EAR file. The assembler or deployer can edit the deployment descriptor directly or can use tools that correctly add XML tags according to interactive selections.

A software developer performs the following tasks to deliver an EAR file containing the Java EE application:

- Assembles EJB JAR and WAR files created in the previous phases into a Java EE application (EAR) file
- Specifies the deployment descriptor for the Java EE application (optional)
- Verifies that the contents of the EAR file are well formed and comply with the Java EE specification

Application Deployer and Administrator

The application deployer and administrator is the company or person who configures and deploys the Java EE application, administers the computing and networking infrastructure where Java EE applications run, and oversees the runtime environment. Duties include setting transaction controls and security attributes and specifying connections to databases.

During configuration, the deployer follows instructions supplied by the application component provider to resolve external dependencies, specify security settings, and assign transaction attributes. During installation, the deployer moves the application components to the server and generates the container-specific classes and interfaces.

A deployer or system administrator performs the following tasks to install and configure a Java EE application:

- Configures the Java EE application for the operational environment

- Verifies that the contents of the EAR file are well formed and comply with the Java EE specification

- Deploys (installs) the Java EE application EAR file into the Java EE server

Java EE 6 APIs

Figure 1–7 shows the relationships among the Java EE containers.

FIGURE 1–7 Java EE Containers

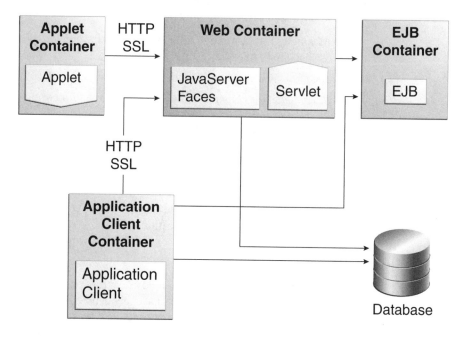

Figure 1–8 shows the availability of the Java EE 6 APIs in the web container.

FIGURE 1–8   Java EE APIs in the Web Container

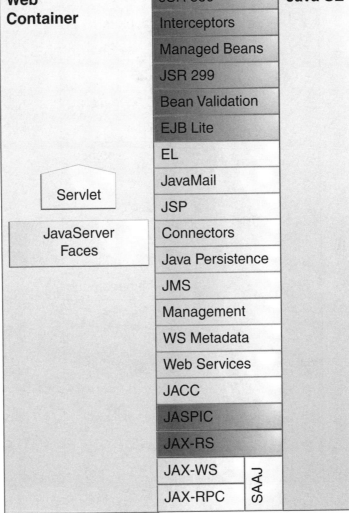

Figure 1–9 shows the availability of the Java EE 6 APIs in the EJB container.

FIGURE 1-9 Java EE APIs in the EJB Container

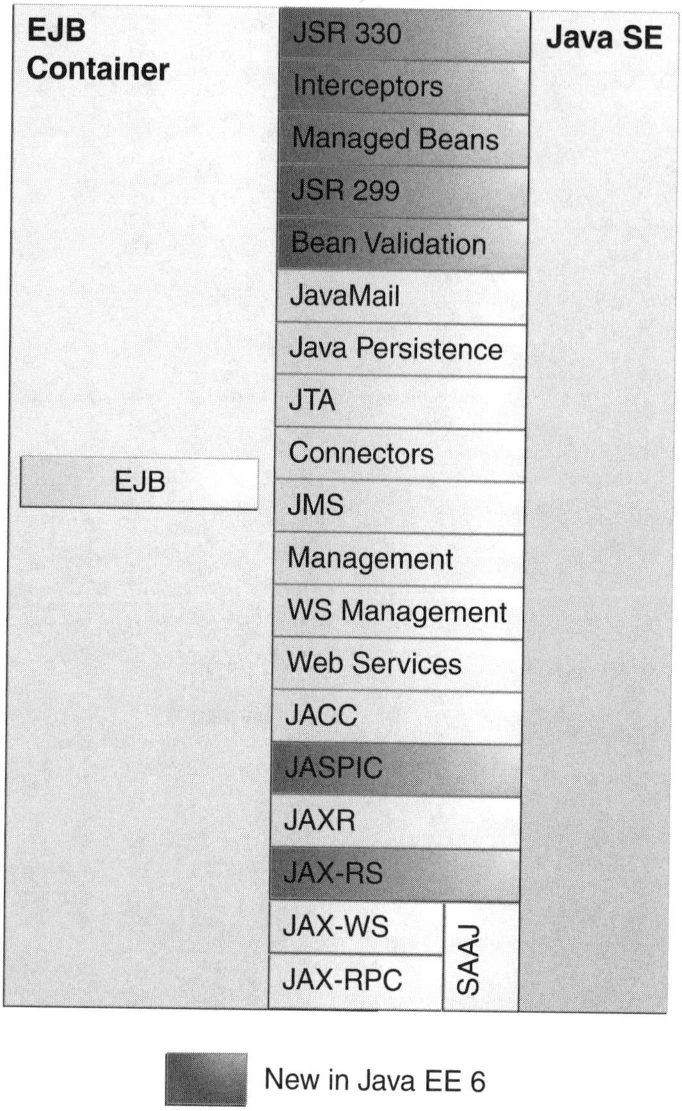

EJB Container		Java SE
	JSR 330	
	Interceptors	
	Managed Beans	
	JSR 299	
	Bean Validation	
	JavaMail	
	Java Persistence	
	JTA	
EJB	Connectors	
	JMS	
	Management	
	WS Management	
	Web Services	
	JACC	
	JASPIC	
	JAXR	
	JAX-RS	
	JAX-WS	SAAJ
	JAX-RPC	

 New in Java EE 6

Figure 1-10 shows the availability of the Java EE 6 APIs in the application client container.

FIGURE 1–10   Java EE APIs in the Application Client Container

Application Client Container	Java Persistence	Java SE
	Management	
	WS Metadata	
	Web Services	
Application Client	JSR 299	
	JMS	
	JAXR	
	JAX-WS / SAAJ	
	JAX-RPC	

New in Java EE 6

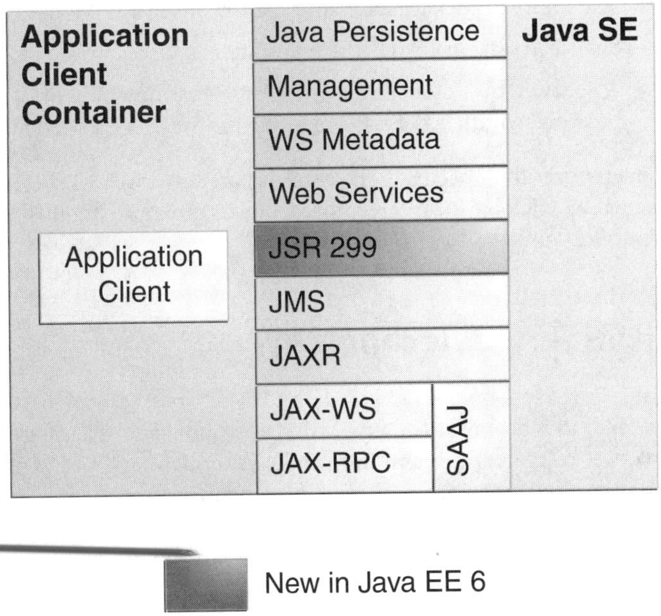

The following sections give a brief summary of the technologies required by the Java EE platform and the APIs used in Java EE applications.

Enterprise JavaBeans Technology

An Enterprise JavaBeans (EJB) component, or *enterprise bean*, is a body of code having fields and methods to implement modules of business logic. You can think of an enterprise bean as a building block that can be used alone or with other enterprise beans to execute business logic on the Java EE server.

Enterprise beans are either session beans or message-driven beans.

- A *session bean* represents a transient conversation with a client. When the client finishes executing, the session bean and its data are gone.

- A *message-driven bean* combines features of a session bean and a message listener, allowing a business component to receive messages asynchronously. Commonly, these are Java Message Service (JMS) messages.

In the Java EE 6 platform, new enterprise bean features include the following:

- The ability to package local enterprise beans in a WAR file
- Singleton session beans, which provide easy access to shared state
- A lightweight subset of Enterprise JavaBeans functionality (EJB Lite) that can be provided within Java EE Profiles, such as the Java EE Web Profile.

The Interceptors specification, which is part of the EJB 3.1 specification, makes more generally available the interceptor facility originally defined as part of the EJB 3.0 specification.

Java Servlet Technology

Java Servlet technology lets you define HTTP-specific servlet classes. A servlet class extends the capabilities of servers that host applications accessed by way of a request-response programming model. Although servlets can respond to any type of request, they are commonly used to extend the applications hosted by web servers.

In the Java EE 6 platform, new Java Servlet technology features include the following:

- Annotation support
- Asynchronous support
- Ease of configuration
- Enhancements to existing APIs
- Pluggability

JavaServer Faces Technology

JavaServer Faces technology is a user interface framework for building web applications. The main components of JavaServer Faces technology are as follows:

- A GUI component framework.
- A flexible model for rendering components in different kinds of HTML or different markup languages and technologies. A Renderer object generates the markup to render the component and converts the data stored in a model object to types that can be represented in a view.
- A standard RenderKit for generating HTML/4.01 markup.

The following features support the GUI components:

- Input validation
- Event handling
- Data conversion between model objects and components
- Managed model object creation

- Page navigation configuration
- Expression Language (EL)

All this functionality is available using standard Java APIs and XML-based configuration files.

In the Java EE 6 platform, new features of JavaServer Faces include the following:

- The ability to use annotations instead of a configuration file to specify managed beans
- Facelets, a display technology that replaces JavaServer Pages (JSP) technology using XHTML files
- Ajax support
- Composite components
- Implicit navigation

JavaServer Pages Technology

JavaServer Pages (JSP) technology lets you put snippets of servlet code directly into a text-based document. A JSP page is a text-based document that contains two types of text:

- Static data, which can be expressed in any text-based format such as HTML or XML
- JSP elements, which determine how the page constructs dynamic content

JavaServer Pages Standard Tag Library

The JavaServer Pages Standard Tag Library (JSTL) encapsulates core functionality common to many JSP applications. Instead of mixing tags from numerous vendors in your JSP applications, you use a single, standard set of tags. This standardization allows you to deploy your applications on any JSP container that supports JSTL and makes it more likely that the implementation of the tags is optimized.

JSTL has iterator and conditional tags for handling flow control, tags for manipulating XML documents, internationalization tags, tags for accessing databases using SQL, and commonly used functions.

Java Persistence API

The Java Persistence API is a Java standards-based solution for persistence. Persistence uses an object/relational mapping approach to bridge the gap between an object-oriented model and a relational database. The Java Persistence API can also be used in Java SE applications, outside of the Java EE environment. Java Persistence consists of the following areas:

- The Java Persistence API
- The query language
- Object/relational mapping metadata

Java Transaction API

The Java Transaction API (JTA) provides a standard interface for demarcating transactions. The Java EE architecture provides a default auto commit to handle transaction commits and rollbacks. An *auto commit* means that any other applications that are viewing data will see the updated data after each database read or write operation. However, if your application performs two separate database access operations that depend on each other, you will want to use the JTA API to demarcate where the entire transaction, including both operations, begins, rolls back, and commits.

Java API for RESTful Web Services

The Java API for RESTful Web Services (JAX-RS) defines APIs for the development of web services built according to the Representational State Transfer (REST) architectural style. A JAX-RS application is a web application that consists of classes that are packaged as a servlet in a WAR file along with required libraries.

The JAX-RS API is new to the Java EE 6 platform.

Managed Beans

Managed Beans, lightweight container-managed objects (POJOs) with minimal requirements, support a small set of basic services, such as resource injection, lifecycle callbacks, and interceptors. Managed Beans represent a generalization of the managed beans specified by JavaServer Faces technology and can be used anywhere in a Java EE application, not just in web modules.

The Managed Beans specification is part of the Java EE 6 platform specification (JSR 316).

Managed Beans are new to the Java EE 6 platform.

Contexts and Dependency Injection for the Java EE Platform (JSR 299)

Contexts and Dependency Injection (CDI) for the Java EE platform defines a set of contextual services, provided by Java EE containers, that make it easy for developers to use enterprise beans along with JavaServer Faces technology in web applications. Designed for use with stateful objects, CDI also has many broader uses, allowing developers a great deal of flexibility to integrate different kinds of components in a loosely coupled but type-safe way.

CDI is new to the Java EE 6 platform.

Dependency Injection for Java (JSR 330)

Dependency Injection for Java defines a standard set of annotations (and one interface) for use on injectable classes.

In the Java EE platform, CDI provides support for Dependency Injection. Specifically, you can use DI injection points only in a CDI-enabled application.

Dependency Injection for Java is new to the Java EE 6 platform.

Bean Validation

The Bean Validation specification defines a metadata model and API for validating data in JavaBeans components. Instead of distributing validation of data over several layers, such as the browser and the server side, you can define the validation constraints in one place and share them across the different layers.

Bean Validation is new to the Java EE 6 platform.

Java Message Service API

The Java Message Service (JMS) API is a messaging standard that allows Java EE application components to create, send, receive, and read messages. It enables distributed communication that is loosely coupled, reliable, and asynchronous.

Java EE Connector Architecture

The Java EE Connector architecture is used by tools vendors and system integrators to create resource adapters that support access to enterprise information systems that can be plugged in to any Java EE product. A *resource adapter* is a software component that allows Java EE application components to access and interact with the underlying resource manager of the EIS. Because a resource adapter is specific to its resource manager, a different resource adapter typically exists for each type of database or enterprise information system.

The Java EE Connector architecture also provides a performance-oriented, secure, scalable, and message-based transactional integration of Java EE based web services with existing EISs that can be either synchronous or asynchronous. Existing applications and EISs integrated through the Java EE Connector architecture into the Java EE platform can be exposed as XML-based web services by using JAX-WS and Java EE component models. Thus JAX-WS and the Java EE Connector architecture are complementary technologies for enterprise application integration (EAI) and end-to-end business integration.

JavaMail API

Java EE applications use the JavaMail API to send email notifications. The JavaMail API has two parts:

- An application-level interface used by the application components to send mail
- A service provider interface

The Java EE platform includes the JavaMail API with a service provider that allows application components to send Internet mail.

Java Authorization Contract for Containers

The Java Authorization Contract for Containers (JACC) specification defines a contract between a Java EE application server and an authorization policy provider. All Java EE containers support this contract.

The JACC specification defines `java.security.Permission` classes that satisfy the Java EE authorization model. The specification defines the binding of container access decisions to operations on instances of these permission classes. It defines the semantics of policy providers that use the new permission classes to address the authorization requirements of the Java EE platform, including the definition and use of roles.

Java Authentication Service Provider Interface for Containers

The Java Authentication Service Provider Interface for Containers (JASPIC) specification defines a service provider interface (SPI) by which authentication providers that implement message authentication mechanisms may be integrated in client or server message-processing containers or runtimes. Authentication providers integrated through this interface operate on network messages provided to them by their calling container. The authentication providers transform outgoing messages so that the source of the message can be authenticated by the receiving container, and the recipient of the message can be authenticated by the message sender. Authentication providers authenticate incoming messages and return to their calling container the identity established as a result of the message authentication.

JASPIC is new to the Java EE 6 platform.

Java EE 6 APIs in the Java Platform, Standard Edition 6.0

Several APIs that are required by the Java EE 6 platform are included in the Java Platform, Standard Edition 6.0 (Java SE 6) platform and are thus available to Java EE applications.

Java Database Connectivity API

The Java Database Connectivity (JDBC) API lets you invoke SQL commands from Java programming language methods. You use the JDBC API in an enterprise bean when you have a session bean access the database. You can also use the JDBC API from a servlet or a JSP page to access the database directly without going through an enterprise bean.

The JDBC API has two parts:

- An application-level interface used by the application components to access a database
- A service provider interface to attach a JDBC driver to the Java EE platform

Java Naming and Directory Interface API

The Java Naming and Directory Interface (JNDI) API provides naming and directory functionality, enabling applications to access multiple naming and directory services, including existing naming and directory services, such as LDAP, NDS, DNS, and NIS. The JNDI API provides applications with methods for performing standard directory operations, such as associating attributes with objects and searching for objects using their attributes. Using JNDI, a Java EE application can store and retrieve any type of named Java object, allowing Java EE applications to coexist with many legacy applications and systems.

Java EE naming services provide application clients, enterprise beans, and web components with access to a JNDI naming environment. A *naming environment* allows a component to be customized without the need to access or change the component's source code. A container implements the component's environment and provides it to the component as a JNDI *naming context*.

A Java EE component can locate its environment naming context by using JNDI interfaces. A component can create a `javax.naming.InitialContext` object and look up the environment naming context in `InitialContext` under the name `java:comp/env`. A component's naming environment is stored directly in the environment naming context or in any of its direct or indirect subcontexts.

A Java EE component can access named system-provided and user-defined objects. The names of system-provided objects, such as JTA `UserTransaction` objects, are stored in the environment naming context `java:comp/env`. The Java EE platform allows a component to name user-defined objects, such as enterprise beans, environment entries, JDBC `DataSource` objects, and message connections. An object should be named within a subcontext of the naming environment according to the type of the object. For example, enterprise beans are named within the subcontext `java:comp/env/ejb`, and JDBC `DataSource` references are named within the subcontext `java:comp/env/jdbc`.

JavaBeans Activation Framework

The JavaBeans Activation Framework (JAF) is used by the JavaMail API. JAF provides standard services to determine the type of an arbitrary piece of data, encapsulate access to it, discover the operations available on it, and create the appropriate JavaBeans component to perform those operations.

Java API for XML Processing

The Java API for XML Processing (JAXP), part of the Java SE platform, supports the processing of XML documents using Document Object Model (DOM), Simple API for XML (SAX), and Extensible Stylesheet Language Transformations (XSLT). JAXP enables applications to parse and transform XML documents independently of a particular XML processing implementation.

JAXP also provides namespace support, which lets you work with schemas that might otherwise have naming conflicts. Designed to be flexible, JAXP lets you use any XML-compliant parser or XSL processor from within your application and supports the Worldwide Web Consortium (W3C) schema. You can find information on the W3C schema at this URL: `http://www.w3.org/XML/Schema`.

Java Architecture for XML Binding

The Java Architecture for XML Binding (JAXB) provides a convenient way to bind an XML schema to a representation in Java language programs. JAXB can be used independently or in combination with JAX-WS, where it provides a standard data binding for web service messages. All Java EE application client containers, web containers, and EJB containers support the JAXB API.

SOAP with Attachments API for Java

The SOAP with Attachments API for Java (SAAJ) is a low-level API on which JAX-WS depends. SAAJ enables the production and consumption of messages that conform to the SOAP 1.1 and 1.2 specifications and SOAP with Attachments note. Most developers do not use the SAAJ API, instead using the higher-level JAX-WS API.

Java API for XML Web Services

The Java API for XML Web Services (JAX-WS) specification provides support for web services that use the JAXB API for binding XML data to Java objects. The JAX-WS specification defines client APIs for accessing web services as well as techniques for implementing web service endpoints. The Implementing Enterprise Web Services specification describes the deployment of JAX-WS-based services and clients. The EJB and Java Servlet specifications also describe aspects of such deployment. It must be possible to deploy JAX-WS-based applications using any of these deployment models.

The JAX-WS specification describes the support for message handlers that can process message requests and responses. In general, these message handlers execute in the same container and with the same privileges and execution context as the JAX-WS client or endpoint component with which they are associated. These message handlers have access to the same JNDI java:comp/env namespace as their associated component. Custom serializers and deserializers, if supported, are treated in the same way as message handlers.

Java Authentication and Authorization Service

The Java Authentication and Authorization Service (JAAS) provides a way for a Java EE application to authenticate and authorize a specific user or group of users to run it.

JAAS is a Java programming language version of the standard Pluggable Authentication Module (PAM) framework, which extends the Java Platform security architecture to support user-based authorization.

GlassFish Server Tools

The GlassFish Server is a compliant implementation of the Java EE 6 platform. In addition to supporting all the APIs described in the previous sections, the GlassFish Server includes a number of Java EE tools that are not part of the Java EE 6 platform but are provided as a convenience to the developer.

This section briefly summarizes the tools that make up the GlassFish Server. Instructions for starting and stopping the GlassFish Server, starting the Administration Console, and starting and stopping the Java DB server are in Chapter 2, "Using the Tutorial Examples."

The GlassFish Server contains the tools listed in Table 1–1. Basic usage information for many of the tools appears throughout the tutorial. For detailed information, see the online help in the GUI tools.

TABLE 1–1 GlassFish Server Tools

Tool	Description
Administration Console	A web-based GUI GlassFish Server administration utility. Used to stop the GlassFish Server and manage users, resources, and applications.
asadmin	A command-line GlassFish Server administration utility. Used to start and stop the GlassFish Server and manage users, resources, and applications.
appclient	A command-line tool that launches the application client container and invokes the client application packaged in the application client JAR file.
capture-schema	A command-line tool to extract schema information from a database, producing a schema file that the GlassFish Server can use for container-managed persistence.
package-appclient	A command-line tool to package the application client container libraries and JAR files.
Java DB database	A copy of the Java DB server.
xjc	A command-line tool to transform, or bind, a source XML schema to a set of JAXB content classes in the Java programming language.
schemagen	A command-line tool to create a schema file for each namespace referenced in your Java classes.

TABLE 1–1 GlassFish Server Tools   *(Continued)*

Tool	Description
wsimport	A command-line tool to generate JAX-WS portable artifacts for a given WSDL file. After generation, these artifacts can be packaged in a WAR file with the WSDL and schema documents, along with the endpoint implementation, and then deployed.
wsgen	A command-line tool to read a web service endpoint class and generate all the required JAX-WS portable artifacts for web service deployment and invocation.

2

Using the Tutorial Examples

This chapter tells you everything you need to know to install, build, and run the examples. The following topics are addressed here:

- "Required Software" on page 37
- "Starting and Stopping the GlassFish Server" on page 41
- "Starting the Administration Console" on page 42
- "Starting and Stopping the Java DB Server" on page 43
- "Building the Examples" on page 44
- "Tutorial Example Directory Structure" on page 44
- "Getting the Latest Updates to the Tutorial" on page 44
- "Debugging Java EE Applications" on page 45

Required Software

The following software is required to run the examples:

- "Java Platform, Standard Edition" on page 37
- "Java EE 6 Software Development Kit" on page 38
- "Java EE 6 Tutorial Component" on page 38
- "NetBeans IDE" on page 40
- "Apache Ant" on page 41

Java Platform, Standard Edition

To build, deploy, and run the examples, you need a copy of the Java Platform, Standard Edition 6.0 Development Kit (JDK 6). You can download the JDK 6 software from http://www.oracle.com/technetwork/java/javase/downloads/index.html.

Download the current JDK update that does not include any other software, such as NetBeans IDE or the Java EE SDK.

Java EE 6 Software Development Kit

GlassFish Server Open Source Edition 3.0.1 is targeted as the build and runtime environment for the tutorial examples. To build, deploy, and run the examples, you need a copy of the GlassFish Server and, optionally, NetBeans IDE. To obtain the GlassFish Server, you must install the Java EE 6 Software Development Kit (SDK), which you can download from http://www.oracle.com/technetwork/java/javaee/downloads/index.html. Make sure you download the Java EE 6 SDK, not the Java EE 6 Web Profile SDK.

SDK Installation Tips

During the installation of the SDK, do the following.

- Configure the GlassFish Server administration user name as admin, and specify no password. This is the default setting.

- Accept the default port values for the Admin Port (4848) and the HTTP Port (8080).

- Allow the installer to download and configure the Update Tool. If you access the Internet through a firewall, provide the proxy host and port.

This tutorial refers to *as-install-parent*, the directory where you install the GlassFish Server. For example, the default installation directory on Microsoft Windows is C:\glassfishv3, so *as-install-parent* is C:\glassfishv3. The GlassFish Server itself is installed in *as-install*, the glassfish directory under *as-install-parent*. So on Microsoft Windows, *as-install* is C:\glassfishv3\glassfish.

After you install the GlassFish Server, add the following directories to your PATH to avoid having to specify the full path when you use commands:

as-install-parent/bin

as-install/bin

Java EE 6 Tutorial Component

The tutorial example source is contained in the tutorial component. To obtain the tutorial component, use the Update Tool.

If you are behind a firewall that prevents you from using the Update Tool to obtain components, you can obtain the tutorial from the java.net web site.

▼ To Obtain the Tutorial Component Using the Update Tool

1 Start the Update Tool.

   - From the command line, type the command `updatetool`.

   - On a Windows system, select Start → All Programs → Java EE 6 SDK → Start Update Tool.

2 Expand the GlassFish Server Open Source Edition node.

3 Select the Available Add-ons node.

4 From the list, select the Java EE 6 Tutorial check box.

5 Click Install.

6 Accept the license agreement.

   After installation, the Java EE 6 Tutorial appears in the list of installed components. The tool is installed in the *as-install*/docs/javaee-tutorial directory. This directory contains two subdirectories: docs and examples. The examples directory contains subdirectories for each of the technologies discussed in the tutorial.

Next Steps Updates to the Java EE 6 Tutorial are published periodically. For details on obtaining these updates, see "Getting the Latest Updates to the Tutorial" on page 44.

▼ To Obtain the Tutorial Component from the `java.net` Web Site

Follow these steps exactly. If you place the tutorial in the wrong location, the examples will not work.

1 Open the following URL in a web browser:

   `https://javaeetutorial.dev.java.net/`

2 Click the Documents & Files link in the left sidebar.

3 In the table on the Documents & Files page, locate the latest stable version of the Java EE 6 Tutorial zip file.

4 Right-click the zip file name and save it to your system.

5 Copy or move the zip file into the GlassFish SDK directory.

   By default, this directory is named glassfishv3.

6   Unzip the zip file.

The tutorial unzips into the directory `glassfish/docs/javaee-tutorial`.

NetBeans IDE

The NetBeans integrated development environment (IDE) is a free, open-source IDE for developing Java applications, including enterprise applications. NetBeans IDE supports the Java EE platform. You can build, package, deploy, and run the tutorial examples from within NetBeans IDE.

To run the tutorial examples, you need the latest version of NetBeans IDE. You can download NetBeans IDE from `http://www.netbeans.org/downloads/index.html`.

▼ To Install NetBeans IDE without GlassFish Server

When you install NetBeans IDE, do not install the version of GlassFish Server that comes with NetBeans IDE. To skip the installation of GlassFish Server, follow these steps.

1   Click Customize on the first page of the NetBeans IDE Installer wizard.

2   In the Customize Installation dialog, deselect the check box for GlassFish Server and click OK.

3   Continue with the installation of NetBeans IDE.

▼ To Add GlassFish Server as a Server in NetBeans IDE

To run the tutorial examples in NetBeans IDE, you must add your GlassFish Server as a server in NetBeans IDE. Follow these instructions to add the GlassFish Server to NetBeans IDE.

1   Select Tools → Servers to open the Servers dialog.

2   Click Add Server.

3   Under Choose Server, select GlassFish v3 and click Next.

4   Under Server Location, browse the location of your GlassFish Server installation and click Next.

5   Under Domain Location, select Register Local Domain.

6   Click Finish.

Apache Ant

Ant is a Java technology-based build tool developed by the Apache Software Foundation (http://ant.apache.org/) and is used to build, package, and deploy the tutorial examples. To run the tutorial examples, you need Ant 1.7.1. If you do not already have Ant 1.7.1, you can install it from the Update Tool that is part of the GlassFish Server.

▼ To Obtain Apache Ant

1   Start the Update Tool.

- From the command line, type the command `updatetool`.

- On a Windows system, select Start → All Programs → Java EE 6 SDK → Start Update Tool.

2   Expand the GlassFish Server Open Source Edition node.

3   Select the Available Add-ons node.

4   From the list, select the Apache Ant Build Tool check box.

5   Click Install.

6   Accept the license agreement.

After installation, Apache Ant appears in the list of installed components. The tool is installed in the *as-install-parent*/ant directory.

Next Steps   To use the ant command, add *as-install*/ant/bin to your PATH environment variable.

Starting and Stopping the GlassFish Server

To start the GlassFish Server, open a terminal window or command prompt and execute the following:

```
asadmin start-domain --verbose
```

A *domain* is a set of one or more GlassFish Server instances managed by one administration server. Associated with a domain are the following:

- The GlassFish Server's port number. The default is 8080.
- The administration server's port number. The default is 4848.
- An administration user name and password.

You specify these values when you install the GlassFish Server. The examples in this tutorial assume that you chose the default ports.

With no arguments, the `start-domain` command initiates the default domain, which is `domain1`. The `--verbose` flag causes all logging and debugging output to appear on the terminal window or command prompt. The output also goes into the server log, which is located in *domain-dir*/`logs/server.log`.

Or, on Windows, choose Start → All Programs → Java EE 6 SDK → Start Application Server.

After the server has completed its startup sequence, you will see the following output:

```
Domain domain1 started.
```

To stop the GlassFish Server, open a terminal window or command prompt and execute:

```
asadmin stop-domain domain1
```

Or, on Windows, choose Start → All Programs → Java EE 6 SDK → Stop Application Server.

When the server has stopped, you will see the following output:

```
Domain domain1 stopped.
```

Starting the Administration Console

To administer the GlassFish Server and manage users, resources, and Java EE applications, use the Administration Console tool. The GlassFish Server must be running before you invoke the Administration Console. To start the Administration Console, open a browser at `http://localhost:4848/`.

Or, on Windows, choose Start → All Programs → Java EE 6 SDK → Administration Console.

▼ To Start the Administration Console in NetBeans IDE

1 Click the Services tab.

2 Expand the Servers node.

3 Right-click the GlassFish Server instance and select View Admin Console.

Note – NetBeans IDE uses your default web browser to open the Administration Console.

Starting and Stopping the Java DB Server

The GlassFish Server includes the Java DB database server.

To start the Java DB server, open a terminal window or command prompt and execute:

```
asadmin start-database
```

To stop the Java DB server, open a terminal window or command prompt and execute:

```
asadmin stop-database
```

For information about the Java DB included with the GlassFish Server, see
http://www.oracle.com/technetwork/java/javadb/overview/index.html.

▼ To Start the Database Server Using NetBeans IDE

1 Click the Services tab.

2 Expand the Databases node.

3 Right-click Java DB and choose Start Server.

Next Steps To stop the database using NetBeans IDE, right-click Java DB and choose Stop Server.

Building the Examples

The tutorial examples are distributed with a configuration file for either NetBeans IDE or Ant. Directions for building the examples are provided in each chapter. Either NetBeans IDE or Ant may be used to build, package, deploy, and run the examples.

Tutorial Example Directory Structure

To facilitate iterative development and keep application source separate from compiled files, the tutorial examples use the Java BluePrints application directory structure.

Each application module has the following structure:

- `build.xml`: Ant build file
- `src/java`: Java source files for the module
- `src/conf`: configuration files for the module, with the exception of web applications
- `web`: web pages, style sheets, tag files, and images (web applications only)
- `web/WEB-INF`: configuration files for web applications (web applications only)
- `nbproject`: NetBeans project files

Examples that have multiple application modules packaged into an EAR file have submodule directories that use the following naming conventions:

- *example-name*-`app-client`: application clients
- *example-name*-`ejb`: enterprise bean JAR files
- *example-name*-`war`: web applications

The Ant build files (`build.xml`) distributed with the examples contain targets to create a `build` subdirectory and to copy and compile files into that directory; a `dist` subdirectory, which holds the packaged module file; and a `client-jar` directory, which holds the retrieved application client JAR.

Getting the Latest Updates to the Tutorial

Check for any updates to the tutorial by using the Update Center included with the Java EE 6 SDK.

▼ To Update the Tutorial Through the Update Center

1   Open the Services tab in NetBeans IDE and expand Servers.

2   Right-click the GlassFish v3 instance and select View Update Center to display the Update Tool.

3   Select Available Updates in the tree to display a list of updated packages.

4   Look for updates to the Java EE 6 Tutorial (javaee-tutorial) package.

5   If there is an updated version of the Tutorial, select Java EE 6 Tutorial (javaee-tutorial) and click Install.

Debugging Java EE Applications

This section explains how to determine what is causing an error in your application deployment or execution.

Using the Server Log

One way to debug applications is to look at the server log in *domain-dir*/logs/server.log. The log contains output from the GlassFish Server and your applications. You can log messages from any Java class in your application with System.out.println and the Java Logging APIs (documented at http://download.oracle.com/ docs/cd/E17409_01/javase/6/docs/technotes/guides/logging/index.html) and from web components with the ServletContext.log method.

If you start the GlassFish Server with the --verbose flag, all logging and debugging output will appear on the terminal window or command prompt and the server log. If you start the GlassFish Server in the background, debugging information is available only in the log. You can view the server log with a text editor or with the Administration Console log viewer.

▼ To Use the Log Viewer

1   Select the GlassFish Server node.

2   Click the View Log Files button.

The log viewer opens and displays the last 40 entries.

3   To display other entries, follow these steps.

    a. Click the Modify Search button.

    b. Specify any constraints on the entries you want to see.

    c. Click the Search button at the top of the log viewer.

Using a Debugger

The GlassFish Server supports the Java Platform Debugger Architecture (JPDA). With JPDA, you can configure the GlassFish Server to communicate debugging information using a socket.

▼ To Debug an Application Using a Debugger

1   Enable debugging in the GlassFish Server using the Administration Console:

    a. Expand the Configuration node.

    b. Select the JVM Settings node. The default debug options are set to:

```
-Xdebug -Xrunjdwp:transport=dt_socket,server=y,suspend=n,address=9009
```

      As you can see, the default debugger socket port is 9009. You can change it to a port not in use by the GlassFish Server or another service.

    c. Select the Debug Enabled check box.

    d. Click the Save button.

2   Stop the GlassFish Server and then restart it.

The Web Tier

Part II introduces the technologies in the web tier. This part contains the following chapters:

- Chapter 3, "Getting Started with Web Applications"
- Chapter 4, "JavaServer Faces Technology"
- Chapter 5, "Introduction to Facelets"
- Chapter 6, "Expression Language"
- Chapter 7, "Using JavaServer Faces Technology in Web Pages"
- Chapter 8, "Using Converters, Listeners, and Validators"
- Chapter 9, "Developing with JavaServer Faces Technology"
- Chapter 10, "Java Servlet Technology"

Getting Started with Web Applications

A *web application* is a dynamic extension of a web or application server. Web applications are of the following types:

- **Presentation-oriented**: A presentation-oriented web application generates interactive web pages containing various types of markup language (HTML, XHTML, XML, and so on) and dynamic content in response to requests. Development of presentation-oriented web applications is covered in Chapter 4, "JavaServer Faces Technology," through Chapter 9, "Developing with JavaServer Faces Technology."

- **Service-oriented**: A service-oriented web application implements the endpoint of a web service. Presentation-oriented applications are often clients of service-oriented web applications. Development of service-oriented web applications is covered in Chapter 12, "Building Web Services with JAX-WS," and Chapter 13, "Building RESTful Web Services with JAX-RS," in Part III, "Web Services."

The following topics are addressed here:

Web Applications

In the Java EE platform, *web components* provide the dynamic extension capabilities for a web server. Web components can be Java servlets, web pages implemented with JavaServer Faces technology, web service endpoints, or JSP pages. Figure 3–1 illustrates the interaction between a web client and a web application that uses a servlet. The client sends an HTTP request to the web server. A web server that implements Java Servlet and JavaServer Pages technology converts the request into an HTTPServletRequest object. This object is delivered to a web component, which can interact with JavaBeans components or a database to generate dynamic content. The web component can then generate an HTTPServletResponse or can pass the request to another web component. A web component eventually generates a HTTPServletResponse object. The web server converts this object to an HTTP response and returns it to the client.

FIGURE 3–1   Java Web Application Request Handling

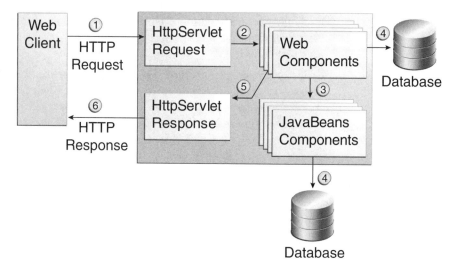

Servlets are Java programming language classes that dynamically process requests and construct responses. Java technologies, such as JavaServer Faces and Facelets, are used for building interactive web applications. (Frameworks can also be used for this purpose.) Although servlets and Java Server Faces and Facelets pages can be used to accomplish similar things, each has its own strengths. Servlets are best suited for service-oriented applications (web service endpoints can be implemented as servlets) and the control functions of a presentation-oriented application, such as dispatching requests and handling nontextual data. Java Server Faces and Facelets pages are more appropriate for generating text-based markup, such as XHTML, and are generally used for presentation–oriented applications.

Web components are supported by the services of a runtime platform called a *web container*. A web container provides such services as request dispatching, security, concurrency, and lifecycle management. A web container also gives web components access to such APIs as naming, transactions, and email.

Certain aspects of web application behavior can be configured when the application is installed, or *deployed*, to the web container. The configuration information can be specified using Java EE annotations or can be maintained in a text file in XML format called a *web application deployment descriptor* (DD). A web application DD must conform to the schema described in the Java Servlet specification.

This chapter gives a brief overview of the activities involved in developing web applications. First, it summarizes the web application lifecycle and explains how to package and deploy very simple web applications on the GlassFish Server. The chapter moves on to configuring web applications and discusses how to specify the most commonly used configuration parameters.

Web Application Lifecycle

A web application consists of web components; static resource files, such as images; and helper classes and libraries. The web container provides many supporting services that enhance the capabilities of web components and make them easier to develop. However, because a web application must take these services into account, the process for creating and running a web application is different from that of traditional stand-alone Java classes.

The process for creating, deploying, and executing a web application can be summarized as follows:

1. Develop the web component code.
2. Develop the web application deployment descriptor, if necessary.
3. Compile the web application components and helper classes referenced by the components.
4. Optionally, package the application into a deployable unit.
5. Deploy the application into a web container.
6. Access a URL that references the web application.

Developing web component code is covered in the later chapters. Steps 2 through 4 are expanded on in the following sections and illustrated with a Hello, World-style presentation-oriented application. This application allows a user to enter a name into an HTML form (Figure 3–2) and then displays a greeting after the name is submitted (Figure 3–3).

FIGURE 3-2   Greeting Form for hello1 Web Application

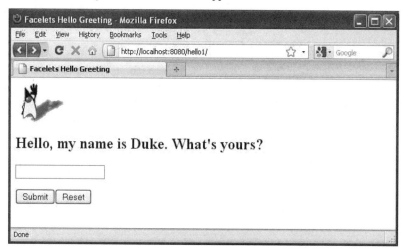

FIGURE 3-3   Response Page for hello1 Web Application

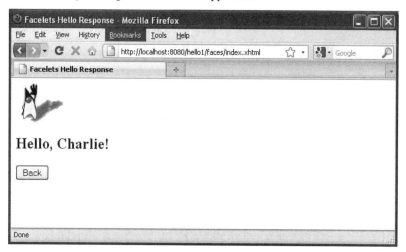

The Hello application contains two web components that generate the greeting and the response. This chapter discusses the following simple applications:

- hello1, a JavaServer Faces technology-based application that uses two XHTML pages and a backing bean

- hello2, a servlet-based web application in which the components are implemented by two servlet classes

The applications are used to illustrate tasks involved in packaging, deploying, configuring, and running an application that contains web components. The source code for the examples is in the *tut-install*/examples/web/hello1/ and *tut-install*/examples/web/hello2/ directories.

Web Modules: The `hello1` Example

In the Java EE architecture, web components and static web content files, such as images, are called *web resources*. A *web module* is the smallest deployable and usable unit of web resources. A Java EE web module corresponds to a web application as defined in the Java Servlet specification.

In addition to web components and web resources, a web module can contain other files:

- Server-side utility classes, such as shopping carts
- Client-side classes, such as applets and utility classes

A web module has a specific structure. The top-level directory of a web module is the *document root* of the application. The document root is where XHTML pages, client-side classes and archives, and static web resources, such as images, are stored.

The document root contains a subdirectory named WEB-INF, which can contain the following files and directories:

- `classes`: A directory that contains server-side classes: servlets, enterprise bean class files, utility classes, and JavaBeans components
- `tags`: A directory that contains tag files, which are implementations of tag libraries
- `lib`: A directory that contains JAR files that contain enterprise beans, and JAR archives of libraries called by server-side classes
- Deployment descriptors, such as web.xml (the web application deployment descriptor) and ejb-jar.xml (an EJB deployment descriptor)

A web module needs a web.xml file if it uses JavaServer Faces technology, if it must specify certain kinds of security information, or if you want to override information specified by web component annotations.

You can also create application-specific subdirectories (that is, package directories) in either the document root or the WEB-INF/classes/ directory.

A web module can be deployed as an unpacked file structure or can be packaged in a JAR file known as a Web Archive (WAR) file. Because the contents and use of WAR files differ from those of JAR files, WAR file names use a .war extension. The web module just described is portable; you can deploy it into any web container that conforms to the Java Servlet specification.

To deploy a WAR on the GlassFish Server, the file must contain a runtime deployment descriptor. The runtime DD is an XML file that contains such information as the context root of the web application and the mapping of the portable names of an application's resources to the GlassFish Server's resources. The GlassFish Server web application runtime DD is named sun-web.xml and is located in the WEB-INF directory. The structure of a web module that can be deployed on the GlassFish Server is shown in Figure 3–4.

For example, the sun-web.xml file for the hello1 application specifies the following context root:

```
<context-root>/hello1</context-root>
```

FIGURE 3–4   Web Module Structure

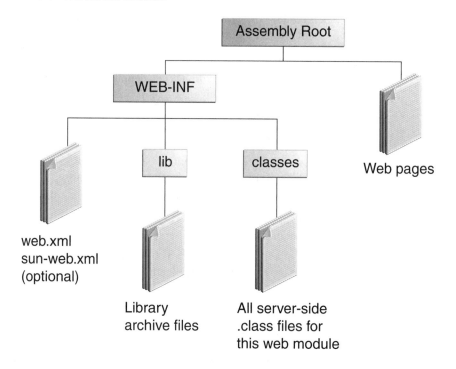

Examining the hello1 Web Module

The hello1 application is a web module that uses JavaServer Faces technology to display a greeting and response. You can use a text editor to view the application files, or you can use NetBeans IDE.

▼ To View the hello1 Web Module Using NetBeans IDE

1 **In NetBeans IDE, select File→Open Project.**

2 **In the Open Project dialog, navigate to:**

tut-install/examples/web/

3 **Select the hello1 folder.**

4 **Select the Open as Main Project check box.**

5 **Expand the Web Pages node and double-click the index.xhtml file to view it in the right-hand pane.**

The index.html file is the default landing page for a Facelets application. For this application, the page uses simple tag markup to display a form with a graphic image, a header, a text field, and two command buttons:

```
<?xml version='1.0' encoding='UTF-8' ?>
<!DOCTYPE html PUBLIC "-//W3C//DTD XHTML 1.0 Transitional//EN"
    "http://www.w3.org/TR/xhtml1/DTD/xhtml1-transitional.dtd">
<html xmlns="http://www.w3.org/1999/xhtml"
    xmlns:h="http://java.sun.com/jsf/html">
    <h:head>
        <title>Facelets Hello Greeting</title>
    </h:head>
    <h:body>
        <h:form>
            <h:graphicImage url="duke.waving.gif"/>
            <h2>Hello, my name is Duke. What's yours?</h2>
            <h:inputText id="username"
                        value="#{hello.name}"
                        required="true"
                        requiredMessage="A name is required."
                        maxlength="25">
            </h:inputText>
            <p></p>
            <h:commandButton id="submit" value="Submit" action="response">
            </h:commandButton>
            <h:commandButton id="reset" value="Reset" type="reset">
            </h:commandButton>
        </h:form>
    </h:body>
</html>
```

The most complex element on the page is the inputText text field. The maxlength attribute specifies the maximum length of the field. The required attribute specifies that the field must be filled out; the requiredMessage attribute provides the error message to be displayed if the field is left empty. Finally, the value attribute contains an expression that will be provided by the Hello backing bean.

The Submit commandButton element specifies the action as response, meaning that when the button is clicked, the response.xhtml page is displayed.

6   Double-click the `response.xhtml` file to view it.

The response page appears. Even simpler than the greeting page, the response page contains a graphic image, a header that displays the expression provided by the backing bean, and a single button whose `action` element transfers you back to the `index.xhtml` page:

```
<?xml version='1.0' encoding='UTF-8' ?>
<!DOCTYPE html PUBLIC "-//W3C//DTD XHTML 1.0 Transitional//EN"
    "http://www.w3.org/TR/xhtml1/DTD/xhtml1-transitional.dtd">
<html xmlns="http://www.w3.org/1999/xhtml"
      xmlns:h="http://java.sun.com/jsf/html">
    <h:head>
        <title>Facelets Hello Response</title>
    </h:head>
    <h:body>
        <h:form>
            <h:graphicImage url="duke.waving.gif"/>
            <h2>Hello, #{hello.name}!</h2>
            <p></p>
            <h:commandButton id="back" value="Back" action="index" />
        </h:form>
    </h:body>
</html>
```

7   Expand the Source Packages node, then the `hello1` node.

8   Double-click the `Hello.java` file to view it.

The `Hello` class, called a backing bean class, provides getter and setter methods for the name property used in the Facelets page expressions. By default, the expression language refers to the class name, with the first letter in lowercase (`hello.name`).

```
package hello1;

import javax.faces.bean.ManagedBean;
import javax.faces.bean.RequestScoped;

@ManagedBean
@RequestScoped
public class Hello {

    private String name;

    public Hello() {
    }

    public String getName() {
        return name;
    }

    public void setName(String user_name) {
        this.name = user_name;
    }
}
```

9   Under the Web Pages node, expand the `WEB-INF` node and double-click the `web.xml` file to view it.

The web.xml file contains several elements that are required for a Facelets application. All these are created automatically when you use NetBeans IDE to create an application:

- A context parameter specifying the project stage:

```
<context-param>
    <param-name>javax.faces.PROJECT_STAGE</param-name>
    <param-value>Development</param-value>
</context-param>
```

A context parameter provides configuration information needed by a web application. An application can define its own context parameters. In addition, JavaServer Faces technology and Java Servlet technology define context parameters that an application can use.

- A servlet element and its servlet-mapping element specifying the FacesServlet:

```
<servlet>
    <servlet-name>Faces Servlet</servlet-name>
    <servlet-class>javax.faces.webapp.FacesServlet</servlet-class>
    <load-on-startup>1</load-on-startup>
</servlet>
<servlet-mapping>
    <servlet-name>Faces Servlet</servlet-name>
    <url-pattern>/faces/*</url-pattern>
</servlet-mapping>
```

- A welcome-file-list element specifying the location of the landing page; note that the location is faces/index.xhtml, not just index.xhtml:

```
<welcome-file-list>
    <welcome-file>faces/index.xhtml</welcome-file>
</welcome-file-list>
```

Packaging a Web Module

A web module must be packaged into a WAR in certain deployment scenarios and whenever you want to distribute the web module. You package a web module into a WAR by executing the jar command in a directory laid out in the format of a web module, by using the Ant utility, or by using the IDE tool of your choice. This tutorial shows you how to use NetBeans IDE or Ant to build, package, and deploy the hello1 sample application.

▼ To Set the Context Root

A *context root* identifies a web application in a Java EE server. A context root must start with a forward slash (/) and end with a string.

In a packaged web module for deployment on the GlassFish Server, the context root is stored in sun-web.xml.

To view or edit the context root, follow these steps.

1 Expand the Web Pages and WEB-INF nodes of the hello1 project.

2 Double-click sun-web.xml.

3 In the General tab, observe that the Context Root field is set to /hello1.

If you needed to edit this value, you could do so here. When you create a new application, you type the context root here.

4 (Optional) Click the XML tab.

Observe that the context root value /hello1 is enclosed by the context-root element. You could also edit the value here.

▼ To Build and Package the hello1 Web Module Using NetBeans IDE

1 Select File→Open Project.

2 In the Open Project dialog, navigate to:

tut-install/examples/web/

3 Select the hello1 folder.

4 Select the Open as Main Project check box.

5 Click Open Project.

6 In the Projects tab, right-click the hello1 project and select Build.

▼ To Build and Package the hello1 Web Module Using Ant

1 In a terminal window, go to:

tut-install/examples/web/hello1/

2 Type the following command:

ant

This command spawns any necessary compilations, copies files to the directory *tut-install*/examples/web/hello1/build/, creates the WAR file, and copies it to the directory *tut-install*/examples/web/hello1/dist/.

Deploying a Web Module

You can deploy a WAR file to the GlassFish Server by

- Using NetBeans IDE
- Using the Ant utility
- Using the asadmin command
- Using the Administration Console
- Copying the WAR file into the *domain-dir*/autodeploy/ directory

Throughout the tutorial, you will use NetBeans IDE or Ant for packaging and deploying.

▼ To Deploy the hello1 Web Module Using NetBeans IDE

● Right-click the hello1 project and select Deploy.

▼ To Deploy the hello1 Web Module Using Ant

1   **In a terminal window, go to:**

tut-install/examples/web/hello1/

2   **Type the following command:**

`ant deploy`

Running a Deployed Web Module

Now that the web module is deployed, you can view it by opening the application in a web browser. By default, the application is deployed to host localhost on port 8080. The context root of the web application is hello1.

▼ To Run a Deployed Web Module

1   **Open a web browser.**

2   **Type the following URL:**

`http://localhost:8080/hello1/`

3   **Type your name and click Submit.**

The response page displays the name you submitted. Click the Back button to try again.

Listing Deployed Web Modules

The GlassFish Server provides two ways to view the deployed web modules: the Administration Console and the asadmin command.

▼ To List Deployed Web Modules Using the Administration Console

1   Open the URL http://localhost:4848/ in a browser.

2   Select the Applications node.
    The deployed web modules appear in the Deployed Applications table.

▼ To List Deployed Web Modules Using the asadmin Command

●   Type the following command:

```
asadmin list-applications
```

Updating a Web Module

A typical iterative development cycle involves deploying a web module and then making changes to the application components. To update a deployed web module, follow these steps.

▼ To Update a Deployed Web Module

1   Recompile any modified classes.

2   Redeploy the module.

3   Reload the URL in the client.

Dynamic Reloading

If dynamic reloading is enabled, you do not have to redeploy an application or module when you change its code or deployment descriptors. All you have to do is copy the changed pages or class files into the deployment directory for the application or module. The deployment directory for a web module named *context-root* is *domain-dir*/applications/*context-root*. The server checks for changes periodically and redeploys the application, automatically and dynamically, with the changes.

This capability is useful in a development environment because it allows code changes to be tested quickly. Dynamic reloading is not recommended for a production environment, however, because it may degrade performance. In addition, whenever a reload is done, the sessions at that time become invalid, and the client must restart the session.

In the GlassFish Server, dynamic reloading is enabled by default.

▼ To Disable or Modify Dynamic Reloading

If for some reason you do not want the default dynamic reloading behavior, follow these steps in the Administration Console.

1   Open the URL `http://localhost:4848/` in a browser.

2   Select the GlassFish Server node.

3   Select the Advanced tab.

4   To disable dynamic reloading, deselect the Reload Enabled check box.

5   To change the interval at which applications and modules are checked for code changes and dynamically reloaded, type a number of seconds in the Reload Poll Interval field.

The default value is 2 seconds.

6   Click the Save button.

Undeploying Web Modules

You can undeploy web modules and other types of enterprise applications by using either NetBeans IDE or the Ant tool.

▼ To Undeploy the hello1 Web Module Using NetBeans IDE

1   Ensure that the GlassFish Server is running.

2   In the Services window, expand the Servers node, GlassFish Server instance, and the Applications node.

3   Right-click the hello1 module and choose Undeploy.

4   To delete the class files and other build artifacts, right-click the project and choose Clean.

▼ **To Undeploy the hello1 Web Module Using Ant**

1   **In a terminal window, go to:**

    tut-install/examples/web/hello1/

2   **Type the following command:**

    `ant undeploy`

3   **To delete the class files and other build artifacts, type the following command:**

    `ant clean`

Configuring Web Applications: The hello2 Example

Web applications are configured by means of annotations or by elements contained in the web application deployment descriptor.

The following sections give a brief introduction to the web application features you will usually want to configure. Examples demonstrate procedures for configuring the Hello, World application.

Mapping URLs to Web Components

When it receives a request, the web container must determine which web component should handle the request. The web container does so by mapping the URL path contained in the request to a web application and a web component. A URL path contains the context root and, optionally, a URL pattern:

`http://host:port/context-root[/url-pattern]`

You set the URL pattern for a servlet by using the @WebServlet annotation in the servlet source file. For example, the GreetingServlet.java file in the hello2 application contains the following annotation, specifying the URL pattern as /greeting:

```
@WebServlet("/greeting")
public class GreetingServlet extends HttpServlet {
    ...
```

This annotation indicates that the URL pattern /greeting follows the context root. Therefore, when the servlet is deployed locally, it is accessed with the following URL:

`http://localhost:8080/hello2/greeting`

To access the servlet by using only the context root, specify "/" as the URL pattern.

Examining the hello2 Web Module

The hello2 application behaves almost identically to the hello1 application, but it is implemented using Java Servlet technology instead of JavaServer Faces technology. You can use a text editor to view the application files, or you can use NetBeans IDE.

▼ To View the hello2 Web Module Using NetBeans IDE

1 In NetBeans IDE, select File→Open Project.

2 In the Open Project dialog, navigate to:

tut-install/examples/web/

3 Select the hello2 folder.

4 Select the Open as Main Project check box.

5 Expand the Source Packages node, then the servlets node.

6 Double-click the GreetingServlet.java file to view it.

This servlet overrides the doGet method, implementing the GET method of HTTP. The servlet displays a simple HTML greeting form whose Submit button, like that of hello1, specifies a response page for its action. The following excerpt begins with the @WebServlet annotation that specifies the URL pattern, relative to the context root:

```
@WebServlet("/greeting")
public class GreetingServlet extends HttpServlet {

    @Override
    public void doGet(HttpServletRequest request,
            HttpServletResponse response)
            throws ServletException, IOException {

        response.setContentType("text/html");
        response.setBufferSize(8192);
        PrintWriter out = response.getWriter();

        // then write the data of the response
        out.println("<html>"
                + "<head><title>Servlet Hello</title></head>");

        // then write the data of the response
        out.println("<body  bgcolor=\"#ffffff\">"
                + "<img src=\"duke.waving.gif\" alt=\"Duke waving\">"
                + "<h2>Hello, my name is Duke. What's yours?</h2>"
                + "<form method=\"get\">"
                + "<input type=\"text\" name=\"username\" size=\"25\">"
                + "<p></p>"
                + "<input type=\"submit\" value=\"Submit\">"
                + "<input type=\"reset\" value=\"Reset\">"
```

```
                                    + "</form>");

                 String username = request.getParameter("username");
                 if (username != null && username.length() > 0) {
                     RequestDispatcher dispatcher =
                             getServletContext().getRequestDispatcher("/response");

                     if (dispatcher != null) {
                         dispatcher.include(request, response);
                     }
                 }
                 out.println("</body></html>");
                 out.close();
             }
             ...
```

7 **Double-click the `ResponseServlet.java` file to view it.**

This servlet also overrides the doGet method, displaying only the response. The following excerpt begins with the @WebServlet annotation, which specifies the URL pattern, relative to the context root:

```
@WebServlet("/response")
public class ResponseServlet extends HttpServlet {

    @Override
    public void doGet(HttpServletRequest request,
            HttpServletResponse response)
            throws ServletException, IOException {
        PrintWriter out = response.getWriter();

        // then write the data of the response
        String username = request.getParameter("username");
        if (username != null && username.length() > 0) {
            out.println("<h2>Hello, " + username + "!</h2>");
        }
    }
    ...
```

8 **Under the Web Pages node, expand the `WEB-INF` node and double-click the `sun-web.xml` file to view it.**

In the General tab, observe that the Context Root field is set to /hello2.

For this simple servlet application, a web.xml file is not required.

Building, Packaging, Deploying, and Running the hello2 Example

You can use either NetBeans IDE or Ant to build, package, deploy, and run the hello2 example.

▼ To Build, Package, Deploy, and Run the hello2 Example Using NetBeans IDE

1 Select File→Open Project.

2 In the Open Project dialog, navigate to:

   tut-install/examples/web/

3 Select the hello2 folder.

4 Select the Open as Main Project check box.

5 Click Open Project.

6 In the Projects tab, right-click the hello2 project and select Build.

7 Right-click the project and select Deploy.

8 In a web browser, open the URL http://localhost:8080/hello2/greeting.

   The URL specifies the context root, followed by the URL pattern.

   The application looks much like the hello1 application shown in Figure 3–2. The major difference is that after you click the Submit button, the response appears below the greeting, not on a separate page.

▼ To Build, Package, Deploy, and Run the hello2 Example Using Ant

1 In a terminal window, go to:

   tut-install/examples/web/hello2/

2 Type the following command:

   ant

   This target builds the WAR file and copies it to the *tut-install*/examples/web/hello2/dist/ directory.

3 Type ant deploy.

   Ignore the URL shown in the deploy target output.

4 In a web browser, open the URL http://localhost:8080/hello2/greeting.

   The URL specifies the context root, followed by the URL pattern.

The application looks much like the hello1 application shown in Figure 3–2. The major difference is that after you click the Submit button, the response appears below the greeting, not on a separate page.

Declaring Welcome Files

The *welcome files* mechanism allows you to specify a list of files that the web container will use for appending to a request for a URL (called a valid partial request) that is not mapped to a web component. For example, suppose that you define a welcome file welcome.html. When a client requests a URL such as *host:port/webapp/directory*, where *directory* is not mapped to a servlet or XHTML page, the file *host:port/webapp/directory/*welcome.html is returned to the client.

If a web container receives a valid partial request, the web container examines the welcome file list and appends to the partial request each welcome file in the order specified and checks whether a static resource or servlet in the WAR is mapped to that request URL. The web container then sends the request to the first resource that matches in the WAR.

If no welcome file is specified, the GlassFish Server will use a file named index.html as the default welcome file. If there is no welcome file and no file named index.html, the GlassFish Server returns a directory listing.

By convention, you specify the welcome file for a JavaServer Faces application as faces/*file-name*.xhtml.

Setting Context and Initialization Parameters

The web components in a web module share an object that represents their application context. You can pass initialization parameters to the context or to a web component.

▼ To Add a Context Parameter Using NetBeans IDE

1   Open the project if you haven't already.

2   Expand the project's node in the Projects pane.

3   Expand the Web Pages node and then the WEB-INF node.

4   Double-click web.xml.

5   Click General at the top of the editor pane.

6   Expand the Context Parameters node.

7   **Click Add.**

An Add Context Parameter dialog opens.

8   **In the Parameter Name field, type the name that specifies the context object.**

9   **In the Parameter Value field, type the parameter to pass to the context object.**

10 **Click OK.**

▼ **To Add an Initialization Parameter Using NetBeans IDE**

You can use the `@WebServlet` annotation to specify web component initialization parameters by using the `initParams` attribute and the `@WebInitParam` annotation. For example:

```
@WebServlet(urlPatterns="/MyPattern", initParams=
  {@WebInitParam(name="ccc", value="333")})
```

Alternatively, you can add an initialization parameter to the `web.xml` file. To do this using NetBeans IDE, follow these steps.

1   **Open the project if you haven't already.**

2   **Expand the project's node in the Projects pane.**

3   **Expand the Web Pages node and then the WEB-INF node.**

4   **Double-click `web.xml`.**

5   **Click Servlets at the top of the editor pane.**

6   **Click the Add button under the Initialization Parameters table.**

An Add Initialization Parameter dialog opens.

7   **In the Parameter Name field, type the name of the parameter.**

8   **In the Parameter Value Field, type the parameter's value.**

9   **Click OK.**

Mapping Errors to Error Screens

When an error occurs during execution of a web application, you can have the application display a specific error screen according to the type of error. In particular, you can specify a mapping between the status code returned in an HTTP response or a Java programming language exception returned by any web component and any type of error screen.

You can have multiple error-page elements in your deployment descriptor. Each element identifies a different error that causes an error page to open. This error page can be the same for any number of error-page elements.

▼ To Set Up Error Mapping Using NetBeans IDE

1   Open the project if you haven't already.

2   Expand the project's node in the Projects pane.

3   Expand the Web Pages node and then the WEB-INF node.

4   Double-click web.xml.

5   Click Pages at the top of the editor pane.

6   Expand the Error Pages node.

7   Click Add.

The Add Error Page dialog opens.

8   Click Browse to locate the page that you want to act as the error page.

9   In the Error Code field, type the HTTP status code that will cause the error page to be opened.

10   In the Exception Type field, type the exception that will cause the error page to load.

11   Click OK.

Declaring Resource References

If your web component uses such objects as enterprise beans, data sources, or web services, you use Java EE annotations to inject these resources into your application. Annotations eliminate a lot of the boilerplate lookup code and configuration elements that previous versions of Java EE required.

Although resource injection using annotations can be more convenient for the developer, there are some restrictions on using it in web applications. First, you can inject resources only into container-managed objects, since a container must have control over the creation of a component so that it can perform the injection into a component. As a result, you cannot inject resources into such objects as simple JavaBeans components. However, JavaServer Faces managed beans are managed by the container; therefore, they can accept resource injections.

Components that can accept resource injections are listed in Table 3–1.

This section explains how to use a couple of the annotations supported by a servlet container to inject resources. Chapter 20, "Running the Persistence Examples," explains how web applications use annotations supported by the Java Persistence API. Chapter 24, "Getting Started Securing Web Applications," explains how to use annotations to specify information about securing web applications.

TABLE 3–1 Web Components That Accept Resource Injections

Component	Interface/Class
Servlets	`javax.servlet.Servlet`
Servlet filters	`javax.servlet.ServletFilter`
Event listeners	`javax.servlet.ServletContextListener`
	`javax.servlet.ServletContextAttributeListener`
	`javax.servlet.ServletRequestListener`
	`javax.servlet.ServletRequestAttributeListener`
	`javax.servlet.http.HttpSessionListener`
	`javax.servlet.http.HttpSessionAttributeListener`
	`javax.servlet.http.HttpSessionBindingListener`
Taglib listeners	Same as above
Taglib tag handlers	`javax.servlet.jsp.tagext.JspTag`
Managed beans	Plain Old Java Objects

Declaring a Reference to a Resource

The @Resource annotation is used to declare a reference to a resource, such as a data source, an enterprise bean, or an environment entry.

The @Resource annotation is specified on a class, a method, or a field. The container is responsible for injecting references to resources declared by the @Resource annotation and mapping it to the proper JNDI resources.

In the following example, the @Resource annotation is used to inject a data source into a component that needs to make a connection to the data source, as is done when using JDBC technology to access a relational database:

```
@Resource javax.sql.DataSource catalogDS;
public getProductsByCategory() {
    // get a connection and execute the query
    Connection conn = catalogDS.getConnection();
    ..
}
```

The container injects this data source prior to the component's being made available to the application. The data source JNDI mapping is inferred from the field name catalogDS and the type, javax.sql.DataSource.

If you have multiple resources that you need to inject into one component, you need to use the @Resources annotation to contain them, as shown by the following example:

```
@Resources ({
    @Resource (name="myDB" type=java.sql.DataSource),
    @Resource(name="myMQ" type=javax.jms.ConnectionFactory)
})
```

The web application examples in this tutorial use the Java Persistence API to access relational databases. This API does not require you to explicitly create a connection to a data source. Therefore, the examples do not use the @Resource annotation to inject a data source. However, this API supports the @PersistenceUnit and @PersistenceContext annotations for injecting EntityManagerFactory and EntityManager instances, respectively. Chapter 20, "Running the Persistence Examples," describes these annotations and the use of the Java Persistence API in web applications.

Declaring a Reference to a Web Service

The @WebServiceRef annotation provides a reference to a web service. The following example shows uses the @WebServiceRef annotation to declare a reference to a web service. WebServiceRef uses the wsdlLocation element to specify the URI of the deployed service's WSDL file:

```
...
import javax.xml.ws.WebServiceRef;
...
public class ResponseServlet extends HTTPServlet {
@WebServiceRef(wsdlLocation=
    "http://localhost:8080/helloservice/hello?wsdl")
static HelloService service;
```

Further Information about Web Applications

For more information on web applications, see

- JavaServer Faces 2.0 specification:

  `http://jcp.org/en/jsr/detail?id=314`

- JavaServer Faces technology web site:

  `http://www.oracle.com/`
  `technetwork/java/javaee/javaserverfaces-139869.html`

- Java Servlet 3.0 specification:

  `http://jcp.org/en/jsr/detail?id=315`

- Java Servlet web site:

  `http://www.oracle.com/technetwork/java/index-jsp-135475.html`

CHAPTER 4

JavaServer Faces Technology

JavaServer Faces technology is a server-side component framework for building Java technology-based web applications.

JavaServer Faces technology consists of the following:

- An API for representing components and managing their state; handling events, server-side validation, and data conversion; defining page navigation; supporting internationalization and accessibility; and providing extensibility for all these features
- Tag libraries for adding components to web pages and for connecting components to server-side objects

JavaServer Faces technology provides a well-defined programming model and various tag libraries. These features significantly ease the burden of building and maintaining web applications with server-side user interfaces (UIs). With minimal effort, you can complete the following tasks.

- Create a web page.
- Drop components onto a web page by adding component tags.
- Bind components on a page to server-side data.
- Wire component-generated events to server-side application code.
- Save and restore application state beyond the life of server requests.
- Reuse and extend components through customization.

This chapter provides an overview of JavaServer Faces technology. After explaining what a JavaServer Faces application is and reviewing some of the primary benefits of using JavaServer Faces technology, this chapter describes the process of creating a simple JavaServer Faces application. This chapter also introduces the JavaServer Faces lifecycle by describing the example JavaServer Faces application progressing through the lifecycle stages.

The following topics are addressed here:

- "What Is a JavaServer Faces Application?" on page 74
- "JavaServer Faces Technology Benefits" on page 75
- "Creating a Simple JavaServer Faces Application" on page 77
- "Further Information about JavaServer Faces Technology" on page 81

What Is a JavaServer Faces Application?

The functionality provided by a JavaServer Faces application is similar to that of any other Java web application. A typical JavaServer Faces application includes the following parts:

- A set of web pages in which components are laid out

- A set of tags to add components to the web page

- A set of *backing beans*, which are JavaBeans components that define properties and functions for components on a page

- A web deployment descriptor (web.xml file)

- Optionally, one or more application configuration resource files, such as a faces-config.xml file, which can be used to define page navigation rules and configure beans and other custom objects, such as custom components

- Optionally, a set of custom objects, which can include custom components, validators, converters, or listeners, created by the application developer

- A set of custom tags for representing custom objects on the page

Figure 4–1 shows the interaction between client and server in a typical JavaServer Faces application. In response to a client request, a web page is rendered by the web container that implements JavaServer Faces technology.

FIGURE 4–1   Responding to a Client Request for a JavaServer Faces Page

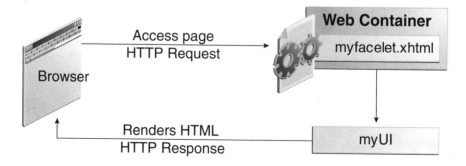

The web page, `myfacelet.xhtml`, is built using JavaServer Faces component tags. Component tags are used to add components to the `view` (represented by `myUI` in the diagram), which is the server-side representation of the page. In addition to components, the web page can also reference objects, such as the following:

- Any event listeners, validators, and converters that are registered on the components
- The JavaBeans components that capture the data and process the application-specific functionality of the components

On request from the client, the view is rendered as a response. Rendering is the process whereby, based on the server-side view, the web container generates output, such as HTML or XHTML, that can be read by the client, such as a browser.

JavaServer Faces Technology Benefits

One of the greatest advantages of JavaServer Faces technology is that it offers a clean separation between behavior and presentation for web applications. A JavaServer Faces application can map HTTP requests to component-specific event handling and manage components as stateful objects on the server. JavaServer Faces technology allows you to build web applications that implement the finer-grained separation of behavior and presentation that is traditionally offered by client-side UI architectures.

The separation of logic from presentation also allows each member of a web application development team to focus on a single piece of the development process and provides a simple programming model to link the pieces. For example, page authors with no programming expertise can use JavaServer Faces technology tags in a web page to link to server-side objects without writing any scripts.

Another important goal of JavaServer Faces technology is to leverage familiar component and web-tier concepts without limiting you to a particular scripting technology or markup language. JavaServer Faces technology APIs are layered directly on top of the Servlet API, as shown in Figure 4–2.

FIGURE 4–2 Java Web Application Technologies

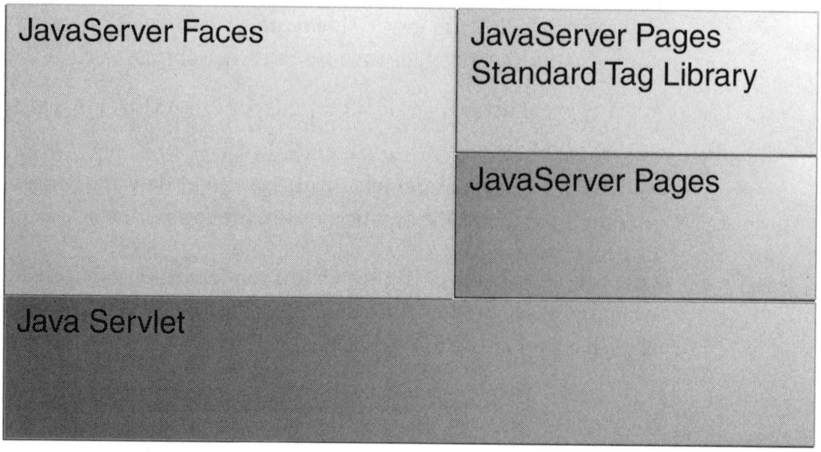

This layering of APIs enables several important application use cases, such as using different presentation technologies, creating your own custom components directly from the component classes, and generating output for various client devices.

Facelets technology, available as part of JavaServer Faces 2.0, is now the preferred presentation technology for building JavaServer Faces technology-based web applications. For more information on Facelets technology features, see Chapter 5, "Introduction to Facelets."

Facelets technology offers several advantages.

- Code can be reused and extended for components through the templating and composite component features.

- When you use the JavaServer Faces Annotations feature, you can automatically register the backing bean as a resource available for JavaServer Faces applications. In addition, *implicit navigation* rules allow developers to quickly configure page navigation. These features reduce the manual configuration process for applications.

- Most important, JavaServer Faces technology provides a rich architecture for managing component state, processing component data, validating user input, and handling events.

Creating a Simple JavaServer Faces Application

JavaServer Faces technology provides an easy and user-friendly process for creating web applications. Developing a simple JavaServer Faces application typically requires the following tasks:

- Developing backing beans
- Adding managed bean declarations
- Creating web pages using component tags
- Mapping the FacesServlet instance

This section describes those tasks through the process of creating a simple JavaServer Faces Facelets application.

The example is a Hello application that includes a backing bean and a web page. When accessed by a client, the web page prints out a Hello World message. The example application is located in the directory *tut-install*/examples/web/hello. The tasks involved in developing this application can be examined by looking at the application components in detail.

Developing the Backing Bean

As mentioned earlier in this chapter, a backing bean, a type of managed bean, is a JavaBeans component that is managed by JavaServer Faces technology. Components in a page are associated with backing beans that provide application logic. The example backing bean, Hello.java, contains the following code:

```
package hello;

import javax.faces.bean.ManagedBean;

@ManagedBean
public class Hello {

    final String world = "Hello World!";

    public String getworld() {
        return world;
    }
}
```

The example backing bean sets the value of the variable world with the string "Hello World!". The @ManagedBean annotation registers the backing bean as a resource with the JavaServer Faces implementation. For more information on managed beans and annotations, see Chapter 9, "Developing with JavaServer Faces Technology."

Creating the Web Page

In a typical Facelets application, web pages are created in XHTML. The example web page, beanhello.xhtml, is a simple XHTML page. It has the following content:

```
<html xmlns="http://www.w3.org/1999/xhtml"
      xmlns:h="http://java.sun.com/jsf/html">
    <h:head>
        <title>Facelets Hello World</title>
    </h:head>
    <h:body>
        #{hello.world}
    </h:body>
</html>
```

A Facelets XHTML web page can also contain several other elements, which are covered later in this tutorial.

The web page connects to the backing bean through the Expression Language (EL) value expression #{hello.world}, which retrieves the value of the world property from the backing bean Hello. Note the use of hello to reference the backing bean Hello. If no name is specified in the @ManagedBean annotation, the backing bean is always accessed with the first letter of the class name in lowercase.

For more information on using EL expressions, see Chapter 6, "Expression Language." For more information about Facelets technology, see Chapter 5, "Introduction to Facelets." For more information about the JavaServer Faces programming model and building web pages using JavaServer Faces technology, see Chapter 7, "Using JavaServer Faces Technology in Web Pages."

Mapping the FacesServlet Instance

The final task requires mapping the FacesServlet, which is done through the web deployment descriptor (web.xml). A typical mapping of FacesServlet is as follows:

```
<servlet>
    <servlet-name>Faces Servlet</servlet-name>
    <servlet-class>javax.faces.webapp.FacesServlet</servlet-class>
    <load-on-startup>1</load-on-startup>
</servlet>
<servlet-mapping>
    <servlet-name>Faces Servlet</servlet-name>
    <url-pattern>/faces/*</url-pattern>
</servlet-mapping>
```

The preceding file segment represents part of a typical JavaServer Faces web deployment descriptor. The web deployment descriptor can also contain other content relevant to a JavaServer Faces application configuration, but that information is not covered here.

Mapping the `FacesServlet` is automatically done for you if you are using an IDE such as NetBeans IDE.

The Lifecycle of the `hello` Application

Every web application has a lifecycle. Common tasks, such as handling incoming requests, decoding parameters, modifying and saving state, and rendering web pages to the browser, are all performed during a web application lifecycle. Some web application frameworks hide the details of the lifecycle from you, whereas others require you to manage them manually.

By default, JavaServer Faces automatically handles most of the lifecycle actions for you. However, it also exposes the various stages of the request lifecycle, so that you can modify or perform different actions if your application requirements warrant it.

It is not necessary for the beginning user to understand the lifecycle of a JavaServer Faces application, but the information can be useful for creating more complex applications.

The lifecycle of a JavaServer Faces application starts and ends with the following activity: The client makes a request for the web page, and the server responds with the page. The lifecycle consists of two main phases: *execute* and *render*.

During the execute phase, several actions can take place:

- The application view is built or restored.
- The request parameter values are applied.
- Conversions and validations are performed for component values.
- Backing beans are updated with component values.
- Application logic is invoked.

For a first (initial) request, only the view is built. For subsequent (postback) requests, some or all of the other actions can take place.

In the render phase, the requested view is rendered as a response to the client. Rendering is typically the process of generating output, such as HTML or XHTML, that can be read by the client, usually a browser.

The following short description of the example JavaServer Faces application passing through its lifecycle summarizes the activity that takes place behind the scenes.

The `hello` example application goes through the following stages when it is deployed on the GlassFish Server.

1. When the `hello` application is built and deployed on the GlassFish Server, the application is in an uninitiated state.

2. When a client makes an initial request for the `beanhello.xhtml` web page, the `hello` Facelets application is compiled.

3. The compiled Facelets application is executed, and a new component tree is constructed for the `hello` application and is placed in a `FacesContext`.

4. The component tree is populated with the component and the backing bean property associated with it, represented by the EL expression `hello.world`.

5. A new view is built, based on the component tree.

6. The view is rendered to the requesting client as a response.

7. The component tree is destroyed automatically.

8. On subsequent (postback) requests, the component tree is rebuilt, and the saved state is applied.

For more detailed information on the JavaServer Faces lifecycle, see the JavaServer Faces Specification, Version 2.0.

▼ To Build, Package, Deploy, and Run the Application in NetBeans IDE

1 In NetBeans IDE, select File→Open Project.

2 In the Open Project dialog box, navigate to:

tut-install/examples/web

3 Select the `hello` folder.

4 Select the Open as Main Project check box.

5 Click Open Project.

6 In the Projects tab, right-click the `hello` project and select Run.

This step compiles, assembles, and deploys the application and then brings up a web browser window displaying the following URL:

```
http://localhost:8080/hello
```

The output looks like this:

```
Hello World!
```

Further Information about JavaServer Faces Technology

For more information on JavaServer Faces technology, see

- JavaServer Faces 2.0 specification:

  ```
  http://jcp.org/en/jsr/detail?id=314
  ```

- JavaServer Faces technology web site:

  ```
  http://www.oracle.com/
  technetwork/java/javaee/javaserverfaces-139869.html
  ```

- JavaServer Faces 2.0 technology download web site:

  ```
  http://www.oracle.com/technetwork/java/javaee/download-139288.html
  ```

- Mojarra (JavaServer Faces 2.0) Release Notes:

  ```
  https://javaserverfaces.dev.java.net/nonav/rlnotes/2.0.0/index.html
  ```

5

Introduction to Facelets

The term *Facelets* refers to the view declaration language for JavaServer Faces technology. JavaServer Pages (JSP) technology, previously used as the presentation technology for JavaServer Faces, does not support all the new features available in JavaServer Faces 2.0. JSP technology is considered to be a deprecated presentation technology for JavaServer Faces 2.0. Facelets is a part of the JavaServer Faces specification and also the preferred presentation technology for building JavaServer Faces technology-based applications.

The following topics are addressed here:

What Is Facelets?

Facelets is a powerful but lightweight page declaration language that is used to build JavaServer Faces views using HTML style templates and to build component trees. Facelets features include the following:

- Use of XHTML for creating web pages

- Support for Facelets tag libraries in addition to JavaServer Faces and JSTL tag libraries

- Support for the Expression Language (EL)

- Templating for components and pages

Advantages of Facelets for large-scale development projects include the following:

- Support for code reuse through templating and composite components
- Functional extensibility of components and other server-side objects through customization
- Faster compilation time
- Compile-time EL validation
- High-performance rendering

In short, the use of Facelets reduces the time and effort that needs to be spent on development and deployment.

Facelets views are usually created as XHTML pages. JavaServer Faces implementations support XHTML pages created in conformance with the XHTML Transitional Document Type Definition (DTD), as listed at `http://www.w3.org/TR/xhtml1/#a_dtd_XHTML-1.0-Transitional`. By convention, web pages built with XHTML have an `.xhtml` extension.

JavaServer Faces technology supports various tag libraries to add components to a web page. To support the JavaServer Faces tag library mechanism, Facelets uses XML namespace declarations. Table 5–1 lists the tag libraries supported by Facelets.

TABLE 5–1   Tag Libraries Supported by Facelets

Tag Library	URI	Prefix	Example	Contents
JavaServer Faces Facelets Tag Library	`http://java.sun.com/jsf/facelets`	`ui:`	`ui:component` `ui:insert`	Tags for templating
JavaServer Faces HTML Tag Library	`http://java.sun.com/jsf/html`	`h:`	`h:head` `h:body` `h:outputText` `h:inputText`	JavaServer Faces component tags for all UIComponents
JavaServer Faces Core Tag Library	`http://java.sun.com/jsf/core`	`f:`	`f:actionListener` `f:attribute`	Tags for JavaServer Faces custom actions that are independent of any particular RenderKit

TABLE 5–1   Tag Libraries Supported by Facelets   *(Continued)*

Tag Library	URI	Prefix	Example	Contents

JSTL Core Tag Library	`http://java.sun.com/jsp/jstl/core`	`c:`	`c:forEach`
			
			`c:catch`
				JSTL 1.1 Core Tags

JSTL Functions Tag Library	`http://java.sun.com/jsp/jstl/functions`	`fn:`	`fn:toUpperCase`
			
			`fn:toLowerCase`
				JSTL 1.1 Functions Tags

In addition, Facelets supports tags for composite components for which you can declare custom prefixes. For more information on composite components, see "Composite Components" on page 94.

Based on the JavaServer Faces support for Expression Language (EL) syntax defined by JSP 2.1, Facelets uses EL expressions to reference properties and methods of backing beans. EL expressions can be used to bind component objects or values to methods or properties of managed beans. For more information on using EL expressions, see "Using the EL to Reference Backing Beans" on page 161.

Developing a Simple Facelets Application

This section describes the general steps involved in developing a JavaServer Faces application. The following tasks are usually required:

- Developing the backing beans
- Creating the pages using the component tags
- Defining page navigation
- Mapping the `FacesServlet` instance
- Adding managed bean declarations

Creating a Facelets Application

The example used in this tutorial is the `guessnumber` application. The application presents you with a page that asks you to guess a number between 0 and 10, validates your input against a random number, and responds with another page that informs you whether you guessed the number correctly or incorrectly.

Developing a Backing Bean

In a typical JavaServer Faces application, each page of the application connects to a backing bean, a type of managed bean. The backing bean defines the methods and properties that are associated with the components.

The following managed bean class, `UserNumberBean.java`, generates a random number from 0 to 10:

```java
package guessNumber;

import java.util.Random;
import javax.faces.bean.ManagedBean;
import javax.faces.bean.SessionScoped;

@ManagedBean
@SessionScoped
public class UserNumberBean {

    Integer randomInt = null;
    Integer userNumber = null;
    String response = null;
    private long maximum=10;
    private long minimum=0;

    public UserNumberBean() {
        Random randomGR = new Random();
        randomInt = new Integer(randomGR.nextInt(10));
        System.out.println("Duke's number: " + randomInt);
    }
    public void setUserNumber(Integer user_number) {
        userNumber = user_number;
    }

    public Integer getUserNumber() {
        return userNumber;
    }

    public String getResponse() {
        if ((userNumber != null) && (userNumber.compareTo(randomInt) == 0)) {
            return "Yay! You got it!";
        } else {
            return "Sorry, " + userNumber + " is incorrect.";
        }
    }

    public long getMaximum() {
        return (this.maximum);
    }

    public void setMaximum(long maximum) {
        this.maximum = maximum;
    }

    public long getMinimum() {
        return (this.minimum);
    }

    public void setMinimum(long minimum) {
        this.minimum = minimum;
    }
}
```

Note the use of the @ManagedBean annotation, which registers the backing bean as a resource with JavaServer Faces implementation. The @SessionScoped annotation registers the bean scope as session.

Creating Facelets Views

Creating a page or view is the responsibility of a page author. This task involves adding components on the pages, wiring the components to backing bean values and properties, and registering converters, validators, or listeners onto the components.

For the example application, XHTML web pages serve as the front end. The first page of the example application is a page called greeting.xhtml. A closer look at various sections of this web page provides more information.

The first section of the web page declares the content type for the page, which is XHTML:

```
<!DOCTYPE html PUBLIC "-//W3C//DTD XHTML 1.0 Transitional//EN"
  "http://www.w3.org/TR/xhtml1/DTD/xhtml1-transitional.dtd">
```

The next section declares the XML namespace for the tag libraries that are used in the web page:

```
<html xmlns="http://www.w3.org/1999/xhtml"
      xmlns:h="http://java.sun.com/jsf/html"
      xmlns:f="http://java.sun.com/jsf/core">
```

The next section uses various tags to insert components into the web page:

```
h:head>
        <title>Guess Number Facelets Application</title>
    </h:head>
    <h:body>
        <h:form>
            <h:graphicImage value="#{resource['images:wave.med.gif']}"/>
            <h2>
                Hi, my name is Duke. I am thinking of a number from
                #{userNumberBean.minimum} to #{userNumberBean.maximum}.
                Can you guess it?
                <p></p>
                <h:inputText
                    id="userNo"
                    value="#{userNumberBean.userNumber}">
                    <f:validateLongRange
                        minimum="#{userNumberBean.minimum}"
                        maximum="#{userNumberBean.maximum}"/>
                </h:inputText>

                <h:commandButton id="submit" value="Submit"
                            action="response.xhtml"/>
                <h:message showSummary="true" showDetail="false"
                        style="color: red;
```

```
                                    font-family: 'New Century Schoolbook', serif;
                                    font-style: oblique;
                                    text-decoration: overline"
                                    id="errors1"
                                    for="userNo"/>
                    </h2>
                </h:form>
            </h:body>
```

Note the use of the following tags:

- Facelets HTML tags (those beginning with h:) to add components
- The Facelets core tag f:validateLongRange to validate the user input

An inputText component accepts user input and sets the value of the backing bean property userNumber through the EL expression #{userNumberBean.userNumber}. The input value is validated for value range by the JavaServer Faces standard validator f:validateLongRange.

The image file, wave.med.gif, is added to the page as a resource. For more details about the resources facility, see "Resources" on page 96.

A commandButton component with the ID submit starts validation of the input data when a user clicks the button. Using implicit navigation, the component redirects the client to another page, response.xhtml, which shows the response to your input.

You can now create the second page, response.xhtml, with the following content:

```
<!DOCTYPE html PUBLIC "-//W3C//DTD XHTML 1.0 Transitional//EN"
     "http://www.w3.org/TR/xhtml1/DTD/xhtml1-transitional.dtd">

<html xmlns="http://www.w3.org/1999/xhtml"
      xmlns:h="http://java.sun.com/jsf/html">

    <h:head>
        <title>Guess Number Facelets Application</title>
    </h:head>
    <h:body>
        <h:form>
            <h:graphicImage value="#{resource['images:wave.med.gif']}"/>
            <h2>
                <h:outputText id="result" value="#{userNumberBean.response}"/>
            </h2>
            <h:commandButton id="back" value="Back" action="greeting.xhtml"/>
        </h:form>
    </h:body>
</html>
```

Configuring the Application

Configuring a JavaServer Faces application involves mapping the Faces Servlet in the web deployment descriptor file, such as a web.xml file, and possibly adding managed bean declarations, navigation rules, and resource bundle declarations to the application configuration resource file, faces-config.xml.

If you are using NetBeans IDE, a web deployment descriptor file is automatically created for you. In such an IDE-created web.xml file, change the default greeting page, which is index.xhtml, to greeting.xhtml. Here is an example web.xml file, showing this change in bold.

```xml
<?xml version="1.0" encoding="UTF-8"?>
<web-app version="3.0" xmlns="http://java.sun.com/xml/ns/javaee"
  xmlns:xsi="http://www.w3.org/2001/XMLSchema-instance"
  xsi:schemaLocation="http://java.sun.com/xml/ns/javaee
  http://java.sun.com/xml/ns/javaee/web-app_3_0.xsd">
    <context-param>
        <param-name>javax.faces.PROJECT_STAGE</param-name>
        <param-value>Development</param-value>
    </context-param>
    <servlet>
        <servlet-name>Faces Servlet</servlet-name>
        <servlet-class>javax.faces.webapp.FacesServlet</servlet-class>
        <load-on-startup>1</load-on-startup>
    </servlet>
    <servlet-mapping>
        <servlet-name>Faces Servlet</servlet-name>
        <url-pattern>/faces/*</url-pattern>
    </servlet-mapping>
    <session-config>
        <session-timeout>
            30
        </session-timeout>
    </session-config>
    <welcome-file-list>
        <welcome-file>faces/greeting.xhtml</welcome-file>
    </welcome-file-list>
</web-app>
```

Note the use of the context parameter PROJECT_STAGE. This parameter identifies the status of a JavaServer Faces application in the software lifecycle.

The stage of an application can affect the behavior of the application. For example, if the project stage is defined as Development, debugging information is automatically generated for the user. If not defined by the user, the default project stage is Production.

Building, Packaging, Deploying, and Running the guessnumber Facelets Example

You can use either NetBeans IDE or Ant to build, package, deploy, and run the guessnumber example. The source code for this example is available in the *tut-install*/examples/web/guessnumber directory.

▼ **To Build, Package, and Deploy the** guessnumber **Example Using NetBeans IDE**

1   In NetBeans IDE, select File→Open Project.

2   In the Open Project dialog, navigate to:

    tut-install/examples/web/

3   Select the guessnumber folder.

4   Select the Open as Main Project check box.

5   Click Open Project.

6   In the Projects tab, right-click the guessnumber project and select Deploy.

    This option builds and deploys the example application to your GlassFish Server instance.

▼ **To Build, Package, and Deploy the** guessnumber **Example Using Ant**

1   In a terminal window, go to:

    tut-install/examples/web/guessnumber/

2   Type the following command:

    ```
    ant
    ```

    This command calls the default target, which builds and packages the application into a WAR file, guessnumber.war, that is located in the dist directory.

3   Make sure that the GlassFish Server is started.

4   To deploy the application, type the following command:

    ```
    ant deploy
    ```

▼ **To Run the** guessnumber **Example**

1   Open a web browser.

2   Type the following URL in your web browser:

    ```
    http://localhost:8080/guessnumber
    ```

    The web page shown in Figure 5–1 appears.

FIGURE 5-1 Running the guessnumber Application

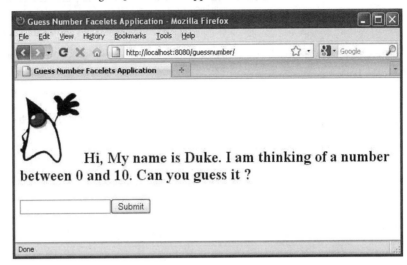

3 **In the text field, type a number from 0 to 10 and click Submit.**

Another page appears, reporting whether your guess is correct or incorrect.

4 **If you guessed incorrectly, click the Back button to return to the main page.**

You can continue to guess until you get the correct answer.

Templating

JavaServer Faces technology provides the tools to implement user interfaces that are easy to extend and reuse. Templating is a useful Facelets feature that allows you to create a page that will act as the base, or *template*, for the other pages in an application. By using templates, you can reuse code and avoid recreating similarly constructed pages. Templating also helps in maintaining a standard look and feel in an application with a large number of pages.

Table 5–2 lists Facelets tags that are used for templating and their respective functionality.

TABLE 5-2 Facelets Templating Tags

Tag	Function
ui:component	Defines a component that is created and added to the component tree.
ui:composition	Defines a page composition that optionally uses a template. Content outside of this tag is ignored.

TABLE 5–2 Facelets Templating Tags *(Continued)*

Tag	Function
ui:debug	Defines a debug component that is created and added to the component tree.
ui:decorate	Similar to the composition tag but does not disregard content outside this tag.
ui:define	Defines content that is inserted into a page by a template.
ui:fragment	Similar to the component tag but does not disregard content outside this tag.
ui:include	Encapsulate and reuse content for multiple pages.
ui:insert	Inserts content into a template.
ui:param	Used to pass parameters to an included file.
ui:repeat	Used as an alternative for loop tags, such as c:forEach or h:dataTable.
ui:remove	Removes content from a page.

For more information on Facelets templating tags, see the documentation at
`http://download.oracle.com/`
`docs/cd/E17410_01/javaee/6/javaserverfaces/2.0/docs/pdldocs/facelets/`.

The Facelets tag library includes the main templating tag ui:insert. A template page that is created with this tag allows you to define a default structure for a page. A template page is used as a template for other pages, usually referred to as client pages.

Here is an example of a template saved as `template.xhtml`:

```
<!DOCTYPE html PUBLIC "-//W3C//DTD XHTML 1.0 Transitional//EN"
    "http://www.w3.org/TR/xhtml1/DTD/xhtml1-transitional.dtd">
<html xmlns="http://www.w3.org/1999/xhtml"
    xmlns:ui="http://java.sun.com/jsf/facelets"
    xmlns:h="http://java.sun.com/jsf/html">

    <h:head>
        <meta http-equiv="Content-Type"
            content="text/html; charset=UTF-8" />
        <link href="./resources/css/default.css"
            rel="stylesheet" type="text/css" />
        <link href="./resources/css/cssLayout.css"
            rel="stylesheet" type="text/css" />
        <title>Facelets Template</title>
    </h:head>

    <h:body>
        <div id="top" class="top">
            <ui:insert name="top">Top Section</ui:insert>
        </div>
        <div>
        <div id="left">
            <ui:insert name="left">Left Section</ui:insert>
```

```
            </div>
            <div id="content" class="left_content">
                <ui:insert name="content">Main Content</ui:insert>
            </div>
        </div>
    </h:body>
</html>
```

The example page defines an XHTML page that is divided into three sections: a top section, a left section, and a main section. The sections have style sheets associated with them. The same structure can be reused for the other pages of the application.

The client page invokes the template by using the ui:composition tag. In the following example, a client page named templateclient.xhtml invokes the template page named template.xhtml from the preceding example. A client page allows content to be inserted with the help of the ui:define tag.

```
<!DOCTYPE html PUBLIC "-//W3C//DTD XHTML 1.0 Transitional//EN"
  "http://www.w3.org/TR/xhtml1/DTD/xhtml1-transitional.dtd">
<html xmlns="http://www.w3.org/1999/xhtml"
      xmlns:ui="http://java.sun.com/jsf/facelets"
      xmlns:h="http://java.sun.com/jsf/html">

    <h:body>
        <ui:composition template="./template.xhtml">
            <ui:define name="top">
                Welcome to Template Client Page
            </ui:define>

            <ui:define name="left">
                <h:outputLabel value="You are in the Left Section"/>
            </ui:define>

            <ui:define name="content">
                <h:graphicImage value="#{resource['images:wave.med.gif']}"/>
                <h:outputText value="You are in the Main Content Section"/>
            </ui:define>
        </ui:composition>
    </h:body>
</html>
```

You can use NetBeans IDE to create Facelets template and client pages. For more information on creating these pages, see http://netbeans.org/kb/docs/web/jsf20-intro.html.

Composite Components

JavaServer Faces technology offers the concept of composite components with Facelets. A composite component is a special type of template that acts as a component.

Any component is essentially a piece of reusable code that behaves in a particular way. For example, an inputText component accepts user input. A component can also have validators, converters, and listeners attached to it to perform certain defined actions.

A composite component consists of a collection of markup tags and other existing components. This reusable, user-created component has a customized, defined functionality and can have validators, converters, and listeners attached to it like any other component.

With Facelets, any XHTML page that contains markup tags and other components can be converted into a composite component. Using the resources facility, the composite component can be stored in a library that is available to the application from the defined resources location.

Table 5–3 lists the most commonly used composite tags and their functions.

TABLE 5–3 Composite Component Tags

Tag	Function
composite:interface	Declares the usage contract for a composite component. The composite component can be used as a single component whose feature set is the union of the features declared in the usage contract.
composite:implementation	Defines the implementation of the composite component. If a composite:interface element appears, there must be a corresponding composite:implementation.
composite:attribute	Declares an attribute that may be given to an instance of the composite component in which this tag is declared.
composite:insertChildren	Any child components or template text within the composite component tag in the using page will be reparented into the composite component at the point indicated by this tag's placement within the composite:implementation section.
composite:valueHolder	Declares that the composite component whose contract is declared by the composite:interface in which this element is nested exposes an implementation of ValueHolder suitable for use as the target of attached objects in the using page.

TABLE 5–3 Composite Component Tags *(Continued)*

Tag	Function
composite:editableValueHolder	Declares that the composite component whose contract is declared by the composite:interface in which this element is nested exposes an implementation of EditableValueHolder suitable for use as the target of attached objects in the using page.
composite:actionSource	Declares that the composite component whose contract is declared by the composite:interface in which this element is nested exposes an implementation of ActionSource2 suitable for use as the target of attached objects in the using page.

For more information and a complete list of Facelets composite tags, see the documentation at `http://download.oracle.com/docs/cd/E17410_01/javaee/6/javaserverfaces/2.0/docs/pdldocs/facelets/`.

The following example shows a composite component that accepts an email address as input:

```
<!DOCTYPE html PUBLIC "-//W3C//DTD XHTML 1.0 Transitional//EN"
  "http://www.w3.org/TR/xhtml1/DTD/xhtml1-transitional.dtd">
<html xmlns="http://www.w3.org/1999/xhtml"
  xmlns:composite="http://java.sun.com/jsf/composite"
  xmlns:h="http://java.sun.com/jsf/html">

    <h:head>
        <title>This content will not be displayed</title>
    </h:head>
    <h:body>
        <composite:interface>
            <composite:attribute name="value" required="false"/>
        </composite:interface>

        <composite:implementation>
            <h:outputLabel value="Email id: "></h:outputLabel>
            <h:inputText value="#{cc.attrs.value}"></h:inputText>
        </composite:implementation>
    </h:body>
</html>
```

Note the use of cc.attrs.value when defining the value of the inputText component. The word cc in JavaServer Faces is a reserved word for composite components. The #{cc.attrs.*attribute-name*} expression is used to access the attributes defined for the composite component's interface, which in this case happens to be value.

The preceding example content is stored as a file named email.xhtml in a folder named resources/emcomp, under the application web root directory. This directory is considered a library by JavaServer Faces, and a component can be accessed from such a library. For more information on resources, see "Resources" on page 96.

The web page that uses this composite component is generally called a *using page*. The using page includes a reference to the composite component, in the xml namespace declarations:

```
<!DOCTYPE html PUBLIC "-//W3C//DTD XHTML 1.0 Transitional//EN"
  "http://www.w3.org/TR/xhtml1/DTD/xhtml1-transitional.dtd">
<html xmlns="http://www.w3.org/1999/xhtml"
  xmlns:h="http://java.sun.com/jsf/html"
  xmlns:em="http://java.sun.com/jsf/composite/emcomp/">

    <h:head>
        <title>Using a sample composite component</title>
    </h:head>

    <body>
        <h:form>
            <em:email value="Enter your email id" />
        </h:form>
    </body>
</html>
```

The local composite component library is defined in the xml namespace with the declaration xmlns:em="http://java.sun.com/jsf/composite/emcomp/". The component itself is accessed through the use of em:email tag. The preceding example content can be stored as a web page named emuserpage.xhtml under the web root directory. When compiled and deployed on a server, it can be accessed with the following URL:

```
http://localhost:8080/application-name/faces/emuserpage.xhtml
```

Resources

Web resources are any software artifacts that the web application requires for proper rendering, including images, script files, and any user-created component libraries. Resources must be collected in a standard location, which can be one of the following.

- A resource packaged in the web application root must be in a subdirectory of a resources directory at the web application root: resources/*resource-identifier*.

- A resource packaged in the web application's classpath must be in a subdirectory of the META-INF/resources directory within a web application: META-INF/resources/*resource-identifier*.

The JavaServer Faces runtime will look for the resources in the preceding listed locations, in that order.

Resource identifiers are unique strings that conform to the following format:

[locale-prefix/] *[library-name/]* *[library-version/]* *resource-name*[*/resource-version*]

Elements of the resource identifier in brackets ([ ]) are optional, indicating that only a *resource-name*, which is usually a file name, is a required element.

Resources can be considered as a library location. Any artifact, such as a composite component or a template that is stored in the `resources` directory, becomes accessible to the other application components, which can use it to create a resource instance.

6

Expression Language

This chapter introduces the Expression Language (also referred to as the EL), which provides an important mechanism for enabling the presentation layer (web pages) to communicate with the application logic (backing beans). The EL is used by both JavaServer Faces technology and JavaServer Pages (JSP) technology. The EL represents a union of the expression languages offered by JavaServer Faces technology and JSP technology.

The following topics are addressed here:

Overview of the EL

The EL allows page authors to use simple expressions to dynamically access data from JavaBeans components. For example, the test attribute of the following conditional tag is supplied with an EL expression that compares 0 with the number of items in the session-scoped bean named cart.

```
<c:if test="${sessionScope.cart.numberOfItems > 0}">
   ...
</c:if>
```

JavaServer Faces technology uses the EL for the following functions:

- Deferred and immediate evaluation of expressions
- The ability to set as well as get data
- The ability to invoke methods

See "Using the EL to Reference Backing Beans" on page 161 for more information on how to use the EL in JavaServer Faces applications.

To summarize, the EL provides a way to use simple expressions to perform the following tasks:

- Dynamically read application data stored in JavaBeans components, various data structures, and implicit objects

- Dynamically write data, such as user input into forms, to JavaBeans components

- Invoke arbitrary static and public methods

- Dynamically perform arithmetic operations

The EL is also used to specify the following kinds of expressions that a custom tag attribute will accept:

- **Immediate evaluation expressions** or **deferred evaluation expressions**. An immediate evaluation expression is evaluated at once by the underlying technology, such as JavaServer Faces. A deferred evaluation expression can be evaluated later by the underlying technology using the EL.

- **Value expression** or **method expression**. A value expression references data, whereas a method expression invokes a method.

- **Rvalue expression** or **lvalue expression**. An rvalue expression can only read a value, whereas an lvalue expression can both read and write that value to an external object.

Finally, the EL provides a pluggable API for resolving expressions so custom resolvers that can handle expressions not already supported by the EL can be implemented.

Immediate and Deferred Evaluation Syntax

The EL supports both immediate and deferred evaluation of expressions. Immediate evaluation means that the expression is evaluated and the result returned as soon as the page is first rendered. Deferred evaluation means that the technology using the expression language can use its own machinery to evaluate the expression sometime later during the page's lifecycle, whenever it is appropriate to do so.

Those expressions that are evaluated immediately use the ${} syntax. Expressions whose evaluation is deferred use the #{} syntax.

Because of its multiphase lifecycle, JavaServer Faces technology uses mostly deferred evaluation expressions. During the lifecycle, component events are handled, data is validated, and other tasks are performed in a particular order. Therefore, a JavaServer Faces implementation must defer evaluation of expressions until the appropriate point in the lifecycle.

Other technologies using the EL might have different reasons for using deferred expressions.

Immediate Evaluation

All expressions using the ${} syntax are evaluated immediately. These expressions can be used only within template text or as the value of a tag attribute that can accept runtime expressions.

The following example shows a tag whose value attribute references an immediate evaluation expression that gets the total price from the session-scoped bean named cart:

```
<fmt:formatNumber value="${sessionScope.cart.total}"/>
```

The JavaServer Faces implementation evaluates the expression ${sessionScope.cart.total}, converts it, and passes the returned value to the tag handler.

Immediate evaluation expressions are always read-only value expressions. The preceding example expression cannot set the total price, but instead can only get the total price from the cart bean.

Deferred Evaluation

Deferred evaluation expressions take the form #{expr} and can be evaluated at other phases of a page lifecycle as defined by whatever technology is using the expression. In the case of JavaServer Faces technology, its controller can evaluate the expression at different phases of the lifecycle, depending on how the expression is being used in the page.

The following example shows a JavaServer Faces inputText tag, which represents a text field component into which a user enters a value. The inputText tag's value attribute references a deferred evaluation expression that points to the name property of the customer bean:

```
<h:inputText id="name" value="#{customer.name}" />
```

For an initial request of the page containing this tag, the JavaServer Faces implementation evaluates the #{customer.name} expression during the render-response phase of the lifecycle. During this phase, the expression merely accesses the value of name from the customer bean, as is done in immediate evaluation.

For a postback request, the JavaServer Faces implementation evaluates the expression at different phases of the lifecycle, during which the value is retrieved from the request, validated, and propagated to the customer bean.

As shown in this example, deferred evaluation expressions can be

- Value expressions that can be used to both read and write data
- Method expressions

Value expressions (both immediate and deferred) and method expressions are explained in the next section.

Value and Method Expressions

The EL defines two kinds of expressions: value expressions and method expressions. Value expressions can either yield a value or set a value. Method expressions reference methods that can be invoked and can return a value.

Value Expressions

Value expressions can be further categorized into rvalue and lvalue expressions. Rvalue expressions can read data but cannot write it. Lvalue expressions can both read and write data.

All expressions that are evaluated immediately use the ${} delimiters and are always rvalue expressions. Expressions whose evaluation can be deferred use the #{} delimiters and can act as both rvalue and lvalue expressions. Consider the following two value expressions:

```
${customer.name}
```

```
#{customer.name}
```

The former uses immediate evaluation syntax, whereas the latter uses deferred evaluation syntax. The first expression accesses the name property, gets its value, adds the value to the response, and gets rendered on the page. The same can happen with the second expression. However, the tag handler can defer the evaluation of this expression to a later time in the page lifecycle, if the technology using this tag allows.

In the case of JavaServer Faces technology, the latter tag's expression is evaluated immediately during an initial request for the page. In this case, this expression acts as an rvalue expression. During a postback request, this expression can be used to set the value of the name property with user input. In this case, the expression acts as an lvalue expression.

Referencing Objects Using Value Expressions

Both rvalue and lvalue expressions can refer to the following objects and their properties or attributes:

- JavaBeans components
- Collections
- Java SE enumerated types
- Implicit objects

To refer to these objects, you write an expression using a variable that is the name of the object. The following expression references a backing bean (a JavaBeans component) called customer:

```
${customer}
```

The web container evaluates the variable that appears in an expression by looking up its value according to the behavior of PageContext.findAttribute(String), where the String argument is the name of the variable. For example, when evaluating the expression ${customer}, the container will look for customer in the page, request, session, and application scopes and will return its value. If customer is not found, a null value is returned.

You can use a custom EL resolver to alter the way variables are resolved. For instance, you can provide an EL resolver that intercepts objects with the name customer, so that ${customer} returns a value in the EL resolver instead.

To reference an enum constant with an expression, use a String literal. For example, consider this Enum class:

```
public enum Suit {hearts, spades, diamonds, clubs}
```

To refer to the Suit constant Suit.hearts with an expression, use the String literal "hearts". Depending on the context, the String literal is converted to the enum constant automatically. For example, in the following expression in which mySuit is an instance of Suit, "hearts" is first converted to Suit.hearts before it is compared to the instance:

```
${mySuit == "hearts"}
```

Referring to Object Properties Using Value Expressions

To refer to properties of a bean or an enum instance, items of a collection, or attributes of an implicit object, you use the . or [ ] notation.

To reference the name property of the `customer` bean, use either the expression `${customer.name}` or the expression `${customer["name"]}`. The part inside the brackets is a `String` literal that is the name of the property to reference.

You can use double or single quotes for the `String` literal. You can also combine the [ ] and . notations, as shown here:

```
${customer.address["street"]}
```

Properties of an enum constant can also be referenced in this way. However, as with JavaBeans component properties, the properties of an `Enum` class must follow JavaBeans component conventions. This means that a property must at least have an accessor method called get*Property*, where *Property* is the name of the property that can be referenced by an expression.

For example, consider an `Enum` class that encapsulates the names of the planets of our galaxy and includes a method to get the mass of a planet. You can use the following expression to reference the method `getMass` of the `Enum` class `Planet`:

```
${myPlanet.mass}
```

If you are accessing an item in an array or list, you must use either a literal value that can be converted to `int` or the [ ] notation with an `int` and without quotes. The following examples could resolve to the same item in a list or array, assuming that `socks` can be converted to `int`:

- `${customer.orders[1]}`
- `${customer.orders.socks}`

In contrast, an item in a `Map` can be accessed using a string literal key; no coercion is required:

```
${customer.orders["socks"]}
```

An rvalue expression also refers directly to values that are not objects, such as the result of arithmetic operations and literal values, as shown by these examples:

- `${"literal"}`
- `${customer.age + 20}`
- `${true}`
- `${57}`

The EL defines the following literals:

- Boolean: `true` and `false`
- Integer: as in Java
- Floating-point: as in Java
- String: with single and double quotes; " is escaped as \", ' is escaped as \ ', and \ is escaped as \\
- Null: `null`

You can also write expressions that perform operations on an enum constant. For example, consider the following Enum class:

```
public enum Suit {club, diamond, heart, spade}
```

After declaring an enum constant called `mySuit`, you can write the following expression to test whether `mySuit` is `spade`:

```
${mySuit == "spade"}
```

When it resolves this expression, the EL resolving mechanism will invoke the `valueOf` method of the Enum class with the `Suit` class and the `spade` type, as shown here:

```
mySuit.valueOf(Suit.class, "spade"}
```

Where Value Expressions Can Be Used

Value expressions using the ${} delimiters can be used in

- Static text
- Any standard or custom tag attribute that can accept an expression

The value of an expression in static text is computed and inserted into the current output. Here is an example of an expression embedded in static text:

```
<some:tag>
    some text ${expr} some text
</some:tag>
```

If the static text appears in a tag body, note that an expression *will not* be evaluated if the body is declared to be `tagdependent`.

Lvalue expressions can be used only in tag attributes that can accept lvalue expressions.

A tag attribute value using either an rvalue or lvalue expression can be set in the following ways:

- With a single expression construct:

```
<some:tag value="${expr}"/>

<another:tag value="#{expr}"/>
```

These expressions are evaluated, and the result is converted to the attribute's expected type.

- With one or more expressions separated or surrounded by text:

```
<some:tag value="some${expr}${expr}text${expr}"/>

<another:tag value="some#{expr}#{expr}text#{expr}"/>
```

These kinds of expression, called *composite expressions*, are evaluated from left to right. Each expression embedded in the composite expression is converted to a String and then concatenated with any intervening text. The resulting String is then converted to the attribute's expected type.

- With text only:

```
<some:tag value="sometext"/>
```

This expression is called a *literal expression*. In this case, the attribute's String value is converted to the attribute's expected type. Literal value expressions have special syntax rules. See "Literal Expressions" on page 109 for more information. When a tag attribute has an enum type, the expression that the attribute uses must be a literal expression. For example, the tag attribute can use the expression "hearts" to mean Suit.hearts. The literal is converted to Suit, and the attribute gets the value Suit.hearts.

All expressions used to set attribute values are evaluated in the context of an expected type. If the result of the expression evaluation does not match the expected type exactly, a type conversion will be performed. For example, the expression ${1.2E4} provided as the value of an attribute of type float will result in the following conversion:

```
Float.valueOf("1.2E4").floatValue()
```

See Section 1.18 of the JavaServer Pages 2.2 Expression Language specification (available from http://jcp.org/aboutJava/communityprocess/final/jsr245/) for the complete type conversion rules.

Method Expressions

Another feature of the EL is its support of deferred method expressions. A method expression is used to invoke an arbitrary public method of a bean, which can return a result.

In JavaServer Faces technology, a component tag represents a component on a page. The component tag uses method expressions to invoke methods that perform some processing for the component. These methods are necessary for handling events that the components generate and for validating component data, as shown in this example:

```
<h:form>
    <h:inputText
        id="name"
        value="#{customer.name}"
        validator="#{customer.validateName}"/>
    <h:commandButton
        id="submit"
        action="#{customer.submit}" />
</h:form>
```

The inputText tag displays as a text field. The validator attribute of this inputText tag references a method, called validateName, in the bean, called customer.

Because a method can be invoked during different phases of the lifecycle, method expressions must always use the deferred evaluation syntax.

Like lvalue expressions, method expressions can use the . and the [] operators. For example, #{object.method} is equivalent to #{object["method"]}. The literal inside the [] is converted to String and is used to find the name of the method that matches it. Once the method is found, it is invoked, or information about the method is returned.

Method expressions can be used only in tag attributes and only in the following ways:

- With a single expression construct, where *bean* refers to a JavaBeans component and *method* refers to a method of the JavaBeans component:

  `<some:tag value="#{`*bean.method*`}"/>`

  The expression is evaluated to a method expression, which is passed to the tag handler. The method represented by the method expression can then be invoked later.

- With text only:

  `<some:tag value="sometext"/>`

  Method expressions support literals primarily to support action attributes in JavaServer Faces technology. When the method referenced by this method expression is invoked, the method returns the String literal, which is then converted to the expected return type, as defined in the tag's tag library descriptor.

Parameterized Method Calls

The EL offers support for parameterized method calls. Method calls can use parameters without having to use static EL functions.

Both the . and [ ] operators can be used for invoking method calls with parameters, as shown in the following expression syntax:

- *expr-a*[*expr-b*] (*parameters*)
- *expr-a*.*identifier-b*(*parameters*)

In the first expression syntax, *expr-a* is evaluated to represent a bean object. The expression *expr-b* is evaluated and cast to a string that represents a method in the bean represented by *expr-a*. In the second expression syntax, *expr-a* is evaluated to represent a bean object, and *identifier-b* is a string that represents a method in the bean object. The *parameters* in parentheses are the arguments for the method invocation. Parameters can be zero or more values or expressions, separated by commas.

Parameters are supported for both value expressions and method expressions. In the following example, which is a modified tag from the guessnumber application, a random number is provided as an argument rather than from user input to the method call:

```
<h:inputText value="#{userNumberBean.userNumber('5')}">
```

The preceding example uses a value expression.

Consider the following example of a JavaServer Faces component tag that uses a method expression:

```
<h:commandButton action="#{trader.buy}" value="buy"/>
```

The EL expression trader.buy calls the trader bean's buy method. You can modify the tag to pass on a parameter. Here is the revised tag where a parameter is passed:

```
<h:commandButton action="#{trader.buy('SOMESTOCK')}" value="buy"/>
```

In the preceding example, you are passing the string 'SOMESTOCK' (a stock symbol) as a parameter to the buy method.

For more information on the updated EL, see https://uel.dev.java.net.

Defining a Tag Attribute Type

As explained in the previous section, all kinds of expressions can be used in tag attributes. Which kind of expression and how it is evaluated, whether immediately or deferred, are determined by the type attribute of the tag's definition in the Page Description Language (PDL) that defines the tag.

If you plan to create custom tags, for each tag in the PDL, you need to specify what kind of expression to accept. Table 6–1 shows the kinds of tag attributes that accept EL expressions, gives examples of expressions they accept, and provides the type definitions of the attributes that must be added to the PDL. You cannot use #{} syntax for a dynamic attribute, meaning an attribute that accepts dynamically calculated values at runtime. Similarly, you also cannot use the ${} syntax for a deferred attribute.

TABLE 6–1 Definitions of Tag Attributes That Accept EL Expressions

Attribute Type	Example Expression	Type Attribute Definition
Dynamic	`"literal"`	`<rtexprvalue>true</rtexprvalue>`
	`${literal}`	`<rtexprvalue>true</rtexprvalue>`

Deferred value	`"literal"`	`<deferred-value>`
		`    <type>java.lang.String</type>`
		`</deferred-value>`

	`#{customer.age}`	`<deferred-value>`
		`    <type>int</type>`
		`</deferred-value>`

Deferred method	`"literal"`	`<deferred-method>`
		`    <method-signature>`
		`        java.lang.String submit()`
		`    </method-signature>`
		`<deferred-method>`

	`#{customer.calcTotal}`	`<deferred-method>`
		`    <method-signature>`
		`        double calcTotal(int, double)`
		`    </method-signature>`
		`</deferred-method>`

In addition to the tag attribute types shown in Table 6–1, you can define an attribute to accept both dynamic and deferred expressions. In this case, the tag attribute definition contains both an `rtexprvalue` definition set to `true` and either a `deferred-value` or `deferred-method` definition.

Literal Expressions

A literal expression is evaluated to the text of the expression, which is of type `String`. A literal expression does not use the ${} or #{} delimiters.

If you have a literal expression that includes the reserved ${} or #{} syntax, you need to escape these characters as follows:

- By creating a composite expression as shown here:

  ```
  ${'${'}exprA}
  #{'#{'}exprB}
  ```

  The resulting values would then be the strings ${exprA} and #{exprB}.

- By using the escape characters \$ and \# to escape what would otherwise be treated as an eval-expression:

  ```
  \${exprA}
  \#{exprB}
  ```

  The resulting values would again be the strings ${exprA} and #{exprB}.

When a literal expression is evaluated, it can be converted to another type. Table 6–2 shows examples of various literal expressions and their expected types and resulting values.

TABLE 6–2 Literal Expressions

Expression	Expected Type	Result
Hi	String	Hi
true	Boolean	Boolean.TRUE
42	int	42

Literal expressions can be evaluated immediately or deferred and can be either value or method expressions. At what point a literal expression is evaluated depends on where it is being used. If the tag attribute that uses the literal expression is defined to accept a deferred value expression, when referencing a value, the literal expression is evaluated at a point in the lifecycle that is determined by other factors, such as where the expression is being used and to what it is referring.

In the case of a method expression, the method that is referenced is invoked and returns the specified String literal. For example, the commandButton tag of the guessnumber application uses a literal method expression as a logical outcome to tell the JavaServer Faces navigation system which page to display next.

Operators

In addition to the . and [ ] operators discussed in "Value and Method Expressions" on page 102, the EL provides the following operators, which can be used in rvalue expressions only:

- **Arithmetic**: +, - (binary), *, / and div, % and mod, - (unary)
- **Logical**: and, &&, or, | |, not, !
- **Relational**: ==, eq, !=, ne, <, lt, >, gt, <=, ge, >=, le. Comparisons can be made against other values or against Boolean, string, integer, or floating-point literals.
- **Empty**: The empty operator is a prefix operation that can be used to determine whether a value is null or empty.
- **Conditional**: A ? B : C. Evaluate B or C, depending on the result of the evaluation of A.

The precedence of operators highest to lowest, left to right is as follows:

- [ ] .
- ( ) (used to change the precedence of operators)
- - (unary) not ! empty
- * / div % mod
- + - (binary)
- < > <= >= lt gt le ge
- == != eq ne
- && and
- | | or
- ? :

Reserved Words

The following words are reserved for the EL and should not be used as identifiers:

and	or	not	eq
ne	lt	gt	le
ge	true	false	null
instanceof	empty	div	mod

Examples of EL Expressions

Table 6–3 contains example EL expressions and the result of evaluating them.

TABLE 6–3 Example Expressions

EL Expression	Result
`${1 > (4/2)}`	false
`${4.0 >= 3}`	true
`${100.0 == 100}`	true
`${(10*10) ne 100}`	false
`${'a' < 'b'}`	true
`${'hip' gt 'hit'}`	false
`${4 > 3}`	true
`${1.2E4 + 1.4}`	12001.4
`${3 div 4}`	0.75
`${10 mod 4}`	2
`${!empty param.Add}`	False if the request parameter named `Add` is `null` or an empty string.
`${pageContext.request.contextPath}`	The context path.
`${sessionScope.cart.numberOfItems}`	The value of the `numberOfItems` property of the session-scoped attribute named `cart`.
`${param['mycom.productId']}`	The value of the request parameter named `mycom.productId`.
`${header["host"]}`	The host.
`${departments[deptName]}`	The value of the entry named `deptName` in the `departments` map.
`${requestScope['javax.servlet.forward.servlet_path']}`	The value of the request-scoped attribute named `javax.servlet.forward.servlet_path`.
`#{customer.lName}`	Gets the value of the property `lName` from the `customer` bean during an initial request. Sets the value of `lName` during a postback.
`#{customer.calcTotal}`	The return value of the method `calcTotal` of the `customer` bean.

7

Using JavaServer Faces Technology in Web Pages

Web pages represent the presentation layer for web applications. The process of creating web pages of a JavaServer Faces application includes adding components to the page and wiring them to backing beans, validators, converters, and other server-side objects that are associated with the page.

This chapter explains how to create web pages using various types of component and core tags. In the next chapter, you will learn about adding converters, validators, and listeners to component tags to provide additional functionality to components.

The following topics are addressed here:

Setting Up a Page

A typical JavaServer Faces web page includes the following elements:

- A set of namespace declarations that declare the JavaServer Faces tag libraries
- Optionally, the new HTML head (h:head) and body (h:body) tags
- A form tag (h:form) that represents the user input components

To add the JavaServer Faces components to your web page, you need to provide the page access to the two standard tag libraries: the JavaServer Faces HTML tag library and the JavaServer Faces core tag library. The JavaServer Faces standard HTML tag library defines tags that represent common HTML user interface components. This library is linked to the HTML render kit at http://download.oracle.com/docs/cd/E17410_01/javaee/6/javaserverfaces/2.0/docs/renderkitdocs/. The JavaServer Faces core tag library defines tags that perform core actions.

For a complete list of JavaServer Faces Facelets tags and their attributes, refer to the documentation at `http://download.oracle.com/docs/cd/E17410_01/javaee/6/javaserverfaces/2.0/docs/pdldocs/facelets/`.

To use any of the JavaServer Faces tags, you need to include appropriate directives at the top of each page specifying the tag libraries.

For Facelets applications, the XML namespace directives uniquely identify the tag library URI and the tag prefix.

For example, when creating a Facelets XHTML page, include namespace directives as follows:

```
<html xmlns="http://www.w3.org/1999/xhtml"
  xmlns:h="http://java.sun.com/jsf/html"
  xmlns:f="http://java.sun.com/jsf/core">
```

The XML namespace URI identifies the tag library location, and the prefix value is used to distinguish the tags belonging to that specific tag library. You can also use other prefixes instead of the standard h or f. However, when including the tag in the page, you must use the prefix that you have chosen for the tag library. For example, in the following web page, the form tag must be referenced using the h prefix because the preceding tag library directive uses the h prefix to distinguish the tags defined in HTML tag library:

```
<h:form ...>
```

The sections "Adding Components to a Page Using HTML Tags" on page 114 and "Using Core Tags" on page 143 describe how to use the component tags from the JavaServer Faces standard HTML tag library and the core tags from the JavaServer Faces core tag library.

Adding Components to a Page Using HTML Tags

The tags defined by the JavaServer Faces standard HTML tag library represent HTML form components and other basic HTML elements. These components display data or accept data from the user. This data is collected as part of a form and is submitted to the server, usually when the user clicks a button. This section explains how to use each of the component tags shown in Table 7–1.

TABLE 7–1 The Component Tags

Tag	Functions	Rendered as	Appearance
column	Represents a column of data in a data component	A column of data in an HTML table	A column in a table
commandButton	Submits a form to the application	An HTML `<input type=type>` element, where the `type` value can be `submit`, `reset`, or `image`	A button
commandLink	Links to another page or location on a page	An HTML `<a href>` element	A hyperlink
dataTable	Represents a data wrapper	An HTML `<table>` element	A table that can be updated dynamically
form	Represents an input form (inner tags of the form receive the data that will be submitted with the form)	An HTML `<form>` element	No appearance
graphicImage	Displays an image	An HTML `<img>` element	An image
inputHidden	Allows a page author to include a hidden variable in a page	An HTML `<input type=hidden>` element	No appearance
inputSecret	Allows a user to input a string without the actual string appearing in the field	An HTML `<input type=password>` element	A text field, which displays a row of characters instead of the actual string entered
inputText	Allows a user to input a string	An HTML `<input type=text>` element	A text field
inputTextarea	Allows a user to enter a multiline string	An HTML `<textarea>` element	A multi-row text field
message	Displays a localized message	An HTML `<span>` tag if styles are used	A text string
messages	Displays localized messages	A set of HTML `<span>` tags if styles are used	A text string
outputFormat	Displays a localized message	Plain text	Plain text

TABLE 7–1 The Component Tags   *(Continued)*

Tag	Functions	Rendered as	Appearance
outputLabel	Displays a nested component as a label for a specified input field	An HTML <label> element	Plain text
outputLink	Links to another page or location on a page without generating an action event	An HTML <a> element	A hyperlink
outputText	Displays a line of text	Plain text	Plain text
panelGrid	Displays a table	An HTML <table> element with <tr> and <td> elements	A table
panelGroup	Groups a set of components under one parent	A HTML <div> or <span> element	A row in a table
selectBooleanCheckbox	Allows a user to change the value of a Boolean choice	An HTML <input type=checkbox> element.	A check box
selectItem	Represents one item in a list of items from which the user must select one	An HTML <option> element	No appearance
selectItems	Represents a list of items from which the user must select one	A list of HTML <option> elements	No appearance
selectManyCheckbox	Displays a set of check boxes from which the user can select multiple values	A set of HTML <input> elements of type checkbox	A set of check boxes
selectManyListbox	Allows a user to select multiple items from a set of items, all displayed at once	An HTML <select> element	A list box
selectManyMenu	Allows a user to select multiple items from a set of items	An HTML <select> element	A scrollable combo box
selectOneListbox	Allows a user to select one item from a set of items, all displayed at once	An HTML <select> element	A list box

TABLE 7–1 The Component Tags   *(Continued)*

Tag	Functions	Rendered as	Appearance
selectOneMenu	Allows a user to select one item from a set of items	An HTML <select> element	A scrollable combo box
selectOneRadio	Allows a user to select one item from a set of items	An HTML <input type=radio> element	A set of radio buttons

The next section explains the important tag attributes that are common to most component tags. For each of the components discussed in the following sections, "Writing Bean Properties" on page 162 explains how to write a bean property bound to a particular component or its value.

Common Component Tag Attributes

Most of the component tags support the attributes shown in Table 7–2.

TABLE 7–2 Common Component Tag Attributes

Attribute	Description
binding	Identifies a bean property and binds the component instance to it.
id	Uniquely identifies the component.
immediate	If set to true, indicates that any events, validation, and conversion associated with the component should happen when request parameter values are applied,
rendered	Specifies a condition under which the component should be rendered. If the condition is not satisfied, the component is not rendered.
style	Specifies a Cascading Style Sheet (CSS) style for the tag.
styleClass	Specifies a CSS class that contains definitions of the styles.
value	Identifies an external data source and binds the component's value to it.

All the tag attributes (except id) can accept expressions, as defined by the EL, described in Chapter 6, "Expression Language."

The id Attribute

The id attribute is not usually required for a component tag but is used when another component or a server-side class must refer to the component. If you don't include an id attribute, the JavaServer Faces implementation automatically generates a component ID. Unlike most other JavaServer Faces tag attributes, the id attribute takes expressions using only the evaluation syntax described in "The `immediate` Attribute" on page 118, which uses the `${}` delimiters. For more information on expression syntax, see "Value Expressions" on page 102.

The `immediate` Attribute

Input components and command components (those that implement the `ActionSource` interface, such as buttons and hyperlinks) can set the `immediate` attribute to `true` to force events, validations, and conversions to be processed when request parameter values are applied.

You need to carefully consider how the combination of an input component's `immediate` value and a command component's `immediate` value determines what happens when the command component is activated.

Assume that you have a page with a button and a field for entering the quantity of a book in a shopping cart. If the `immediate` attributes of both the button and the field are set to `true`, the new value entered in the field will be available for any processing associated with the event that is generated when the button is clicked. The event associated with the button as well as the event validation and conversion associated with the field are all handled when request parameter values are applied.

If the button's `immediate` attribute is set to `true` but the field's `immediate` attribute is set to `false`, the event associated with the button is processed without updating the field's local value to the model layer. The reason is that any events, conversion, or validation associated with the field occurs *after* request parameter values are applied.

The `rendered` Attribute

A component tag uses a Boolean EL expression along with the `rendered` attribute to determine whether the component will be rendered. For example, the `commandLink` component in the following section of a page is not rendered if the cart contains no items:

```
<h:commandLink id="check"
    ...
    rendered="#{cart.numberOfItems > 0}">
    <h:outputText
        value="#{bundle.CartCheck}"/>
</h:commandLink>
```

Unlike nearly every other JavaServer Faces tag attribute, the `rendered` attribute is restricted to using rvalue expressions. As explained in "Value and Method Expressions" on page 102, these rvalue expressions can only read data; they cannot write the data back to the data source. Therefore, expressions used with `rendered` attributes can use the arithmetic operators and literals that rvalue expressions can use but lvalue expressions cannot use. For example, the expression in the preceding example uses the `>` operator.

The `style` and `styleClass` Attributes

The `style` and `styleClass` attributes allow you to specify CSS styles for the rendered output of your tags. "Displaying Error Messages with the `h:message` and `h:messages` Tags" on page 138 describes an example of using the `style` attribute to specify styles directly in the attribute. A component tag can instead refer to a CSS class.

The following example shows the use of a `dataTable` tag that references the style class `list-background`:

```
<h:dataTable id="books"
    ...
    styleClass="list-background"
    value="#{bookDBAO.books}"
    var="book">
```

The style sheet that defines this class is `stylesheet.css`, which will be included in the application. For more information on defining styles, see *Cascading Style Sheets Specification* at `http://www.w3.org/Style/CSS/`.

The `value` and `binding` Attributes

A tag representing an output component uses the `value` and `binding` attributes to bind its component's value or instance, respectively, to an external data source.

Adding HTML Head and Body Tags

The HTML head (`h:head`) and body (`h:body`) tags add HTML page structure to JavaServer Faces web pages.

- The `h:head` tag represents the head element of an HTML page
- The `h:body` tag represents the body element of an HTML page

The following is an example of an XHTML page using the usual head and body markup tags:

```
<!DOCTYPE html PUBLIC "-//W3C//DTD XHTML 1.0 Transitional//EN"
  "http://www.w3.org/TR/xhtml1/DTD/xhtml1-transitional.dtd">
  <html xmlns="http://www.w3.org/1999/xhtml">
  <head>
    <title>Add a title</title>
  </head>
  <body>
    Add Content
  </body>
```

The following is an example of an XHTML page using `h:head` and `h:body` tags:

```
<!DOCTYPE html PUBLIC "-//W3C//DTD XHTML 1.0 Transitional//EN"
  "http://www.w3.org/TR/xhtml1/DTD/xhtml1-transitional.dtd">
  <html xmlns="http://www.w3.org/1999/xhtml"
```

```
        xmlns:h="http://java.sun.com/jsf/html">
<h:head>
  Add a title
</h:head>
<h:body>
  Add Content
</h:body>
```

Both of the preceding example code segments render the same HTML elements. The head and body tags are useful mainly for resource relocation. For more information on resource relocation, see "Resource Relocation Using h:output Tags" on page 141.

Adding a Form Component

An h:form tag represents an input form, which includes child components that can contain data that is either presented to the user or submitted with the form.

Figure 7–1 shows a typical login form in which a user enters a user name and password, then submits the form by clicking the Login button.

FIGURE 7–1   A Typical Form

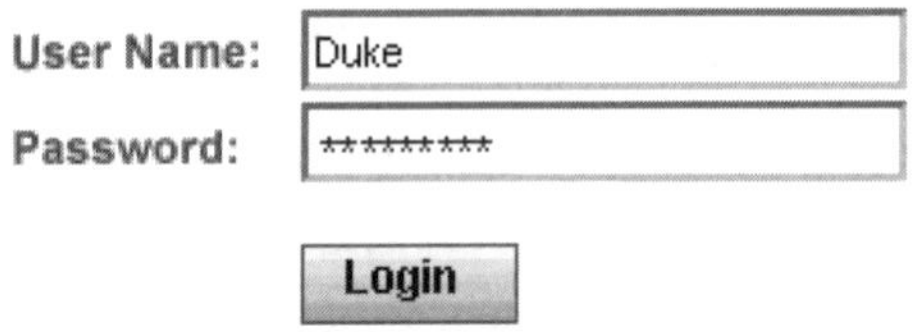

User Name:	Duke
Password:	********

Login

The h:form tag represents the form on the page and encloses all the components that display or collect data from the user, as shown here:

```
<h:form>
... other JavaServer Faces tags and other content...
</h:form>
```

The h:form tag can also include HTML markup to lay out the components on the page. Note that the h:form tag itself does not perform any layout; its purpose is to collect data and to declare attributes that can be used by other components in the form.

A page can include multiple h:form tags, but only the values from the form submitted by the user will be included in the postback request.

Using Text Components

Text components allow users to view and edit text in web applications. The basic types of text components are as follows:

- Label, which displays read-only text
- Text field, which allows users to enter text, often to be submitted as part of a form
- Text area, which is a type of text field that allows users to enter multiple lines of text
- Password field, which is a type of text field that displays a set of characters, such as asterisks, instead of the password text that the user enters

Figure 7–2 shows examples of these text components.

FIGURE 7-2   Example Text Components

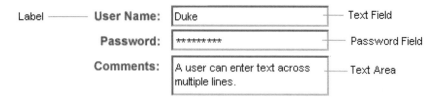

Text components can be categorized as either input or output. A JavaServer Faces output component is rendered as read-only text. An example is a label. A JavaServer Faces input component is rendered as editable text. An example is a text field.

The input and output components can each be rendered in various ways to display more specialized text.

Table 7–3 lists the tags that represent the input components.

TABLE 7-3   Input Tags

Tag	Function
h:inputHidden	Allows a page author to include a hidden variable in a page
h:inputSecret	The standard password field: accepts one line of text with no spaces and displays it as a set of asterisks as it is typed
h:inputText	The standard text field: accepts a one-line text string
h:inputTextarea	The standard text area: accepts multiple lines of text

The input tags support the tag attributes shown in Table 7–4 in addition to those described in "Common Component Tag Attributes" on page 117. Note that this table does not include all the attributes supported by the input tags but just those that are used most often. For the complete list of attributes, refer to the documentation at `http://download.oracle.com/` `docs/cd/E17410_01/javaee/6/javaserverfaces/2.0/docs/pdldocs/facelets/`.

TABLE 7–4 Input Tag Attributes

Attribute	Description
converter	Identifies a converter that will be used to convert the component's local data. See "Using the Standard Converters" on page 145 for more information on how to use this attribute.
converterMessage	Specifies an error message to display when the converter registered on the component fails.
dir	Specifies the direction of the text displayed by this component. Acceptable values are LTR, meaning left-to-right, and RTL, meaning right-to-left.
label	Specifies a name that can be used to identify this component in error messages.
lang	Specifies the code for the language used in the rendered markup, such as en_US.
required	Takes a boolean value that indicates whether the user must enter a value in this component.
requiredMessage	Specifies an error message to display when the user does not enter a value into the component.
validator	Identifies a method expression pointing to a backing bean method that performs validation on the component's data. See "Referencing a Method That Performs Validation" on page 156 for an example of using the f:validator tag.
f:validatorMessage	Specifies an error message to display when the validator registered on the component fails to validate the component's local value.
valueChangeListener	Identifies a method expression that points to a backing bean method that handles the event of entering a value in this component. See "Referencing a Method That Handles a Value-Change Event" on page 156 for an example of using valueChangeListener.

Table 7–5 lists the tags that represent the output components.

TABLE 7–5 Output Tags

Tag	Function
h:outputFormat	Displays a localized message
h:outputLabel	The standard read-only label: displays a component as a label for a specified input field
h:outputLink	Displays an <a href> tag that links to another page without generating an action event
h:outputText	Displays a one-line text string

The output tags support the `converter` tag attribute in addition to those listed in "Common Component Tag Attributes" on page 117.

The rest of this section explains how to use some of the tags listed in Table 7–3 and Table 7–5. The other tags are written in a similar way.

Rendering a Text Field with the h:inputText Tag

The h:inputText tag is used to display a text field. A similar tag, the h:outputText tag, displays a read-only, single-line string. This section shows you how to use the h:inputText tag. The h:outputText tag is written in a similar way.

Here is an example of an h:inputText tag:

```
<h:inputText id="name" label="Customer Name" size="50"
    value="#{cashier.name}"
    required="true"
    requiredMessage="#{customMessages.CustomerName}">
    <f:valueChangeListener
        type="com.sun.bookstore6.listeners.NameChanged" />
 </h:inputText>
```

The label attribute specifies a user-friendly name that will be used in the substitution parameters of error messages displayed for this component.

The value attribute refers to the name property of a backing bean named CashierBean. This property holds the data for the name component. After the user submits the form, the value of the name property in CashierBean will be set to the text entered in the field corresponding to this tag.

The required attribute causes the page to reload, displaying errors, if the user does not enter a value in the name text field. The JavaServer Faces implementation checks whether the value of the component is null or is an empty string.

If your component must have a non-null value or a String value at least one character in length, you should add a required attribute to your tag and set its value to true. If your tag has a required attribute that is set to true and the value is null or a zero-length string, no other validators that are registered on the tag are called. If your tag does not have a required attribute set to true, other validators that are registered on the tag are called, but those validators must handle the possibility of a null or zero-length string. See "Validating Null and Empty Strings" on page 177 for more information.

Rendering a Password Field with the h:inputSecret Tag

The h:inputSecret tag renders an <input type="password"> HTML tag. When the user types a string into this field, a row of asterisks is displayed instead of the text typed by the user. Here is an example:

```
<h:inputSecret redisplay="false"
    value="#{LoginBean.password}" />
```

In this example, the redisplay attribute is set to false. This will prevent the password from being displayed in a query string or in the source file of the resulting HTML page.

Rendering a Label with the h:outputLabel Tag

The h:outputLabel tag is used to attach a label to a specified input field for the purpose of making it accessible. The following page uses an h:outputLabel tag to render the label of a check box:

```
<h:selectBooleanCheckbox
    id="fanClub"
    binding="#{cashier.specialOffer}" />
<h:outputLabel for="fanClub"
    binding="#{cashier.specialOfferText}" >
  <h:outputText id="fanClubLabel"
      value="#{bundle.DukeFanClub}" />
</h:outputLabel>
...
```

The for attribute of the h:outputLabel tag maps to the id of the input field to which the label is attached. The h:outputText tag nested inside the h:outputLabel tag represents the label component. The value attribute on the h:outputText tag indicates the text that is displayed next to the input field.

Instead of using an h:outputText tag for the text displayed as a label, you can simply use the h:outputLabel tag's value attribute. The following code snippet shows what the previous code snippet would look like if it used the value attribute of the h:outputLabel tag to specify the text of the label:

```
<h:selectBooleanCheckbox
    id="fanClub"
    binding="#{cashier.specialOffer}" />
<h:outputLabel for="fanClub"
    binding="#{cashier.specialOfferText}"
```

```
    value="#{bundle.DukeFanClub}" />
</h:outputLabel>
...
```

Rendering a Hyperlink with the h:outputLink Tag

The h:outputLink tag is used to render a hyperlink that, when clicked, loads another page but does not generate an action event. You should use this tag instead of the h:commandLink tag if you always want the URL specified by the h:outputLink tag's value attribute to open and do not want any processing to be performed when the user clicks the link. Here is an example:

```
<h:outputLink value="javadocs">
    Documentation for this demo
</h:outputLink>
```

The text in the body of the outputLink tag identifies the text that the user clicks to get to the next page.

Displaying a Formatted Message with the h:outputFormat Tag

The h:outputFormat tag allows display of concatenated messages as a MessageFormat pattern, as described in the API documentation for java.text.MessageFormat. Here is an example of an outputFormat tag:

```
<h:outputFormat value="Hello, {0}!">
    <f:param value="#{hello.name}"/>
</h:outputFormat>
```

The value attribute specifies the MessageFormat pattern. The param tag specifies the substitution parameters for the message. The value of the parameter replaces the {0} in the sentence. If the value of "#{hello.name}" is "Bill", the message displayed in the page is as follows:

```
Hello, Bill!
```

An h:outputFormat tag can include more than one param tag for those messages that have more than one parameter that must be concatenated into the message. If you have more than one parameter for one message, make sure that you put the param tags in the proper order so that the data is inserted in the correct place in the message. Here is the preceding example modified with an additional parameter:

```
<h:outputFormat value="Hello, {0}! You are visitor number {1} to the page.">
<f:param value="#{hello.name}" />
<f:param value="#{bean.numVisitor}"/>
</h:outputFormat>
```

The value of {1} is replaced by the second parameter. The parameter is an EL expression, bean.numVisitor, where the property numVisitor of the backing bean

bean keeps track of visitors to the page. This is an example of a value-expression-enabled tag attribute accepting an EL expression. The message displayed in the page is now as follows:

```
Hello, Bill! You are visitor number 10 to the page.
```

Using Command Component Tags for Performing Actions and Navigation

In JavaServer Faces applications, the button and hyperlink component tags are used to perform actions, such as submitting a form, and for navigating to another page. These tags are called command component tags because they perform an action when activated.

The h:commandButton tag is rendered as a button. The h:commandLink tag is rendered as a hyperlink.

In addition to the tag attributes listed in "Common Component Tag Attributes" on page 117, the h:commandButton and h:commandLink tags can use the following attributes:

- action, which is either a logical outcome String or a method expression pointing to a bean method that returns a logical outcome String. In either case, the logical outcome String is used to determine what page to access when the command component tag is activated.

- actionListener, which is a method expression pointing to a bean method that processes an action event fired by the command component tag.

See "Referencing a Method That Performs Navigation" on page 155 for more information on using the action attribute. See "Referencing a Method That Handles an Action Event" on page 156 for details on using the actionListener attribute.

Rendering a Button with the h:commandButton Tag

If you are using a commandButton component tag, the data from the current page is processed when a user clicks the button, and the next page is opened. Here is an example of the h:commandButton tag:

```
<h:commandButton value="Submit"
      action="#{cashier.submit}"/>
```

Clicking the button will cause the submit method of CashierBean to be invoked because the action attribute references this method. The submit method performs some processing and returns a logical outcome.

The `value` attribute of the example `commandButton` tag references the button's label. For information on how to use the `action` attribute, see "Referencing a Method That Performs Navigation" on page 155.

Rendering a Hyperlink with the `h:commandLink` Tag

The `h:commandLink` tag represents an HTML hyperlink and is rendered as an HTML `<a>` element. This tag acts like a form's Submit button and is used to submit an action event to the application.

A `h:commandLink` tag must include a nested `h:outputText` tag, which represents the text that the user clicks to generate the event. Here is an example:

```
<h:commandLink id="NAmerica" action="bookstore"
    actionListener="#{localeBean.chooseLocaleFromLink}">
        <h:outputText value="#{bundle.English}" />
</h:commandLink>
```

This tag will render the following HTML:

```
<a id="_id3:NAmerica" href="#"
    onclick="document.forms['_id3']['_id3:NAmerica'].
    value='_id3:NAmerica';
    document.forms['_id3'].submit();
    return false;">English</a>
```

Note – The `h:commandLink` tag will render JavaScript programming language. If you use this tag, make sure that your browser is enabled for JavaScript technology.

Adding Graphics and Images with the `h:graphicImage` Tag

In a JavaServer Faces application, use the `h:graphicImage` tag to render an image on a page:

```
<h:graphicImage id="mapImage" url="/template/world.jpg"/>
```

The `url` attribute specifies the path to the image. The URL of the example tag begins with a /, which adds the relative context path of the web application to the beginning of the path to the image.

Alternatively, you can use the facility described in "Resources" on page 96 to point to the image location. Here is an example:

```
<h:graphicImage value="#{resource['images:wave.med.gif']}"/>
```

Laying Out Components with the `h:panelGrid` and `h:panelGroup` Tags

In a JavaServer Faces application, you use a panel as a layout container for a set of other components. A panel is rendered as an HTML table. Table 7–6 lists the tags used to create panels.

TABLE 7–6 Panel Component Tags

Tag	Attributes	Function
h:panelGrid	columns, columnClasses, footerClass, headerClass, panelClass, rowClasses	Displays a table
h:panelGroup	layout	Groups a set of components under one parent

The `h:panelGrid` tag is used to represent an entire table. The `h:panelGroup` tag is used to represent rows in a table. Other tags are used to represent individual cells in the rows.

The `columns` attribute defines how to group the data in the table and therefore is required if you want your table to have more than one column. The `h:panelGrid` tag also has a set of optional attributes that specify CSS classes: `columnClasses`, `footerClass`, `headerClass`, `panelClass`, and `rowClasses`.

If the `headerClass` attribute value is specified, the `panelGrid` must have a header as its first child. Similarly, if a `footerClass` attribute value is specified, the `panelGrid` must have a footer as its last child.

Here is an example:

```
<h:panelGrid columns="3" headerClass="list-header"
    rowClasses="list-row-even, list-row-odd"
    styleClass="list-background"
    title="#{bundle.Checkout}">
    <f:facet name="header">
        <h:outputText value="#{bundle.Checkout}"/>
    </f:facet>
    <h:outputText value="#{bundle.Name}" />
    <h:inputText id="name" size="50"
        value="#{cashier.name}"
        required="true">
        <f:valueChangeListener
            type="listeners.NameChanged" />
    </h:inputText>
    <h:message styleClass="validationMessage" for="name"/>
    <h:outputText value="#{bundle.CCNumber}"/>
    <h:inputText id="ccno" size="19"
        converter="CreditCardConverter" required="true">
```

```
            <bookstore:formatValidator
                formatPatterns="9999999999999999|
                    9999 9999 9999 9999|9999-9999-9999-9999"/>
        </h:inputText>
        <h:message styleClass="validationMessage"  for="ccno"/>
        ...
</h:panelGrid>
```

The preceding h:panelGrid tag is rendered as a table that contains components in which a customer inputs personal information. This h:panelGrid tag uses style sheet classes to format the table. The following code shows the list-header definition:

```
.list-header {
    background-color: #ffffff;
    color: #000000;
    text-align: center;
}
```

Because the h:panelGrid tag specifies a headerClass, the panelGrid must contain a header. The example panelGrid tag uses a facet tag for the header. Facets can have only one child, so an h:panelGroup tag is needed if you want to group more than one component within a facet. The example h:panelGrid tag has only one cell of data, so an h:panelGroup tag is not needed.

The h:panelGroup tag has an attribute, layout, in addition to those listed in "Common Component Tag Attributes" on page 117. If the layout attribute has the value block, an HTML div element is rendered to enclose the row; otherwise, an HTML span element is rendered to enclose the row. If you are specifying styles for the h:panelGroup tag, you should set the layout attribute to block in order for the styles to be applied to the components within the h:panelGroup tag. You should do this because styles, such as those that set width and height, are not applied to inline elements, which is how content enclosed by the span element is defined.

An h:panelGroup tag can also be used to encapsulate a nested tree of components so that the tree of components appears as a single component to the parent component.

Data, represented by the nested tags, is grouped into rows according to the value of the columns attribute of the h:panelGrid tag. The columns attribute in the example is set to 3, and therefore the table will have three columns. The column in which each component is displayed is determined by the order in which the component is listed on the page modulo 3. So, if a component is the fifth one in the list of components, that component will be in the 5 modulo 3 column, or column 2.

Displaying Components for Selecting One Value

Another commonly used component is one that allows a user to select one value, whether it is the only value available or one of a set of choices. The most common tags for this kind of component are as follows:

- An h:selectBooleanCheckbox tag, displayed as a check box, which represents a Boolean state
- An h:selectOneRadio tag, displayed as a set of radio buttons
- An h:selectOneMenu tag, displayed as a drop-down menu, with a scrollable list
- An h:selectOneListbox tag, displayed as a list box, with an unscrollable list

Figure 7–3 shows examples of these components.

FIGURE 7–3   Example Components for Selecting One Item

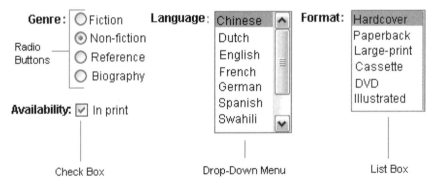

Displaying a Check Box Using the h:selectBooleanCheckbox Tag

The h:selectBooleanCheckbox tag is the only tag that JavaServer Faces technology provides for representing a Boolean state.

Here is an example that shows how to use the h:selectBooleanCheckbox tag:

```
<h:selectBooleanCheckbox
    id="fanClub"
    rendered="false"
    binding="#{cashier.specialOffer}" />
<h:outputLabel
    for="fanClub"
    rendered="false"
    binding="#{cashier.specialOfferText}">
    <h:outputText
        id="fanClubLabel"
        value="#{bundle.DukeFanClub}" />
</h:outputLabel>
```

This example tag displays a check box to allow users to indicate whether they want to join the Duke Fan Club. The label for the check box is rendered by the outputLabel tag. The text is represented by the nested outputText tag.

Displaying a Menu Using the h:selectOneMenu Tag

A component that allows the user to select one value from a set of values can be rendered as a list box, a set of radio buttons, or a menu. This section describes the h:selectOneMenu tag. The h:selectOneRadio and h:selectOneListbox tags are used in a similar way. The h:selectOneListbox tag is similar to the h:selectOneMenu tag except that h:selectOneListbox defines a size attribute that determines how many of the items are displayed at once.

The h:selectOneMenu tag represents a component that contains a list of items from which a user can choose one item. This menu component is also commonly known as a drop-down list or a combo box. The following code snippet shows how the h:selectOneMenu tag is used to allow the user to select a shipping method:

```
<h:selectOneMenu id="shippingOption"
    required="true"
    value="#{cashier.shippingOption}">
    <f:selectItem
        itemValue="2"
        itemLabel="#{bundle.QuickShip}"/>
    <f:selectItem
        itemValue="5"
        itemLabel="#{bundle.NormalShip}"/>
    <f:selectItem
        itemValue="7"
        itemLabel="#{bundle.SaverShip}"/>
 </h:selectOneMenu>
```

The value attribute of the h:selectOneMenu tag maps to the property that holds the currently selected item's value. You are not required to provide a value for the currently selected item. If you don't provide a value, the first item in the list is selected by default.

Like the h:selectOneRadio tag, the selectOneMenu tag must contain either an f:selectItems tag or a set of f:selectItem tags for representing the items in the list. "Using the f:selectItem and f:selectItems Tags" on page 133 describes these tags.

Displaying Components for Selecting Multiple Values

In some cases, you need to allow your users to select multiple values rather than just one value from a list of choices. You can do this using one of the following component tags:

- An h:selectManyCheckbox tag, displayed as a set of check boxes
- An h:selectManyMenu tag, displayed as a drop-down menu
- An h:selectManyListbox tag, displayed as a list box

Figure 7–4 shows examples of these components.

FIGURE 7–4   Example Components for Selecting Multiple Values

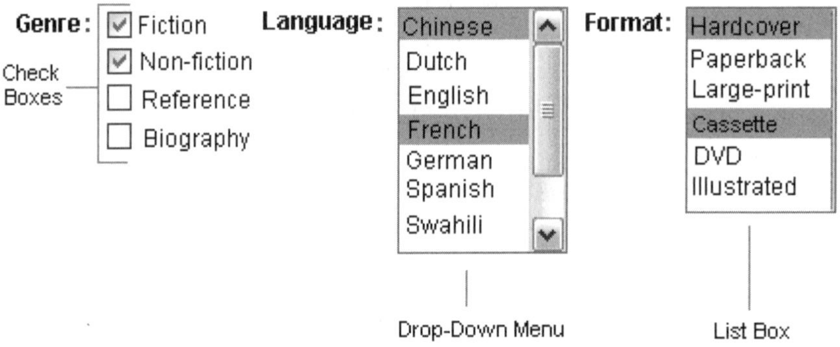

These tags allow the user to select zero or more values from a set of values. This section explains the h:selectManyCheckbox tag. The h:selectManyListbox and h:selectManyMenu tags are used in a similar way.

Unlike a menu, a list box displays a subset of items in a box; a menu displays only one item at a time when the user is not selecting the menu. The size attribute of the h:selectManyListbox tag determines the number of items displayed at one time. The list box includes a scroll bar for scrolling through any remaining items in the list.

The h:selectManyCheckbox tag renders a set of check boxes, with each check box representing one value that can be selected:

```
<h:selectManyCheckbox
    id="newsletters"
    layout="pageDirection"
    value="#{cashier.newsletters}">
    <f:selectItems
        value="#{newsletters}"/>
</h:selectManyCheckbox>
```

The `value` attribute of the `h:selectManyCheckbox` tag identifies the `newsletters` property of the `Cashier` backing bean. This property holds the values of the currently selected items from the set of check boxes. You are not required to provide a value for the currently selected items. If you don't provide a value, the first item in the list is selected by default.

The `layout` attribute indicates how the set of check boxes is arranged on the page. Because layout is set to `pageDirection`, the check boxes are arranged vertically. The default is `lineDirection`, which aligns the check boxes horizontally.

The `h:selectManyCheckbox` tag must also contain a tag or set of tags representing the set of check boxes. To represent a set of items, you use the `f:selectItems` tag. To represent each item individually, you use a `f:selectItem` tag. The following subsection explains these tags in more detail.

Using the `f:selectItem` and `f:selectItems` Tags

The `f:selectItem` and `f:selectItems` tags represent components that can be nested inside a component that allows you to select one or multiple items. An `f:selectItem` tag contains the value, label, and description of a single item. An `f:selectItems` tag contains the values, labels, and descriptions of the entire list of items.

You can use either a set of `f:selectItem` tags or a single `f:selectItems` tag within your component tag.

The advantages of using the `f:selectItems` tag are as follows.

- Items can be represented by using different data structures, including `Array`, `Map`, and `Collection`. The value of the `f:selectItems` tag can represent even a generic collection of POJOs.
- Different lists can be concatenated into a single component, and the lists can be grouped within the component.
- Values can be generated dynamically at runtime.

The advantages of using `f:selectItem` are as follows:

- Items in the list can be defined from the page.
- Less code is needed in the bean for the `selectItem` properties.

The rest of this section shows you how to use the `f:selectItems` and `f:selectItem` tags.

Using the f:selectItems Tag

The following example from "Displaying Components for Selecting Multiple Values" on page 132 shows how to use the h:selectManyCheckbox tag:

```
<h:selectManyCheckbox
    id="newsletters"
    layout="pageDirection"
    value="#{cashier.newsletters}">
    <f:selectItems
        value="#{newsletters}"/>
</h:selectManyCheckbox>
```

The value attribute of the f:selectItems tag is bound to the backing bean newsletters.

You can also create the list of items programmatically in the backing bean. See "Writing Bean Properties" on page 162 for information on how to write a backing bean property for one of these tags.

Using the f:selectItem Tag

The f:selectItem tag represents a single item in a list of items. Here is the example from "Displaying a Menu Using the h:selectOneMenu Tag" on page 131 once again:

```
<h:selectOneMenu
      id="shippingOption" required="true"
      value="#{cashier.shippingOption}">
    <f:selectItem
        itemValue="2"
        itemLabel="#{bundle.QuickShip}"/>
    <f:selectItem
        itemValue="5"
        itemLabel="#{bundle.NormalShip}"/>
    <f:selectItem
        itemValue="7"
        itemLabel="#{bundle.SaverShip}"/>
 </h:selectOneMenu>
```

The itemValue attribute represents the default value for the selectItem tag. The itemLabel attribute represents the String that appears in the drop-down menu component on the page.

The itemValue and itemLabel attributes are value-binding-enabled, meaning that they can use value-binding expressions to refer to values in external objects. These attributes can also define literal values, as shown in the example h:selectOneMenu tag.

Using Data-Bound Table Components

Data-bound table components display relational data in a tabular format. In a JavaServer Faces application, the h:dataTable component tag supports binding to a collection of data objects and displays the data as an HTML table. The h:column tag represents a column of data within the table, iterating over each record in the data source, which is displayed as a row. Here is an example:

```
<h:dataTable id="items"
    captionClass="list-caption"
    columnClasses="list-column-center, list-column-left,
        list-column-right, list-column-center"
    footerClass="list-footer"
    headerClass="list-header"
    rowClasses="list-row-even, list-row-odd"
    styleClass="list-background">
    <h:column headerClass="list-header-left">
        <f:facet name="header">
            <h:outputText value=Quantity"" />
        </f:facet>
        <h:inputText id="quantity" size="4"
            value="#{item.quantity}" >
            ...
        </h:inputText>
        ...
    </h:column>
    <h:column>
        <f:facet name="header">
            <h:outputText value="Title"/>
        </f:facet>
        <h:commandLink>
            <h:outputText value="#{item.title}"/>
        </h:commandLink>
    </h:column>
    ...
    <f:facet name="footer">
        <h:panelGroup>
            <h:outputText value="Total}"/>
            <h:outputText value="#{cart.total}" />
                <f:convertNumber type="currency" />
            </h:outputText>
        </h:panelGroup>
    </f:facet>
</h:dataTable>
```

Figure 7–5 shows a data grid that this h:dataTable tag can display.

FIGURE 7–5   Table on a Web Page

Quantity	Title	Price	
1	Web Servers for Fun and Profit	$40.75	Remove Item
3	Web Components for Web Developers	$27.75	Remove Item
1	From Oak to Java: The Revolution of a Language	$10.75	Remove Item
2	My Early Years: Growing up on *7	$30.75	Remove Item
1	Java Intermediate Bytecodes	$30.95	Remove Item
3	Duke: A Biography of the Java Evangelist	$45.00	Remove Item
	Subtotal:$362.20		

Update Quantities

The example h:dataTable tag displays the books in the shopping cart, as well as the quantity of each book in the shopping cart, the prices, and a set of buttons the user can click to remove books from the shopping cart.

The h:column tags represent columns of data in a data component. While the data component is iterating over the rows of data, it processes the column component associated with each h:column tag for each row in the table.

The h:dataTable tag shown in the preceding code example iterates through the list of books (cart.items) in the shopping cart and displays their titles, authors, and prices. Each time the h:dataTable tag iterates through the list of books, it renders one cell in each column.

The h:dataTable and h:column tags use facets to represent parts of the table that are not repeated or updated. These parts include headers, footers, and captions.

In the preceding example, h:column tags include f:facet tags for representing column headers or footers. The h:column tag allows you to control the styles of these headers and footers by supporting the headerClass and footerClass attributes. These attributes accept space-separated lists of CSS classes, which will be applied to the header and footer cells of the corresponding column in the rendered table.

Facets can have only one child, so an h:panelGroup tag is needed if you want to group more than one component within an f:facet. Because the facet tag representing the footer includes more than one tag, the panelGroup is needed to group those tags. Finally, this h:dataTable tag includes an f:facet tag with its name attribute set to caption, causing a table caption to be rendered below the table.

This table is a classic use case for a data component because the number of books might not be known to the application developer or the page author when that application is developed. The data component can dynamically adjust the number of rows of the table to accommodate the underlying data.

The `value` attribute of an `h:dataTable` tag references the data to be included in the table. This data can take the form of any of the following:

- A list of beans
- An array of beans
- A single bean
- A `javax.faces.model.DataModel` object
- A `java.sql.ResultSet` object
- A `javax.servlet.jsp.jstl.sql.Result` object
- A `javax.sql.RowSet` object

All data sources for data components have a `DataModel` wrapper. Unless you explicitly construct a `DataModel` wrapper, the JavaServer Faces implementation will create one around data of any of the other acceptable types. See "Writing Bean Properties" on page 162 for more information on how to write properties for use with a data component.

The `var` attribute specifies a name that is used by the components within the `h:dataTable` tag as an alias to the data referenced in the `value` attribute of `dataTable`.

In the example `h:dataTable` tag, the `value` attribute points to a list of books. The `var` attribute points to a single book in that list. As the `h:dataTable` tag iterates through the list, each reference to `item` points to the current book in the list.

The `h:dataTable` tag also has the ability to display only a subset of the underlying data. This feature is not shown in the preceding example. To display a subset of the data, you use the optional `first` and `rows` attributes.

The `first` attribute specifies the first row to be displayed. The `rows` attribute specifies the number of rows, starting with the first row, to be displayed. For example, if you wanted to display records 2 through 10 of the underlying data, you would set `first` to 2 and `rows` to 9. When you display a subset of the data in your pages, you might want to consider including a link or button that causes subsequent rows to display when clicked. By default, both `first` and `rows` are set to zero, and this causes all the rows of the underlying data to display.

Table 7–7 shows the optional attributes for the `h:dataTable` tag.

TABLE 7–7 Optional Attributes for the `h:dataTable` Tag

Attribute	Defines Styles for
`captionClass`	Table caption
`columnClasses`	All the columns
`footerClass`	Footer
`headerClass`	Header

TABLE 7–7 Optional Attributes for the h:dataTable Tag *(Continued)*

Attribute	Defines Styles for
rowClasses	Rows
styleClass	The entire table

Each of the attributes in Table 7–7 can specify more than one style. If columnClasses or rowClasses specifies more than one style, the styles are applied to the columns or rows in the order that the styles are listed in the attribute. For example, if columnClasses specifies styles list-column-center and list-column-right and if the table has two columns, the first column will have style list-column-center, and the second column will have style list-column-right.

If the style attribute specifies more styles than there are columns or rows, the remaining styles will be assigned to columns or rows starting from the first column or row. Similarly, if the style attribute specifies fewer styles than there are columns or rows, the remaining columns or rows will be assigned styles starting from the first style.

Displaying Error Messages with the h:message and h:messages Tags

The h:message and h:messages tags are used to display error messages when conversion or validation fails. The h:message tag displays error messages related to a specific input component, whereas the h:messages tag displays the error messages for the entire page.

Here is an example h:message tag from the guessnumber application:

```
<h:inputText id="userNo" value="#{UserNumberBean.userNumber}">
    <f:validateLongRange minimum="0" maximum="10" />
 <h:commandButton id="submit"
        action="success" value="Submit" /><p>
<h:message
    style="color: red;
    font-family: 'New Century Schoolbook', serif;
    font-style: oblique;
    text-decoration: overline" id="errors1" for="userNo"/>
```

The for attribute refers to the ID of the component that generated the error message. The error message is displayed at the same location that the h:message tag appears in the page. In this case, the error message will appear after the Submit button.

The style attribute allows you to specify the style of the text of the message. In the example in this section, the text will be red, New Century Schoolbook, serif font family, and oblique style, and a line will appear over the text. The message and messages tags support many other attributes for defining styles. For more information on these attributes, refer to the documentation at `http://download.oracle.com/docs/cd/E17410_01/javaee/6/javaserverfaces/2.0/docs/pdldocs/facelets/`.

Another attribute supported by the `h:messages` tag is the `layout` attribute. Its default value is `list`, which indicates that the messages are displayed in a bullet list using the HTML `ul` and `li` elements. If you set the attribute value to `table`, the messages will be rendered in a table using the HTML `table` element.

The preceding example shows a standard validator that is registered on the input component. The message tag displays the error message that is associated with this validator when the validator cannot validate the input component's value. In general, when you register a converter or validator on a component, you are queueing the error messages associated with the converter or validator on the component. The `h:message` and `h:messages` tags display the appropriate error messages that are queued on the component when the validators or converters registered on that component fail to convert or validate the component's value.

Standard error messages are provided with standard converters and standard validators. An application architect can override these standard messages and supply error messages for custom converters and validators by registering custom error messages with the application.

Creating Bookmarkable URLs with the `h:button` and `h:link` Tags

The ability to create bookmarkable URLs refers to the ability to generate hyperlinks based on a specified navigation outcome and on component parameters.

In HTTP, most browsers by default send GET requests for URL retrieval and POST requests for data processing. The GET requests can have query parameters and can be cached, which is not advised for POST requests, which send data to the external servers. The other JavaServer Faces tags capable of generating hyperlinks use either simple GET requests, as in the case of `h:outputlink`, or POST requests, as in the case of `h:commandLink` or `h:commandButton` tags. GET requests with query parameters provide finer granularity to URL strings. These URLs are created with one or more `name=value` parameters appended to the simple URL after a ? character and separated by either `&;` or `&amp;` strings.

To create a bookmarkable URL, use an `h:link` or `h:button` tag. Both of these tags can generate a hyperlink based on the `outcome` attribute of the component. For example:

```
<h:link outcome="response" value="Message">
  <f:param name="Result" value="#{sampleBean.result}"/>
</h:link>
```

The h:link tag will generate a URL link that points to the response.xhtml file on the same server, appended with the single query parameter created by the f:param tag. When processed, the parameter Result is assigned the value of backing bean's result method #{sampleBean.result}. The following sample HTML is generated from the preceding set of tags, assuming that the value of the parameter is success:

```
<a href="http://localhost:8080/guessnumber/response.xhtml?Result=success">Response</a>
```

This is a simple GET request. To create more complex GET requests and utilize the complete functionality of the h:link tag, you can use view parameters.

Using View Parameters to Configure Bookmarkable URLs

The core tags f:metadata and f:viewparam are used as a source of parameters for configuring the URLs. View parameters are declared as part of f:metadata for a page, as shown in the following example:

```
<h:body>
<f:metadata>
  <f:viewParam id="name" name="Name" value="#{sampleBean.username}"/>
  <f:viewParam id="ID" name="uid" value="#{sampleBean.useridentity}"/>
</f:metadata>
<h:link outcome="response" value="Message" includeViewParams="true">
</h:link>
</h:body>
```

View parameters are declared with the f:viewparam tag and are placed inside the f:metadata tag. If the includeViewParams attribute is set on the component, the view parameters are added to the hyperlink.

The resulting URL will look like this:

```
http://localhost:8080/guessnumber/response.xhtml?Name=Duke&;uid=2001
```

Because the URL can be the result of various parameter values, the order of the URL creation has been predefined. The order in which the various parameter values are read is as follows:

1. Component
2. Navigation-case parameters
3. View parameters

Resource Relocation Using h:output Tags

Resource relocation refers to the ability of a JavaServer Faces application to specify the location where a resource can be rendered. Resource relocation can be defined with the following HTML tags:

- h:outputScript
- h:outputStylesheet

These tags have name and target attributes, which can be used to define the render location. For a complete list of attributes for these tags, see the documentation at http://download.oracle.com/
docs/cd/E17410_01/javaee/6/javaserverfaces/2.0/docs/pdldocs/facelets/.

For the h:outputScript tag, the name and target attributes define where the output of a resource may appear. Here is an example:

```
<html xmlns="http://www.w3.org/1999/xhtml"
    xmlns:h="http://java.sun.com/jsf/html">
    <h:head id="head">
        <title>Resource Relocation</title>
    </h:head>
    <h:body id="body">
        <h:form id="form">
            <h:outputScript name="hello.js"/>
            <h:outputStylesheet name="hello.css"/>
        </h:form>
    </h:body>
</html>
```

Since the target attribute is not defined in the tag, the style sheet hello.css is rendered in the head, and the hello.js script is rendered in the body of the page as defined by the h:head tag.

Here is the HTML generated by the preceding code:

```
<html xmlns="http://www.w3.org/1999/xhtml">
    <head>
        <title>Resource Relocation</title>
        <link type="text/css" rel="stylesheet"
            href="/ctx/faces/javax.faces.resource/hello.css"/>
    </head>
    <body>
        <form id="form" name="form" method="post" action="..." enctype="...">
            <script type="text/javascript"
              src="/ctx/faces/javax.faces.resource/hello.js">
            </script>
        </form>
    </body>
</html>
```

The original page can be recreated by setting the `target` attribute for the `h:outputScript` tag, which allows the incoming GET request to provide the location parameter. Here is an example:

```
<html xmlns="http://www.w3.org/1999/xhtml"
    xmlns:h="http://java.sun.com/jsf/html">
    <h:head id="head">
        <title>Resource Relocation</title>
    </h:head>
    <h:body id="body">
        <h:form id="form">
            <h:outputScript name="hello.js" target="#{param.location}"/>
            <h:outputStylesheet name="hello.css"/>
        </h:form>
    </h:body>
</html>
```

In this case, if the incoming request does not provide a location parameter, the default locations will still apply: The style sheet is rendered in the head, and the script is rendered inline. However, if the incoming request provides the location parameter as the head, both the style sheet and the script will be rendered in the head element.

The HTML generated by the preceding code is as follows:

```
<html xmlns="http://www.w3.org/1999/xhtml">
    <head>
        <title>Resource Relocation</title>
        <link type="text/css" rel="stylesheet"
            href="/ctx/faces/javax.faces.resource/hello.css"/>
        <script type="text/javascript"
          src="/ctx/faces/javax.faces.resource/hello.js">
        </script>
    </head>
    <body>
        <form id="form" name="form" method="post" action="..." enctype="...">
        </form>
    </body>
</html>
```

Similarly, if the incoming request provides the location parameter as the body, the script will be rendered in the body element.

The preceding section describes simple uses for resource relocation. That feature can add even more functionality for the components and pages. A page author does not have to know the location of a resource or its placement.

By using a `@ResourceDependency` annotation for the components, component authors can define the resources for the component, such as a style sheet and script. This allows the page authors freedom from defining resource locations.

Using Core Tags

The tags included in the JavaServer Faces core tag library are used to perform core actions that are not performed by HTML tags. Commonly used core tags, along with the functions they perform, are listed in Table 7–8.

TABLE 7–8 The Core Tags

Tag Categories	Tags	Functions
Event handling	f:actionListener	Adds an action listener to a parent component
	f:phaseListener	Adds a PhaseListener to a page
	f:setPropertyActionListener	Registers a special action listener whose sole purpose is to push a value into a backing bean when a form is submitted
	f:valueChangeListener	Adds a value-change listener to a parent component
Attribute configuration	f:attribute	Adds configurable attributes to a parent component
Data conversion	f:converter	Adds an arbitrary converter to the parent component
	f:convertDateTime	Adds a DateTimeConverter instance to the parent component
	f:convertNumber	Adds a NumberConverter instance to the parent component
Facet	f:facet	Adds a nested component that has a special relationship to its enclosing tag
	f:metadata	Registers a facet on a parent component
Localization	f:loadBundle	Specifies a ResourceBundle that is exposed as a Map
Parameter substitution	f:param	Substitutes parameters into a MessageFormat instance and adds query string name-value pairs to a URL
Representing items in a list	f:selectItem	Represents one item in a list of items
	f:selectItems	Represents a set of items

TABLE 7–8 The Core Tags *(Continued)*

Tag Categories	Tags	Functions
Validator	f:validateDoubleRange	Adds a DoubleRangeValidator to a component
	f:validateLength	Adds a LengthValidator to a component
	f:validateLongRange	Adds a LongRangeValidator to a component
	f:validator	Adds a custom validator to a component
	f:validateRegEx	Adds a RegExValidator to a component
	f:validateBean	Delegates the validation of a local value to a BeanValidator
	f:validateRequired	Enforces the presence of a value in a component
Ajax	f:ajax	Associates an Ajax action with a single component or a group of components based on placement
Event	f:event	Allows installing a ComponentSystemEventListener on a component

These tags, which are used in conjunction with component tags, are explained in other sections of this tutorial. Table 7–9 lists the sections that explain how to use specific core tags.

TABLE 7–9 Where the Core Tags Are Explained

Tags	Where Explained
Event handling tags	"Registering Listeners on Components" on page 151
Data conversion tags	"Using the Standard Converters" on page 145
facet	"Using Data-Bound Table Components" on page 135 and "Laying Out Components with the h:panelGrid and h:panelGroup Tags" on page 128
loadBundle	"Displaying Components for Selecting Multiple Values" on page 132
param	"Displaying a Formatted Message with the h:outputFormat Tag" on page 125
selectItem and selectItems	"Using the f:selectItem and f:selectItems Tags" on page 133
Validator tags	"Using the Standard Validators" on page 152

◆ ◆ ◆   C H A P T E R   8

8

Using Converters, Listeners, and Validators

The previous chapter described components and explained how to add them to a web page. This chapter provides information on adding more functionality to the components through converters, listeners, and validators.

- Converters are used to convert data that is received from the input components.
- Listeners are used to listen to the events happening in the page and perform actions as defined.
- Validators are used to validate the data that is received from the input components.

The following topics are addressed here:

Using the Standard Converters

The JavaServer Faces implementation provides a set of Converter implementations that you can use to convert component data. The standard Converter implementations, located in the javax.faces.convert package, are as follows:

- BigDecimalConverter
- BigIntegerConverter
- BooleanConverter
- ByteConverter
- CharacterConverter
- DateTimeConverter
- DoubleConverter
- EnumConverter
- FloatConverter

- `IntegerConverter`
- `LongConverter`
- `NumberConverter`
- `ShortConverter`

A standard error message is associated with each of these converters. If you have registered one of these converters onto a component on your page, and the converter is not able to convert the component's value, the converter's error message will display on the page. For example, the following error message appears if `BigIntegerConverter` fails to convert a value:

```
{0} must be a number consisting of one or more digits
```

In this case, the {0} substitution parameter will be replaced with the name of the input component on which the converter is registered.

Two of the standard converters (`DateTimeConverter` and `NumberConverter`) have their own tags, which allow you to configure the format of the component data using the tag attributes. For more information about using `DateTimeConverter`, see "Using `DateTimeConverter`" on page 147. For more information about using `NumberConverter`, see "Using `NumberConverter`" on page 149. The following section explains how to convert a component's value, including how to register other standard converters with a component.

Converting a Component's Value

To use a particular converter to convert a component's value, you need to register the converter onto the component. You can register any of the standard converters in one of the following ways:

- Nest one of the standard converter tags inside the component's tag. These tags are `convertDateTime` and `convertNumber`, which are described in "Using `DateTimeConverter`" on page 147 and "Using `NumberConverter`" on page 149, respectively.

- Bind the value of the component to a backing bean property of the same type as the converter.

- Refer to the converter from the component tag's `converter` attribute.

- Nest a `converter` tag inside of the component tag, and use either the `converter` tag's `converterId` attribute or its `binding` attribute to refer to the converter.

As an example of the second method, if you want a component's data to be converted to an `Integer`, you can simply bind the component's value to a backing bean property. Here is an example:

```
Integer age = 0;
public Integer getAge(){ return age;}
public void setAge(Integer age) {this.age = age;}
```

If the component is not bound to a bean property, you can use the third method by using the `converter` attribute directly on the component tag:

```
<h:inputText
    converter="javax.faces.convert.IntegerConverter" />
```

This example shows the `converter` attribute referring to the fully qualified class name of the converter. The `converter` attribute can also take the ID of the component.

The data from the `inputText` tag in the this example will be converted to a `java.lang.Integer` value. The `Integer` type is a supported type of `NumberConverter`. If you don't need to specify any formatting instructions using the `convertNumber` tag attributes, and if one of the standard converters will suffice, you can simply reference that converter by using the component tag's `converter` attribute.

Finally, you can nest a `converter` tag within the component tag and use either the converter tag's `converterId` attribute or its `binding` attribute to reference the converter.

The `converterId` attribute must reference the converter's ID. Here is an example:

```
<h:inputText value="#{LoginBean.Age}" />
    <f:converter converterId="Integer" />
</h:inputText>
```

Instead of using the `converterId` attribute, the converter tag can use the `binding` attribute. The `binding` attribute must resolve to a bean property that accepts and returns an appropriate `Converter` instance.

Using `DateTimeConverter`

You can convert a component's data to a `java.util.Date` by nesting the `convertDateTime` tag inside the component tag. The `convertDateTime` tag has several attributes that allow you to specify the format and type of the data. Table 8–1 lists the attributes.

Here is a simple example of a `convertDateTime` tag:

```
<h:outputText id= "shipDate" value="#{cashier.shipDate}">
    <f:convertDateTime dateStyle="full" />
</h:outputText>
```

When binding the `DateTimeConverter` to a component, ensure that the backing bean property to which the component is bound is of type `java.util.Date`. In the preceding example, `cashier.shipDate` must be of type `java.util.Date`.

The example tag can display the following output:

```
Saturday, September 25, 2010
```

You can also display the same date and time by using the following tag where the date format is specified:

```
<h:outputText value="#{cashier.shipDate}">
    <f:convertDateTime
        pattern="EEEEEEEE, MMM dd, yyyy" />
</h:outputText>
```

If you want to display the example date in Spanish, you can use the locale attribute:

```
<h:inputText value="#{cashier.shipDate}">
    <f:convertDateTime dateStyle="full"
        locale="Locale.SPAIN"
        timeStyle="long" type="both" />
</h:inputText>
```

This tag would display the following output:

```
sabado 25 de septiembre de 2010
```

Refer to the "Customizing Formats" lesson of the *Java Tutorial* at
http://download.oracle.com/
docs/cd/E17409_01/javase/tutorial/i18n/format/simpleDateFormat.html for
more information on how to format the output using the pattern attribute of the
convertDateTime tag.

TABLE 8–1   Attributes for the convertDateTime Tag

Attribute	Type	Description
binding	DateTimeConverter	Used to bind a converter to a backing bean property.
dateStyle	String	Defines the format, as specified by java.text.DateFormat, of a date or the date part of a date string. Applied only if type is date or both and if pattern is not defined. Valid values: default, short, medium, long, and full. If no value is specified, default is used.
for	String	Used with composite components. Refers to one of the objects within the composite component inside which this tag is nested.
locale	String or Locale	Locale whose predefined styles for dates and times are used during formatting or parsing. If not specified, the Locale returned by FacesContext.getLocale will be used.

TABLE 8-1   Attributes for the `convertDateTime` Tag   *(Continued)*

Attribute	Type	Description
`pattern`	`String`	Custom formatting pattern that determines how the date/time string should be formatted and parsed. If this attribute is specified, `dateStyle`, `timeStyle`, and `type` attributes are ignored.
`timeStyle`	`String`	Defines the format, as specified by `java.text.DateFormat`, of a `time` or the time part of a date string. Applied only if `type` is `time` and `pattern` is not defined. Valid values: `default`, `short`, `medium`, `long`, and `full`. If no value is specified, `default` is used.
`timeZone`	`String or TimeZone`	Time zone in which to interpret any time information in the date string.
`type`	`String`	Specifies whether the string value will contain a date, a time, or both. Valid values are `date`, `time`, or `both`. If no value is specified, `date` is used.

Using `NumberConverter`

You can convert a component's data to a `java.lang.Number` by nesting the `convertNumber` tag inside the component tag. The `convertNumber` tag has several attributes that allow you to specify the format and type of the data. Table 8–2 lists the attributes.

The following example uses a `convertNumber` tag to display the total prices of the contents of a shopping cart:

```
<h:outputText value="#{cart.total}" >
    <f:convertNumber type="currency"/>
</h:outputText>
```

When binding the `NumberConverter` to a component, ensure that the backing bean property to which the component is bound is of a primitive type or has a type of `java.lang.Number`. In the preceding example, `cart.total` is of type `java.lang.Number`.

Here is an example of a number that this tag can display:

$934

This result can also be displayed by using the following tag, where the currency pattern is specified:

```
<h:outputText id="cartTotal"
    value="#{cart.Total}" >
```

```
    <f:convertNumber pattern="$####" />
</h:outputText>
```

See the "Customizing Formats" lesson of the *Java Tutorial* at `http://`
`download.oracle.com/`
`docs/cd/E17409_01/javase/tutorial/i18n/format/decimalFormat.html` for
more information on how to format the output by using the `pattern` attribute of the
`convertNumber` tag.

TABLE 8–2   Attributes for the `convertNumber` Tag

Attribute	Type	Description
binding	NumberConverter	Used to bind a converter to a backing bean property.
currencyCode	String	ISO 4217 currency code, used only when formatting currencies.
currencySymbol	String	Currency symbol, applied only when formatting currencies.
for	String	Used with composite components. Refers to one of the objects within the composite component inside which this tag is nested.
groupingUsed	Boolean	Specifies whether formatted output contains grouping separators.
integerOnly	Boolean	Specifies whether only the integer part of the value will be parsed.
locale	String or Locale	`Locale` whose number styles are used to format or parse data.
maxFractionDigits	int	Maximum number of digits formatted in the fractional part of the output.
maxIntegerDigits	int	Maximum number of digits formatted in the integer part of the output.
minFractionDigits	int	Minimum number of digits formatted in the fractional part of the output.
minIntegerDigits	int	Minimum number of digits formatted in the integer part of the output.
pattern	String	Custom formatting pattern that determines how the number string is formatted and parsed.
type	String	Specifies whether the string value is parsed and formatted as a `number`, `currency`, or `percentage`. If not specified, `number` is used.

Registering Listeners on Components

An application developer can implement listeners as classes or as backing bean methods. If a listener is a backing bean method, the page author references the method from either the component's `valueChangeListener` attribute or its `actionListener` attribute. If the listener is a class, the page author can reference the listener from either a `valueChangeListener` tag or an `actionListener` tag and nest the tag inside the component tag to register the listener on the component.

"Referencing a Method That Handles an Action Event" on page 156 and "Referencing a Method That Handles a Value-Change Event" on page 156 explain how a page author uses the `valueChangeListener` and `actionListener` attributes to reference backing bean methods that handle events.

This section explains how to register the `NameChanged` value-change listener and a hypothetical `LocaleChange` action listener implementation on components.

Registering a Value-Change Listener on a Component

A `ValueChangeListener` implementation can be registered on a component that implements `EditableValueHolder` by nesting a `valueChangeListener` tag within the component's tag on the page. The `valueChangeListener` tag supports the attributes shown in Table 8–3, one of which must be used.

TABLE 8–3   Attributes for the `valueChangeListener` Tag

Attribute	Description
type	References the fully qualified class name of a `ValueChangeListener` implementation. Can accept a literal or a value expression.
binding	References an object that implements `ValueChangeListener`. Can accept only a value expression, which must point to a backing bean property that accepts and returns a `ValueChangeListener` implementation.

The following example shows a value-change listener registered on a component:

```
<h:inputText id="name" size="50" value="#{cashier.name}"
    required="true">
    <f:valueChangeListener type="listeners.NameChanged" />
</h:inputText>
```

In the example, the core tag `type` attribute specifies the custom `NameChanged` listener as the `ValueChangeListener` implementation registered on the name component.

After this component tag is processed and local values have been validated, its corresponding component instance will queue the `ValueChangeEvent` associated with the specified `ValueChangeListener` to the component.

The `binding` attribute is used to bind a `ValueChangeListener` implementation to a backing bean property. This attribute works in a similar way to the `binding` attribute supported by the standard converter tags.

Registering an Action Listener on a Component

A page author can register an `ActionListener` implementation on a command component by nesting an `actionListener` tag within the component's tag on the page. Similarly to the `valueChangeListener` tag, the `actionListener` tag supports both the type and `binding` attributes. One of these attributes must be used to reference the action listener.

Here is an example of a `commandLink` tag that references an `ActionListener` implementation rather than a backing bean method:

```
<h:commandLink id="NAmerica" action="bookstore">
    <f:actionListener type="listeners.LocaleChange" />
</h:commandLink>
```

The type attribute of the `actionListener` tag specifies the fully qualified class name of the `ActionListener` implementation. Similarly to the `valueChangeListener` tag, the `actionListener` tag also supports the `binding` attribute.

Using the Standard Validators

JavaServer Faces technology provides a set of standard classes and associated tags that page authors and application developers can use to validate a component's data. Table 8–4 lists all the standard validator classes and the tags that allow you to use the validators from the page.

TABLE 8–4 The Validator Classes

Validator Class	Tag	Function
BeanValidator	validateBean	Registers a bean validator for the component.
DoubleRangeValidator	validateDoubleRange	Checks whether the local value of a component is within a certain range. The value must be floating-point or convertible to floating-point.
LengthValidator	validateLength	Checks whether the length of a component's local value is within a certain range. The value must be a `java.lang.String`.

TABLE 8–4 The Validator Classes *(Continued)*

Validator Class	Tag	Function
LongRangeValidator	validateLongRange	Checks whether the local value of a component is within a certain range. The value must be any numeric type or String that can be converted to a long.
RegexValidator	validateRegEx	Checks whether the local value of a component is a match against a regular expression from the java.util.regex package.
RequiredValidator	validateRequired	Ensures that the local value is not empty on an EditableValueHolder component.

Similar to the standard converters, each of these validators has one or more standard error messages associated with it. If you have registered one of these validators onto a component on your page, and the validator is unable to validate the component's value, the validator's error message will display on the page. For example, the error message that displays when the component's value exceeds the maximum value allowed by LongRangeValidator is as follows:

```
{1}: Validation Error: Value is greater than allowable maximum of "{0}"
```

In this case, the {1} substitution parameter is replaced by the component's label or id, and the {0} substitution parameter is replaced with the maximum value allowed by the validator.

Instead of using the standard validators, you can use Bean Validation to validate data. See "Using Bean Validation" on page 174 for more information.

Validating a Component's Value

To validate a component's value using a particular validator, you need to register that validator on the component. You can do this in one of the following ways:

- Nest the validator's corresponding tag (shown in Table 8–4) inside the component's tag. "Using LongRangeValidator" on page 154 explains how to use the validateLongRange tag. You can use the other standard tags in the same way.

- Refer to a method that performs the validation from the component tag's validator attribute.

- Nest a validator tag inside the component tag, and use either the validator tag's validatorId attribute or its binding attribute to refer to the validator.

See "Referencing a Method That Performs Validation" on page 156 for more information on using the `validator` attribute.

The `validatorId` attribute works similarly to the `converterId` attribute of the `converter` tag, as described in "Converting a Component's Value" on page 146.

Keep in mind that validation can be performed only on components that implement `EditableValueHolder`, because these components accept values that can be validated.

Using `LongRangeValidator`

The following example shows how to use the `validateLongRange` validator on an input component named `quantity`:

```
<h:inputText id="quantity" size="4"
      value="#{item.quantity}" >
   <f:validateLongRange minimum="1"/>
</h:inputText>
<h:message for="quantity"/>
```

This tag requires the user to enter a number that is at least 1. The `size` attribute specifies that the number can have no more than four digits. The `validateLongRange` tag also has a `maximum` attribute, which sets a maximum value for the input.

The attributes of all the standard validator tags accept EL value expressions. This means that the attributes can reference backing bean properties rather than specify literal values. For example, the `validateLongRange` tag in the preceding example can reference a backing bean property called `minimum` to get the minimum value acceptable to the validator implementation, as shown here:

```
<f:validateLongRange minimum="#{ShowCartBean.minimum}" />
```

Referencing a Backing Bean Method

A component tag has a set of attributes for referencing backing bean methods that can perform certain functions for the component associated with the tag. These attributes are summarized in Table 8–5.

TABLE 8–5   Component Tag Attributes That Reference Backing Bean Methods

Attribute	Function
`action`	Refers to a backing bean method that performs navigation processing for the component and returns a logical outcome `String`
`actionListener`	Refers to a backing bean method that handles action events

TABLE 8–5 Component Tag Attributes That Reference Backing Bean Methods   *(Continued)*

Attribute	Function
validator	Refers to a backing bean method that performs validation on the component's value
valueChangeListener	Refers to a backing bean method that handles value-change events

Only components that implement `ActionSource` can use the `action` and `actionListener` attributes. Only components that implement `EditableValueHolder` can use the `validator` or `valueChangeListener` attributes.

The component tag refers to a backing bean method using a method expression as a value of one of the attributes. The method referenced by an attribute must follow a particular signature, which is defined by the tag attribute's definition in the documentation at `http://download.oracle.com/docs/cd/E17410_01/javaee/6/javaserverfaces/2.0/docs/pdldocs/jsp/`. For example, the definition of the `validator` attribute of the `inputText` tag is the following:

```
void validate(javax.faces.context.FacesContext,
    javax.faces.component.UIComponent, java.lang.Object)
```

The following sections give examples of how to use the attributes.

Referencing a Method That Performs Navigation

If your page includes a component, such as a button or a hyperlink, that causes the application to navigate to another page when the component is activated, the tag corresponding to this component must include an `action` attribute. This attribute does one of the following:

- Specifies a logical outcome `String` that tells the application which page to access next

- References a backing bean method that performs some processing and returns a logical outcome `String`

The following example shows how to reference a navigation method:

```
<h:commandButton
    value="#{bundle.Submit}"
    action="#{cashier.submit}" />
```

Referencing a Method That Handles an Action Event

If a component on your page generates an action event, and if that event is handled by a backing bean method, you refer to the method by using the component's `actionListener` attribute.

The following example shows how the method is referenced:

```
<h:commandLink id="NAmerica" action="bookstore"
    actionListener="#{localeBean.chooseLocaleFromLink}">
```

The `actionListener` attribute of this component tag references the `chooseLocaleFromLink` method using a method expression. The `chooseLocaleFromLink` method handles the event when the user clicks the hyperlink rendered by this component.

Referencing a Method That Performs Validation

If the input of one of the components on your page is validated by a backing bean method, refer to the method from the component's tag by using the `validator` attribute.

The following example shows how to reference a method that performs validation on `email`, an input component:

```
<h:inputText id="email" value="#{checkoutFormBean.email}"
    size="25" maxlength="125"
    validator="#{checkoutFormBean.validateEmail}"/>
```

Referencing a Method That Handles a Value-Change Event

If you want a component on your page to generate a value-change event and you want that event to be handled by a backing bean method, you refer to the method by using the component's `valueChangeListener` attribute.

The following example shows how a component references a `ValueChangeListener` implementation that handles the event when a user enters a name in the name input field:

```
<h:inputText
    id="name"
    size="50"
    value="#{cashier.name}"
    required="true">
    <f:valueChangeListener type="listeners.NameChanged" />
</h:inputText>
```

To refer to this backing bean method, the tag uses the `valueChangeListener` attribute:

```
<h:inputText
     id="name"
     size="50"
     value="#{cashier.name}"
     required="true"
     valueChangeListener="#{cashier.processValueChange}" />
</h:inputText>
```

The `valueChangeListener` attribute of this component tag references the `processValueChange` method of `CashierBean` by using a method expression. The `processValueChange` method handles the event of a user entering a name in the input field rendered by this component.

9

Developing with JavaServer Faces Technology

Chapter 7, "Using JavaServer Faces Technology in Web Pages," and Chapter 8, "Using Converters, Listeners, and Validators," show how to add components to a page and connect them to server-side objects by using component tags and core tags, as well as how to provide additional functionality to the components through converters, listeners, and validators. Developing a JavaServer Faces application also involves the task of programming the server-side objects: backing beans, converters, event handlers, and validators.

This chapter provides an overview of backing beans and explains how to write methods and properties of backing beans that are used by a JavaServer Faces application. This chapter also introduces the Bean Validation feature.

The following topics are addressed here:

Backing Beans

A typical JavaServer Faces application includes one or more backing beans, each of which is a type of JavaServer Faces managed bean that can be associated with the components used in a particular page. This section introduces the basic concepts of creating, configuring, and using backing beans in an application.

Creating a Backing Bean

A backing bean is created with a constructor with no arguments (like all JavaBeans components) and a set of properties and a set of methods that perform functions for a component. Each of the backing bean properties can be bound to one of the following:

- A component value
- A component instance
- A converter instance
- A listener instance
- A validator instance

The most common functions that backing bean methods perform include the following:

- Validating a component's data

- Handling an event fired by a component

- Performing processing to determine the next page to which the application must navigate

As with all JavaBeans components, a property consists of a private data field and a set of accessor methods, as shown by this code:

```
Integer userNumber = null;
...
public void setUserNumber(Integer user_number) {
    userNumber = user_number;
}
public Integer getUserNumber() {
    return userNumber;
}
public String getResponse() {
    ...
}
```

When bound to a component's value, a bean property can be any of the basic primitive and numeric types or any Java object type for which the application has access to an appropriate converter. For example, a property can be of type Date if the application has access to a converter that can convert the Date type to a String and back again. See "Writing Bean Properties" on page 162 for information on which types are accepted by which component tags.

When a bean property is bound to a component instance, the property's type must be the same as the component object. For example, if a javax.faces.component.UISelectBoolean component is bound to the property, the property must accept and return a UISelectBoolean object. Likewise, if the property is bound to a converter, validator, or listener instance, the property must be of the appropriate converter, validator, or listener type.

For more information on writing beans and their properties, see "Writing Bean Properties" on page 162.

Using the EL to Reference Backing Beans

To bind component values and objects to backing bean properties or to reference backing bean methods from component tags, page authors use the Expression Language syntax. As explained in "Overview of the EL" on page 99, the following are some of the features that EL offers:

- Deferred evaluation of expressions
- The ability to use a value expression to both read and write data
- Method expressions

Deferred evaluation of expressions is important because the JavaServer Faces lifecycle is split into several phases in which component event handling, data conversion and validation, and data propagation to external objects are all performed in an orderly fashion. The implementation must be able to delay the evaluation of expressions until the proper phase of the lifecycle has been reached. Therefore, the implementation's tag attributes always use deferred-evaluation syntax, which is distinguished by the #{} delimiter.

To store data in external objects, almost all JavaServer Faces tag attributes use lvalue expressions, which are expressions that allow both getting and setting data on external objects.

Finally, some component tag attributes accept method expressions that reference methods that handle component events or validate or convert component data.

To illustrate a JavaServer Faces tag using the EL, suppose that a tag of an application referenced a method to perform the validation of user input:

```
<h:inputText id="userNo"
    value="#{UserNumberBean.userNumber}"
    validator="#{UserNumberBean.validate}" />
```

This tag binds the userNo component's value to the UserNumberBean.userNumber backing bean property by using an lvalue expression. The tag uses a method expression to refer to the UserNumberBean.validate method, which performs validation of the component's local value. The local value is whatever the user enters into the field corresponding to this tag. This method is invoked when the expression is evaluated.

Nearly all JavaServer Faces tag attributes accept value expressions. In addition to referencing bean properties, value expressions can reference lists, maps, arrays, implicit objects, and resource bundles.

Another use of value expressions is binding a component instance to a backing bean property. A page author does this by referencing the property from the binding attribute:

```
<inputText binding="#{UserNumberBean.userNoComponent}" />
```

In addition to using expressions with the standard component tags, you can configure your custom component properties to accept expressions by creating javax.el.ValueExpression or javax.el.MethodExpression instances for them.

For information on the EL, see Chapter 6, "Expression Language."

For information on referencing backing bean methods from component tags, see "Referencing a Backing Bean Method" on page 154.

Writing Bean Properties

As explained in "Backing Beans" on page 159, a backing bean property can be bound to one of the following items:

- A component value
- A component instance
- A converter implementation
- A listener implementation
- A validator implementation

These properties follow the conventions of JavaBeans components (also called beans). For more information on JavaBeans components, see the *JavaBeans Tutorial* at http://download.oracle.com/ docs/cd/E17409_01/javase/tutorial/javabeans/index.html.

The component's tag binds the component's value to a backing bean property by using its value attribute and binds the component's instance to a backing bean property by using its binding attribute. Likewise, all the converter, listener, and validator tags use their binding attributes to bind their associated implementations to backing bean properties.

To bind a component's value to a backing bean property, the type of the property must match the type of the component's value to which it is bound. For example, if a backing bean property is bound to a UISelectBoolean component's value, the property should accept and return a boolean value or a Boolean wrapper Object instance.

To bind a component instance to a backing bean property, the property must match the type of component. For example, if a backing bean property is bound to a UISelectBoolean instance, the property should accept and return a UISelectBoolean value.

Similarly, to bind a converter, listener, or validator implementation to a backing bean property, the property must accept and return the same type of converter, listener, or validator object. For example, if you are using the convertDateTime tag to bind a DateTimeConverter to a property, that property must accept and return a DateTimeConverter instance.

The rest of this section explains how to write properties that can be bound to component values, to component instances for the component objects described in "Adding Components to a Page Using HTML Tags" on page 114, and to converter, listener, and validator implementations.

Writing Properties Bound to Component Values

To write a backing bean property that is bound to a component's value, you must match the property type to the component's value.

Table 9–1 lists the javax.faces.component classes and the acceptable types of their values.

TABLE 9–1   Acceptable Types of Component Values

Component Class	Acceptable Types of Component Values
UIInput, UIOutput, UISelectItem, UISelectOne	Any of the basic primitive and numeric types or any Java programming language object type for which an appropriate Converter implementation is available
UIData	array of beans, List of beans, single bean, java.sql.ResultSet, javax.servlet.jsp.jstl.sql.Result, javax.sql.RowSet
UISelectBoolean	boolean or Boolean
UISelectItems	java.lang.String, Collection, Array, Map
UISelectMany	array or List, though elements of the array or List can be any of the standard types

When they bind components to properties by using the value attributes of the component tags, page authors need to ensure that the corresponding properties match the types of the components' values.

UIInput and UIOutput Properties

In the following example, an h:inputText tag binds the name component to the name property of a backing bean called CashierBean.

```
<h:inputText id="name" size="50"
    value="#{cashier.name}">
</h:inputText>
```

The following code snippet from the backing bean `CashierBean` shows the bean property type bound by the preceding component tag:

```
protected String name = null;

public void setName(String name) {
    this.name = name;
}
public String getName() {
    return this.name;
}
```

As described in "Using the Standard Converters" on page 145, to convert the value of an input or output component, you can either apply a converter or create the bean property bound to the component with the matching type. Here is the example tag, from "Using `DateTimeConverter`" on page 147, that displays the date when items will be shipped.

```
<h:outputText value="#{cashier.shipDate}">
    <f:convertDateTime dateStyle="full" />
</h:outputText>
```

The bean property represented by this tag must have a type of `java.util.Date`. The following code snippet shows the `shipDate` property, from the backing bean `CashierBean`, that is bound by the tag's value in the preceding example:

```
protected Date shipDate;

public Date getShipDate() {
    return this.shipDate;
}
public void setShipDate(Date shipDate) {
    this.shipDate = shipDate;
}
```

UIData **Properties**

Data components must be bound to one of the backing bean property types listed in Table 9–1. Data components are discussed in "Using Data-Bound Table Components" on page 135. Here is part of the start tag of `dataTable` from that section:

```
<h:dataTable id="items"
    ...
    value="#{cart.items}"
    var="item" >
```

The value expression points to the `items` property of a shopping cart bean named `cart`. The `cart` bean maintains a map of `ShoppingCartItem` beans.

The `getItems` method from the `cart` bean populates a `List` with `ShoppingCartItem` instances that are saved in the items map when the customer adds items to the cart, as shown in the following code segment:

```
public synchronized List getItems() {
    List results = new ArrayList();
    results.addAll(this.items.values());
    return results;
}
```

All the components contained in the data component are bound to the properties of the cart bean that is bound to the entire data component. For example, here is the h:outputText tag that displays the item name in the table:

```
<h:commandLink action="#{showcart.details}">
    <h:outputText value="#{item.item.name}"/>
</h:commandLink>
```

UISelectBoolean Properties

Backing bean properties that hold a UISelectBoolean component's data must be of boolean or Boolean type. The example selectBooleanCheckbox tag from the section "Displaying Components for Selecting One Value" on page 130 binds a component to a property. The following example shows a tag that binds a component value to a boolean property:

```
<h:selectBooleanCheckbox title="#{bundle.receiveEmails}"
    value="#{custFormBean.receiveEmails}" >
</h:selectBooleanCheckbox>
<h:outputText value="#{bundle.receiveEmails}">
```

Here is an example property that can be bound to the component represented by the example tag:

```
protected boolean receiveEmails = false;
    ...
    public void setReceiveEmails(boolean receiveEmails) {
        this.receiveEmails = receiveEmails;
    }
    public boolean getReceiveEmails() {
        return receiveEmails;
    }
```

UISelectMany Properties

Because a UISelectMany component allows a user to select one or more items from a list of items, this component must map to a bean property of type List or array. This bean property represents the set of currently selected items from the list of available items.

The following example of the selectManyCheckbox tag comes from "Displaying Components for Selecting Multiple Values" on page 132:

```
<h:selectManyCheckbox
    id="newsletters"
    layout="pageDirection"
```

```
    value="#{cashier.newsletters}">
    <f:selectItems value="#{newsletters}"/>
</h:selectManyCheckbox>
```

Here is the bean property that maps to the value of the selectManyCheckbox tag from the preceding example:

```
protected String newsletters[] = new String[0];

public void setNewsletters(String newsletters[]) {
    this.newsletters = newsletters;
}
public String[] getNewsletters() {
    return this.newsletters;
}
```

The UISelectItem and UISelectItems components are used to represent all the values in a UISelectMany component. See "UISelectItem Properties" on page 167 and "UISelectItems Properties" on page 167 for information on writing the bean properties for the UISelectItem and UISelectItems components.

UISelectOne Properties

UISelectOne properties accept the same types as UIInput and UIOutput properties, because a UISelectOne component represents the single selected item from a set of items. This item can be any of the primitive types and anything else for which you can apply a converter.

Here is an example of the selectOneMenu tag from "Displaying a Menu Using the h:selectOneMenu Tag" on page 131:

```
<h:selectOneMenu   id="shippingOption"
    required="true"
    value="#{cashier.shippingOption}">
    <f:selectItem
        itemValue="2"
        itemLabel="#{bundle.QuickShip}"/>
    <f:selectItem
        itemValue="5"
        itemLabel="#{bundle.NormalShip}"/>
    <f:selectItem
        itemValue="7"
        itemLabel="#{bundle.SaverShip}"/>
 </h:selectOneMenu>
```

Here is the bean property corresponding to this tag:

```
protected String shippingOption = "2";

public void setShippingOption(String shippingOption) {
    this.shippingOption = shippingOption;
}
public String getShippingOption() {
```

```
    return this.shippingOption;
}
```

Note that shippingOption represents the currently selected item from the list of items in the UISelectOne component.

The UISelectItem and UISelectItems components are used to represent all the values in a UISelectOne component. This is explained in the section "Displaying a Menu Using the h:selectOneMenu Tag" on page 131.

For information on how to write the backing bean properties for the UISelectItem and UISelectItems components, see "UISelectItem Properties" on page 167 and "UISelectItems Properties" on page 167.

UISelectItem Properties

A UISelectItem component represents a single value in a set of values in a UISelectMany or a UISelectOne component. A UISelectItem component must be bound to a backing bean property of type javax.faces.model.SelectItem. A SelectItem object is composed of an Object representing the value, along with two Strings representing the label and description of the UISelectItem object.

The example selectOneMenu tag from "Displaying a Menu Using the h:selectOneMenu Tag" on page 131 contains selectItem tags that set the values of the list of items in the page. Here is an example of a bean property that can set the values for this list in the bean:

```
SelectItem itemOne = null;

SelectItem getItemOne(){
    return itemOne;
}
void setItemOne(SelectItem item) {
    itemOne = item;
}
```

UISelectItems Properties

UISelectItems components are children of UISelectMany and UISelectOne components. Each UISelectItems component is composed of a set of either javax.faces.model.SelectItem instances or any collection of objects, such as an array, a list, or even POJOs.

This section explains how to write the properties for selectItems tags containing SelectItem instances.

You can populate the UISelectItems with SelectItem instances programmatically in the backing bean.

1. In your backing bean, create a list that is bound to the SelectItem component.

2. Define a set of SelectItem objects, set their values, and populate the list with the SelectItem objects.

The following example code snippet from a backing bean shows how to create a SelectItems property:

```
import javax.faces.model.SelectItem;
...
protected ArrayList options = null;
protected SelectItem newsletter0 =
    new SelectItem("200", "Duke's Quarterly", "");
...
//in constructor, populate the list
    options.add(newsletter0);
    options.add(newsletter1);
    options.add(newsletter2);
...
public SelectItem getNewsletter0(){
    return newsletter0;
}

void setNewsletter0(SelectItem firstNL) {
    newsletter0 = firstNL;
}
// Other SelectItem properties

public Collection[] getOptions(){
    return options;
}
public void setOptions(Collection[] options){
    this.options = new ArrayList(options);
}
```

The code first initializes options as a list. Each newsletter property is defined with values. Then each newsletter SelectItem is added to the list. Finally, the code includes the obligatory setOptions and getOptions accessor methods.

Writing Properties Bound to Component Instances

A property bound to a component instance returns and accepts a component instance rather than a component value. The following components bind a component instance to a backing bean property:

```
<h:selectBooleanCheckbox
    id="fanClub"
    rendered="false"
    binding="#{cashier.specialOffer}" />
```

```
<h:outputLabel for="fanClub"
    rendered="false"
    binding="#{cashier.specialOfferText}"  >
    <h:outputText id="fanClubLabel"
        value="#{bundle.DukeFanClub}" />
</h:outputLabel>
```

The selectBooleanCheckbox tag renders a check box and binds the fanClub
UISelectBoolean component to the specialOffer property of CashierBean. The
outputLabel tag binds the fanClubLabel component, which represents the check
box's label, to the specialOfferText property of CashierBean. If the user orders more
than $100 worth of items and clicks the Submit button, the submit method of
CashierBean sets both components' rendered properties to true, causing the check
box and label to display when the page is rerendered.

Because the components corresponding to the example tags are bound to the backing
bean properties, these properties must match the components' types. This means that
the specialOfferText property must be of type UIOutput, and the specialOffer
property must be of type UISelectBoolean:

```
UIOutput specialOfferText = null;

public UIOutput getSpecialOfferText() {
    return this.specialOfferText;
}
public void setSpecialOfferText(UIOutput specialOfferText) {
    this.specialOfferText = specialOfferText;
}

UISelectBoolean specialOffer = null;

public UISelectBoolean getSpecialOffer() {
    return this.specialOffer;
}
public void setSpecialOffer(UISelectBoolean specialOffer) {
    this.specialOffer = specialOffer;
}
```

For more general information on component binding, see "Backing Beans" on
page 159.

For information on how to reference a backing bean method that performs navigation
when a button is clicked, see "Referencing a Method That Performs Navigation" on
page 155.

For more information on writing backing bean methods that handle navigation, see
"Writing a Method to Handle Navigation" on page 171.

Writing Properties Bound to Converters, Listeners, or Validators

All the standard converter, listener, and validator tags included with JavaServer Faces technology support binding attributes that allow you to bind converter, listener, or validator implementations to backing bean properties.

The following example shows a standard `convertDateTime` tag using a value expression with its `binding` attribute to bind the `DateTimeConverter` instance to the `convertDate` property of `LoginBean`:

```
<h:inputText value="#{LoginBean.birthDate}">
    <f:convertDateTime binding="#{LoginBean.convertDate}" />
</h:inputText>
```

The `convertDate` property must therefore accept and return a `DateTimeConverter` object, as shown here:

```
private DateTimeConverter convertDate;
public DateTimeConverter getConvertDate() {
    ...
    return convertDate;
{
public void setConvertDate(DateTimeConverter convertDate) {
    convertDate.setPattern("EEEEEEEE, MMM dd, yyyy");
    this.convertDate = convertDate;
}
```

Because the converter is bound to a backing bean property, the backing bean property can modify the attributes of the converter or add new functionality to it. In the case of the preceding example, the property sets the date pattern that the converter uses to parse the user's input into a `Date` object.

The backing bean properties that are bound to validator or listener implementations are written in the same way and have the same general purpose.

Writing Backing Bean Methods

Methods of a backing bean can perform several application-specific functions for components on the page. These functions include

- Performing processing associated with navigation
- Handling action events
- Performing validation on the component's value
- Handling value-change events

By using a backing bean to perform these functions, you eliminate the need to implement the `Validator` interface to handle the validation or one of the listener interfaces to handle events. Also, by using a backing bean instead of a Validator implementation to perform validation, you eliminate the need to create a custom tag for the Validator implementation.

In general, it's good practice to include these methods in the same backing bean that defines the properties for the components referencing these methods. The reason for doing so is that the methods might need to access the component's data to determine how to handle the event or to perform the validation associated with the component.

The following sections explain how to write various types of backing bean methods.

Writing a Method to Handle Navigation

An action method, a backing bean method that handles navigation processing, must be a public method that takes no parameters and returns an Object, which is the logical outcome that the navigation system uses to determine the page to display next. This method is referenced using the component tag's action attribute.

The following action method is from a backing bean named CashierBean, which is invoked when a user clicks the Submit button on the page. If the user has ordered more than $100 worth of items, this method sets the rendered properties of the fanClub and specialOffer components to true, causing them to be displayed on the page the next time that page is rendered.

After setting the components' rendered properties to true, this method returns the logical outcome null. This causes the JavaServer Faces implementation to rerender the page without creating a new view of the page, retaining the customer's input. If this method were to return purchase, which is the logical outcome to use to advance to a payment page, the page would rerender without retaining the customer's input.

If the user does not purchase more than $100 worth of items, or if the thankYou component has already been rendered, the method returns receipt. The JavaServer Faces implementation loads the page after this method returns:

```
public String submit() {
    ...
    if(cart().getTotal() > 100.00 &&
        !specialOffer.isRendered())
    {
        specialOfferText.setRendered(true);
        specialOffer.setRendered(true);
        return null;
    } else if (specialOffer.isRendered() &&
        !thankYou.isRendered()){
        thankYou.setRendered(true);
        return null;
    } else {
        clear();
```

```
        return ("receipt");
    }
}
```

Typically, an action method will return a String outcome, as shown in the previous example. Alternatively, you can define an Enum class that encapsulates all possible outcome strings and then make an action method return an enum constant, which represents a particular String outcome defined by the Enum class.

The following example uses an Enum class to encapsulate all logical outcomes:

```
public enum Navigation  {
    main, accountHist, accountList, atm, atmAck, transferFunds,
      transferAck, error
}
```

When it returns an outcome, an action method uses the dot notation to reference the outcome from the Enum class:

```
public Object submit(){
    ...
    return Navigation.accountHist;
}
```

The section "Referencing a Method That Performs Navigation" on page 155 explains how a component tag references this method. The section "Writing Properties Bound to Component Instances" on page 168 explains how to write the bean properties to which the components are bound.

Writing a Method to Handle an Action Event

A backing bean method that handles an action event must be a public method that accepts an action event and returns void. This method is referenced using the component tag's actionListener attribute. Only components that implement javax.faces.component.ActionSource can refer to this method.

In the following example, a method from a backing bean named LocaleBean processes the event of a user clicking one of the hyperlinks on the page:

```
public void chooseLocaleFromLink(ActionEvent event) {
    String current = event.getComponent().getId();
    FacesContext context = FacesContext.getCurrentInstance();
    context.getViewRoot().setLocale((Locale)
        locales.get(current));
}
```

This method gets the component that generated the event from the event object; then it gets the component's ID, which indicates a region of the world. The method matches the ID against a HashMap object that contains the locales available for the application. Finally, the method sets the locale by using the selected value from the HashMap object.

"Referencing a Method That Handles an Action Event" on page 156 explains how a component tag references this method.

Writing a Method to Perform Validation

Instead of implementing the Validator interface to perform validation for a component, you can include a method in a backing bean to take care of validating input for the component. A backing bean method that performs validation must accept a FacesContext, the component whose data must be validated, and the data to be validated, just as the validate method of the Validator interface does. A component refers to the backing bean method by using its validator attribute. Only values of UIInput components or values of components that extend UIInput can be validated.

Here is an example of a backing bean method that validates user input:

```
public void validateEmail(FacesContext context,
    UIComponent toValidate, Object value) {

    String message = "";
    String email = (String) value;
    if (email.contains('@')) {
        ((UIInput)toValidate).setValid(false);
        message = CoffeeBreakBean.loadErrorMessage(context,
            CoffeeBreakBean.CB_RESOURCE_BUNDLE_NAME,
            "EMailError");
        context.addMessage(toValidate.getClientId(context),
            new FacesMessage(message));
    }
}
```

Take a closer look at the preceding code segment:

1. The validateEmail method first gets the local value of the component.

2. The method then checks whether the @ character is contained in the value.

3. If not, the method sets the component's valid property to false.

4. The method then loads the error message and queues it onto the FacesContext instance, associating the message with the component ID.

See "Referencing a Method That Performs Validation" on page 156 for information on how a component tag references this method.

Writing a Method to Handle a Value-Change Event

A backing bean that handles a value-change event must use a public method that accepts a value-change event and returns void. This method is referenced using the component's valueChangeListener attribute. This section explains how to write a backing bean method to replace the ValueChangeListener implementation.

The following example tag comes from "Registering a Value-Change Listener on a Component" on page 151, where the h:inputText tag with the id of name has a ValueChangeListener instance registered on it. This ValueChangeListener instance handles the event of entering a value in the field corresponding to the component. When the user enters a value, a value-change event is generated, and the processValueChange(ValueChangeEvent) method of the ValueChangeListener class is invoked:

```
<h:inputText  id="name" size="50" value="#{cashier.name}"
      required="true">
      <f:valueChangeListener type="listeners.NameChanged" />
</h:inputText>
```

Instead of implementing ValueChangeListener, you can write a backing bean method to handle this event. To do this, you move the processValueChange(ValueChangeEvent) method from the ValueChangeListener class, called NameChanged, to your backing bean.

Here is the backing bean method that processes the event of entering a value in the name field on the page:

```
public void processValueChange(ValueChangeEvent event)
    throws AbortProcessingException {
    if (null != event.getNewValue()) {
        FacesContext.getCurrentInstance().
            getExternalContext().getSessionMap().
                put("name", event.getNewValue());
    }
}
```

To make this method handle the ValueChangeEvent generated by an input component, reference this method from the component tag's valueChangeListener attribute. See "Referencing a Method That Handles a Value-Change Event" on page 156 for more information.

Using Bean Validation

Validating input received from the user to maintain data integrity is an important part of application logic. Validation of data can take place at different layers in even the simplest of applications, as shown in the guessnumber example application from an earlier chapter. The guessnumber example application validates the user input (in the h:inputText tag) for numerical data at the presentation layer and for a valid range of numbers at the business layer.

JavaBeans Validation (Bean Validation) is a new validation model available as part of Java EE 6 platform. The Bean Validation model is supported by constraints in the form of annotations placed on a field, method, or class of a JavaBeans component, such as a backing bean.

Constraints can be built in or user defined. User-defined constraints are called custom constraints. Several built-in constraints are available in the `javax.validation.constraints` package. Table 9–2 lists all the built-in constraints.

TABLE 9–2 Built-In Bean Validation Constraints

Constraint	Description	Example
`@AssertFalse`	The value of the field or property must be false.	`@AssertFalse` `boolean isUnsupported;`
`@AssertTrue`	The value of the field or property must be true.	`@AssertTrue` `boolean isActive;`
`@DecimalMax`	The value of the field or property must be a decimal value lower than or equal to the number in the value element.	`@DecimalMax("30.00")` `BigDecimal discount;`
`@DecimalMin`	The value of the field or property must be a decimal value greater than or equal to the number in the value element.	`@DecimalMin("5.00")` `BigDecimal discount;`
`@Digits`	The value of the field or property must be a number within a specified range. The `integer` element specifies the maximum integral digits for the number, and the `fraction` element specifies the maximum fractional digits for the number.	`@Digits(integer=6, fraction=2)` `BigDecimal price;`
`@Future`	The value of the field or property must be a date in the future.	`@Future` `Date eventDate;`
`@Max`	The value of the field or property must be an integer value lower than or equal to the number in the value element.	`@Max(10)` `int quantity;`

TABLE 9–2 Built-In Bean Validation Constraints *(Continued)*

Constraint	Description	Example
@Min	The value of the field or property must be an integer value greater than or equal to the number in the value element.	`@Min(5)` `int quantity;`
@NotNull	The value of the field or property must not be null.	`@NotNull` `String username;`
@Null	The value of the field or property must be null.	`@Null` `String unusedString;`
@Past	The value of the field or property must be a date in the past.	`@Past` `Date birthday;`
@Pattern	The value of the field or property must match the regular expression defined in the regexp element.	`@Pattern(regexp="\\(\\d{3}\\)\\d{3}-\\d{4}")` `String phoneNumber;`
@Size	The size of the field or property is evaluated and must match the specified boundaries. If the field or property is a `String`, the size of the string is evaluated. If the field or property is a `Collection`, the size of the `Collection` is evaluated. If the field or property is a `Map`, the size of the `Map` is evaluated. If the field or property is an array, the size of the array is evaluated. Use one of the optional `max` or `min` elements to specify the boundaries.	`@Size(min=2, max=240)` `String briefMessage;`

In the following example, a constraint is placed on a field using the built-in `@NotNull` constraint:

```
public class Name {
    @NotNull
    private String firstname;

    @NotNull
    private String lastname;
}
```

You can also place more than one constraint on a single JavaBeans component object. For example, you can place an additional constraint for size of field on the firstname and the lastname fields:

```
public class Name {
    @NotNull
    @Size(min=1, max=16)
    private String firstname;

    @NotNull
    @Size(min=1, max=16)
    private String lastname;
}
```

The following example shows a method with a user-defined constraint that checks for a predefined email address pattern such as a corporate email account:

```
@ValidEmail
public String getEmailAddress() {
    return emailAddress;
}
```

For a built-in constraint, a default implementation is available. A user-defined or custom constraint needs a validation implementation. In the above example, the @ValidEmail custom constraint needs an implementation class.

Any validation failures are gracefully handled and can be displayed by the h:messages tag.

Any backing bean that contains Bean Validation annotations automatically gets validation constraints placed on the fields on a JavaServer Faces application's web pages.

See "Validating Persistent Fields and Properties" on page 337 for more information on using validation constraints.

Validating Null and Empty Strings

The Java programming language distinguishes between null and empty strings. An empty string is a string instance of zero length, whereas a null string has no value at all.

An empty string is represented as "". It is a character array of zero characters. A null string is represented by null. It can be described as the absence of a string instance.

Backing bean elements represented as a JavaServer Faces text component such as inputText are initialized with the value of the empty string by the JavaServer Faces implementation. Validating these strings can be an issue when user input for such fields is not required. Consider the following example, where the string testString is a bean variable that will be set using input typed by the user. In this case, the user input for the field is not required.

```
if (testString.equals(null)) {
  doSomething();
} else  {
  doAnotherThing();
}
```

By default, the doAnotherThing method is called even when the user enters no data, because the testString element has been initialized with the value of an empty string.

In order for the Bean Validation model to work as intended, you must set the context parameter javax.faces.INTERPRET_EMPTY_STRING_SUBMITTED_VALUES_AS_NULL to true in the web deployment descriptor file, web.xml:

```
<context-param>
    <param-name>
        javax.faces.INTERPRET_EMPTY_STRING_SUBMITTED_VALUES_AS_NULL
    </param-name>
    <param-value>true</param-value>
</context-param>
```

This parameter enables the JavaServer Faces implementation to treat empty strings as null.

Suppose, on the other hand, that you have a @NotNull constraint on an element, meaning that input is required. In this case, an empty string will pass this validation constraint. However, if you set the context parameter javax.faces.INTERPRET_EMPTY_STRING_SUBMITTED_VALUES_AS_NULL to true, the value of the backing bean attribute is passed to the Bean Validation runtime as a null value, causing the @NotNull constraint to fail.

10

Java Servlet Technology

Shortly after the Web began to be used for delivering services, service providers recognized the need for dynamic content. Applets, one of the earliest attempts toward this goal, focused on using the client platform to deliver dynamic user experiences. At the same time, developers also investigated using the server platform for the same purpose. Initially, Common Gateway Interface (CGI) server-side scripts were the main technology used to generate dynamic content. Although widely used, CGI scripting technology had many shortcomings, including platform dependence and lack of scalability. To address these limitations, Java Servlet technology was created as a portable way to provide dynamic, user-oriented content.

The following topics are addressed here:

- "What Is a Servlet?" on page 180
- "Servlet Lifecycle" on page 180
- "Sharing Information" on page 182
- "Creating and Initializing a Servlet" on page 183
- "Writing Service Methods" on page 184
- "Filtering Requests and Responses" on page 187
- "Invoking Other Web Resources" on page 191
- "Accessing the Web Context" on page 193
- "Maintaining Client State" on page 193
- "Finalizing a Servlet" on page 195
- "The mood Example Application" on page 198
- "Further Information about Java Servlet Technology" on page 200

What Is a Servlet?

A servlet is a Java programming language class used to extend the capabilities of servers that host applications accessed by means of a request-response programming model. Although servlets can respond to any type of request, they are commonly used to extend the applications hosted by web servers. For such applications, Java Servlet technology defines HTTP-specific servlet classes.

The `javax.servlet` and `javax.servlet.http` packages provide interfaces and classes for writing servlets. All servlets must implement the `Servlet` interface, which defines lifecycle methods. When implementing a generic service, you can use or extend the `GenericServlet` class provided with the Java Servlet API. The `HttpServlet` class provides methods, such as `doGet` and `doPost`, for handling HTTP-specific services.

Servlet Lifecycle

The lifecycle of a servlet is controlled by the container in which the servlet has been deployed. When a request is mapped to a servlet, the container performs the following steps.

1. If an instance of the servlet does not exist, the web container

   a. Loads the servlet class.

   b. Creates an instance of the servlet class.

   c. Initializes the servlet instance by calling the `init` method. Initialization is covered in "Creating and Initializing a Servlet" on page 183.

2. Invokes the `service` method, passing request and response objects. Service methods are discussed in "Writing Service Methods" on page 184.

If it needs to remove the servlet, the container finalizes the servlet by calling the servlet's `destroy` method. For more information, see "Finalizing a Servlet" on page 195.

Handling Servlet Lifecycle Events

You can monitor and react to events in a servlet's lifecycle by defining listener objects whose methods get invoked when lifecycle events occur. To use these listener objects, you must define and specify the listener class.

Defining the Listener Class

You define a listener class as an implementation of a listener interface. Table 10–1 lists the events that can be monitored and the corresponding interface that must be implemented. When a listener method is invoked, it is passed an event that contains information appropriate to the event. For example, the methods in the `HttpSessionListener` interface are passed an `HttpSessionEvent`, which contains an `HttpSession`.

TABLE 10-1   Servlet Lifecycle Events

Object	Event	Listener Interface and Event Class
Web context (see "Accessing the Web Context" on page 193)	Initialization and destruction	`javax.servlet.ServletContextListener` and `ServletContextEvent`
	Attribute added, removed, or replaced	`javax.servlet.ServletContextAttributeListener` and `ServletContextAttributeEvent`
Session (See "Maintaining Client State" on page 193)	Creation, invalidation, activation, passivation, and timeout	`javax.servlet.http.HttpSessionListener`, `javax.servlet.http.HttpSessionActivationListener`, and `HttpSessionEvent`
	Attribute added, removed, or replaced	`javax.servlet.http.HttpSessionAttributeListener` and `HttpSessionBindingEvent`
Request	A servlet request has started being processed by web components	`javax.servlet.ServletRequestListener` and `ServletRequestEvent`
	Attribute added, removed, or replaced	`javax.servlet.ServletRequestAttributeListener` and `ServletRequestAttributeEvent`

Use the `@WebListener` annotation to define a listener to get events for various operations on the particular web application context. Classes annotated with `@WebListener` must implement one of the following interfaces:

```
javax.servlet.ServletContextListener
javax.servlet.ServletContextAttributeListener
javax.servlet.ServletRequestListener
javax.servlet.ServletRequestAttributeListener
javax.servlet..http.HttpSessionListener
javax.servlet..http.HttpSessionAttributeListener
```

For example, the following code snippet defines a listener that implements two of these interfaces:

```
import javax.servlet.ServletContextAttributeListener;
import javax.servlet.ServletContextListener;
import javax.servlet.annotation.WebListener;
```

```
@WebListener()
public class SimpleServletListener implements ServletContextListener,
        ServletContextAttributeListener {
    ...
```

Handling Servlet Errors

Any number of exceptions can occur when a servlet executes. When an exception occurs, the web container generates a default page containing the following message:

```
A Servlet Exception Has Occurred
```

But you can also specify that the container should return a specific error page for a given exception.

Sharing Information

Web components, like most objects, usually work with other objects to accomplish their tasks. Web components can do so by

- Using private helper objects (for example, JavaBeans components).
- Sharing objects that are attributes of a public scope.
- Using a database.
- Invoking other web resources. The Java Servlet technology mechanisms that allow a web component to invoke other web resources are described in "Invoking Other Web Resources" on page 191.

Using Scope Objects

Collaborating web components share information by means of objects that are maintained as attributes of four scope objects. You access these attributes by using the getAttribute and setAttribute methods of the class representing the scope. Table 10–2 lists the scope objects.

TABLE 10–2 Scope Objects

Scope Object	Class	Accessible from
Web context	javax.servlet.ServletContext	Web components within a web context. See "Accessing the Web Context" on page 193.
Session	javax.servlet.http.HttpSession	Web components handling a request that belongs to the session. See "Maintaining Client State" on page 193.

TABLE 10–2 Scope Objects *(Continued)*

Scope Object	Class	Accessible from
Request	Subtype of `javax.servlet.ServletRequest`	Web components handling the request.
Page	`javax.servlet.jsp.JspContext`	The JSP page that creates the object.

Controlling Concurrent Access to Shared Resources

In a multithreaded server, shared resources can be accessed concurrently. In addition to scope object attributes, shared resources include in-memory data, such as instance or class variables, and external objects, such as files, database connections, and network connections.

Concurrent access can arise in several situations:

- Multiple web components accessing objects stored in the web context.
- Multiple web components accessing objects stored in a session.
- Multiple threads within a web component accessing instance variables. A web container will typically create a thread to handle each request. To ensure that a servlet instance handles only one request at a time, a servlet can implement the `SingleThreadModel` interface. If a servlet implements this interface, no two threads will execute concurrently in the servlet's service method. A web container can implement this guarantee by synchronizing access to a single instance of the servlet or by maintaining a pool of web component instances and dispatching each new request to a free instance. This interface does not prevent synchronization problems that result from web components' accessing shared resources, such as static class variables or external objects.

When resources can be accessed concurrently, they can be used in an inconsistent fashion. You prevent this by controlling the access using the synchronization techniques described in the Threads lesson at `http://download.oracle.com/docs/cd/E17409_01/javase/tutorial/essential/concurrency/index.html` in *The Java Tutorial, Fourth Edition*, by Sharon Zakhour et al. (Addison-Wesley, 2006).

Creating and Initializing a Servlet

Use the `@WebServlet` annotation to define a servlet component in a web application. This annotation is specified on a class and contains metadata about the servlet being declared. The annotated servlet must specify at least one URL pattern. This is done by using the `urlPatterns` or `value` attribute on the annotation. All other attributes are optional, with default settings. Use the value attribute when the only attribute on the annotation is the URL pattern; otherwise use the urlPatterns attribute when other attributes are also used.

Classes annotated with @WebServlet must extend the javax.servlet.http.HttpServlet class. For example, the following code snippet defines a servlet with the URL pattern /report:

```
import javax.servlet.annotation.WebServlet;
import javax.servlet.http.HttpServlet;

@WebServlet("/report")
public class MoodServlet extends HttpServlet {
    ...
```

The web container initializes a servlet after loading and instantiating the servlet class and before delivering requests from clients. To customize this process to allow the servlet to read persistent configuration data, initialize resources, and perform any other one-time activities, you can either override the init method of the Servlet interface or specify the initParams attribute of the @WebServlet annotation. The initParams attribute contains a @WebInitParam annotation. If it cannot complete its initialization process, a servlet throws an UnavailableException.

Writing Service Methods

The service provided by a servlet is implemented in the service method of a GenericServlet, in the do*Method* methods (where *Method* can take the value Get, Delete, Options, Post, Put, or Trace) of an HttpServlet object, or in any other protocol-specific methods defined by a class that implements the Servlet interface. The term *service method* is used for any method in a servlet class that provides a service to a client.

The general pattern for a service method is to extract information from the request, access external resources, and then populate the response, based on that information. For HTTP servlets, the correct procedure for populating the response is to do the following:

1. Retrieve an output stream from the response.
2. Fill in the response headers.
3. Write any body content to the output stream.

Response headers must always be set before the response has been committed. The web container will ignore any attempt to set or add headers after the response has been committed. The next two sections describe how to get information from requests and generate responses.

Getting Information from Requests

A request contains data passed between a client and the servlet. All requests implement the ServletRequest interface. This interface defines methods for accessing the following information:

- Parameters, which are typically used to convey information between clients and servlets

- Object-valued attributes, which are typically used to pass information between the servlet container and a servlet or between collaborating servlets

- Information about the protocol used to communicate the request and about the client and server involved in the request

- Information relevant to localization

You can also retrieve an input stream from the request and manually parse the data. To read character data, use the BufferedReader object returned by the request's getReader method. To read binary data, use the ServletInputStream returned by getInputStream.

HTTP servlets are passed an HTTP request object, HttpServletRequest, which contains the request URL, HTTP headers, query string, and so on. An HTTP request URL contains the following parts:

http://[*host*]:[*port*][*request-path*]?[*query-string*]

The request path is further composed of the following elements:

- **Context path**: A concatenation of a forward slash (/) with the context root of the servlet's web application.

- **Servlet path**: The path section that corresponds to the component alias that activated this request. This path starts with a forward slash (/).

- **Path info**: The part of the request path that is not part of the context path or the servlet path.

You can use the getContextPath, getServletPath, and getPathInfo methods of the HttpServletRequest interface to access this information. Except for URL encoding differences between the request URI and the path parts, the request URI is always comprised of the context path plus the servlet path plus the path info.

Query strings are composed of a set of parameters and values. Individual parameters are retrieved from a request by using the getParameter method. There are two ways to generate query strings.

- A query string can explicitly appear in a web page.

- A query string is appended to a URL when a form with a GET HTTP method is submitted.

Constructing Responses

A response contains data passed between a server and the client. All responses implement the ServletResponse interface. This interface defines methods that allow you to

- Retrieve an output stream to use to send data to the client. To send character data, use the PrintWriter returned by the response's getWriter method. To send binary data in a Multipurpose Internet Mail Extensions (MIME) body response, use the ServletOutputStream returned by getOutputStream. To mix binary and text data, as in a multipart response, use a ServletOutputStream and manage the character sections manually.

- Indicate the content type (for example, text/html) being returned by the response with the setContentType(String) method. This method must be called before the response is committed. A registry of content type names is kept by the Internet Assigned Numbers Authority (IANA) at http://www.iana.org/assignments/media-types/.

- Indicate whether to buffer output with the setBufferSize(int) method. By default, any content written to the output stream is immediately sent to the client. Buffering allows content to be written before anything is sent back to the client, thus providing the servlet with more time to set appropriate status codes and headers or forward to another web resource. The method must be called before any content is written or before the response is committed.

- Set localization information, such as locale and character encoding.

HTTP response objects, javax.servlet.http.HttpServletResponse, have fields representing HTTP headers, such as the following:

- Status codes, which are used to indicate the reason a request is not satisfied or that a request has been redirected.

- Cookies, which are used to store application-specific information at the client. Sometimes, cookies are used to maintain an identifier for tracking a user's session (see "Session Tracking" on page 195).

Filtering Requests and Responses

A *filter* is an object that can transform the header and content (or both) of a request or response. Filters differ from web components in that filters usually do not themselves create a response. Instead, a filter provides functionality that can be "attached" to any kind of web resource. Consequently, a filter should not have any dependencies on a web resource for which it is acting as a filter; this way, it can be composed with more than one type of web resource.

The main tasks that a filter can perform are as follows:

- Query the request and act accordingly.
- Block the request-and-response pair from passing any further.
- Modify the request headers and data. You do this by providing a customized version of the request.
- Modify the response headers and data. You do this by providing a customized version of the response.
- Interact with external resources.

Applications of filters include authentication, logging, image conversion, data compression, encryption, tokenizing streams, XML transformations, and so on.

You can configure a web resource to be filtered by a chain of zero, one, or more filters in a specific order. This chain is specified when the web application containing the component is deployed and is instantiated when a web container loads the component.

Programming Filters

The filtering API is defined by the `Filter`, `FilterChain`, and `FilterConfig` interfaces in the `javax.servlet` package. You define a filter by implementing the `Filter` interface.

Use the `@WebFilter` annotation to define a filter in a web application. This annotation is specified on a class and contains metadata about the filter being declared. The annotated filter must specify at least one URL pattern. This is done by using the `urlPatterns` or `value` attribute on the annotation. All other attributes are optional, with default settings. Use the `value` attribute when the only attribute on the annotation is the URL pattern; use the `urlPatterns` attribute when other attributes are also used.

Classes annotated with the `@WebFilter` annotation must implement the `javax.servlet.Filter` interface.

To add configuration data to the filter, specify the initParams attribute of the @WebFilter annotation. The initParams attribute contains a @WebInitParam annotation. The following code snippet defines a filter, specifying an initialization parameter:

```
import javax.servlet.Filter;
import javax.servlet.annotation.WebFilter;
import javax.servlet.annotation.WebInitParam;

@WebFilter(filterName = "TimeOfDayFilter",
urlPatterns = {"/*"},
initParams = {
    @WebInitParam(name = "mood", value = "awake")})
public class TimeOfDayFilter implements Filter {
    ....
```

The most important method in the Filter interface is doFilter, which is passed request, response, and filter chain objects. This method can perform the following actions:

- Examine the request headers.
- Customize the request object if the filter wishes to modify request headers or data.
- Customize the response object if the filter wishes to modify response headers or data.
- Invoke the next entity in the filter chain. If the current filter is the last filter in the chain that ends with the target web component or static resource, the next entity is the resource at the end of the chain; otherwise, it is the next filter that was configured in the WAR. The filter invokes the next entity by calling the doFilter method on the chain object, passing in the request and response it was called with or the wrapped versions it may have created. Alternatively, the filter can choose to block the request by not making the call to invoke the next entity. In the latter case, the filter is responsible for filling out the response.
- Examine response headers after invoking the next filter in the chain.
- Throw an exception to indicate an error in processing.

In addition to doFilter, you must implement the init and destroy methods. The init method is called by the container when the filter is instantiated. If you wish to pass initialization parameters to the filter, you retrieve them from the FilterConfig object passed to init.

Programming Customized Requests and Responses

There are many ways for a filter to modify a request or a response. For example, a filter can add an attribute to the request or can insert data in the response.

A filter that modifies a response must usually capture the response before it is returned to the client. To do this, you pass a stand-in stream to the servlet that generates the response. The stand-in stream prevents the servlet from closing the original response stream when it completes and allows the filter to modify the servlet's response.

To pass this stand-in stream to the servlet, the filter creates a response wrapper that overrides the getWriter or getOutputStream method to return this stand-in stream. The wrapper is passed to the doFilter method of the filter chain. Wrapper methods default to calling through to the wrapped request or response object.

To override request methods, you wrap the request in an object that extends either ServletRequestWrapper or HttpServletRequestWrapper. To override response methods, you wrap the response in an object that extends either ServletResponseWrapper or HttpServletResponseWrapper.

Specifying Filter Mappings

A web container uses filter mappings to decide how to apply filters to web resources. A filter mapping matches a filter to a web component by name or to web resources by URL pattern. The filters are invoked in the order in which filter mappings appear in the filter mapping list of a WAR. You specify a filter mapping list for a WAR in its deployment descriptor by either using NetBeans IDE or coding the list by hand with XML.

If you want to log every request to a web application, you map the hit counter filter to the URL pattern /*.

You can map a filter to one or more web resources, and you can map more than one filter to a web resource. This is illustrated in Figure 10–1, where filter F1 is mapped to servlets S1, S2, and S3; filter F2 is mapped to servlet S2; and filter F3 is mapped to servlets S1 and S2.

FIGURE 10–1   Filter-to-Servlet Mapping

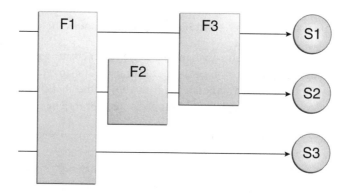

Recall that a filter chain is one of the objects passed to the doFilter method of a filter. This chain is formed indirectly by means of filter mappings. The order of the filters in the chain is the same as the order in which filter mappings appear in the web application deployment descriptor.

When a filter is mapped to servlet S1, the web container invokes the doFilter method of F1. The doFilter method of each filter in S1's filter chain is invoked by the preceding filter in the chain by means of the chain.doFilter method. Because S1's filter chain contains filters F1 and F3, F1's call to chain.doFilter invokes the doFilter method of filter F3. When F3's doFilter method completes, control returns to F1's doFilter method.

▼ To Specify Filter Mappings Using NetBeans IDE

1   Expand the application's project node in the Project pane.

2   Expand the Web Pages and WEB-INF nodes under the project node.

3   Double-click web.xml.

4   Click Filters at the top of the editor pane.

5   Expand the Servlet Filters node in the editor pane.

6   Click Add Filter Element to map the filter to a web resource by name or by URL pattern.

7   In the Add Servlet Filter dialog, enter the name of the filter in the Filter Name field.

8   Click Browse to locate the servlet class to which the filter applies.

You can include wildcard characters so that you can apply the filter to more than one servlet.

9   Click OK.

10   To constrain how the filter is applied to requests, follow these steps.

a.   Expand the Filter Mappings node.

b.   Select the filter from the list of filters.

c.   Click Add.

d.   In the Add Filter Mapping dialog, select one of the following dispatcher types:

- REQUEST: Only when the request comes directly from the client
- ASYNC: Only when the asynchronous request comes from the client
- FORWARD: Only when the request has been forwarded to a component (see "Transferring Control to Another Web Component" on page 192)
- INCLUDE: Only when the request is being processed by a component that has been included (see "Including Other Resources in the Response" on page 192)
- ERROR: Only when the request is being processed with the error page mechanism (see "Handling Servlet Errors" on page 182)

You can direct the filter to be applied to any combination of the preceding situations by selecting multiple dispatcher types. If no types are specified, the default option is REQUEST.

Invoking Other Web Resources

Web components can invoke other web resources both indirectly and directly. A web component indirectly invokes another web resource by embedding a URL that points to another web component in content returned to a client. While it is executing, a web component directly invokes another resource by either including the content of another resource or forwarding a request to another resource.

To invoke a resource available on the server that is running a web component, you must first obtain a RequestDispatcher object by using the getRequestDispatcher("URL") method. You can get a RequestDispatcher object from either a request or the web context; however, the two methods have slightly different behavior. The method takes the path to the requested resource as an argument. A request can take a relative path (that is, one that does not begin with a /), but the web context requires an absolute path. If the resource is not available or if the server has not implemented a RequestDispatcher object for that type of resource, getRequestDispatcher will return null. Your servlet should be prepared to deal with this condition.

Including Other Resources in the Response

It is often useful to include another web resource, such as banner content or copyright information) in the response returned from a web component. To include another resource, invoke the include method of a RequestDispatcher object:

```
include(request, response);
```

If the resource is static, the include method enables programmatic server-side includes. If the resource is a web component, the effect of the method is to send the request to the included web component, execute the web component, and then include the result of the execution in the response from the containing servlet. An included web component has access to the request object but is limited in what it can do with the response object.

- It can write to the body of the response and commit a response.

- It cannot set headers or call any method, such as setCookie, that affects the headers of the response.

Transferring Control to Another Web Component

In some applications, you might want to have one web component do preliminary processing of a request and have another component generate the response. For example, you might want to partially process a request and then transfer to another component, depending on the nature of the request.

To transfer control to another web component, you invoke the forward method of a RequestDispatcher. When a request is forwarded, the request URL is set to the path of the forwarded page. The original URI and its constituent parts are saved as request attributes
javax.servlet.forward.[*request-uri* | *context-path* | *servlet-path* | *path-info* | *query-string*].

The forward method should be used to give another resource responsibility for replying to the user. If you have already accessed a ServletOutputStream or PrintWriter object within the servlet, you cannot use this method; doing so throws an IllegalStateException.

Accessing the Web Context

The context in which web components execute is an object that implements the ServletContext interface. You retrieve the web context by using the getServletContext method. The web context provides methods for accessing

- Initialization parameters
- Resources associated with the web context
- Object-valued attributes
- Logging capabilities

The counter's access methods are synchronized to prevent incompatible operations by servlets that are running concurrently. A filter retrieves the counter object by using the context's getAttribute method. The incremented value of the counter is recorded in the log.

Maintaining Client State

Many applications require that a series of requests from a client be associated with one another. For example, a web application can save the state of a user's shopping cart across requests. Web-based applications are responsible for maintaining such state, called a *session*, because HTTP is stateless. To support applications that need to maintain state, Java Servlet technology provides an API for managing sessions and allows several mechanisms for implementing sessions.

Accessing a Session

Sessions are represented by an HttpSession object. You access a session by calling the getSession method of a request object. This method returns the current session associated with this request; or, if the request does not have a session, this method creates one.

Associating Objects with a Session

You can associate object-valued attributes with a session by name. Such attributes are accessible by any web component that belongs to the same web context *and* is handling a request that is part of the same session.

Recall that your application can notify web context and session listener objects of servlet lifecycle events ("Handling Servlet Lifecycle Events" on page 180). You can also notify objects of certain events related to their association with a session such as the following:

- When the object is added to or removed from a session. To receive this notification, your object must implement the `javax.servlet.http.HttpSessionBindingListener` interface.

- When the session to which the object is attached will be passivated or activated. A session will be passivated or activated when it is moved between virtual machines or saved to and restored from persistent storage. To receive this notification, your object must implement the `javax.servlet.http.HttpSessionActivationListener` interface.

Session Management

Because an HTTP client has no way to signal that it no longer needs a session, each session has an associated timeout so that its resources can be reclaimed. The timeout period can be accessed by using a session's `getMaxInactiveInterval` and `setMaxInactiveInterval` methods.

- To ensure that an active session is not timed out, you should periodically access the session by using service methods because this resets the session's time-to-live counter.

- When a particular client interaction is finished, you use the session's `invalidate` method to invalidate a session on the server side and remove any session data.

▼ To Set the Timeout Period Using NetBeans IDE

To set the timeout period in the deployment descriptor using NetBeans IDE, follow these steps.

1   Open the project if you haven't already.

2   Expand the project's node in the Projects pane.

3   Expand the Web Pages node and then the WEB-INF node.

4   Double-click `web.xml`.

5   Click General at the top of the editor.

6 In the Session Timeout field, type an integer value.

The integer value represents the number of minutes of inactivity that must pass before the session times out.

Session Tracking

To associate a session with a user, a web container can use several methods, all of which involve passing an identifier between the client and the server. The identifier can be maintained on the client as a cookie, or the web component can include the identifier in every URL that is returned to the client.

If your application uses session objects, you must ensure that session tracking is enabled by having the application rewrite URLs whenever the client turns off cookies. You do this by calling the response's encodeURL(URL) method on all URLs returned by a servlet. This method includes the session ID in the URL only if cookies are disabled; otherwise, the method returns the URL unchanged.

Finalizing a Servlet

A servlet container may determine that a servlet should be removed from service (for example, when a container wants to reclaim memory resources or when it is being shut down). In such a case, the container calls the destroy method of the Servlet interface. In this method, you release any resources the servlet is using and save any persistent state. The destroy method releases the database object created in the init method .

A servlet's service methods should all be complete when a servlet is removed. The server tries to ensure this by calling the destroy method only after all service requests have returned or after a server-specific grace period, whichever comes first. If your servlet has operations that may run longer than the server's grace period, the operations could still be running when destroy is called. You must make sure that any threads still handling client requests complete.

The remainder of this section explains how to do the following:

- Keep track of how many threads are currently running the service method.
- Provide a clean shutdown by having the destroy method notify long-running threads of the shutdown and wait for them to complete.
- Have the long-running methods poll periodically to check for shutdown and, if necessary, stop working, clean up, and return.

Tracking Service Requests

To track service requests, include in your servlet class a field that counts the number of service methods that are running. The field should have synchronized access methods to increment, decrement, and return its value:

```
public class ShutdownExample extends HttpServlet {
    private int serviceCounter = 0;
    ...
    // Access methods for serviceCounter
    protected synchronized void enteringServiceMethod() {
        serviceCounter++;
    }
    protected synchronized void leavingServiceMethod() {
        serviceCounter--;
    }
    protected synchronized int numServices() {
        return serviceCounter;
    }
}
```

The service method should increment the service counter each time the method is entered and should decrement the counter each time the method returns. This is one of the few times that your HttpServlet subclass should override the service method. The new method should call super.service to preserve the functionality of the original service method:

```
protected void service(HttpServletRequest req,
                       HttpServletResponse resp)
                       throws ServletException,IOException {
    enteringServiceMethod();
    try {
        super.service(req, resp);
    } finally {
        leavingServiceMethod();
    }
}
```

Notifying Methods to Shut Down

To ensure a clean shutdown, your destroy method should not release any shared resources until all the service requests have completed. One part of doing this is to check the service counter. Another part is to notify the long-running methods that it is time to shut down. For this notification, another field is required. The field should have the usual access methods:

```
public class ShutdownExample extends HttpServlet {
    private boolean shuttingDown;
    ...
    //Access methods for shuttingDown
    protected synchronized void setShuttingDown(boolean flag) {
```

```
        shuttingDown = flag;
    }
    protected synchronized boolean isShuttingDown() {
        return shuttingDown;
    }
}
```

Here is an example of the destroy method using these fields to provide a clean shutdown:

```
public void destroy() {
    /* Check to see whether there are still service methods /*
    /* running, and if there are, tell them to stop. */
    if (numServices() > 0) {
        setShuttingDown(true);
    }

    /* Wait for the service methods to stop. */
    while(numServices() > 0) {
        try {
            Thread.sleep(interval);
        } catch (InterruptedException e) {
        }
    }
}
```

Creating Polite Long-Running Methods

The final step in providing a clean shutdown is to make any long-running methods behave politely. Methods that might run for a long time should check the value of the field that notifies them of shutdowns and should interrupt their work, if necessary:

```
public void doPost(...) {
    ...
    for(i = 0; ((i < lotsOfStuffToDo) &&
        !isShuttingDown()); i++) {
        try {
            partOfLongRunningOperation(i);
        } catch (InterruptedException e) {
            ...
        }
    }
}
```

The mood **Example Application**

The mood example application, located in *tut-install*/examples/web/mood, is a simple example that displays Duke's moods at different times during the day. The example shows how to develop a simple application by using the @WebServlet, @WebFilter, and @WebListener annotations to create a servlet, a listener, and a filter.

Components of the mood **Example Application**

The mood example application is comprised of three components: mood.web.MoodServlet, mood.web.TimeOfDayFilter, and mood.web.SimpleServletListener.

MoodServlet, the presentation layer of the application, displays Duke's mood in a graphic, based on the time of day. The @WebServlet annotation specifies the URL pattern:

```
@WebServlet("/report")
public class MoodServlet extends HttpServlet {
    ...
```

TimeOfDayFilter sets an initialization parameter indicating that Duke is awake:

```
@WebFilter(filterName = "TimeOfDayFilter",
urlPatterns = {"/*"},
initParams = {
    @WebInitParam(name = "mood", value = "awake")})
public class TimeOfDayFilter implements Filter {
    ...
```

The filter calls the doFilter method, which contains a switch statement that sets Duke's mood based on the current time.

SimpleServletListener logs changes in the servlet's lifecycle. The log entries appear in the server log.

Building, Packaging, Deploying, and Running the mood **Example**

You can use either NetBeans IDE or Ant to build, package, deploy, and run the mood example.

▼ To Build, Package, Deploy, and Run the mood Example Using NetBeans IDE

1 Select File→Open Project.

2 In the Open Project dialog, navigate to:

tut-install/examples/web/

3 Select the mood folder.

4 Select the Open as Main Project check box.

5 Click Open Project.

6 In the Projects tab, right-click the mood project and select Build.

7 Right-click the project and select Deploy.

8 In a web browser, open the URL `http://localhost:8080/mood/report`.

The URL specifies the context root, followed by the URL pattern specified for the servlet.

A web page appears with the title "Servlet MoodServlet at /mood" a text string describing Duke's mood, and an illustrative graphic.

▼ To Build, Package, Deploy, and Run the mood Example Using Ant

1 In a terminal window, go to:

tut-install/examples/web/mood/

2 Type the following command:

`ant`

This target builds the WAR file and copies it to the *tut-install*/examples/web/mood/dist/ directory.

3 Type `ant deploy`.

Ignore the URL shown in the deploy target output.

4 In a web browser, open the URL `http://localhost:8080/mood/report`.

The URL specifies the context root, followed by the URL pattern.

A web page appears with the title "Servlet MoodServlet at /mood" a text string describing Duke's mood, and an illustrative graphic.

Further Information about Java Servlet Technology

For more information on Java Servlet technology, see

- Java Servlet 3.0 specification:

  `http://jcp.org/en/jsr/detail?id=315`

- Java Servlet web site:

  `http://www.oracle.com/technetwork/java/index-jsp-135475.html`

Web Services

Part III introduces web services. This part contains the following chapters:

- Chapter 11, "Introduction to Web Services"
- Chapter 12, "Building Web Services with JAX-WS"
- Chapter 13, "Building RESTful Web Services with JAX-RS"

◆ ◆ ◆ **CHAPTER 11**

Introduction to Web Services

Part III of the tutorial discusses Java EE 6 web services technologies. For this book, these technologies include Java API for XML Web Services (JAX-WS) and Java API for RESTful Web Services (JAX-RS).

The following topics are addressed here:

- "What Are Web Services?" on page 203
- "Types of Web Services" on page 203
- "Deciding Which Type of Web Service to Use" on page 206

What Are Web Services?

Web services are client and server applications that communicate over the World Wide Web's (WWW) HyperText Transfer Protocol (HTTP). As described by the World Wide Web Consortium (W3C), web services provide a standard means of interoperating between software applications running on a variety of platforms and frameworks. Web services are characterized by their great interoperability and extensibility, as well as their machine-processable descriptions, thanks to the use of XML. Web services can be combined in a loosely coupled way to achieve complex operations. Programs providing simple services can interact with each other to deliver sophisticated added-value services.

Types of Web Services

On the conceptual level, a service is a software component provided through a network-accessible endpoint. The service consumer and provider use messages to exchange invocation request and response information in the form of self-containing documents that make very few assumptions about the technological capabilities of the receiver.

On a technical level, web services can be implemented in various ways. The two types of web services discussed in this section can be distinguished as "big" web services and "RESTful" web services.

"Big" Web Services

In Java EE 6, JAX-WS provides the functionality for "big" web services, which are described in Chapter 12, "Building Web Services with JAX-WS." Big web services use XML messages that follow the Simple Object Access Protocol (SOAP) standard, an XML language defining a message architecture and message formats. Such systems often contain a machine-readable description of the operations offered by the service, written in the Web Services Description Language (WSDL), an XML language for defining interfaces syntactically.

The SOAP message format and the WSDL interface definition language have gained widespread adoption. Many development tools, such as NetBeans IDE, can reduce the complexity of developing web service applications.

A SOAP-based design must include the following elements.

- A formal contract must be established to describe the interface that the web service offers. WSDL can be used to describe the details of the contract, which may include messages, operations, bindings, and the location of the web service. You may also process SOAP messages in a JAX-WS service without publishing a WSDL.

- The architecture must address complex nonfunctional requirements. Many web service specifications address such requirements and establish a common vocabulary for them. Examples include transactions, security, addressing, trust, coordination, and so on.

- The architecture needs to handle asynchronous processing and invocation. In such cases, the infrastructure provided by standards, such as Web Services Reliable Messaging (WSRM), and APIs, such as JAX-WS, with their client-side asynchronous invocation support, can be leveraged out of the box.

RESTful Web Services

In Java EE 6, JAX-RS provides the functionality for Representational State Transfer (RESTful) web services. REST is well suited for basic, ad hoc integration scenarios. RESTful web services, often better integrated with HTTP than SOAP-based services are, do not require XML messages or WSDL service–API definitions.

Project Jersey is the production-ready reference implementation for the JAX-RS specification. Jersey implements support for the annotations defined in the JAX-RS specification, making it easy for developers to build RESTful web services with Java and the Java Virtual Machine (JVM).

Because RESTful web services use existing well-known W3C and Internet Engineering Task Force (IETF) standards (HTTP, XML, URI, MIME) and have a lightweight infrastructure that allows services to be built with minimal tooling, developing RESTful web services is inexpensive and thus has a very low barrier for adoption. You can use a development tool such as NetBeans IDE to further reduce the complexity of developing RESTful web services.

A RESTful design may be appropriate when the following conditions are met.

- The web services are completely stateless. A good test is to consider whether the interaction can survive a restart of the server.

- A caching infrastructure can be leveraged for performance. If the data that the web service returns is not dynamically generated and can be cached, the caching infrastructure that web servers and other intermediaries inherently provide can be leveraged to improve performance. However, the developer must take care because such caches are limited to the HTTP GET method for most servers.

- The service producer and service consumer have a mutual understanding of the context and content being passed along. Because there is no formal way to describe the web services interface, both parties must agree out of band on the schemas that describe the data being exchanged and on ways to process it meaningfully. In the real world, most commercial applications that expose services as RESTful implementations also distribute so-called value-added toolkits that describe the interfaces to developers in popular programming languages.

- Bandwidth is particularly important and needs to be limited. REST is particularly useful for limited-profile devices, such as PDAs and mobile phones, for which the overhead of headers and additional layers of SOAP elements on the XML payload must be restricted.

- Web service delivery or aggregation into existing web sites can be enabled easily with a RESTful style. Developers can use such technologies as JAX-RS and Asynchronous JavaScript with XML (AJAX) and such toolkits as Direct Web Remoting (DWR) to consume the services in their web applications. Rather than starting from scratch, services can be exposed with XML and consumed by HTML pages without significantly refactoring the existing web site architecture. Existing developers will be more productive because they are adding to something they are already familiar with rather than having to start from scratch with new technology.

RESTful web services are discussed in Chapter 13, "Building RESTful Web Services with JAX-RS." This chapter contains information about generating the skeleton of a RESTful web service using both NetBeans IDE and the Maven project management tool.

Deciding Which Type of Web Service to Use

Basically, you would want to use RESTful web services for integration over the web and use big web services in enterprise application integration scenarios that have advanced quality of service (QoS) requirements.

- **JAX-WS**: addresses advanced QoS requirements commonly occurring in enterprise computing. When compared to JAX-RS, JAX-WS makes it easier to support the WS-* set of protocols, which provide standards for security and reliability, among other things, and interoperate with other WS-* conforming clients and servers.

- **JAX-RS**: makes it easier to write web applications that apply some or all of the constraints of the REST style to induce desirable properties in the application, such as loose coupling (evolving the server is easier without breaking existing clients), scalability (start small and grow), and architectural simplicity (use off-the-shelf components, such as proxies or HTTP routers). You would choose to use JAX-RS for your web application because it is easier for many types of clients to consume RESTful web services while enabling the server side to evolve and scale. Clients can choose to consume some or all aspects of the service and mash it up with other web-based services.

Note – For an article that provides more in-depth analysis of this issue, see "RESTful Web Services vs. "Big" Web Services: Making the Right Architectural Decision," by Cesare Pautasso, Olaf Zimmermann, and Frank Leymann from *WWW '08: Proceedings of the 17th International Conference on the World Wide Web* (2008), pp. 805–814 (http://www2008.org/papers/pdf/p805-pautassoA.pdf).

12

Building Web Services with JAX-WS

Java API for XML Web Services (JAX-WS) is a technology for building web services and clients that communicate using XML. JAX-WS allows developers to write message-oriented as well as Remote Procedure Call-oriented (RPC-oriented) web services.

In JAX-WS, a web service operation invocation is represented by an XML-based protocol, such as SOAP. The SOAP specification defines the envelope structure, encoding rules, and conventions for representing web service invocations and responses. These calls and responses are transmitted as SOAP messages (XML files) over HTTP.

Although SOAP messages are complex, the JAX-WS API hides this complexity from the application developer. On the server side, the developer specifies the web service operations by defining methods in an interface written in the Java programming language. The developer also codes one or more classes that implement those methods. Client programs are also easy to code. A client creates a proxy (a local object representing the service) and then simply invokes methods on the proxy. With JAX-WS, the developer does not generate or parse SOAP messages. It is the JAX-WS runtime system that converts the API calls and responses to and from SOAP messages.

With JAX-WS, clients and web services have a big advantage: the platform independence of the Java programming language. In addition, JAX-WS is not restrictive: A JAX-WS client can access a web service that is not running on the Java platform, and vice versa. This flexibility is possible because JAX-WS uses technologies defined by the W3C: HTTP, SOAP, and WSDL. WSDL specifies an XML format for describing a service as a set of endpoints operating on messages.

Note – Several files in the JAX-WS examples depend on the port that you specified when you installed the GlassFish Server. These tutorial examples assume that the server runs on the default port, 8080. They do not run with a nondefault port setting.

The following topics are addressed here:

- "Creating a Simple Web Service and Clients with JAX-WS" on page 208
- "Types Supported by JAX-WS" on page 217
- "Web Services Interoperability and JAX-WS" on page 217
- "Further Information about JAX-WS" on page 217

Creating a Simple Web Service and Clients with JAX-WS

This section shows how to build and deploy a simple web service and two clients: an application client and a web client. The source code for the service is in the directory *tut-install*/examples/jaxws/helloservice/, and the clients are in the directories *tut-install*/examples/jaxws/appclient/ and *tut-install*/examples/jaxws/webclient/.

Figure 12–1 illustrates how JAX-WS technology manages communication between a web service and a client.

FIGURE 12–1 Communication between a JAX-WS Web Service and a Client

The starting point for developing a JAX-WS web service is a Java class annotated with the javax.jws.WebService annotation. The @WebService annotation defines the class as a web service endpoint.

A *service endpoint interface* or *service endpoint implementation* (SEI) is a Java interface or class, respectively, that declares the methods that a client can invoke on the service. An interface is not required when building a JAX-WS endpoint. The web service implementation class implicitly defines an SEI.

You may specify an explicit interface by adding the endpointInterface element to the @WebService annotation in the implementation class. You must then provide an interface that defines the public methods made available in the endpoint implementation class.

The basic steps for creating a web service and client are as follows:

1. Code the implementation class.

2. Compile the implementation class.

3. Package the files into a WAR file.

4. Deploy the WAR file. The web service artifacts, which are used to communicate with clients, are generated by the GlassFish Server during deployment.

5. Code the client class.

6. Use a `wsimport` Ant task to generate and compile the web service artifacts needed to connect to the service.

7. Compile the client class.

8. Run the client.

If you use NetBeans IDE to create a service and client, the IDE performs the `wsimport` task for you.

The sections that follow cover these steps in greater detail.

Requirements of a JAX-WS Endpoint

JAX-WS endpoints must follow these requirements.

- The implementing class must be annotated with either the `javax.jws.WebService` or the `javax.jws.WebServiceProvider` annotation.

- The implementing class may explicitly reference an SEI through the `endpointInterface` element of the `@WebService` annotation but is not required to do so. If no `endpointInterface` is specified in `@WebService`, an SEI is implicitly defined for the implementing class.

- The business methods of the implementing class must be public and must not be declared `static` or `final`.

- Business methods that are exposed to web service clients must be annotated with `javax.jws.WebMethod`.

- Business methods that are exposed to web service clients must have JAXB-compatible parameters and return types. See the list of JAXB default data type bindings at `http://download.oracle.com/docs/cd/E17477_01/javaee/5/tutorial/doc/bnazq.html#bnazs`.

- The implementing class must not be declared `final` and must not be `abstract`.

- The implementing class must have a default public constructor.

- The implementing class must not define the `finalize` method.

- The implementing class may use the `javax.annotation.PostConstruct` or the `javax.annotation.PreDestroy` annotations on its methods for lifecycle event callbacks.

  The `@PostConstruct` method is called by the container before the implementing class begins responding to web service clients.

The @PreDestroy method is called by the container before the endpoint is removed from operation.

Coding the Service Endpoint Implementation Class

In this example, the implementation class, Hello, is annotated as a web service endpoint using the @WebService annotation. Hello declares a single method named sayHello, annotated with the @WebMethod annotation, which exposes the annotated method to web service clients. The sayHello method returns a greeting to the client, using the name passed to it to compose the greeting. The implementation class also must define a default, public, no-argument constructor.

```
package helloservice.endpoint;

import javax.jws.WebService;
import javax.jws.webMethod;

@WebService
public class Hello {
    private String message = new String("Hello, ");

    public void Hello() {
    }

    @WebMethod
    public String sayHello(String name) {
        return message + name + ".";
    }
}
```

Building, Packaging, and Deploying the Service

You can build, package, and deploy the helloservice application by using either NetBeans IDE or Ant.

▼ To Build, Package, and Deploy the Service Using NetBeans IDE

1 In NetBeans IDE, select File→Open Project.

2 In the Open Project dialog, navigate to:

tut-install/examples/jaxws/

3 Select the helloservice folder.

4 Select the Open as Main Project check box.

5 Click Open Project.

6   **In the Projects tab, right-click the `helloservice` project and select Deploy.**

This command builds and packages the application into `helloservice.war`, located in *tut-install*/examples/jaxws/helloservice/dist/, and deploys this WAR file to the GlassFish Server.

Next Steps   You can view the WSDL file of the deployed service by requesting the URL `http://localhost:8080/helloservice/HelloService?wsdl` in a web browser. Now you are ready to create a client that accesses this service.

▼ To Build, Package, and Deploy the Service Using Ant

1   **In a terminal window, go to:**

tut-install/examples/jaxws/helloservice/

2   **Type the following command:**

`ant`

This command calls the `default` target, which builds and packages the application into a WAR file, `helloservice.war`, located in the `dist` directory.

3   **Make sure that the GlassFish Server is started.**

4   **Type the following:**

`ant deploy`

Next Steps   You can view the WSDL file of the deployed service by requesting the URL `http://localhost:8080/helloservice/HelloService?wsdl` in a web browser. Now you are ready to create a client that accesses this service.

Testing the Methods of a Web Service Endpoint

GlassFish Server allows you to test the methods of a web service endpoint.

▼ To Test the Service without a Client

To test the `sayHello` method of `HelloService`, follow these steps.

1   **Open the web service test interface by typing the following URL in a web browser:**

`http://localhost:8080/helloservice/HelloService?Tester`

2   **Under Methods, type a name as the parameter to the `sayHello` method.**

3 **Click the `sayHello` button.**

This takes you to the `sayHello` Method invocation page.

Under Method returned, you'll see the response from the endpoint.

A Simple JAX-WS Application Client

The `HelloAppClient` class is a stand-alone application client that accesses the `sayHello` method of `HelloService`. This call is made through a port, a local object that acts as a proxy for the remote service. The port is created at development time by the `wsimport` task, which generates JAX-WS portable artifacts based on a WSDL file.

Coding the Application Client

When invoking the remote methods on the port, the client performs these steps:

1. Uses the generated `helloservice.endpoint.HelloService` class, which represents the service at the URI of the deployed service's WSDL file:

   ```
   import helloservice.endpoint.HelloService;
   import javax.xml.ws.WebServiceRef;

   public class HelloAppClient {
       @WebServiceRef(wsdlLocation =
         "META-INF/wsdl/localhost_8080/helloservice/HelloService.wsdl")
       private static HelloService service;
   ```

2. Retrieves a proxy to the service, also known as a port, by invoking `getHelloPort` on the service:

   ```
   helloservice.endpoint.Hello port = service.getHelloPort();
   ```

   The port implements the SEI defined by the service.

3. Invokes the port's `sayHello` method, passing a string to the service:

   ```
   return port.sayHello(arg0);
   ```

Here is the full source of `HelloAppClient`, which is located in the following directory:

tut-install/examples/jaxws/appclient/src/appclient/

```
package appclient;

import helloservice.endpoint.HelloService;
import javax.xml.ws.WebServiceRef;

public class HelloAppClient {
    @WebServiceRef(wsdlLocation =
      "META-INF/wsdl/localhost_8080/helloservice/HelloService.wsdl")
    private static HelloService service;

    /**
```

```
 * @param args the command line arguments
 */
public static void main(String[] args) {
    System.out.println(sayHello("world"));
}

private static String sayHello(java.lang.String arg0) {
    helloservice.endpoint.Hello port = service.getHelloPort();
    return port.sayHello(arg0);
}
}
```

Building, Packaging, Deploying, and Running the Application Client

You can build, package, deploy, and run the appclient application by using either NetBeans IDE or Ant. To build the client, you must first have deployed helloservice, as described in "Building, Packaging, and Deploying the Service" on page 210.

▼ To Build, Package, Deploy, and Run the Application Client Using NetBeans IDE

1 In NetBeans IDE, select File→Open Project.

2 In the Open Project dialog, navigate to:

   tut-install/examples/jaxws/

3 Select the appclient folder.

4 Select the Open as Main Project check box.

5 Click Open Project.

6 In the Projects tab, right-click the appclient project and select Run.

   You will see the output of the application client in the Output pane.

▼ To Build, Package, Deploy, and Run the Application Client Using Ant

1 In a terminal window, go to:

   tut-install/examples/jaxws/appclient/

2 Type the following command:

   ant

This command calls the `default` target, which runs the `wsimport` task and builds and packages the application into a JAR file, `appclient.jar`, located in the `dist` directory.

3 To run the client, type the following command:

```
ant run
```

A Simple JAX-WS Web Client

`HelloServlet` is a servlet that, like the Java client, calls the `sayHello` method of the web service. Like the application client, it makes this call through a port.

Coding the Servlet

To invoke the method on the port, the client performs these steps:

1. Imports the `HelloService` endpoint and the `WebServiceRef` annotation:

   ```
   import helloservice.endpoint.HelloService;
   ...
   import javax.xml.ws.WebServiceRef;
   ```

2. Defines a reference to the web service by specifying the WSDL location:

   ```
   @WebServiceRef(wsdlLocation =
     "WEB-INF/wsdl/localhost_8080/helloservice/HelloService.wsdl")
   ```

3. Declares the web service, then defines a private method that calls the `sayHello` method on the port:

   ```
   private HelloService service;
   ...
   private String sayHello(java.lang.String arg0) {
       helloservice.endpoint.Hello port = service.getHelloPort();
       return port.sayHello(arg0);
   }
   ```

4. In the servlet, calls this private method:

   ```
   out.println("<p>" + sayHello("world") + "</p>");
   ```

The significant parts of the `HelloServlet` code follow. The code is located in the *tut-install*/examples/jaxws/src/java/webclient directory.

```
package webclient;

import helloservice.endpoint.HelloService;
import java.io.IOException;
import java.io.PrintWriter;
import javax.servlet.ServletException;
import javax.servlet.annotation.WebServlet;
import javax.servlet.http.HttpServlet;
import javax.servlet.http.HttpServletRequest;
import javax.servlet.http.HttpServletResponse;
import javax.xml.ws.WebServiceRef;
```

```java
@WebServlet(name="HelloServlet", urlPatterns={"/HelloServlet"})
public class HelloServlet extends HttpServlet {
    @WebServiceRef(wsdlLocation =
      "WEB-INF/wsdl/localhost_8080/helloservice/HelloService.wsdl")
    private HelloService service;

    /**
     * Processes requests for both HTTP <code>GET</code>
     *    and <code>POST</code> methods.
     * @param request servlet request
     * @param response servlet response
     * @throws ServletException if a servlet-specific error occurs
     * @throws IOException if an I/O error occurs
     */
    protected void processRequest(HttpServletRequest request,
            HttpServletResponse response)
    throws ServletException, IOException {
        response.setContentType("text/html;charset=UTF-8");
        PrintWriter out = response.getWriter();
        try {

            out.println("<html>");
            out.println("<head>");
            out.println("<title>Servlet HelloServlet</title>");
            out.println("</head>");
            out.println("<body>");
            out.println("<h1>Servlet HelloServlet at " +
                    request.getContextPath () + "</h1>");
            out.println("<p>" + sayHello("world") + "</p>");
            out.println("</body>");
            out.println("</html>");

        } finally {
            out.close();
        }
    }

    // doGet and doPost methods, which call processRequest, and
    //    getServletInfo method

    private String sayHello(java.lang.String arg0) {
        helloservice.endpoint.Hello port = service.getHelloPort();
        return port.sayHello(arg0);
    }
}
```

Building, Packaging, Deploying, and Running the Web Client

You can build, package, deploy, and run the webclient application by using either NetBeans IDE or Ant. To build the client, you must first have deployed helloservice, as described in "Building, Packaging, and Deploying the Service" on page 210.

▼ To Build, Package, Deploy, and Run the Web Client Using NetBeans IDE

1   In NetBeans IDE, select File→Open Project.

2   In the Open Project dialog, navigate to:

   tut-install/examples/jaxws/

3   Select the `webclient` folder.

4   Select the Open as Main Project check box.

5   Click Open Project.

6   In the Projects tab, right-click the `webclient` project and select Deploy.

   This task runs the `wsimport` tasks, builds and packages the application into a WAR file, `webclient.war`, located in the `dist` directory, and deploys it to the server.

7   In a web browser, navigate to the following URL:

   `http://localhost:8080/webclient/HelloServlet`

   The output of the `sayHello` method appears in the window.

▼ To Build, Package, Deploy, and Run the Web Client Using Ant

1   In a terminal window, go to:

   tut-install/examples/jaxws/webclient/

2   Type the following command:

   `ant`

   This command calls the `default` target, which runs the `wsimport` tasks, then builds and packages the application into a WAR file, `webclient.war`, located in the `dist` directory.

3   Type the following command:

   `ant deploy`

   This task deploys the WAR file to the server.

4   In a web browser, navigate to the following URL:

   `http://localhost:8080/webclient/HelloServlet`

   The output of the `sayHello` method appears in the window.

Types Supported by JAX-WS

JAX-WS delegates the mapping of Java programming language types to and from XML definitions to JAXB. Application developers don't need to know the details of these mappings but should be aware that not every class in the Java language can be used as a method parameter or return type in JAX-WS. For information on which types are supported by JAXB, see the list of JAXB default data type bindings at `http://download.oracle.com/` `docs/cd/E17477_01/javaee/5/tutorial/doc/bnazq.html#bnazs`.

Web Services Interoperability and JAX-WS

JAX-WS supports the Web Services Interoperability (WS-I) Basic Profile Version 1.1. The WS-I Basic Profile is a document that clarifies the SOAP 1.1 and WSDL 1.1 specifications to promote SOAP interoperability. For links related to WS-I, see "Further Information about JAX-WS" on page 217.

To support WS-I Basic Profile Version 1.1, the JAX-WS runtime supports doc/literal and rpc/literal encodings for services, static ports, dynamic proxies, and the Dynamic Invocation Interface (DII).

Further Information about JAX-WS

For more information about JAX-WS and related technologies, see

- Java API for XML Web Services 2.2 specification:

  `https://jax-ws.dev.java.net/spec-download.html`

- JAX-WS home:

  `https://jax-ws.dev.java.net/`

- Simple Object Access Protocol (SOAP) 1.2 W3C Note:

  `http://www.w3.org/TR/soap/`

- Web Services Description Language (WSDL) 1.1 W3C Note:

  `http://www.w3.org/TR/wsdl`

- WS-I Basic Profile 1.1:

  `http://www.ws-i.org`

13

Building RESTful Web Services with JAX-RS

This chapter describes the REST architecture, RESTful web services, and the Java API for RESTful Web Services (JAX-RS, defined in JSR 311).

Jersey, the reference implementation of JAX-RS, implements support for the annotations defined in JSR 311, making it easy for developers to build RESTful web services by using the Java programming language.

If you are developing with GlassFish Server, you can install the Jersey samples and documentation by using the Update Tool. Instructions for using the Update Tool can be found in "Java EE 6 Tutorial Component" on page 38. The Jersey samples and documentation are provided in the Available Add-ons area of the Update Tool.

The following topics are addressed here:

What Are RESTful Web Services?

RESTful web services are built to work best on the Web. Representational State Transfer (REST) is an architectural style that specifies constraints, such as the uniform interface, that if applied to a web service induce desirable properties, such as performance, scalability, and modifiability, that enable services to work best on the Web. In the REST architectural style, data and functionality are considered resources and are accessed using *Uniform Resource Identifiers (URIs)*, typically links on the Web. The resources are acted upon by using a set of simple, well-defined operations. The REST architectural style constrains an architecture to a client/server architecture and is designed to use a stateless communication protocol, typically HTTP. In the REST architecture style, clients and servers exchange representations of resources by using a standardized interface and protocol.

The following principles encourage RESTful applications to be simple, lightweight, and fast:

- **Resource identification through URI**: A RESTful web service exposes a set of resources that identify the targets of the interaction with its clients. Resources are identified by URIs, which provide a global addressing space for resource and service discovery. See "The @Path Annotation and URI Path Templates" on page 223 for more information.

- **Uniform interface**: Resources are manipulated using a fixed set of four create, read, update, delete operations: PUT, GET, POST, and DELETE. PUT creates a new resource, which can be then deleted by using DELETE. GET retrieves the current state of a resource in some representation. POST transfers a new state onto a resource. See "Responding to HTTP Resources" on page 226 for more information.

- **Self-descriptive messages**: Resources are decoupled from their representation so that their content can be accessed in a variety of formats, such as HTML, XML, plain text, PDF, JPEG, JSON, and others. Metadata about the resource is available and used, for example, to control caching, detect transmission errors, negotiate the appropriate representation format, and perform authentication or access control. See "Responding to HTTP Resources" on page 226 and "Using Entity Providers to Map HTTP Response and Request Entity Bodies" on page 227 for more information.

- **Stateful interactions through hyperlinks**: Every interaction with a resource is stateless; that is, request messages are self-contained. Stateful interactions are based on the concept of explicit state transfer. Several techniques exist to exchange state, such as URI rewriting, cookies, and hidden form fields. State can be embedded in response messages to point to valid future states of the interaction. See "Using Entity Providers to Map HTTP Response and Request Entity Bodies" on page 227 and "Building URIs" in the JAX-RS Overview document for more information.

Creating a RESTful Root Resource Class

Root resource classes are POJOs that are either annotated with @Path or have at least one method annotated with @Path or a *request method designator*, such as @GET, @PUT, @POST, or @DELETE. *Resource methods* are methods of a resource class annotated with a request method designator. This section explains how to use JAX-RS to annotate Java classes to create RESTful web services.

Developing RESTful Web Services with JAX-RS

JAX-RS is a Java programming language API designed to make it easy to develop applications that use the REST architecture.

The JAX-RS API uses Java programming language annotations to simplify the development of RESTful web services. Developers decorate Java programming language class files with JAX-RS annotations to define resources and the actions that can be performed on those resources. JAX-RS annotations are runtime annotations; therefore, runtime reflection will generate the helper classes and artifacts for the resource. A Java EE application archive containing JAX-RS resource classes will have the resources configured, the helper classes and artifacts generated, and the resource exposed to clients by deploying the archive to a Java EE server.

Table 13–1 lists some of the Java programming annotations that are defined by JAX-RS, with a brief description of how each is used. Further information on the JAX-RS APIs can be viewed at `http://download.oracle.com/docs/cd/E17410_01/javaee/6/api/`.

TABLE 13–1   Summary of JAX-RS Annotations

Annotation	Description
@Path	The @Path annotation's value is a relative URI path indicating where the Java class will be hosted: for example, /helloworld. You can also embed variables in the URIs to make a URI path template. For example, you could ask for the name of a user and pass it to the application as a variable in the URI: /helloworld/{username}.
@GET	The @GET annotation is a request method designator and corresponds to the similarly named HTTP method. The Java method annotated with this request method designator will process HTTP GET requests. The behavior of a resource is determined by the HTTP method to which the resource is responding.
@POST	The @POST annotation is a request method designator and corresponds to the similarly named HTTP method. The Java method annotated with this request method designator will process HTTP POST requests. The behavior of a resource is determined by the HTTP method to which the resource is responding.
@PUT	The @PUT annotation is a request method designator and corresponds to the similarly named HTTP method. The Java method annotated with this request method designator will process HTTP PUT requests. The behavior of a resource is determined by the HTTP method to which the resource is responding.

TABLE 13-1 Summary of JAX-RS Annotations *(Continued)*

Annotation	Description
@DELETE	The @DELETE annotation is a request method designator and corresponds to the similarly named HTTP method. The Java method annotated with this request method designator will process HTTP DELETE requests. The behavior of a resource is determined by the HTTP method to which the resource is responding.
@HEAD	The @HEAD annotation is a request method designator and corresponds to the similarly named HTTP method. The Java method annotated with this request method designator will process HTTP HEAD requests. The behavior of a resource is determined by the HTTP method to which the resource is responding.
@PathParam	The @PathParam annotation is a type of parameter that you can extract for use in your resource class. URI path parameters are extracted from the request URI, and the parameter names correspond to the URI path template variable names specified in the @Path class-level annotation.
@QueryParam	The @QueryParam annotation is a type of parameter that you can extract for use in your resource class. Query parameters are extracted from the request URI query parameters.
@Consumes	The @Consumes annotation is used to specify the MIME media types of representations a resource can consume that were sent by the client.
@Produces	The @Produces annotation is used to specify the MIME media types of representations a resource can produce and send back to the client: for example, "text/plain".
@Provider	The @Provider annotation is used for anything that is of interest to the JAX-RS runtime, such as MessageBodyReader and MessageBodyWriter. For HTTP requests, the MessageBodyReader is used to map an HTTP request entity body to method parameters. On the response side, a return value is mapped to an HTTP response entity body by using a MessageBodyWriter. If the application needs to supply additional metadata, such as HTTP headers or a different status code, a method can return a Response that wraps the entity and that can be built using Response.ResponseBuilder.

Overview of a JAX-RS Application

The following code sample is a very simple example of a root resource class that uses JAX-RS annotations:

```
package com.sun.jersey.samples.helloworld.resources;

import javax.ws.rs.GET;
import javax.ws.rs.Produces;
import javax.ws.rs.Path;
```

```
// The Java class will be hosted at the URI path "/helloworld"
@Path("/helloworld")
public class HelloWorldResource {

    // The Java method will process HTTP GET requests
    @GET
    // The Java method will produce content identified by the MIME Media
    // type "text/plain"
    @Produces("text/plain")
    public String getClichedMessage() {
        // Return some cliched textual content
        return "Hello World";
    }
}
```

The following sections describe the annotations used in this example.

- The @Path annotation's value is a relative URI path. In the preceding example, the Java class will be hosted at the URI path /helloworld. This is an extremely simple use of the @Path annotation, with a static URI path. Variables can be embedded in the URIs. *URI path templates* are URIs with variables embedded within the URI syntax.

- The @GET annotation is a request method designator, along with @POST, @PUT, @DELETE, and @HEAD, defined by JAX-RS and corresponding to the similarly named HTTP methods. In the example, the annotated Java method will process HTTP GET requests. The behavior of a resource is determined by the HTTP method to which the resource is responding.

- The @Produces annotation is used to specify the MIME media types a resource can produce and send back to the client. In this example, the Java method will produce representations identified by the MIME media type "text/plain".

- The @Consumes annotation is used to specify the MIME media types a resource can consume that were sent by the client. The example could be modified to set the message returned by the getClichedMessage method, as shown in this code example:

```
@POST
@Consumes("text/plain")
public void postClichedMessage(String message) {
    // Store the message
}
```

The @Path Annotation and URI Path Templates

The @Path annotation identifies the URI path template to which the resource responds and is specified at the class or method level of a resource. The @Path annotation's value is a partial URI path template relative to the base URI of the server on which the resource is deployed, the context root of the application, and the URL pattern to which the JAX-RS runtime responds.

URI path templates are URIs with variables embedded within the URI syntax. These variables are substituted at runtime in order for a resource to respond to a request based on the substituted URI. Variables are denoted by braces ({ and }). For example, look at the following @Path annotation:

```
@Path("/users/{username}")
```

In this kind of example, a user is prompted to type his or her name, and then a JAX-RS web service configured to respond to requests to this URI path template responds. For example, if the user types the user name "Galileo," the web service responds to the following URL:

```
http://example.com/users/Galileo
```

To obtain the value of the user name, the @PathParam annotation may be used on the method parameter of a request method, as shown in the following code example:

```
@Path("/users/{username}")
public class UserResource {

    @GET
    @Produces("text/xml")
    public String getUser(@PathParam("username") String userName) {
        ...
    }
}
```

By default, the URI variable must match the regular expression "[^/]+?". This variable may be customized by specifying a different regular expression after the variable name. For example, if a user name must consist only of lowercase and uppercase alphanumeric characters, override the default regular expression in the variable definition:

```
@Path("users/{username: [a-zA-Z][a-zA-Z_0-9]}")
```

In this example the username variable will match only user names that begin with one uppercase or lowercase letter and zero or more alphanumeric characters and the underscore character. If a user name does not match that template, a 404 (Not Found) response will be sent to the client.

A @Path value isn't required to have leading or trailing slashes (/). The JAX-RS runtime parses URI path templates the same whether or not they have leading or trailing spaces.

A URI path template has one or more variables, with each variable name surrounded by braces: { to begin the variable name and } to end it. In the preceding example, username is the variable name. At runtime, a resource configured to respond to the preceding URI path template will attempt to process the URI data that corresponds to the location of {username} in the URI as the variable data for username.

For example, if you want to deploy a resource that responds to the URI path template
`http://example.com/myContextRoot/resources/{name1}/{name2}/`, you must
deploy the application to a Java EE server that responds to requests to the
`http://example.com/myContextRoot` URI and then decorate your resource with the
following @Path annotation:

```
@Path("/{name1}/{name2}/")
public class SomeResource {
    ...
}
```

In this example, the URL pattern for the JAX-RS helper servlet, specified in web.xml, is
the default:

```
<servlet-mapping>
    <servlet-name>My JAX-RS Resource</servlet-name>
    <url-pattern>/resources/*</url-pattern>
</servlet-mapping>
```

A variable name can be used more than once in the URI path template.

If a character in the value of a variable would conflict with the reserved characters of a
URI, the conflicting character should be substituted with percent encoding. For
example, spaces in the value of a variable should be substituted with %20.

When defining URI path templates, be careful that the resulting URI after substitution
is valid.

Table 13–2 lists some examples of URI path template variables and how the URIs are
resolved after substitution. The following variable names and values are used in the
examples:

- name1: james
- name2: gatz
- name3:
- location: Main%20Street
- question: why

Note – The value of the name3 variable is an empty string.

TABLE 13–2   Examples of URI Path Templates

URI Path Template	URI After Substitution
`http://example.com/{name1}/{name2}/`	`http://example.com/james/gatz/`
`http://example.com/{question}/` `{question}/{question}/`	`http://example.com/why/why/why/`

TABLE 13–2 Examples of URI Path Templates *(Continued)*

URI Path Template	URI After Substitution
`http://example.com/maps/{location}`	`http://example.com/maps/Main%20Street`
`http://example.com/{name3}/home/`	`http://example.com//home/`

Responding to HTTP Resources

The behavior of a resource is determined by the HTTP methods (typically, GET, POST, PUT, DELETE) to which the resource is responding.

The Request Method Designator Annotations

Request method designator annotations are runtime annotations, defined by JAX-RS, that correspond to the similarly named HTTP methods. Within a resource class file, HTTP methods are mapped to Java programming language methods by using the request method designator annotations. The behavior of a resource is determined by which HTTP method the resource is responding to. JAX-RS defines a set of request method designators for the common HTTP methods @GET, @POST, @PUT, @DELETE, and @HEAD; you can also create your own custom request method designators. Creating custom request method designators is outside the scope of this document.

The following example, an extract from the storage service sample, shows the use of the PUT method to create or update a storage container:

```
@PUT
public Response putContainer() {
    System.out.println("PUT CONTAINER " + container);

    URI uri = uriInfo.getAbsolutePath();
    Container c = new Container(container, uri.toString());

    Response r;
    if (!MemoryStore.MS.hasContainer(c)) {
        r = Response.created(uri).build();
    } else {
        r = Response.noContent().build();
    }

    MemoryStore.MS.createContainer(c);
    return r;
}
```

By default, the JAX-RS runtime will automatically support the methods HEAD and OPTIONS if not explicitly implemented. For HEAD, the runtime will invoke the implemented GET method, if present, and ignore the response entity, if set. For OPTIONS, the Allow response header will be set to the set of HTTP methods supported by the resource. In addition, the JAX-RS runtime will return a Web Application

Definition Language (WADL) document describing the resource; see
https://wadl.dev.java.net/ for more information.

Methods decorated with request method designators must return void, a Java
programming language type, or a javax.ws.rs.core.Response object. Multiple
parameters may be extracted from the URI by using the PathParam or QueryParam
annotations as described in "Extracting Request Parameters" on page 231. Conversion
between Java types and an entity body is the responsibility of an entity provider, such
as MessageBodyReader or MessageBodyWriter. Methods that need to provide
additional metadata with a response should return an instance of the Response class.
The ResponseBuilder class provides a convenient way to create a Response instance
using a builder pattern. The HTTP PUT and POST methods expect an HTTP request
body, so you should use a MessageBodyReader for methods that respond to PUT and
POST requests.

Both @PUT and @POST can be used to create or update a resource. POST can mean
anything, so when using POST, it is up to the application to define the semantics. PUT
has well-defined semantics. When using PUT for creation, the client declares the URI
for the newly created resource.

PUT has very clear semantics for creating and updating a resource. The representation
the client sends must be the same representation that is received using a GET, given the
same media type. PUT does not allow a resource to be partially updated, a common
mistake when attempting to use the PUT method. A common application pattern is to
use POST to create a resource and return a 201 response with a location header whose
value is the URI to the newly created resource. In this pattern, the web service declares
the URI for the newly created resource.

Using Entity Providers to Map HTTP Response and Request Entity Bodies

Entity providers supply mapping services between representations and their associated
Java types. The two types of entity providers are MessageBodyReader and
MessageBodyWriter. For HTTP requests, the MessageBodyReader is used to map an
HTTP request entity body to method parameters. On the response side, a return value
is mapped to an HTTP response entity body by using a MessageBodyWriter. If the
application needs to supply additional metadata, such as HTTP headers or a different
status code, a method can return a Response that wraps the entity and that can be built
by using Response.ResponseBuilder.

Table 13–3 shows the standard types that are supported automatically for entities. You
need to write an entity provider only if you are not choosing one of these standard
types.

TABLE 13–3 Types Supported for Entities

Java Type	Supported Media Types
byte[]	All media types (*/*)
java.lang.String	All text media types (text/*)
java.io.InputStream	All media types (*/*)
java.io.Reader	All media types (*/*)
java.io.File	All media types (*/*)
javax.activation.DataSource	All media types (*/*)
javax.xml.transform.Source	XML media types (text/xml, application/xml, and application/*+xml)
javax.xml.bind.JAXBElement and application-supplied JAXB classes	XML media types (text/xml, application/xml, and application/*+xml)
MultivaluedMap<String, String>	Form content (application/x-www-form-urlencoded)
StreamingOutput	All media types (*/*), MessageBodyWriter only

The following example shows how to use MessageBodyReader with the @Consumes and @Provider annotations:

```
@Consumes("application/x-www-form-urlencoded")
@Provider
public class FormReader implements MessageBodyReader<NameValuePair> {
```

The following example shows how to use MessageBodyWriter with the @Produces and @Provider annotations:

```
@Produces("text/html")
@Provider
public class FormWriter implements
        MessageBodyWriter<Hashtable<String, String>> {
```

The following example shows how to use ResponseBuilder:

```
@GET
public Response getItem() {
    System.out.println("GET ITEM " + container + " " + item);

    Item i = MemoryStore.MS.getItem(container, item);
    if (i == null)
        throw new NotFoundException("Item not found");
    Date lastModified = i.getLastModified().getTime();
    EntityTag et = new EntityTag(i.getDigest());
    ResponseBuilder rb = request.evaluatePreconditions(lastModified, et);
```

```
    if (rb != null)
        return rb.build();

    byte[] b = MemoryStore.MS.getItemData(container, item);
    return Response.ok(b, i.getMimeType()).
            lastModified(lastModified).tag(et).build();
}
```

Using @Consumes and @Produces to Customize Requests and Responses

The information sent to a resource and then passed back to the client is specified as a MIME media type in the headers of an HTTP request or response. You can specify which MIME media types of representations a resource can respond to or produce by using the following annotations:

- `javax.ws.rs.Consumes`
- `javax.ws.rs.Produces`

By default, a resource class can respond to and produce all MIME media types of representations specified in the HTTP request and response headers.

The @Produces Annotation

The @Produces annotation is used to specify the MIME media types or representations a resource can produce and send back to the client. If @Produces is applied at the class level, all the methods in a resource can produce the specified MIME types by default. If applied at the method level, the annotation overrides any @Produces annotations applied at the class level.

If no methods in a resource are able to produce the MIME type in a client request, the JAX-RS runtime sends back an HTTP "406 Not Acceptable" error.

The value of @Produces is an array of String of MIME types. For example:

```
@Produces({"image/jpeg,image/png"})
```

The following example shows how to apply @Produces at both the class and method levels:

```
@Path("/myResource")
@Produces("text/plain")
public class SomeResource {
    @GET
    public String doGetAsPlainText() {
        ...
    }

    @GET
```

```
@Produces("text/html")
public String doGetAsHtml() {
    ...
}
}
```

The doGetAsPlainText method defaults to the MIME media type of the @Produces annotation at the class level. The doGetAsHtml method's @Produces annotation overrides the class-level @Produces setting and specifies that the method can produce HTML rather than plain text.

If a resource class is capable of producing more than one MIME media type, the resource method chosen will correspond to the most acceptable media type as declared by the client. More specifically, the Accept header of the HTTP request declares what is most acceptable. For example, if the Accept header is Accept: text/plain, the doGetAsPlainText method will be invoked. Alternatively, if the Accept header is Accept: text/plain;q=0.9, text/html, which declares that the client can accept media types of text/plain and text/html but prefers the latter, the doGetAsHtml method will be invoked.

More than one media type may be declared in the same @Produces declaration. The following code example shows how this is done:

```
@Produces({"application/xml", "application/json"})
public String doGetAsXmlOrJson() {
    ...
}
```

The doGetAsXmlOrJson method will get invoked if either of the media types application/xml and application/json is acceptable. If both are equally acceptable, the former will be chosen because it occurs first. The preceding examples refer explicitly to MIME media types for clarity. It is possible to refer to constant values, which may reduce typographical errors. For more information, see the constant field values of MediaType at https://jsr311.dev.java.net/nonav/releases/1.0/javax/ws/rs/core/MediaType.html.

The @Consumes Annotation

The @Consumes annotation is used to specify which MIME media types of representations a resource can accept, or consume, from the client. If @Consumes is applied at the class level, all the response methods accept the specified MIME types by default. If applied at the method level, @Consumes overrides any @Consumes annotations applied at the class level.

If a resource is unable to consume the MIME type of a client request, the JAX-RS runtime sends back an HTTP 415 ("Unsupported Media Type") error.

The value of @Consumes is an array of String of acceptable MIME types. For example:

```
@Consumes({"text/plain,text/html"})
```

The following example shows how to apply @Consumes at both the class and method levels:

```
@Path("/myResource")
@Consumes("multipart/related")
public class SomeResource {
    @POST
    public String doPost(MimeMultipart mimeMultipartData) {
        ...
    }

    @POST
    @Consumes("application/x-www-form-urlencoded")
    public String doPost2(FormURLEncodedProperties formData) {
        ...
    }
}
```

The doPost method defaults to the MIME media type of the @Consumes annotation at the class level. The doPost2 method overrides the class level @Consumes annotation to specify that it can accept URL-encoded form data.

If no resource methods can respond to the requested MIME type, an HTTP 415 ("Unsupported Media Type") error is returned to the client.

The HelloWorld example discussed previously in this section can be modified to set the message by using @Consumes, as shown in the following code example:

```
@POST
@Consumes("text/plain")
public void postClichedMessage(String message) {
    // Store the message
}
```

In this example, the Java method will consume representations identified by the MIME media type text/plain. Note that the resource method returns void. This means that no representation is returned and that a response with a status code of HTTP 204 ("No Content") will be returned.

Extracting Request Parameters

Parameters of a resource method may be annotated with parameter-based annotations to extract information from a request. A previous example presented the use of the @PathParam parameter to extract a path parameter from the path component of the request URL that matched the path declared in @Path.

You can extract the following types of parameters for use in your resource class:

- Query
- URI path
- Form
- Cookie
- Header
- Matrix

Query parameters are extracted from the request URI query parameters and are specified by using the javax.ws.rs.QueryParam annotation in the method parameter arguments. The following example, from the sparklines sample application, demonstrates using @QueryParam to extract query parameters from the Query component of the request URL:

```
@Path("smooth")
@GET
public Response smooth(
        @DefaultValue("2") @QueryParam("step") int step,
        @DefaultValue("true") @QueryParam("min-m") boolean hasMin,
        @DefaultValue("true") @QueryParam("max-m") boolean hasMax,
        @DefaultValue("true") @QueryParam("last-m") boolean hasLast,
        @DefaultValue("blue") @QueryParam("min-color") ColorParam minColor,
        @DefaultValue("green") @QueryParam("max-color") ColorParam maxColor,
        @DefaultValue("red") @QueryParam("last-color") ColorParam lastColor
        ) { ... }
```

If the query parameter step exists in the query component of the request URI, the value of step will be extracted and parsed as a 32-bit signed integer and assigned to the step method parameter. If step does not exist, a default value of 2, as declared in the @DefaultValue annotation, will be assigned to the step method parameter. If the step value cannot be parsed as a 32-bit signed integer, an HTTP 400 ("Client Error") response is returned.

User-defined Java programming language types may be used as query parameters. The following code example shows the ColorParam class used in the preceding query parameter example:

```
public class ColorParam extends Color {
    public ColorParam(String s) {
        super(getRGB(s));
    }

    private static int getRGB(String s) {
        if (s.charAt(0) == '#') {
            try {
                Color c = Color.decode("0x" + s.substring(1));
                return c.getRGB();
            } catch (NumberFormatException e) {
                throw new WebApplicationException(400);
            }
```

```
        } else {
            try {
                Field f = Color.class.getField(s);
                return ((Color)f.get(null)).getRGB();
            } catch (Exception e) {
                throw new WebApplicationException(400);
            }
        }
    }
}
```

The constructor for ColorParam takes a single String parameter.

Both @QueryParam and @PathParam can be used only on the following Java types:

- All primitive types except char
- All wrapper classes of primitive types except Character
- Any class with a constructor that accepts a single String argument
- Any class with the static method named valueOf(String) that accepts a single String argument
- Any class with a constructor that takes a single String as a parameter
- List<T>, Set<T>, or SortedSet<T>, where *T* matches the already listed criteria. Sometimes, parameters may contain more than one value for the same name. If this is the case, these types may be used to obtain all values

If @DefaultValue is not used in conjunction with @QueryParam, and the query parameter is not present in the request, the value will be an empty collection for List, Set, or SortedSet; null for other object types; and the default for primitive types.

URI path parameters are extracted from the request URI, and the parameter names correspond to the URI path template variable names specified in the @Path class-level annotation. URI parameters are specified using the javax.ws.rs.PathParam annotation in the method parameter arguments. The following example shows how to use @Path variables and the @PathParam annotation in a method:

```
@Path("/{username}")
public class MyResourceBean {
    ...
    @GET
    public String printUsername(@PathParam("username") String userId) {
        ...
    }
}
```

In the preceding snippet, the URI path template variable name username is specified as a parameter to the printUsername method. The @PathParam annotation is set to the variable name username. At runtime, before printUsername is called, the value of username is extracted from the URI and cast to a String. The resulting String is then available to the method as the userId variable.

If the URI path template variable cannot be cast to the specified type, the JAX-RS runtime returns an HTTP 400 ("Bad Request") error to the client. If the @PathParam annotation cannot be cast to the specified type, the JAX-RS runtime returns an HTTP 404 ("Not Found") error to the client.

The @PathParam parameter and the other parameter-based annotations (@MatrixParam, @HeaderParam, @CookieParam, and @FormParam) obey the same rules as @QueryParam.

Cookie parameters, indicated by decorating the parameter with javax.ws.rs.CookieParam, extract information from the cookies declared in cookie-related HTTP headers. *Header parameters*, indicated by decorating the parameter with javax.ws.rs.HeaderParam, extract information from the HTTP headers. *Matrix parameters*, indicated by decorating the parameter with javax.ws.rs.MatrixParam, extract information from URL path segments.

Form parameters, indicated by decorating the parameter with javax.ws.rs.FormParam, extract information from a request representation that is of the MIME media type application/x-www-form-urlencoded and conforms to the encoding specified by HTML forms, as described in http://www.w3.org/TR/html401/interact/forms.html#h-17.13.4.1. This parameter is very useful for extracting information sent by POST in HTML forms.

The following example extracts the name form parameter from the POST form data:

```
@POST
@Consumes("application/x-www-form-urlencoded")
public void post(@FormParam("name") String name) {
    // Store the message
}
```

To obtain a general map of parameter names and values for query and path parameters, use the following code:

```
@GET
public String get(@Context UriInfo ui) {
    MultivaluedMap<String, String> queryParams = ui.getQueryParameters();
    MultivaluedMap<String, String> pathParams = ui.getPathParameters();
}
```

The following method extracts header and cookie parameter names and values into a map:

```
@GET
public String get(@Context HttpHeaders hh) {
    MultivaluedMap<String, String> headerParams = ui.getRequestHeaders();
    Map<String, Cookie> pathParams = ui.getCookies();
}
```

In general, @Context can be used to obtain contextual Java types related to the request or response.

For form parameters, it is possible to do the following:

```
@POST
@Consumes("application/x-www-form-urlencoded")
public void post(MultivaluedMap<String, String> formParams) {
    // Store the message
}
```

Example Applications for JAX-RS

This section provides an introduction to creating, deploying, and running your own JAX-RS applications. This section demonstrates the steps that are needed to create, build, deploy, and test a very simple web application that uses JAX-RS annotations.

A RESTful Web Service

This section explains how to use NetBeans IDE to create a RESTful web service. NetBeans IDE generates a skeleton for the application, and you simply need to implement the appropriate methods. If you do not use an IDE, try using one of the example applications that ship with Jersey as a template to modify.

▼ To Create a RESTful Web Service Using NetBeans IDE

1 In NetBeans IDE, create a simple web application. This example creates a very simple "Hello, World" web application.

 a. In NetBeans IDE, select File → New Project.

 b. From Categories, select Java Web. From Projects, select Web Application. Click Next.

 Note – For this step, you could also create a RESTful web service in a Maven web project by selecting Maven as the category and Maven Web Project as the project. The remaining steps would be the same.

---

 c. Type a project name, `HelloWorldApplication`, and click Next.

 d. Make sure that the Server is GlassFish Server (or similar wording.)

 e. Click Finish.

 The project is created. The file `index.jsp` appears in the Source pane.

2   Right-click the project and select New; then select RESTful Web Services from Patterns.

   a.   Select Simple Root Resource and click Next.

   b.   Type a Resource Package name, such as `helloWorld`.

   c.   Type `helloworld` in the Path field. Type `HelloWorld` in the Class Name field. For MIME Type, select `text/html`.

   d.   Click Finish.

      The REST Resources Configuration page appears.

   e.   Click OK.

      A new resource, `HelloWorld.java`, is added to the project and appears in the Source pane. This file provides a template for creating a RESTful web service.

3   In `HelloWorld.java`, find the `getHtml()` method. Replace the `//TODO` comment and the exception with the following text, so that the finished product resembles the following method.

Note – Because the MIME type produced is HTML, you can use HTML tags in your return statement.

```
/**
 * Retrieves representation of an instance of helloWorld.HelloWorld
 * @return an instance of java.lang.String
 */
@GET
@Produces("text/html")
public String getHtml() {
    return "<html><body><h1>Hello, World!!</body></h1></html>";
}
```

4   Test the web service. To do this, right-click the project node and click Test RESTful Web Services.

This step deploys the application and brings up a test client in the browser.

5   When the test client appears, select the `helloworld` resource in the left pane, and click the Test button in the right pane.

The words `Hello, World!!` appear in the Response window below.

6   Set the Run Properties:

   a.   Right-click the project node and select Properties.

b. In the dialog, select the Run category.

c. Set the Relative URL to the location of the RESTful web service relative to the
    Context Path, which for this example is `resources/helloworld`.

Tip – You can find the value for the Relative URL in the Test RESTful Web Services
browser window. In the top of the right pane, after Resource, is the URL for the
RESTful web service being tested. The part following the Context Path
(`http://localhost:8080/HelloWorldApp`) is the Relative URL that needs to be
entered here.

If you don't set this property, the file `index.jsp` will appear by default when the
application is run. As this file also contains `Hello World` as its default value, you might
not notice that your RESTful web service isn't running, so just be aware of this default
and the need to set this property, or update `index.jsp` to provide a link to the RESTful
web service.

---

7 **Right-click the project and select Deploy.**

8 **Right-click the project and select Run.**

A browser window opens and displays the return value of `Hello, World!!`

See Also   For other sample applications that demonstrate deploying and running JAX-RS
applications using NetBeans IDE, see "The `rsvp` Example Application" on page 237
and *Your First Cup: An Introduction to the Java EE Platform* at
`http://download.oracle.com/docs/cd/E17410_01/javaee/6/firstcup/doc/`.
You may also look at the tutorials on the NetBeans IDE tutorial site, such as the one
titled "Getting Started with RESTful Web Services" at `http://www.netbeans.org/`
`kb/docs/websvc/rest.html`. This tutorial includes a section on creating a CRUD
application from a database. Create, read, update, and delete (CRUD) are the four
basic functions of persistent storage and relational databases.

The `rsvp` Example Application

The `rsvp` example application, located in *tut-install*`/examples/jaxrs/rsvp`, allows
invitees to an event to indicate whether they will attend. The events, people invited to
the event, and the responses to the invite are stored in a Java DB database using the
Java Persistence API. The JAX-RS resources in `rsvp` are exposed in a stateless session
enterprise bean.

Components of the `rsvp` Example Application

The three enterprise beans in the `rsvp` example application are
`rsvp.ejb.ConfigBean`, `rsvp.ejb.StatusBean`, and `rsvp.ejb.ResponseBean`.

`ConfigBean` is a singleton session bean that initializes the data in the database.

`StatusBean` exposes a JAX-RS resource for displaying the current status of all invitees
to an event. The URI path template is declared as follows:

```
@Path("/status/{eventId}/"}
```

The URI path variable `eventId` is a `@PathParam` variable in the `getResponse` method,
which responds to HTTP `GET` requests and has been annotated with `@GET`. The
`eventId` variable is used to look up all the current responses in the database for that
particular event.

`ResponseBean` exposes a JAX-RS resource for setting an invitee's response to a
particular event. The URI path template for `ResponseBean` is declared as follows:

```
@Path("/{eventId}/{inviteId}
```

Two URI path variables are declared in the path template: `eventId` and `inviteId`. As
in `StatusBean`, `eventId` is the unique ID for a particular event. Each invitee to that
event has a unique ID for the invitation, and that is the `inviteId`. Both of these path
variables are used in two JAX-RS methods in `ResponseBean`: `getResponse` and
`putResponse`. The `getResponse` method responds to HTTP `GET` requests and displays
the invitee's current response and a form to change the response.

An invitee who wants to change his or her response selects the new response and
submits the form data, which is processed as an HTTP `PUT` request by the `putResponse`
method. One of the parameters to the `putResponse` method, the `userResponse` string,
is annotated with `@FormParam("attendeeResponse")`. The HTML form created by
`getResponse` stores the changed response in the select list with an ID of
`attendeeResponse`. The annotation `@FormParam("attendeeResponse")` indicates that
the value of the select response is extracted from the HTTP `PUT` request and stored as
the `userResponse` string. The `putResponse` method uses `userResponse`, `eventId`, and
`inviteId` to update the invitee's response in the database.

The events, people, and responses in `rsvp` are encapsulated in Java Persistence API
entities. The `rsvp.entity.Event`, `rsvp.entity.Person`, and `rsvp.entity.Response`
entities respectively represent events, invitees, and responses to an event.

The `rsvp.util.ResponseEnum` class declares an enumerated type that represents all
the possible response statuses an invitee may have.

Running the rsvp Example Application

Both NetBeans IDE and Ant can be used to deploy and run the rsvp example application.

▼ To Run the rsvp Example Application in NetBeans IDE

1 In NetBeans IDE, select File→Open Project.

2 In the Open Project dialog, navigate to:

   tut-install/examples/jaxrs/

3 Select the rsvp folder.

4 Select the Open as Main Project check box.

5 Click Open Project.

6 Right-click the rsvp project in the left pane and select Run.

   The project will be compiled, assembled, and deployed to GlassFish Server. A web browser window will open to http://localhost:8080/rsvp.

7 In the web browser window, click the Event Status link for the Duke's Birthday event.

   You'll see the current invitees and their responses.

8 Click on the name of one of the invitees, select a response, and click Submit response; then click Back to event page.

   The invitee's new status should now be displayed in the table of invitees and their response statuses.

▼ To Run the rsvp Example Application Using Ant

Before You Begin You must have started the Java DB database before running rsvp.

1 In a terminal window, go to:

   tut-install/examples/jaxrs/rsvp

2 Type the following command:

   `ant all`

   This command builds, assembles, and deploys rsvp to GlassFish Server.

3 Open a web browser window to http://localhost:8080/rsvp.

4 **In the web browser window, click the Event Status link for the Duke's Birthday event.**

You'll see the current invitees and their responses.

5 **Click on the name of one of the invitees, select a response, and click Submit response, then click Back to event page.**

The invitee's new status should now be displayed in the table of invitees and their response statuses.

Real-World Examples

Most blog sites use RESTful web services. These sites involve downloading XML files, in RSS or Atom format, that contain lists of links to other resources. Other web sites and web applications that use REST-like developer interfaces to data include Twitter and Amazon S3 (Simple Storage Service). With Amazon S3, buckets and objects can be created, listed, and retrieved using either a REST-style HTTP interface or a SOAP interface. The examples that ship with Jersey include a storage service example with a RESTful interface. The tutorial at `http://netbeans.org/kb/docs/websvc/twitter-swing.html` uses NetBeans IDE to create a simple, graphical, REST-based client that displays Twitter public timeline messages and lets you view and update your Twitter status.

Further Information about JAX-RS

For more information about RESTful web services and JAX-RS, see

- "RESTful Web Services vs. 'Big' Web Services: Making the Right Architectural Decision":

  `http://www2008.org/papers/pdf/p805-pautassoA.pdf`

- The Community Wiki for Project Jersey, the JAX-RS reference implementation:

  `http://wikis.sun.com/display/Jersey/Main`

- "Fielding Dissertation: Chapter 5: Representational State Transfer (REST)":

  `http://www.ics.uci.edu/~fielding/pubs/dissertation/rest_arch_style.htm`

- *RESTful Web Services*, by Leonard Richardson and Sam Ruby, available from O'Reilly Media at `http://oreilly.com/catalog/9780596529260/`

- JSR 311: JAX-RS: The Java API for RESTful Web Services:

  `http://jcp.org/en/jsr/detail?id=311`

- JAX-RS project:

  `https://jsr311.dev.java.net/`

- Jersey project:

  `https://jersey.dev.java.net/`

- JAX-RS Overview document:

  `http://wikis.sun.com/display/Jersey/Overview+of+JAX-RS+1.0+Features`

Enterprise Beans

Part IV introduces Enterprise JavaBeans components. This part contains the following chapters:

- Chapter 14, "Enterprise Beans"
- Chapter 15, "Getting Started with Enterprise Beans"
- Chapter 16, "Running the Enterprise Bean Examples"

14

Enterprise Beans

Enterprise beans are Java EE components that implement Enterprise JavaBeans (EJB) technology. Enterprise beans run in the EJB container, a runtime environment within the GlassFish Server (see "Container Types" on page 14). Although transparent to the application developer, the EJB container provides system-level services, such as transactions and security, to its enterprise beans. These services enable you to quickly build and deploy enterprise beans, which form the core of transactional Java EE applications.

The following topics are addressed here:

What Is an Enterprise Bean?

Written in the Java programming language, an enterprise bean is a server-side component that encapsulates the business logic of an application. The business logic is the code that fulfills the purpose of the application. In an inventory control application, for example, the enterprise beans might implement the business logic in methods called checkInventoryLevel and orderProduct. By invoking these 32–bit methods, clients can access the inventory services provided by the application.

Benefits of Enterprise Beans

For several reasons, enterprise beans simplify the development of large, distributed applications. First, because the EJB container provides system-level services to enterprise beans, the bean developer can concentrate on solving business problems. The EJB container, rather than the bean developer, is responsible for system-level services, such as transaction management and security authorization.

Second, because the beans rather than the clients contain the application's business logic, the client developer can focus on the presentation of the client. The client developer does not have to code the routines that implement business rules or access databases. As a result, the clients are thinner, a benefit that is particularly important for clients that run on small devices.

Third, because enterprise beans are portable components, the application assembler can build new applications from existing beans. Provided that they use the standard APIs, these applications can run on any compliant Java EE server.

When to Use Enterprise Beans

You should consider using enterprise beans if your application has any of the following requirements.

- The application must be scalable. To accommodate a growing number of users, you may need to distribute an application's components across multiple machines. Not only can the enterprise beans of an application run on different machines, but also their location will remain transparent to the clients.
- Transactions must ensure data integrity. Enterprise beans support transactions, the mechanisms that manage the concurrent access of shared objects.
- The application will have a variety of clients. With only a few lines of code, remote clients can easily locate enterprise beans. These clients can be thin, various, and numerous.

Types of Enterprise Beans

Table 14–1 summarizes the two types of enterprise beans. The following sections discuss each type in more detail.

TABLE 14–1 Enterprise Bean Types

Enterprise Bean Type	Purpose
Session	Performs a task for a client; optionally, may implement a web service
Message-driven	Acts as a listener for a particular messaging type, such as the Java Message Service API

What Is a Session Bean?

A *session bean* encapsulates business logic that can be invoked programmatically by a client over local, remote, or web service client views. To access an application that is deployed on the server, the client invokes the session bean's methods. The session bean performs work for its client, shielding it from complexity by executing business tasks inside the server.

A session bean is not persistent. (That is, its data is not saved to a database.)

For code samples, see Chapter 16, "Running the Enterprise Bean Examples."

Types of Session Beans

Session beans are of three types: stateful, stateless, and singleton.

Stateful Session Beans

The state of an object consists of the values of its instance variables. In a *stateful session bean*, the instance variables represent the state of a unique client/bean session. Because the client interacts ("talks") with its bean, this state is often called the *conversational state*.

As its name suggests, a session bean is similar to an interactive session. A session bean is not shared; it can have only one client, in the same way that an interactive session can have only one user. When the client terminates, its session bean appears to terminate and is no longer associated with the client.

The state is retained for the duration of the client/bean session. If the client removes the bean, the session ends and the state disappears. This transient nature of the state is not a problem, however, because when the conversation between the client and the bean ends, there is no need to retain the state.

Stateless Session Beans

A *stateless session bean* does not maintain a conversational state with the client. When a client invokes the methods of a stateless bean, the bean's instance variables may contain a state specific to that client but only for the duration of the invocation. When the method is finished, the client-specific state should not be retained. Clients may, however, change the state of instance variables in pooled stateless beans, and this state is held over to the next invocation of the pooled stateless bean. Except during method invocation, all instances of a stateless bean are equivalent, allowing the EJB container to assign an instance to any client. That is, the state of a stateless session bean should apply across all clients.

Because they can support multiple clients, stateless session beans can offer better scalability for applications that require large numbers of clients. Typically, an application requires fewer stateless session beans than stateful session beans to support the same number of clients.

A stateless session bean can implement a web service, but a stateful session bean cannot.

Singleton Session Beans

A *singleton session bean* is instantiated once per application and exists for the lifecycle of the application. Singleton session beans are designed for circumstances in which a single enterprise bean instance is shared across and concurrently accessed by clients.

Singleton session beans offer similar functionality to stateless session beans but differ from them in that there is only one singleton session bean per application, as opposed to a pool of stateless session beans, any of which may respond to a client request. Like stateless session beans, singleton session beans can implement web service endpoints.

Singleton session beans maintain their state between client invocations but are not required to maintain their state across server crashes or shutdowns.

Applications that use a singleton session bean may specify that the singleton should be instantiated upon application startup, which allows the singleton to perform initialization tasks for the application. The singleton may perform cleanup tasks on application shutdown as well, because the singleton will operate throughout the lifecycle of the application.

When to Use Session Beans

Stateful session beans are appropriate if any of the following conditions are true.

- The bean's state represents the interaction between the bean and a specific client.

- The bean needs to hold information about the client across method invocations.

- The bean mediates between the client and the other components of the application, presenting a simplified view to the client.

- Behind the scenes, the bean manages the work flow of several enterprise beans.

To improve performance, you might choose a stateless session bean if it has any of these traits.

- The bean's state has no data for a specific client.

- In a single method invocation, the bean performs a generic task for all clients. For example, you might use a stateless session bean to send an email that confirms an online order.

- The bean implements a web service.

Singleton session beans are appropriate in the following circumstances.

- State needs to be shared across the application.

- A single enterprise bean needs to be accessed by multiple threads concurrently.

- The application needs an enterprise bean to perform tasks upon application startup and shutdown.

- The bean implements a web service.

What Is a Message-Driven Bean?

A *message-driven bean* is an enterprise bean that allows Java EE applications to process messages asynchronously. This type of bean normally acts as a JMS message listener, which is similar to an event listener but receives JMS messages instead of events. The messages can be sent by any Java EE component (an application client, another enterprise bean, or a web component) or by a JMS application or system that does not use Java EE technology. Message-driven beans can process JMS messages or other kinds of messages.

What Makes Message-Driven Beans Different from Session Beans?

The most visible difference between message-driven beans and session beans is that clients do not access message-driven beans through interfaces. Interfaces are described in the section "Accessing Enterprise Beans" on page 251. Unlike a session bean, a message-driven bean has only a bean class.

In several respects, a message-driven bean resembles a stateless session bean.

- A message-driven bean's instances retain no data or conversational state for a specific client.

- All instances of a message-driven bean are equivalent, allowing the EJB container to assign a message to any message-driven bean instance. The container can pool these instances to allow streams of messages to be processed concurrently.

- A single message-driven bean can process messages from multiple clients.

The instance variables of the message-driven bean instance can contain some state across the handling of client messages, such as a JMS API connection, an open database connection, or an object reference to an enterprise bean object.

Client components do not locate message-driven beans and invoke methods directly on them. Instead, a client accesses a message-driven bean through, for example, JMS by sending messages to the message destination for which the message-driven bean class is the `MessageListener`. You assign a message-driven bean's destination during deployment by using GlassFish Server resources.

Message-driven beans have the following characteristics.

- They execute upon receipt of a single client message.

- They are invoked asynchronously.

- They are relatively short-lived.

- They do not represent directly shared data in the database, but they can access and update this data.

- They can be transaction-aware.

- They are stateless.

When a message arrives, the container calls the message-driven bean's `onMessage` method to process the message. The `onMessage` method normally casts the message to one of the five JMS message types and handles it in accordance with the application's business logic. The `onMessage` method can call helper methods or can invoke a session bean to process the information in the message or to store it in a database.

A message can be delivered to a message-driven bean within a transaction context, so all operations within the `onMessage` method are part of a single transaction. If message processing is rolled back, the message will be redelivered. For more information, see Chapter 27, "Transactions."

When to Use Message-Driven Beans

Session beans allow you to send JMS messages and to receive them synchronously but not asynchronously. To avoid tying up server resources, do not to use blocking synchronous receives in a server-side component; in general, JMS messages should not be sent or received synchronously. To receive messages asynchronously, use a message-driven bean.

Accessing Enterprise Beans

Note – The material in this section applies only to session beans and not to message-driven beans. Because they have a different programming model, message-driven beans do not have interfaces or no-interface views that define client access.

Clients access enterprise beans either through a *no-interface view* or through a *business interface*. A no-interface view of an enterprise bean exposes the public methods of the enterprise bean implementation class to clients. Clients using the no-interface view of an enterprise bean may invoke any public methods in the enterprise bean implementation class or any superclasses of the implementation class. A business interface is a standard Java programming language interface that contains the business methods of the enterprise bean.

A client can access a session bean only through the methods defined in the bean's business interface or through the public methods of an enterprise bean that has a no-interface view. The business interface or no-interface view defines the client's view of an enterprise bean. All other aspects of the enterprise bean (method implementations and deployment settings) are hidden from the client.

Well-designed interfaces and no-interface views simplify the development and maintenance of Java EE applications. Not only do clean interfaces and no-interface views shield the clients from any complexities in the EJB tier, but they also allow the enterprise beans to change internally without affecting the clients. For example, if you change the implementation of a session bean business method, you won't have to alter the client code. But if you were to change the method definitions in the interfaces, you might have to modify the client code as well. Therefore, it is important that you design the interfaces and no-interface views carefully to isolate your clients from possible changes in the enterprise beans.

Session beans can have more than one business interface. Session beans should, but are not required to, implement their business interface or interfaces.

Using Enterprise Beans in Clients

The client of an enterprise bean obtains a reference to an instance of an enterprise bean through either *dependency injection*, using Java programming language annotations, or *JNDI lookup*, using the Java Naming and Directory Interface syntax to find the enterprise bean instance.

Dependency injection is the simplest way of obtaining an enterprise bean reference. Clients that run within a Java EE server-managed environment, JavaServer Faces web applications, JAX-RS web services, other enterprise beans, or Java EE application clients, support dependency injection using the `javax.ejb.EJB` annotation.

Applications that run outside a Java EE server-managed environment, such as Java SE applications, must perform an explicit lookup. JNDI supports a global syntax for identifying Java EE components to simplify this explicit lookup.

Portable JNDI Syntax

Three JNDI namespaces are used for portable JNDI lookups: `java:global`, `java:module`, and `java:app`.

- The `java:global` JNDI namespace is the portable way of finding remote enterprise beans using JNDI lookups. JNDI addresses are of the following form:

  `java:global[/`*application name*`]/`*module name*`/`*enterprise bean name*`[/`*interface name*`]`

  Application name and module name default to the name of the application and module minus the file extension. Application names are required only if the application is packaged within an EAR. The interface name is required only if the enterprise bean implements more than one business interface.

- The `java:module` namespace is used to look up local enterprise beans within the same module. JNDI addresses using the `java:module` namespace are of the following form:

  `java:module/`*enterprise bean name*`/[`*interface name*`]`

  The interface name is required only if the enterprise bean implements more than one business interface.

- The `java:app` namespace is used to look up local enterprise beans packaged within the same application. That is, the enterprise bean is packaged within an EAR file containing multiple Java EE modules. JNDI addresses using the `java:app` namespace are of the following form:

  `java:app[/`*module name*`]/`*enterprise bean name*`[/`*interface name*`]`

  The module name is optional. The interface name is required only if the enterprise bean implements more than one business interface.

For example, if an enterprise bean, MyBean, is packaged within the web application archive myApp.war, the module name is myApp. The portable JNDI name is java:module/MyBean An equivalent JNDI name using the java:global namespace is java:global/myApp/MyBean.

Deciding on Remote or Local Access

When you design a Java EE application, one of the first decisions you make is the type of client access allowed by the enterprise beans: remote, local, or web service.

Whether to allow local or remote access depends on the following factors.

- **Tight or loose coupling of related beans**: Tightly coupled beans depend on one another. For example, if a session bean that processes sales orders calls a session bean that emails a confirmation message to the customer, these beans are tightly coupled. Tightly coupled beans are good candidates for local access. Because they fit together as a logical unit, they typically call each other often and would benefit from the increased performance that is possible with local access.

- **Type of client**: If an enterprise bean is accessed by application clients, it should allow remote access. In a production environment, these clients almost always run on machines other than those on which the GlassFish Server is running. If an enterprise bean's clients are web components or other enterprise beans, the type of access depends on how you want to distribute your components.

- **Component distribution**: Java EE applications are scalable because their server-side components can be distributed across multiple machines. In a distributed application, for example, the server that the web components run on may not be the one on which the enterprise beans they access are deployed. In this distributed scenario, the enterprise beans should allow remote access.

- **Performance**: Owing to such factors as network latency, remote calls may be slower than local calls. On the other hand, if you distribute components among different servers, you may improve the application's overall performance. Both of these statements are generalizations; performance can vary in different operational environments. Nevertheless, you should keep in mind how your application design might affect performance.

If you aren't sure which type of access an enterprise bean should have, choose remote access. This decision gives you more flexibility. In the future, you can distribute your components to accommodate the growing demands on your application.

Although it is uncommon, it is possible for an enterprise bean to allow both remote and local access. If this is the case, either the business interface of the bean must be explicitly designated as a business interface by being decorated with the @Remote or @Local annotations, or the bean class must explicitly designate the business interfaces by using the @Remote and @Local annotations. The same business interface cannot be both a local and a remote business interface.

Local Clients

A local client has these characteristics.

- It must run in the same application as the enterprise bean it accesses.
- It can be a web component or another enterprise bean.
- To the local client, the location of the enterprise bean it accesses is not transparent.

The no-interface view of an enterprise bean is a local view. The public methods of the enterprise bean implementation class are exposed to local clients that access the no-interface view of the enterprise bean. Enterprise beans that use the no-interface view do not implement a business interface.

The *local business interface* defines the bean's business and lifecycle methods. If the bean's business interface is not decorated with @Local or @Remote, and if the bean class does not specify the interface using @Local or @Remote, the business interface is by default a local interface.

To build an enterprise bean that allows only local access, you may, but are not required to, do one of the following:

- Create an enterprise bean implementation class that does not implement a business interface, indicating that the bean exposes a no-interface view to clients. For example:

```
@Session
public class MyBean { ... }
```

- Annotate the business interface of the enterprise bean as a @Local interface. For example:

```
@Local
public interface InterfaceName { ... }
```

- Specify the interface by decorating the bean class with @Local and specify the interface name. For example:

```
@Local(InterfaceName.class)
public class BeanName implements InterfaceName { ... }
```

Accessing Local Enterprise Beans Using the No-Interface View

Client access to an enterprise bean that exposes a local, no-interface view is accomplished through either dependency injection or JNDI lookup.

- To obtain a reference to the no-interface view of an enterprise bean through dependency injection, use the `javax.ejb.EJB` annotation and specify the enterprise bean's implementation class:

```
@EJB
ExampleBean exampleBean;
```

- To obtain a reference to the no-interface view of an enterprise bean through JNDI lookup, use the `javax.naming.InitialContext` interface's `lookup` method:

```
ExampleBean exampleBean = (ExampleBean)
        InitialContext.lookup("java:module/ExampleBean");
```

Clients *do not* use the new operator to obtain a new instance of an enterprise bean that uses a no-interface view.

Accessing Local Enterprise Beans That Implement Business Interfaces

Client access to enterprise beans that implement local business interfaces is accomplished through either dependency injection or JNDI lookup.

- To obtain a reference to the local business interface of an enterprise bean through dependency injection, use the `javax.ejb.EJB` annotation and specify the enterprise bean's local business interface name:

```
@EJB
Example example;
```

- To obtain a reference to a local business interface of an enterprise bean through JNDI lookup, use the `javax.naming.InitialContext` interface's `lookup` method:

```
ExampleLocal example = (ExampleLocal)
        InitialContext.lookup("java:module/ExampleLocal");
```

Remote Clients

A remote client of an enterprise bean has the following traits.

- It can run on a different machine and a different JVM from the enterprise bean it accesses. (It is not required to run on a different JVM.)

- It can be a web component, an application client, or another enterprise bean.

- To a remote client, the location of the enterprise bean is transparent.

- The enterprise bean must implement a business interface. That is, remote clients *may not* access an enterprise bean through a no-interface view.

To create an enterprise bean that allows remote access, you must either

- Decorate the business interface of the enterprise bean with the @Remote annotation:

```
@Remote
public interface InterfaceName { ... }
```

- Decorate the bean class with @Remote, specifying the business interface or interfaces:

```
@Remote(InterfaceName.class)
public class BeanName implements InterfaceName { ... }
```

The *remote interface* defines the business and lifecycle methods that are specific to the bean. For example, the remote interface of a bean named BankAccountBean might have business methods named deposit and credit. Figure 14–1 shows how the interface controls the client's view of an enterprise bean.

FIGURE 14–1   Interfaces for an Enterprise Bean with Remote Access

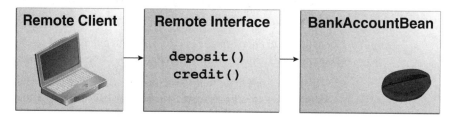

Client access to an enterprise bean that implements a remote business interface is accomplished through either dependency injection or JNDI lookup.

- To obtain a reference to the remote business interface of an enterprise bean through dependency injection, use the javax.ejb.EJB annotation and specify the enterprise bean's remote business interface name:

```
@EJB
Example example;
```

- To obtain a reference to a remote business interface of an enterprise bean through JNDI lookup, use the javax.naming.InitialContext interface's lookup method:

```
ExampleRemote example = (ExampleRemote)
        InitialContext.lookup("java:global/myApp/ExampleRemote");
```

Web Service Clients

A web service client can access a Java EE application in two ways. First, the client can access a web service created with JAX-WS. (For more information on JAX-WS, see

Chapter 12, "Building Web Services with JAX-WS.") Second, a web service client can invoke the business methods of a stateless session bean. Message beans cannot be accessed by web service clients.

Provided that it uses the correct protocols (SOAP, HTTP, WSDL), any web service client can access a stateless session bean, whether or not the client is written in the Java programming language. The client doesn't even "know" what technology implements the service: stateless session bean, JAX-WS, or some other technology. In addition, enterprise beans and web components can be clients of web services. This flexibility enables you to integrate Java EE applications with web services.

A web service client accesses a stateless session bean through the bean's web service endpoint implementation class. By default, all public methods in the bean class are accessible to web service clients. The @WebMethod annotation may be used to customize the behavior of web service methods. If the @WebMethod annotation is used to decorate the bean class's methods, only those methods decorated with @WebMethod are exposed to web service clients.

For a code sample, see "A Web Service Example: `helloservice`" on page 286.

Method Parameters and Access

The type of access affects the parameters of the bean methods that are called by clients. The following sections apply not only to method parameters but also to method return values.

Isolation

The parameters of remote calls are more isolated than those of local calls. With remote calls, the client and the bean operate on different copies of a parameter object. If the client changes the value of the object, the value of the copy in the bean does not change. This layer of isolation can help protect the bean if the client accidentally modifies the data.

In a local call, both the client and the bean can modify the same parameter object. In general, you should not rely on this side effect of local calls. Perhaps someday you will want to distribute your components, replacing the local calls with remote ones.

As with remote clients, web service clients operate on different copies of parameters than does the bean that implements the web service.

Granularity of Accessed Data

Because remote calls are likely to be slower than local calls, the parameters in remote methods should be relatively coarse-grained. A coarse-grained object contains more data than a fine-grained one, so fewer access calls are required. For the same reason, the parameters of the methods called by web service clients should also be coarse-grained.

The Contents of an Enterprise Bean

To develop an enterprise bean, you must provide the following files:

- **Enterprise bean class**: Implements the business methods of the enterprise bean and any lifecycle callback methods.

- **Business interfaces**: Define the business methods implemented by the enterprise bean class. A business interface is not required if the enterprise bean exposes a local, no-interface view.

- **Helper classes**: Other classes needed by the enterprise bean class, such as exception and utility classes.

Package the programming artifacts in the preceding list either into an EJB JAR file (a stand-alone module that stores the enterprise bean) or within a web application archive (WAR) module.

Packaging Enterprise Beans in EJB JAR Modules

An EJB JAR file is portable and can be used for various applications.

To assemble a Java EE application, package one or more modules, such as EJB JAR files, into an EAR file, the archive file that holds the application. When deploying the EAR file that contains the enterprise bean's EJB JAR file, you also deploy the enterprise bean to the GlassFish Server. You can also deploy an EJB JAR that is not contained in an EAR file. Figure 14–2 shows the contents of an EJB JAR file.

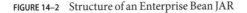

FIGURE 14–2   Structure of an Enterprise Bean JAR

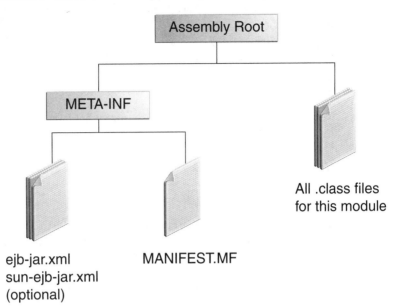

ejb-jar.xml
sun-ejb-jar.xml
(optional)

MANIFEST.MF

All .class files
for this module

Packaging Enterprise Beans in WAR Modules

Enterprise beans often provide the business logic of a web application. In these cases, packaging the enterprise bean within the web application's WAR module simplifies deployment and application organization. Enterprise beans may be packaged within a WAR module as Java programming language class files or within a JAR file that is bundled within the WAR module.

To include enterprise bean class files in a WAR module, the class files should be in the WEB-INF/classes directory.

To include a JAR file that contains enterprise beans in a WAR module, add the JAR to the WEB-INF/lib directory of the WAR module.

WAR modules that contain enterprise beans do not require an ejb-jar.xml deployment descriptor. If the application uses ejb-jar.xml, it must be located in the WAR module's WEB-INF directory.

JAR files that contain enterprise bean classes packaged within a WAR module are not considered EJB JAR files, even if the bundled JAR file conforms to the format of an EJB JAR file. The enterprise beans contained within the JAR file are semantically equivalent to enterprise beans located in the WAR module's WEB-INF/classes directory, and the environment namespace of all the enterprise beans are scoped to the WAR module.

For example, suppose that a web application consists of a shopping cart enterprise bean, a credit card processing enterprise bean, and a Java servlet front end. The shopping cart bean exposes a local, no-interface view and is defined as follows:

```
package com.example.cart;

@Stateless
public class CartBean { ... }
```

The credit card processing bean is packaged within its own JAR file, cc.jar, exposes a local, no-interface view, and is defined as follows:

```
package com.example.cc;

@Stateless
public class CreditCardBean { ... }
```

The servlet, com.example.web.StoreServlet, handles the web front end and uses both CartBean and CreditCardBean. The WAR module layout for this application looks as follows:

```
WEB-INF/classes/com/example/cart/CartBean.class
WEB-INF/classes/com/example/web/StoreServlet
WEB-INF/lib/cc.jar
WEB-INF/ejb-jar.xml
WEB-INF/web.xml
```

Naming Conventions for Enterprise Beans

Because enterprise beans are composed of multiple parts, it's useful to follow a naming convention for your applications. Table 14–2 summarizes the conventions for the example beans in this tutorial.

TABLE 14–2   Naming Conventions for Enterprise Beans

Item	Syntax	Example
Enterprise bean name	*name*Bean	AccountBean
Enterprise bean class	*name*Bean	AccountBean
Business interface	*name*	Account

The Lifecycles of Enterprise Beans

An enterprise bean goes through various stages during its lifetime, or lifecycle. Each type of enterprise bean (stateful session, stateless session, singleton session, or message-driven) has a different lifecycle.

The descriptions that follow refer to methods that are explained along with the code examples in the next two chapters. If you are new to enterprise beans, you should skip this section and run the code examples first.

The Lifecycle of a Stateful Session Bean

Figure 14–3 illustrates the stages that a session bean passes through during its lifetime. The client initiates the lifecycle by obtaining a reference to a stateful session bean. The container performs any dependency injection and then invokes the method annotated with @PostConstruct, if any. The bean is now ready to have its business methods invoked by the client.

FIGURE 14–3   Lifecycle of a Stateful Session Bean

① Create
② Dependency injection, if any
③ PostConstruct callback, if any
④ Init method, or ejbCreate<METHOD>, if any

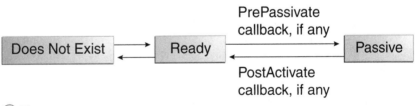

① Remove
② PreDestroy callback, if any

While in the ready stage, the EJB container may decide to deactivate, or *passivate*, the bean by moving it from memory to secondary storage. (Typically, the EJB container uses a least-recently-used algorithm to select a bean for passivation.) The EJB container invokes the method annotated @PrePassivate, if any, immediately before passivating it. If a client invokes a business method on the bean while it is in the passive stage, the EJB container activates the bean, calls the method annotated @PostActivate, if any, and then moves it to the ready stage.

At the end of the lifecycle, the client invokes a method annotated @Remove, and the EJB container calls the method annotated @PreDestroy, if any. The bean's instance is then ready for garbage collection.

Your code controls the invocation of only one lifecycle method: the method annotated @Remove. All other methods in Figure 14–3 are invoked by the EJB container. See Chapter 28, "Resource Connections," for more information.

The Lifecycle of a Stateless Session Bean

Because a stateless session bean is never passivated, its lifecycle has only two stages: nonexistent and ready for the invocation of business methods. Figure 14–4 illustrates the stages of a stateless session bean.

FIGURE 14–4   Lifecycle of a Stateless Session Bean

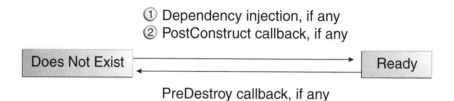

The EJB container typically creates and maintains a pool of stateless session beans, beginning the stateless session bean's lifecycle. The container performs any dependency injection and then invokes the method annotated @PostConstruct, if it exists. The bean is now ready to have its business methods invoked by a client.

At the end of the lifecycle, the EJB container calls the method annotated @PreDestroy, if it exists. The bean's instance is then ready for garbage collection.

The Lifecycle of a Singleton Session Bean

Like a stateless session bean, a singleton session bean is never passivated and has only two stages, nonexistent and ready for the invocation of business methods, as shown in Figure 14–5.

FIGURE 14-5   Lifecycle of a Singleton Session Bean

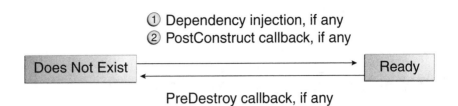

The EJB container initiates the singleton session bean lifecycle by creating the singleton instance. This occurs upon application deployment if the singleton is annotated with the @Startup annotation The container performs any dependency injection and then invokes the method annotated @PostConstruct, if it exists. The singleton session bean is now ready to have its business methods invoked by the client.

At the end of the lifecycle, the EJB container calls the method annotated @PreDestroy, if it exists. The singleton session bean is now ready for garbage collection.

The Lifecycle of a Message-Driven Bean

Figure 14–6 illustrates the stages in the lifecycle of a message-driven bean.

FIGURE 14-6   Lifecycle of a Message-Driven Bean

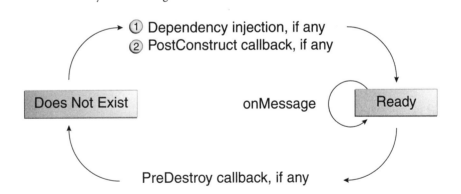

The EJB container usually creates a pool of message-driven bean instances. For each instance, the EJB container performs these tasks.

1. If the message-driven bean uses dependency injection, the container injects these references before instantiating the instance.

2. The container calls the method annotated @PostConstruct, if any.

Like a stateless session bean, a message-driven bean is never passivated and has only two states: nonexistent and ready to receive messages.

At the end of the lifecycle, the container calls the method annotated @PreDestroy, if any. The bean's instance is then ready for garbage collection.

Further Information about Enterprise Beans

For more information on Enterprise JavaBeans technology, see

- Enterprise JavaBeans 3.1 specification:

  `http://jcp.org/en/jsr/summary?id=318`

- Enterprise JavaBeans web site:

  `http://www.oracle.com/technetwork/java/ejb-141389.html`

15

Getting Started with Enterprise Beans

This chapter shows how to develop, deploy, and run a simple Java EE application named converter. The purpose of converter is to calculate currency conversions between Japanese yen and Eurodollars. The converter application consists of an enterprise bean, which performs the calculations, and two types of clients: an application client and a web client.

Here's an overview of the steps you'll follow in this chapter:

1. Create the enterprise bean: ConverterBean.
2. Create the web client.
3. Deploy converter onto the server.
4. Using a browser, run the web client.

Before proceeding, make sure that you've done the following:

- Read Chapter 1, "Overview"
- Become familiar with enterprise beans (see Chapter 14, "Enterprise Beans")
- Started the server (see "Starting and Stopping the GlassFish Server" on page 41)

The following topics are addressed here:

- "Creating the Enterprise Bean" on page 265
- "Modifying the Java EE Application" on page 269

Creating the Enterprise Bean

The enterprise bean in our example is a stateless session bean called ConverterBean. The source code for ConverterBean is in the *tut-install*/examples/ejb/converter/src/java/ directory.

Creating ConverterBean requires these steps:

1. Coding the bean's implementation class (the source code is provided)
2. Compiling the source code

Coding the Enterprise Bean Class

The enterprise bean class for this example is called ConverterBean. This class implements two business methods: dollarToYen and yenToEuro. Because the enterprise bean class doesn't implement a business interface, the enterprise bean exposes a local, no-interface view. The public methods in the enterprise bean class are available to clients that obtain a reference to ConverterBean. The source code for the ConverterBean class is as follows:

```
package com.sun.tutorial.javaee.ejb;

import java.math.BigDecimal;
import javax.ejb.*;

@Stateless
public class ConverterBean {
    private BigDecimal yenRate = new BigDecimal("115.3100");
    private BigDecimal euroRate = new BigDecimal("0.0071");

    public BigDecimal dollarToYen(BigDecimal dollars) {
        BigDecimal result = dollars.multiply(yenRate);
        return result.setScale(2, BigDecimal.ROUND_UP);
    }

    public BigDecimal yenToEuro(BigDecimal yen) {
        BigDecimal result = yen.multiply(euroRate);
        return result.setScale(2, BigDecimal.ROUND_UP);
    }
}
```

Note the @Stateless annotation decorating the enterprise bean class. This annotation lets the container know that ConverterBean is a stateless session bean.

Creating the converter Web Client

The web client is contained in the following servlet class:

tut-install/examples/ejb/converter/src/java/converter/web/ConverterServlet.java

A Java servlet is a web component that responds to HTTP requests.

The ConverterServlet class uses dependency injection to obtain a reference to ConverterBean. The javax.ejb.EJB annotation is added to the declaration of the private member variable converterBean, which is of type ConverterBean. ConverterBean exposes a local, no-interface view, so the enterprise bean implementation class is the variable type:

```
@WebServlet
public class ConverterServlet extends HttpServlet {
  @EJB
  ConverterBean converterBean;
  ...
}
```

When the user enters an amount to be converted to yen and euro, the amount is retrieved from the request parameters; then the ConverterBean.dollarToYen and the ConverterBean.yenToEuro methods are called:

```
...
try {
  String amount = request.getParameter("amount");
  if (amount != null && amount.length() > 0) {
    // convert the amount to a BigDecimal from the request parameter
    BigDecimal d = new BigDecimal(amount);
    // call the ConverterBean.dollarToYen() method to get the amount
    // in Yen
    BigDecimal yenAmount = converter.dollarToYen(d);

    // call the ConverterBean.yenToEuro() method to get the amount
    // in Euros
    BigDecimal euroAmount = converter.yenToEuro(yenAmount);
    ...
  }
  ...
}
```

The results are displayed to the user.

Building, Packaging, Deploying, and Running the converter Example

Now you are ready to compile the enterprise bean class (ConverterBean.java) and the servlet class (ConverterServlet.java) and to package the compiled classes into a WAR file.

▼ To Build, Package, and Deploy the converter Example in NetBeans IDE

1   In NetBeans IDE, select File→Open Project.

2   In the Open Project dialog, navigate to:

    tut-install/examples/ejb/

3   Select the converter folder.

4   Select the Open as Main Project and Open Required Projects check boxes.

5   Click Open Project.

6   In the Projects tab, right-click the converter project and select Deploy.

A web browser window opens the URL `http://localhost:8080/converter`.

▼ To Build, Package, and Deploy the converter Example Using Ant

1   In a terminal window, go to:

tut-install`/examples/ejb/converter/`

2   Type the following command:

`ant all`

This command calls the `default` task, which compiles the source files for the enterprise bean and the servlet, placing the class files in the `build` subdirectory (not the `src` directory) of the project. The default task packages the project into a WAR module: `converter.war`. For more information about the Ant tool, see "Building the Examples" on page 44.

Note – When compiling the code, the `ant` task includes the Java EE API JAR files in the classpath. These JARs reside in the `modules` directory of your GlassFish Server installation. If you plan to use other tools to compile the source code for Java EE components, make sure that the classpath includes the Java EE API JAR files.

▼ To Run the converter Example

1   Open a web browser to the following URL:

`http://localhost:8080/converter`

The screen shown in Figure 15–1 appears.

FIGURE 15–1   The converter Web Client

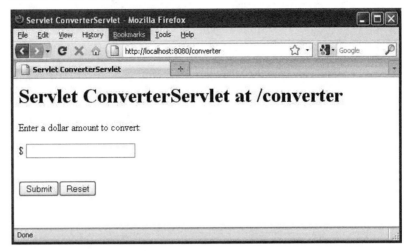

2   **Type 100 in the input field and click Submit.**

A second page appears, showing the converted values.

Modifying the Java EE Application

The GlassFish Server supports iterative development. Whenever you make a change to a Java EE application, you must redeploy the application.

▼ To Modify a Class File

To modify a class file in an enterprise bean, you change the source code, recompile it, and redeploy the application. For example, if you want to change the exchange rate in the `dollarToYen` business method of the `ConverterBean` class, you would follow these steps.

To modify `ConverterServlet`, the procedure is the same.

1   **Edit `ConverterBean.java` and save the file.**

2   **Recompile the source file.**

- **To recompile `ConverterBean.java` in NetBeans IDE, right-click the converter project and select Run.**

  This recompiles the `ConverterBean.java` file, replaces the old class file in the build directory, and redeploys the application to GlassFish Server.

- Recompile `ConverterBean.java` using Ant:

  a. In a terminal window, go to the *tut-install*/**examples/ejb/converter/** subdirectory.

  b. Type the following command:

  ```
  ant all
  ```

  This command repackages, deploys, and runs the application.

16

◆ ◆ ◆ **CHAPTER 16**

Running the Enterprise Bean Examples

Session beans provide a simple but powerful way to encapsulate business logic within an application. They can be accessed from remote Java clients, web service clients, and components running in the same server.

In Chapter 15, "Getting Started with Enterprise Beans," you built a stateless session bean named `ConverterBean`. This chapter examines the source code of four more session beans:

- `CartBean`: a stateful session bean that is accessed by a remote client
- `CounterBean`: a singleton session bean
- `HelloServiceBean`: a stateless session bean that implements a web service
- `TimerSessionBean`: a stateless session bean that sets a timer

The following topics are addressed here:

The cart Example

The cart example represents a shopping cart in an online bookstore and uses a stateful session bean to manage the operations of the shopping cart. The bean's client can add a book to the cart, remove a book, or retrieve the cart's contents. To assemble cart, you need the following code:

- Session bean class (`CartBean`)
- Remote business interface (`Cart`)

All session beans require a session bean class. All enterprise beans that permit remote access must have a remote business interface. To meet the needs of a specific application, an enterprise bean may also need some helper classes. The CartBean session bean uses two helper classes, BookException and IdVerifier, which are discussed in the section "Helper Classes" on page 276.

The source code for this example is in the *tut-install*/examples/ejb/cart/ directory.

The Business Interface

The Cart business interface is a plain Java interface that defines all the business methods implemented in the bean class. If the bean class implements a single interface, that interface is assumed to the business interface. The business interface is a local interface unless it is annotated with the javax.ejb.Remote annotation; the javax.ejb.Local annotation is optional in this case.

The bean class may implement more than one interface. In that case, the business interfaces must either be explicitly annotated @Local or @Remote or be specified by decorating the bean class with @Local or @Remote. However, the following interfaces are excluded when determining whether the bean class implements more than one interface:

- java.io.Serializable
- java.io.Externalizable
- Any of the interfaces defined by the javax.ejb package

The source code for the Cart business interface follows:

```
package com.sun.tutorial.javaee.ejb;

import java.util.List;
import javax.ejb.Remote;

@Remote
public interface Cart {
    public void initialize(String person) throws BookException;
    public void initialize(String person, String id)
        throws BookException;
    public void addBook(String title);
    public void removeBook(String title) throws BookException;
    public List<String> getContents();
    public void remove();
}
```

Session Bean Class

The session bean class for this example is called CartBean. Like any stateful session bean, the CartBean class must meet the following requirements.

- The class is annotated @Stateful.
- The class implements the business methods defined in the business interface.

Stateful session beans also may

- Implement the business interface, a plain Java interface. It is good practice to implement the bean's business interface.

- Implement any optional lifecycle callback methods, annotated @PostConstruct, @PreDestroy, @PostActivate, and @PrePassivate.

- Implement any optional business methods annotated @Remove.

The source code for the CartBean class follows:

```
package com.sun.tutorial.javaee.ejb;

import java.util.ArrayList;
import java.util.List;
import javax.ejb.Remove;
import javax.ejb.Stateful;

@Stateful
public class CartBean implements Cart {
    String customerName;
    String customerId;
    List<String> contents;

    public void initialize(String person) throws BookException {
        if (person == null) {
            throw new BookException("Null person not allowed.");
        } else {
            customerName = person;
        }

        customerId = "0";
        contents = new ArrayList<String>();
    }

    public void initialize(String person, String id)
                throws BookException {
        if (person == null) {
            throw new BookException("Null person not allowed.");
        } else {

            customerName = person;
        }

        IdVerifier idChecker = new IdVerifier();

        if (idChecker.validate(id)) {
```

```
            customerId = id;
        } else {
            throw new BookException("Invalid id: " + id);
        }

        contents = new ArrayList<String>();
    }

    public void addBook(String title) {
        contents.add(title);
    }

    public void removeBook(String title) throws BookException {
        boolean result = contents.remove(title);
        if (result == false) {
            throw new BookException(title + " not in cart.");
        }
    }

    public List<String> getContents() {
        return contents;
    }

    @Remove
    public void remove() {
        contents = null;
    }
}
```

Lifecycle Callback Methods

A method in the bean class may be declared as a lifecycle callback method by annotating the method with the following annotations:

- `javax.annotation.PostConstruct`: Methods annotated with `@PostConstruct` are invoked by the container on newly constructed bean instances after all dependency injection has completed and before the first business method is invoked on the enterprise bean.

- `javax.annotation.PreDestroy`: Methods annotated with `@PreDestroy` are invoked after any method annotated `@Remove` has completed and before the container removes the enterprise bean instance.

- `javax.ejb.PostActivate`: Methods annotated with `@PostActivate` are invoked by the container after the container moves the bean from secondary storage to active status.

- `javax.ejb.PrePassivate`: Methods annotated with `@PrePassivate` are invoked by the container before it passivates the enterprise bean, meaning that the container temporarily removes the bean from the environment and saves it to secondary storage.

Lifecycle callback methods must return `void` and have no parameters.

Business Methods

The primary purpose of a session bean is to run business tasks for the client. The client invokes business methods on the object reference it gets from dependency injection or JNDI lookup. From the client's perspective, the business methods appear to run locally, although they run remotely in the session bean. The following code snippet shows how the CartClient program invokes the business methods:

```
cart.create("Duke DeEarl", "123");
...
cart.addBook("Bel Canto");
 ...
List<String> bookList = cart.getContents();
...
cart.removeBook("Gravity's Rainbow");
```

The CartBean class implements the business methods in the following code:

```
public void addBook(String title) {
   contents.addElement(title);
}

public void removeBook(String title) throws BookException {
   boolean result = contents.remove(title);
   if (result == false) {
      throw new BookException(title + "not in cart.");
   }
}

public List<String> getContents() {
   return contents;
}
```

The signature of a business method must conform to these rules.

- The method name must not begin with ejb, to avoid conflicts with callback methods defined by the EJB architecture. For example, you cannot call a business method ejbCreate or ejbActivate.

- The access control modifier must be public.

- If the bean allows remote access through a remote business interface, the arguments and return types must be legal types for the Java Remote Method Invocation (RMI) API.

- If the bean is a web service endpoint, the arguments and return types for the methods annotated @WebMethod must be legal types for JAX-WS.

- The modifier must not be static or final.

The throws clause can include exceptions that you define for your application. The removeBook method, for example, throws a BookException if the book is not in the cart.

To indicate a system-level problem, such as the inability to connect to a database, a business method should throw a javax.ejb.EJBException. The container will not wrap application exceptions, such as BookException. Because EJBException is a subclass of RuntimeException, you do not need to include it in the throws clause of the business method.

The @Remove Method

Business methods annotated with javax.ejb.Remove in the stateful session bean class can be invoked by enterprise bean clients to remove the bean instance. The container will remove the enterprise bean after a @Remove method completes, either normally or abnormally.

In CartBean, the remove method is a @Remove method:

```
@Remove
public void remove() {
    contents = null;
}
```

Helper Classes

The CartBean session bean has two helper classes: BookException and IdVerifier. The BookException is thrown by the removeBook method, and the IdVerifier validates the customerId in one of the create methods. Helper classes may reside in an EJB JAR file that contains the enterprise bean class, a WAR file if the enterprise bean is packaged within a WAR, or in an EAR that contains an EJB JAR or a WAR file that contains an enterprise bean.

Building, Packaging, Deploying, and Running the cart Example

Now you are ready to compile the remote interface (Cart.java), the home interface (CartHome.java), the enterprise bean class (CartBean.java), the client class (CartClient.java), and the helper classes (BookException.java and IdVerifier.java). Follow these steps.

You can build, package, deploy, and run the cart application using either NetBeans IDE or the Ant tool.

▼ To Build, Package, Deploy, and Run the cart Example Using NetBeans IDE

1 In NetBeans IDE, select File→Open Project.

2 In the Open Project dialog, navigate to:

   tut-install/examples/ejb/

3 Select the cart folder.

4 Select the Open as Main Project and Open Required Projects check boxes.

5 Click Open Project.

6 In the Projects tab, right-click the cart project and select Deploy.

   This builds and packages the application into cart.ear, located in
   tut-install/examples/ejb/cart/dist/, and deploys this EAR file to your GlassFish
   Server instance.

7 To run the cart application client, select Run→Run Main Project.

   You will see the output of the application client in the Output pane:

```
...
Retrieving book title from cart: Infinite Jest
Retrieving book title from cart: Bel Canto
Retrieving book title from cart: Kafka on the Shore
Removing "Gravity's Rainbow" from cart.
Caught a BookException: "Gravity's Rainbow" not in cart.
Java Result: 1
run-cart-app-client:
run-nb:
BUILD SUCCESSFUL (total time: 14 seconds)
```

▼ To Build, Package, Deploy, and Run the cart Example Using Ant

1 In a terminal window, go to:

   tut-install/examples/ejb/cart/

2 Type the following command:

   ant

   This command calls the default target, which builds and packages the application
   into an EAR file, cart.ear, located in the dist directory.

3 **Type the following command:**

```
ant deploy
```

The cart.ear file is deployed to the GlassFish Server.

4 **Type the following command:**

```
ant run
```

This task retrieves the application client JAR, cartClient.jar, and runs the application client. The client JAR, cartClient.jar, contains the application client class, the helper class BookException, and the Cart business interface.

This task is equivalent to running the following command:

```
appclient -client cartClient.jar
```

When you run the client, the application client container injects any component references declared in the application client class, in this case the reference to the Cart enterprise bean.

The all Task

As a convenience, the all task will build, package, deploy, and run the application. To do this, enter the following command:

```
ant all
```

A Singleton Session Bean Example: counter

The counter example demonstrates how to create a singleton session bean.

Creating a Singleton Session Bean

The javax.ejb.Singleton annotation is used to specify that the enterprise bean implementation class is a singleton session bean:

```
@Singleton
public class SingletonBean { ... }
```

Initializing Singleton Session Beans

The EJB container is responsible for determining when to initialize a singleton session bean instance unless the singleton session bean implementation class is annotated with the javax.ejb.Startup annotation. In this case, sometimes called *eager initialization*, the EJB container must initialize the singleton session bean upon application startup. The singleton session bean is initialized before the EJB container delivers client requests to any enterprise beans in the application. This allows the singleton session bean to perform, for example, application startup tasks.

The following singleton session bean stores the status of an application and is eagerly initialized:

```
@Startup
@Singleton
public class StatusBean {
  private String status;

  @PostConstruct
  void init {
    status = "Ready";
  }
  ...
}
```

Sometimes multiple singleton session beans are used to initialize data for an application and therefore must be initialized in a specific order. In these cases, use the `javax.ejb.DependsOn` annotation to declare the startup dependencies of the singleton session bean. The `@DependsOn` annotation's value attribute is one or more strings that specify the name of the target singleton session bean. If more than one dependent singleton bean is specified in `@DependsOn`, the order in which they are listed is not necessarily the order in which the EJB container will initialize the target singleton session beans.

The following singleton session bean, `PrimaryBean`, should be started up first:

```
@Singleton
public class PrimaryBean { ... }
```

`SecondaryBean` depends on `PrimaryBean`:

```
@Singleton
@DependsOn("PrimaryBean")
public class SecondaryBean { ... }
```

This guarantees that the EJB container will initialize `PrimaryBean` before `SecondaryBean`.

The following singleton session bean, `TertiaryBean`, depends on `PrimaryBean` and `SecondaryBean`:

```
@Singleton
@DependsOn("PrimaryBean", "SecondaryBean")
public class TertiaryBean { ... }
```

`SecondaryBean` explicitly requires `PrimaryBean` to be initialized before it is initialized, through its own `@DependsOn` annotation. In this case, the EJB container will first initialize `PrimaryBean`, then `SecondaryBean`, and finally `TertiaryBean`.

If, however, SecondaryBean did not explicitly depend on PrimaryBean, the EJB container may initialize either PrimaryBean or SecondaryBean first. That is, the EJB container could initialize the singletons in the following order: SecondaryBean, PrimaryBean, TertiaryBean.

Managing Concurrent Access in a Singleton Session Bean

Singleton session beans are designed for *concurrent access*, situations in which many clients need to access a single instance of a session bean at the same time. A singleton's client needs only a reference to a singleton in order to invoke any business methods exposed by the singleton and doesn't need to worry about any other clients that may be simultaneously invoking business methods on the same singleton.

When creating a singleton session bean, concurrent access to the singleton's business methods can be controlled in two ways: *container-managed concurrency* and *bean-managed concurrency*.

The javax.ejb.ConcurrencyManagement annotation is used to specify container-managed or bean-managed concurrency for the singleton. With @ConcurrencyManagement, a type attribute must be set to either javax.ejb.ConcurrencyManagementType.CONTAINER or javax.ejb.ConcurrencyManagementType.BEAN. If no @ConcurrencyManagement annotation is present on the singleton implementation class, the EJB container default of container-managed concurrency is used.

Container-Managed Concurrency

If a singleton uses container-managed concurrency, the EJB container controls client access to the business methods of the singleton. The javax.ejb.Lock annotation and a javax.ejb.LockType type are used to specify the access level of the singleton's business methods or @Timeout methods.

Annotate a singleton's business or timeout method with @Lock(READ) if the method can be concurrently accessed, or shared, with many clients. Annotate the business or timeout method with @Lock(WRITE) if the singleton session bean should be locked to other clients while a client is calling that method. Typically, the @Lock(WRITE) annotation is used when clients are modifying the state of the singleton.

Annotating a singleton class with @Lock specifies that all the business methods and any timeout methods of the singleton will use the specified lock type unless they explicitly set the lock type with a method-level @Lock annotation. If no @Lock annotation is present on the singleton class, the default lock type, @Lock(WRITE), is applied to all business and timeout methods.

The following example shows how to use the @ConcurrencyManagement, @Lock(READ), and @Lock(WRITE) annotations for a singleton that uses container-managed concurrency.

Although by default, singletons use container-managed concurrency, the `@ConcurrencyManagement(CONTAINER)` annotation may be added at the class level of the singleton to explicitly set the concurrency management type:

```
@ConcurrencyManagement(CONTAINER)
@Singleton
public class ExampleSingletonBean {
  private String state;

  @Lock(READ)
  public String getState() {
    return state;
  }

  @Lock(WRITE)
  public void setState(String newState) {
    state = newState;
  }
}
```

The `getState` method can be accessed by many clients at the same time because it is annotated with `@Lock(READ)`. When the `setState` method is called, however, all the methods in `ExampleSingletonBean` will be locked to other clients because `setState` is annotated with `@Lock(WRITE)`. This prevents two clients from attempting to simultaneously change the `state` variable of `ExampleSingletonBean`.

The `getData` and `getStatus` methods in the following singleton are of type `READ`, and the `setStatus` method is of type `WRITE`:

```
@Singleton
@Lock(READ)
public class SharedSingletonBean {
  private String data;
  private String status;

  public String getData() {
    return data;
  }

  public String getStatus() {
    return status;
  }

  @Lock(WRITE)
  public void setStatus(String newStatus) {
    status = newStatus;
  }
}
```

If a method is of locking type `WRITE`, client access to all the singleton's methods is blocked until the current client finishes its method call or an access timeout occurs. When an access timeout occurs, the EJB container throws a `javax.ejb.ConcurrentAccessTimeoutException`. The `javax.ejb.AccessTimeout` annotation is used to specify the number of milliseconds before an access timeout occurs. If added at the class level of a singleton, @AccessTimeout specifies the access timeout value for all methods in the singleton unless a method explicitly overrides the default with its own @AccessTimeout annotation.

The @AccessTimeout annotation can be applied to both @Lock(READ) and @Lock(WRITE) methods. The @AccessTimeout annotation has one required element, value, and one optional element, unit. By default, the value is specified in milliseconds. To change the value unit, set unit to one of the java.util.concurrent.TimeUnit constants: NANOSECONDS, MICROSECONDS, MILLISECONDS, or SECONDS.

The following singleton has a default access timeout value of 120,000 milliseconds, or 2 minutes. The doTediousOperation method overrides the default access timeout and sets the value to 360,000 milliseconds, or 6 minutes.

```
@Singleton
@AccessTimeout(value=120000)
public class StatusSingletonBean {
  private String status;

  @Lock(WRITE)
  public void setStatus(String new Status) {
    status = newStatus;
  }

  @Lock(WRITE)
  @AccessTimeout(value=360000)
  public void doTediousOperation {
    ...
  }
}
```

The following singleton has a default access timeout value of 60 seconds, specified using the TimeUnit.SECONDS constant:

```
@Singleton
@AccessTimeout(value=60, timeUnit=SECONDS)
public class StatusSingletonBean { ... }
```

Bean-Managed Concurrency

Singletons that use bean-managed concurrency allow full concurrent access to all the business and timeout methods in the singleton. The developer of the singleton is responsible for ensuring that the state of the singleton is synchronized across all clients. Developers who create singletons with bean-managed concurrency are allowed to use the Java programming language synchronization primitives, such as synchronization and volatile, to prevent errors during concurrent access.

Add a @ConcurrencyManagement annotation at the class level of the singleton to specify bean-managed concurrency:

```
@ConcurrencyManagement(BEAN)
@Singleton
public class AnotherSingletonBean { ... }
```

Handling Errors in a Singleton Session Bean

If a singleton session bean encounters an error when initialized by the EJB container, that singleton instance will be destroyed.

Unlike other enterprise beans, once a singleton session bean instance is initialized, it is not destroyed if the singleton's business or lifecycle methods cause system exceptions. This ensures that the same singleton instance is used throughout the application lifecycle.

The Architecture of the counter Example

The counter example consists of a singleton session bean, CounterBean, and a JavaServer Faces Facelets web front end.

CounterBean is a simple singleton with one method, getHits, that returns an integer representing the number of times a web page has been accessed. Here is the code of CounterBean:

```
package counter.ejb;

import javax.ejb.Singleton;

/**
 * CounterBean is a simple singleton session bean that records the number
 * of hits to a web page.
 */
@Singleton
public class CounterBean {
    private int hits = 1;

    // Increment and return the number of hits
    public int getHits() {
        return hits++;
    }
}
```

The @Singleton annotation marks CounterBean as a singleton session bean. CounterBean uses a local, no-interface view.

CounterBean uses the EJB container's default metadata values for singletons to simplify the coding of the singleton implementation class. There is no @ConcurrencyManagement annotation on the class, so the default of container-managed concurrency access is applied. There is no @Lock annotation on the class or business method, so the default of @Lock(WRITE) is applied to the only business method, getHits.

The following version of CounterBean is functionally equivalent to the preceding version:

```
package counter.ejb;

import javax.ejb.Singleton;
import javax.ejb.ConcurrencyManagement;
import static javax.ejb.ConcurrencyManagementType.CONTAINER;
import javax.ejb.Lock;
import javax.ejb.LockType.WRITE;

/**
 * CounterBean is a simple singleton session bean that records the number
 * of hits to a web page.
 */
@Singleton
@ConcurrencyManagement(CONTAINER)
public class CounterBean {
    private int hits = 1;

    // Increment and return the number of hits
    @Lock(WRITE)
    public int getHits() {
        return hits++;
    }
}
```

The web front end of counter consists of a JavaServer Faces managed bean, Count.java, that is used by the Facelets XHTML files template.xhtml and template-client.xhtml. The Count JavaServer Faces managed bean obtains a reference to CounterBean through dependency injection. Count defines a hitCount JavaBeans property. When the getHitCount getter method is called from the XHTML files, CounterBean's getHits method is called to return the current number of page hits.

Here's the Count managed bean class:

```
@ManagedBean
@SessionScoped
public class Count {
    @EJB
    private CounterBean counterBean;

    private int hitCount;

    public Count() {
        this.hitCount = 0;
    }

    public int getHitCount() {
        hitCount = counterBean.getHits();
        return hitCount;
    }
```

```
        public void setHitCount(int newHits) {
            this.hitCount = newHits;
        }
    }
}
```

The `template.xhtml` and `template-client.xhtml` files are used to render a Facelets view that displays the number of hits to that view. The `template-client.xhtml` file uses an expression language statement, `#{count.hitCount}`, to access the `hitCount` property of the `Count` managed bean. Here is the content of `template-client.xhtml`:

```
<?xml version='1.0' encoding='UTF-8' ?>
<!DOCTYPE html PUBLIC "-//W3C//DTD XHTML 1.0 Transitional//EN"
    "http://www.w3.org/TR/xhtml1/DTD/xhtml1-transitional.dtd">
<html xmlns="http://www.w3.org/1999/xhtml"
      xmlns:ui="http://java.sun.com/jsf/facelets"
      xmlns:h="http://java.sun.com/jsf/html">
    <body>

        This text above will not be displayed.

        <ui:composition template="/template.xhtml">

            This text will not be displayed.

            <ui:define name="title">
                This page has been accessed #{count.hitCount} time(s).
            </ui:define>

            This text will also not be displayed.

            <ui:define name="body">
                Hooray!
            </ui:define>

            This text will not be displayed.

        </ui:composition>

        This text below will also not be displayed.

    </body>
</html>
```

Building, Packaging, Deploying, and Running the counter Example

The counter example application can be built, deployed, and run using NetBeans IDE or Ant.

▼ To Build, Package, Deploy, and Run the `counter` Example Using NetBeans IDE

1   In NetBeans IDE, select File→Open Project.

2   In the Open Project dialog, navigate to:

     tut-install/examples/ejb/

3   Select the `counter` folder.

4   Select the Open as Main Project check box.

5   Click Open Project.

6   In the Projects tab, right-click the `counter` project and select Run.

     A web browser will open the URL `http://localhost:8080/counter`, which displays the number of hits.

7   Click the browser's Refresh button to see the hit count increment.

▼ To Build, Package, Deploy, and Run the `counter` Example Using Ant

1   In a terminal window, go to:

     tut-install/examples/ejb/counter

2   Type the following command:

     `ant all`

     This will build and deploy `counter` to your GlassFish Server instance.

3   In a web browser, type the following URL:

     `http://localhost:8080/counter`

4   Click the browser's Refresh button to see the hit count increment.

A Web Service Example: `helloservice`

This example demonstrates a simple web service that generates a response based on information received from the client. `HelloServiceBean` is a stateless session bean that implements a single method: `sayHello`. This method matches the `sayHello` method invoked by the client described in "A Simple JAX-WS Application Client" on page 212.

The Web Service Endpoint Implementation Class

`HelloServiceBean` is the endpoint implementation class, typically the primary programming artifact for enterprise bean web service endpoints. The web service endpoint implementation class has the following requirements.

- The class must be annotated with either the `javax.jws.WebService` or the `javax.jws.WebServiceProvider` annotation.

- The implementing class may explicitly reference an SEI through the `endpointInterface` element of the `@WebService` annotation but is not required to do so. If no `endpointInterface` is specified in `@WebService`, an SEI is implicitly defined for the implementing class.

- The business methods of the implementing class must be public and must not be declared `static` or `final`.

- Business methods that are exposed to web service clients must be annotated with `javax.jws.WebMethod`.

- Business methods that are exposed to web service clients must have JAXB-compatible parameters and return types. See the list of JAXB default data type bindings at `http://download.oracle.com/ docs/cd/E17477_01/javaee/5/tutorial/doc/bnazq.html#bnazs`.

- The implementing class must not be declared `final` and must not be `abstract`.

- The implementing class must have a default public constructor.

- The endpoint class must be annotated `@Stateless`.

- The implementing class must not define the `finalize` method.

- The implementing class may use the `javax.annotation.PostConstruct` or `javax.annotation.PreDestroy` annotations on its methods for lifecycle event callbacks.

  The `@PostConstruct` method is called by the container before the implementing class begins responding to web service clients.

  The `@PreDestroy` method is called by the container before the endpoint is removed from operation.

Stateless Session Bean Implementation Class

The `HelloServiceBean` class implements the `sayHello` method, which is annotated `@WebMethod`. The source code for the `HelloServiceBean` class follows:

```
package com.sun.tutorial.javaee.ejb;

import javax.ejb.Stateless;
import javax.jws.WebMethod;
```

```
import javax.jws.WebService;

@Stateless
@WebService
public class HelloServiceBean {
    private String message = "Hello, ";

    public void HelloServiceBean() {}

    @WebMethod
    public String sayHello(String name) {
        return message + name + ".";
    }
}
```

Building, Packaging, Deploying, and Testing the `helloservice` Example

You can build, package, and deploy the `helloservice` example using either NetBeans IDE or Ant. You can then use the Administration Console to test the web service endpoint methods.

▼ To Build, Package, and Deploy the `helloservice` Example Using NetBeans IDE

1   In NetBeans IDE, select File→Open Project.

2   In the Open Project dialog, navigate to:

    tut-install/examples/ejb/

3   Select the `helloservice` folder.

4   Select the Open as Main Project and Open Required Projects check boxes.

5   Click Open Project.

6   In the Projects tab, right-click the `helloservice` project and select Deploy.

    This builds and packages the application into `helloservice.ear`, located in *tut-install*/examples/ejb/helloservice/dist, and deploys this EAR file to the GlassFish Server.

▼ **To Build, Package, and Deploy the `helloservice` Example Using Ant**

1   **In a terminal window, go to:**

   tut-install/examples/ejb/helloservice/

2   **Type the following command:**

   `ant`

   This runs the `default` task, which compiles the source files and packages the application into a JAR file located at *tut-install*/examples/ejb/helloservice/dist/helloservice.jar.

3   **To deploy `helloservice`, type the following command:**

   `ant deploy`

   Upon deployment, the GlassFish Server generates additional artifacts required for web service invocation, including the WSDL file.

▼ **To Test the Service without a Client**

   The GlassFish Server Administration Console allows you to test the methods of a web service endpoint. To test the `sayHello` method of `HelloServiceBean`, follow these steps.

1   **Open the Administration Console by opening the following URL in a web browser:**

   `http://localhost:4848/`

2   **In the left pane of the Administration Console, select the Applications node.**

3   **In the Applications table, click `helloservice`.**

4   **In the Modules and Components table, click View Endpoint.**

5   **On the Web Service Endpoint Information page, click the Tester link:**

   `/HelloServiceBeanService/HelloServiceBean?Tester`

   The tester page opens in a browser window or tab.

6   **Under Methods, type a name as the parameter to the `sayHello` method.**

7   **Click the `sayHello` button.**

   The `sayHello` Method invocation page opens. Under Method returned, you'll see the response from the endpoint.

Using the Timer Service

Applications that model business work flows often rely on timed notifications. The timer service of the enterprise bean container enables you to schedule timed notifications for all types of enterprise beans except for stateful session beans. You can schedule a timed notification to occur according to a calendar schedule, at a specific time, after a duration of time, or at timed intervals. For example, you could set timers to go off at 10:30 a.m. on May 23, in 30 days, or every 12 hours.

Enterprise bean timers are either *programmatic timers* or *automatic timers*. Programmatic timers are set by explicitly calling one of the timer creation methods of the TimerService interface. Automatic timers are created upon the successful deployment of an enterprise bean that contains a method annotated with the java.ejb.Schedule or java.ejb.Schedules annotations.

Creating Calendar-Based Timer Expressions

Timers can be set according to a calendar-based schedule, expressed using a syntax similar to the UNIX cron utility. Both programmatic and automatic timers can use calendar-based timer expressions. Table 16–1 shows the calendar-based timer attributes.

TABLE 16–1   Calendar-Based Timer Attributes

Attribute	Description	Allowable Values	Default Value	Examples
second	One or more seconds within a minute	0 to 59	0	second="30"
minute	One or more minutes within an hour	0 to 59	0	minute="15"
hour	One or more hours within a day	0 to 23	0	hour="13"
dayOfWeek	One or more days within a week	0 to 7 (both 0 and 7 refer to Sunday) Sun, Mon, Tue, Wed, Thu, Fri, Sat	*	dayOfWeek="3" dayOfWeek="Mon"

TABLE 16-1 Calendar-Based Timer Attributes   *(Continued)*

Attribute	Description	Allowable Values	Default Value	Examples
dayOfMonth	One or more days within a month	1 to 31 −7 to −1 (a negative number means the *n*th day or days before the end of the month) Last [1st, 2nd, 3rd, 4th, 5th, Last] [Sun, Mon, Tue, Wed, Thu, Fri, Sat]	*	dayOfMonth="15" dayOfMonth="−3" dayOfMonth="Last" dayOfMonth="2nd Fri"
month	One or more months within a year	1 to 12 Jan, Feb, Mar, Apr, May, Jun, Jul, Aug, Sep, Oct, Nov, Dec	*	month="7" month="July"
year	A particular calendar year	A four-digit calendar year	*	year="2010"

Specifying Multiple Values in Calendar Expressions

You can specify multiple values in calendar expressions, as described in the following sections.

Using Wildcards in Calendar Expressions

Setting an attribute to an asterisk symbol (*) represents all allowable values for the attribute.

The following expression represents every minute:

```
minute="*"
```

The following expression represents every day of the week:

```
dayOfWeek="*"
```

Specifying a List of Values

To specify two or more values for an attribute, use a comma (,) to separate the values. A range of values is allowed as part of a list. Wildcards and intervals, however, are not allowed.

Duplicates within a list are ignored.

The following expression sets the day of the week to Tuesday and Thursday:

```
dayOfWeek="Tue, Thu"
```

The following expression represents 4:00 a.m., every hour from 9:00 a.m. to 5:00 p.m. using a range, and 10:00 p.m.:

```
hour="4,9-17,22"
```

Specifying a Range of Values

Use a dash character (–) to specify an inclusive range of values for an attribute. Members of a range cannot be wildcards, lists, or intervals. A range of the form x–x, is equivalent to the single-valued expression x. A range of the form x–y where x is greater than y is equivalent to the expression x–*maximum value*, *minimum value*–y. That is, the expression begins at x, rolls over to the beginning of the allowable values, and continues up to y.

The following expression represents 9:00 a.m. to 5:00 p.m.:

```
hour="9-17"
```

The following expression represents Friday through Monday:

```
dayOfWeek="5-1"
```

The following expression represents the twenty-fifth day of the month to the end of the month, and the beginning of the month to the fifth day of the month:

```
dayOfMonth="25-5"
```

It is equivalent to the following expression:

```
dayOfMonth="25-Last,1-5"
```

Specifying Intervals

The forward slash (/) constrains an attribute to a starting point and an interval and is used to specify every N seconds, minutes, or hours within the minute, hour, or day. For an expression of the form x/y, x represents the starting point and y represents the interval. The wildcard character may be used in the x position of an interval and is equivalent to setting x to 0.

Intervals may be set only for second, minute, and hour attributes.

The following expression represents every 10 minutes within the hour:

```
minute="*/10"
```

It is equivalent to:

```
minute="0,10,20,30,40,50"
```

The following expression represents every 2 hours starting at noon:

```
hour="12/2"
```

Programmatic Timers

When a programmatic timer expires (goes off), the container calls the method annotated @Timeout in the bean's implementation class. The @Timeout method contains the business logic that handles the timed event.

The @Timeout Method

Methods annotated @Timeout in the enterprise bean class must return void and optionally take a javax.ejb.Timer object as the only parameter. They may not throw application exceptions.

```
@Timeout
public void timeout(Timer timer) {
    System.out.println("TimerBean: timeout occurred");
}
```

Creating Programmatic Timers

To create a timer, the bean invokes one of the create methods of the TimerService interface. These methods allow single-action, interval, or calendar-based timers to be created.

For single-action or interval timers, the expiration of the timer can be expressed as either a duration or an absolute time. The duration is expressed as a the number of milliseconds before a timeout event is triggered. To specify an absolute time, create a java.util.Date object and pass it to the TimerService.createSingleActionTimer or the TimerService.createTimer method.

The following code sets a programmatic timer that will expire in 1 minute (6,000 milliseconds):

```
long duration = 6000;
Timer timer =
    timerService.createSingleActionTimer(duration, new TimerConfig());
```

The following code sets a programmatic timer that will expire at 12:05 p.m. on May 1, 2010, specified as a java.util.Date:

```
SimpleDateFormatter formatter =
    new SimpleDateFormatter("MM/dd/yyyy 'at' HH:mm");
Date date = formatter.parse("05/01/2010 at 12:05");
Timer timer = timerService.createSingleActionTimer(date, new TimerConfig());
```

For calendar-based timers, the expiration of the timer is expressed as a `javax.ejb.ScheduleExpression` object, passed as a parameter to the `TimerService.createCalendarTimer` method. The `ScheduleExpression` class represents calendar-based timer expressions and has methods that correspond to the attributes described in "Creating Calendar-Based Timer Expressions" on page 290.

The following code creates a programmatic timer using the `ScheduleExpression` helper class:

```
ScheduleExpression schedule = new ScheduleExpression();
schedule.dayOfWeek("Mon");
schedule.hour("12-17, 23");
Timer timer = timerService.createCalendarTimer(schedule);
```

For details on the method signatures, see the `TimerService` API documentation at `http://download.oracle.com/docs/cd/E17410_01/javaee/6/api/javax/ejb/TimerService.html`.

The bean described in "The `timersession` Example" on page 297 creates a timer as follows:

```
Timer timer = timerService.createTimer(intervalDuration,
        "Created new programmatic timer");
```

In the `timersession` example, `createTimer` is invoked in a business method, which is called by a client.

Timers are persistent by default. If the server is shut down or crashes, persistent timers are saved and will become active again when the server is restarted. If a persistent timer expires while the server is down, the container will call the `@Timeout` method when the server is restarted.

Nonpersistent programmatic timers are created by calling `TimerConfig.setPersistent(false)` and passing the `TimerConfig` object to one of the timer-creation methods.

The `Date` and `long` parameters of the `createTimer` methods represent time with the resolution of milliseconds. However, because the timer service is not intended for real-time applications, a callback to the `@Timeout` method might not occur with millisecond precision. The timer service is for business applications, which typically measure time in hours, days, or longer durations.

Automatic Timers

Automatic timers are created by the EJB container when an enterprise bean that contains methods annotated with the `@Schedule` or `@Schedules` annotations is deployed. An enterprise bean can have multiple automatic timeout methods, unlike a programmatic timer, which allows only one method annotated with the @Timeout annotation in the enterprise bean class.

Automatic timers can be configured through annotations or through the ejb-jar.xml deployment descriptor.

Adding a @Schedule annotation on an enterprise bean marks that method as a timeout method according to the calendar schedule specified in the attributes of @Schedule.

The @Schedule annotation has elements that correspond to the calendar expressions detailed in "Creating Calendar-Based Timer Expressions" on page 290 and the persistent, info, and timezone elements.

The optional persistent element takes a Boolean value and is used to specify whether the automatic timer should survive a server restart or crash. By default, all automatic timers are persistent.

The optional timezone element is used to specify that the automatic timer is associated with a particular time zone. If set, this element will evaluate all timer expressions in relation to the specified time zone, regardless of the time zone in which the EJB container is running. By default, all automatic timers set are in relation to the default time zone of the server.

The optional info element is used to set an informational description of the timer. A timer's information can be retrieved later by using Timer.getInfo.

The following timeout method uses @Schedule to set a timer that will expire every Sunday at midnight:

```
@Schedule(dayOfWeek="Sun", hour="0")
public void cleanupWeekData() { ... }
```

The @Schedules annotation is used to specify multiple calendar-based timer expressions for a given timeout method.

The following timeout method uses the @Schedules annotation to set multiple calendar-based timer expressions. The first expression sets a timer to expire on the last day of every month. The second expression sets a timer to expire every Friday at 11:00 p.m.

```
@Schedules ({
    @Schedule(dayOfMonth="Last"),
    @Schedule(dayOfWeek="Fri", hour="23")
})
public void doPeriodicCleanup() { ... }
```

Canceling and Saving Timers

Timers can be canceled by the following events.

- When a single-event timer expires, the EJB container calls the associated timeout method and then cancels the timer.

- When the bean invokes the cancel method of the Timer interface, the container cancels the timer.

If a method is invoked on a canceled timer, the container throws the javax.ejb.NoSuchObjectLocalException.

To save a Timer object for future reference, invoke its getHandle method and store the TimerHandle object in a database. (A TimerHandle object is serializable.) To reinstantiate the Timer object, retrieve the handle from the database and invoke getTimer on the handle. A TimerHandle object cannot be passed as an argument of a method defined in a remote or web service interface. In other words, remote clients and web service clients cannot access a bean's TimerHandle object. Local clients, however, do not have this restriction.

Getting Timer Information

In addition to defining the cancel and getHandle methods, the Timer interface defines methods for obtaining information about timers:

```
public long getTimeRemaining();
public java.util.Date getNextTimeout();
public java.io.Serializable getInfo();
```

The getInfo method returns the object that was the last parameter of the createTimer invocation. For example, in the createTimer code snippet of the preceding section, this information parameter is a String object with the value created timer.

To retrieve all of a bean's active timers, call the getTimers method of the TimerService interface. The getTimers method returns a collection of Timer objects.

Transactions and Timers

An enterprise bean usually creates a timer within a transaction. If this transaction is rolled back, the timer creation also is rolled back. Similarly, if a bean cancels a timer within a transaction that gets rolled back, the timer cancellation is rolled back. In this case, the timer's duration is reset as if the cancellation had never occurred.

In beans that use container-managed transactions, the @Timeout method usually has the Required or RequiresNew transaction attribute to preserve transaction integrity. With these attributes, the EJB container begins the new transaction before calling the @Timeout method. If the transaction is rolled back, the container will call the @Timeout method at least one more time.

The timersession **Example**

The source code for this example is in the *tut-install*/examples/ejb/timersession/src/java/ directory.

TimerSessionBean is a singleton session bean that shows how to set both an automatic timer and a programmatic timer. In the source code listing of TimerSessionBean that follows, the setTimer and @Timeout methods are used to set a programmatic timer. A TimerService instance is injected by the container when the bean is created. Because it's a business method, setTimer is exposed to the local, no-interface view of TimerSessionBean and can be invoked by the client. In this example, the client invokes setTimer with an interval duration of 30,000 milliseconds. The setTimer method creates a new timer by invoking the createTimer method of TimerService. Now that the timer is set, the EJB container will invoke the programmaticTimeout method of TimerSessionBean when the timer expires, in about 30 seconds.

```
...
    public void setTimer(long intervalDuration) {
        logger.info("Setting a programmatic timeout for " +
                intervalDuration + " milliseconds from now.");
        Timer timer = timerService.createTimer(intervalDuration,
                "Created new programmatic timer");
    }

    @Timeout
    public void programmaticTimeout(Timer timer) {
        this.setLastProgrammaticTimeout(new Date());
        logger.info("Programmatic timeout occurred.");
    }
...
```

TimerSessionBean also has an automatic timer and timeout method, automaticTimeout. The automatic timer is set to expire every 3 minutes and is set by using a calendar-based timer expression in the @Schedule annotation:

```
...
    @Schedule(minute="*/3", hour="*")
    public void automaticTimeout() {
        this.setLastAutomaticTimeout(new Date());
        logger.info("Automatic timeout occured");
    }
...
```

TimerSessionBean also has two business methods: getLastProgrammaticTimeout and getLastAutomaticTimeout. Clients call these methods to get the date and time of the last timeout for the programmatic timer and automatic timer, respectively.

Here's the source code for the TimerSessionBean class:

```java
package timersession.ejb;

import java.util.Date;
import java.util.logging.Logger;
import javax.annotation.Resource;
import javax.ejb.Schedule;
import javax.ejb.Stateless;
import javax.ejb.Timeout;
import javax.ejb.Timer;
import javax.ejb.TimerService;

@Singleton
public class TimerSessionBean {
    @Resource
    TimerService timerService;

    private Date lastProgrammaticTimeout;
    private Date lastAutomaticTimeout;

    private Logger logger = Logger.getLogger(
            "com.sun.tutorial.javaee.ejb.timersession.TimerSessionBean");

    public void setTimer(long intervalDuration) {
        logger.info("Setting a programmatic timeout for "
                + intervalDuration + " milliseconds from now.");
        Timer timer = timerService.createTimer(intervalDuration,
                "Created new programmatic timer");
    }

    @Timeout
    public void programmaticTimeout(Timer timer) {
        this.setLastProgrammaticTimeout(new Date());
        logger.info("Programmatic timeout occurred.");
    }

    @Schedule(minute="*/3", hour="*")
    public void automaticTimeout() {
        this.setLastAutomaticTimeout(new Date());
        logger.info("Automatic timeout occured");
    }

    public String getLastProgrammaticTimeout() {
        if (lastProgrammaticTimeout != null) {
            return lastProgrammaticTimeout.toString();
        } else {
            return "never";
        }

    }

    public void setLastProgrammaticTimeout(Date lastTimeout) {
```

```
        this.lastProgrammaticTimeout = lastTimeout;
    }

    public String getLastAutomaticTimeout() {
        if (lastAutomaticTimeout != null) {
            return lastAutomaticTimeout.toString();
        } else {
            return "never";
        }
    }

    public void setLastAutomaticTimeout(Date lastAutomaticTimeout) {
        this.lastAutomaticTimeout = lastAutomaticTimeout;
    }
}
```

Note – GlassFish Server has a default minimum timeout value of 1,000 milliseconds, or 1 second. If you need to set the timeout value lower than 1,000 milliseconds, change the value of the `minimum-delivery-interval-in-millis` element in *domain-dir*/`config/domain.xml`. The lowest practical value for `minimum-delivery-interval-in-millis` is around 10 milliseconds, owing to virtual machine constraints.

Building, Packaging, Deploying, and Running the `timersession` Example

You can build, package, deploy, and run the `timersession` example by using either NetBeans IDE or Ant.

▼ To Build, Package, Deploy, and Run the `timersession` Example Using NetBeans IDE

1   In NetBeans IDE, select File→Open Project.

2   In the Open Project dialog, navigate to:

    tut-install/examples/ejb/

3   Select the `timersession` folder.

4   Select the Open as Main Project check box.

5   Click Open Project.

6   Select Run→Run Main Project.

This builds and packages the application into `timersession.war`, located in *tut-install*/examples/ejb/timersession/dist/, deploys this WAR file to your GlassFish Server instance, and then runs the web client.

▼ To Build, Package, and Deploy the `timersession` Example Using Ant

1   In a terminal window, go to:

tut-install/examples/ejb/timersession/

2   Type the following command:

`ant build`

This runs the `default` task, which compiles the source files and packages the application into a WAR file located at *tut-install*/examples/ejb/timersession/dist/timersession.war.

3   To deploy the application, type the following command:

`ant deploy`

▼ To Run the Web Client

1   Open a web browser to `http://localhost:8080/timersession`.

2   Click the Set Timer button to set a programmatic timer.

3   Wait for a while and click the browser's Refresh button.

You will see the date and time of the last programmatic and automatic timeouts.

To see the messages that are logged when a timeout occurs, open the `server.log` file located in *domain-dir*/server/logs/.

Handling Exceptions

The exceptions thrown by enterprise beans fall into two categories: system and application.

A *system exception* indicates a problem with the services that support an application. For example, a connection to an external resource cannot be obtained, or an injected resource cannot be found. If it encounters a system-level problem, your enterprise bean should throw a `javax.ejb.EJBException`. Because the `EJBException` is a subclass of the `RuntimeException`, you do not have to specify it in the `throws` clause of the method declaration. If a system exception is thrown, the EJB container might destroy the bean instance. Therefore, a system exception cannot be handled by the bean's client program, but instead requires intervention by a system administrator.

An *application exception* signals an error in the business logic of an enterprise bean. Application exceptions are typically exceptions that you've coded yourself, such as the BookException thrown by the business methods of the CartBean example. When an enterprise bean throws an application exception, the container does not wrap it in another exception. The client should be able to handle any application exception it receives.

If a system exception occurs within a transaction, the EJB container rolls back the transaction. However, if an application exception is thrown within a transaction, the container does not roll back the transaction.

PART V

Contexts and Dependency Injection for the Java EE Platform

Part V introduces Contexts and Dependency Injection for the Java EE Platform. This part contains the following chapters:

- Chapter 17, "Introduction to Contexts and Dependency Injection for the Java EE Platform"
- Chapter 18, "Running the Basic Contexts and Dependency Injection Examples"

17

Introduction to Contexts and Dependency Injection for the Java EE Platform

Contexts and Dependency Injection (CDI) for the Java EE platform is one of several Java EE 6 features that help to knit together the web tier and the transactional tier of the Java EE platform. CDI is a set of services that, used together, make it easy for developers to use enterprise beans along with JavaServer Faces technology in web applications. Designed for use with stateful objects, CDI also has many broader uses, allowing developers a great deal of flexibility to integrate various kinds of components in a loosely coupled but typesafe way.

CDI is specified by JSR 299, formerly known as Web Beans. Related specifications that CDI uses include the following:

- JSR 330, Dependency Injection for Java
- The Managed Beans specification, which is an offshoot of the Java EE 6 platform specification (JSR 316)

The following topics are addressed here:

Overview of CDI

The most fundamental services provided by CDI are as follows:

- **Contexts**: The ability to bind the lifecycle and interactions of stateful components to well-defined but extensible lifecycle contexts
- **Dependency injection**: The ability to inject components into an application in a typesafe way, including the ability to choose at deployment time which implementation of a particular interface to inject

In addition, CDI provides the following services:

- Integration with the Expression Language (EL), which allows any component to be used directly within a JavaServer Faces page or a JavaServer Pages page
- The ability to decorate injected components
- The ability to associate interceptors with components using typesafe interceptor bindings
- An event-notification model
- A web conversation scope in addition to the three standard scopes (request, session, and application) defined by the Java Servlet specification
- A complete Service Provider Interface (SPI) that allows third-party frameworks to integrate cleanly in the Java EE 6 environment

A major theme of CDI is loose coupling. CDI does the following:

- Decouples the server and the client by means of well-defined types and qualifiers, so that the server implementation may vary
- Decouples the lifecycles of collaborating components by doing the following:
  - Making components contextual, with automatic lifecycle management
  - Allowing stateful components to interact like services, purely by message passing
- Completely decouples message producers from consumers, by means of events
- Decouples orthogonal concerns by means of Java EE interceptors

Along with loose coupling, CDI provides strong typing by

- Eliminating lookup using string-based names for wiring and correlations, so that the compiler will detect typing errors
- Allowing the use of declarative Java annotations to specify everything, largely eliminating the need for XML deployment descriptors, and making it easy to provide tools that introspect the code and understand the dependency structure at development time

About Beans

CDI redefines the concept of a *bean* beyond its use in other Java technologies, such as the JavaBeans and Enterprise JavaBeans (EJB) technologies. In CDI, a bean is a source of contextual objects that define application state and/or logic. A Java EE component is a bean if the lifecycle of its instances may be managed by the container according to the lifecycle context model defined in the CDI specification.

More specifically, a bean has the following attributes:

- A (nonempty) set of bean types
- A (nonempty) set of qualifiers (see "Using Qualifiers" on page 309)
- A scope (see "Using Scopes" on page 310)
- Optionally, a bean EL name (see "Giving Beans EL Names" on page 312)
- A set of interceptor bindings
- A bean implementation

A bean type defines a client-visible type of the bean. Almost any Java type may be a bean type of a bean.

- A bean type may be an interface, a concrete class, or an abstract class and may be declared final or have final methods.

- A bean type may be a parameterized type with type parameters and type variables.

- A bean type may be an array type. Two array types are considered identical only if the element type is identical.

- A bean type may be a primitive type. Primitive types are considered to be identical to their corresponding wrapper types in `java.lang`.

- A bean type may be a raw type.

About Managed Beans

A *managed bean* is implemented by a Java class, which is called its bean class. A top-level Java class is a managed bean if it is defined to be a managed bean by any other Java EE technology specification, such as the JavaServer Faces technology specification, or if it meets all the following conditions:

- It is not a nonstatic inner class.

- It is a concrete class or is annotated `@Decorator`.

- It is not annotated with an EJB component-defining annotation or declared as an EJB bean class in `ejb-jar.xml`.

- It has an appropriate constructor. That is, one of the following is the case:
  - The class has a constructor with no parameters.
  - The class declares a constructor annotated @Inject.

No special declaration, such as an annotation, is required to define a managed bean.

Beans as Injectable Objects

The concept of injection has been part of Java technology for some time. Since the Java EE 5 platform was introduced, annotations have made it possible to inject resources and some other kinds of objects into container-managed objects. CDI makes it possible to inject more kinds of objects and to inject them into objects that are not container-managed.

The following kinds of objects can be injected:

- (Almost) any Java class

- Session beans

- Java EE resources: data sources, Java Message Service topics, queues, connection factories, and the like

- Persistence contexts (JPA EntityManager objects)

- Producer fields

- Objects returned by producer methods

- Web service references

- Remote enterprise bean references

For example, suppose that you create a simple Java class with a method that returns a string:

```
package greetings;

public class Greeting {
    public String greet(String name) {
        return "Hello, " + name + ".";
    }
}
```

This class becomes a bean that you can then inject into another class. This bean is not exposed to the EL in this form. "Giving Beans EL Names" on page 312 explains how you can make a bean accessible to the EL.

Using Qualifiers

You can use qualifiers to provide various implementations of a particular bean type. A qualifier is an annotation that you apply to a bean. A qualifier type is a Java annotation defined as `@Target({METHOD, FIELD, PARAMETER, TYPE})` and `@Retention(RUNTIME)`.

For example, you could declare an `@Informal` qualifier type and apply it to another class that extends the `Greeting` class. To declare this qualifier type, you would use the following code:

```
package greetings;

import static java.lang.annotation.ElementType.FIELD;
import static java.lang.annotation.ElementType.METHOD;
import static java.lang.annotation.ElementType.PARAMETER;
import static java.lang.annotation.ElementType.TYPE;
import static java.lang.annotation.RetentionPolicy.RUNTIME;

import java.lang.annotation.Retention;
import java.lang.annotation.Target;

import javax.inject.Qualifier;

@Qualifier
@Retention(RUNTIME)
@Target({TYPE, METHOD, FIELD, PARAMETER})
public @interface Informal {}
```

You can then define a bean class that extends the `Greeting` class and uses this qualifier:

```
package greetings;

@Informal
public class InformalGreeting extends Greeting {
    public String greet(String name) {
        return "Hi, " + name + "!";
    }
}
```

Both implementations of the bean can now be used in the application.

If you define a bean with no qualifier, the bean automatically has the qualifier `@Default`. The unannotated `Greeting` class could be declared as follows:

```
package greetings;

import javax.enterprise.inject.Default;

@Default
public class Greeting {
    public String greet(String name) {
        return "Hello, " + name + ".";
    }
}
```

Injecting Beans

In order to use the beans you create, you inject them into yet another bean that can then be used by an application, such as a JavaServer Faces application. For example, you might create a bean called `Printer` into which you would inject one of the `Greeting` beans:

```
import javax.inject.Inject;

public class Printer {

    @Inject Greeting greeting;
    ...
```

This code injects the `@Default Greeting` implementation into the bean. The following code injects the `@Informal` implementation:

```
import javax.inject.Inject;

public class Printer {

    @Inject @Informal Greeting greeting;
    ...
```

More is needed for the complete picture of this bean. Its use of scope needs to be understood. In addition, for a JavaServer Faces application, the bean needs to be accessible through the EL.

Using Scopes

For a web application to use a bean that injects another bean class, the bean needs to be able to hold state over the duration of the user's interaction with the application. The way to define this state is to give the bean a scope. You can give an object any of the scopes described in Table 17–1, depending on how you are using it.

TABLE 17–1 Scopes

Scope	Annotation	Duration
Request	@RequestScoped	A user's interaction with a web application in a single HTTP request.
Session	@SessionScoped	A user's interaction with a web application across multiple HTTP requests.
Application	@ApplicationScoped	Shared state across all users' interactions with a web application.

TABLE 17–1 Scopes *(Continued)*

Scope	Annotation	Duration
Dependent	`@Dependent`	The default scope if none is specified; it means that an object exists to serve exactly one client (bean) and has the same lifecycle as that client (bean).
Conversation	`@ConversationScoped`	A user's interaction with a JavaServer Faces application, within explicit developer-controlled boundaries that extend the scope across multiple invocations of the JavaServer Faces lifecycle. All long-running conversations are scoped to a particular HTTP servlet session and may not cross session boundaries.

The first three scopes are defined by both JSR 299 and the JavaServer Faces API. The last two are defined by JSR 299.

You can also define and implement custom scopes, but that is an advanced topic. Custom scopes are likely to be used by those who implement and extend the CDI specification.

A scope gives an object a well-defined lifecycle context. A scoped object can be automatically created when it is needed and automatically destroyed when the context in which it was created ends. Moreover, its state is automatically shared by any clients that execute in the same context.

Java EE components, such as servlets and enterprise beans, and JavaBeans components do not by definition have a well-defined scope. These components are one of the following:

- Singletons, such as Enterprise JavaBeans singleton beans, whose state is shared among all clients

- Stateless objects, such as servlets and stateless session beans, which do not contain client-visible state

- Objects that must be explicitly created and destroyed by their client, such as JavaBeans components and stateful session beans, whose state is shared by explicit reference passing between clients

If, however, you create a Java EE component that is a managed bean, it becomes a scoped object, which exists in a well-defined lifecycle context.

The web application for the `Printer` bean will use a simple request and response mechanism, so the managed bean can be annotated as follows:

```
import javax.inject.Inject;
import javax.enterprise.context.RequestScoped;

@RequestScoped
public class Printer {

    @Inject @Informal Greeting greeting;
    ...
```

Beans that use session, application, or conversation scope must be serializable, but beans that use request scope do not have to be serializable.

Giving Beans EL Names

To make a bean accessible through the EL, use the @Named built-in qualifier:

```
import javax.inject.Inject;
import javax.enterprise.context.RequestScoped;
import javax.inject.Named;

@Named
@RequestScoped
public class Printer {

    @Inject @Informal Greeting greeting;
    ...
```

The @Named qualifier allows you to access the bean by using the bean name, with the first letter in lowercase. For example, a Facelets page would refer to the bean as `printer`.

You can specify an argument to the @Named qualifier to use a nondefault name:

```
@Named("MyPrinter")
```

With this annotation, the Facelets page would refer to the bean as `MyPrinter`.

Adding Setter and Getter Methods

To make the state of the managed bean accessible, you need to add setter and getter methods for that state. The `createSalutation` method calls the bean's `greet` method, and the `getSalutation` method retrieves the result.

Once the setter and getter methods have been added, the bean is complete. The final code looks like this:

```
package greetings;

import javax.inject.Inject;
import javax.enterprise.context.RequestScoped;
import javax.inject.Named;

@Named
@RequestScoped
public class Printer {

    @Inject @Informal Greeting greeting;

    private String name;
    private String salutation;

    public void createSalutation() {
        this.salutation = greeting.greet(name);
    }

    public String getSalutation() {
        return salutation;
    }
    public String setName(String name) {
        this.name = name;
    }

    public String getName() {
        return name;
    }
}
```

Using a Managed Bean in a Facelets Page

To use the managed bean in a Facelets page, you typically create a form that uses user interface elements to call its methods and display their results. This example provides a button that asks the user to type a name, retrieves the salutation, and then displays the text in a paragraph below the button:

```
<h:form id="greetme">
    <p><h:outputLabel value="Enter your name: " for="name"/>
        <h:inputText id="name" value="#{printer.name}"/></p>
    <p><h:commandButton value="Say Hello"
                        action="#{printer.createSalutation}"/></p>
    <p><h:outputText value="#{printer.salutation}"/></p>
</h:form>
```

Injecting Objects by Using Producer Methods

Producer methods provide a way to inject objects that are not beans, objects whose values may vary at runtime, and objects that require custom initialization. For example, if you want to initialize a numeric value defined by a qualifier named @MaxNumber, you can define the value in a managed bean and then define a producer method, getMaxNumber, for it:

```
private int maxNumber = 100;
...
@Produces @MaxNumber int getMaxNumber() {
    return maxNumber;
}
```

When you inject the object in another managed bean, the container automatically invokes the producer method, initializing the value to 100:

```
@Inject @MaxNumber private int maxNumber;
```

If the value can vary at runtime, the process is slightly different. For example, the following code defines a producer method that generates a random number defined by a qualifier called @Random:

```
private java.util.Random random =
    new java.util.Random( System.currentTimeMillis() );

java.util.Random getRandom() {
        return random;
}

@Produces @Random int next() {
    return getRandom().nextInt(maxNumber);
}
```

When you inject this object in another managed bean, you declare a contextual instance of the object:

```
@Inject @Random Instance<Integer> randomInt;
```

You then call the get method of the Instance:

```
this.number = randomInt.get();
```

Configuring a CDI Application

An application that uses CDI must have a file named beans.xml. The file can be completely empty (it has content only in certain limited situations), but it must be present. For a web application, the beans.xml file can be in either the WEB-INF directory or the WEB-INF/classes/META-INF directory. For EJB modules or JAR files, the beans.xml file must be in the META-INF directory.

Further Information about CDI

For more information about CDI for the Java EE platform, see

- Contexts and Dependency Injection for the Java EE platform specification:

  http://jcp.org/en/jsr/detail?id=299

- An introduction to Contexts and Dependency Injection for the Java EE platform:

  http://docs.jboss.org/weld/reference/latest/en-US/html/

- Dependency Injection for Java specification:

  http://jcp.org/en/jsr/detail?id=330

18

Running the Basic Contexts and Dependency Injection Examples

This chapter describes in detail how to build and run simple examples that use CDI. The examples are in the following directory:

tut-install/examples/cdi/

To build and run the examples, you will do the following:

1. Use NetBeans IDE or the Ant tool to compile and package the example.
2. Use NetBeans IDE or the Ant tool to deploy the example.
3. Run the example in a web browser.

Each example has a build.xml file that refers to files in the following directory:

tut-install/examples/bp-project/

See Chapter 2, "Using the Tutorial Examples," for basic information on installing, building, and running the examples.

The following topics are addressed here:

- "The simplegreeting CDI Example" on page 317
- "The guessnumber CDI Example" on page 322

The simplegreeting CDI Example

The simplegreeting example illustrates some of the most basic features of CDI: scopes, qualifiers, bean injection, and accessing a managed bean in a JavaServer Faces application. When you run the example, you click a button that presents either a formal or an informal greeting, depending on how you edited one of the classes. The example includes four source files, a Facelets page and template, and configuration files.

The `simplegreeting` Source Files

The four source files for the `simplegreeting` example are

- The default `Greeting` class, shown in "Beans as Injectable Objects" on page 308
- The `@Informal` qualifier interface definition and the `InformalGreeting` class that implements the interface, both shown in "Using Qualifiers" on page 309
- The `Printer` managed bean class, which injects one of the two interfaces, shown in full in "Adding Setter and Getter Methods" on page 312

The source files are located in the following directory:

tut-install/examples/cdi/simplegreeting/src/java/greetings

The Facelets Template and Page

To use the managed bean in a simple Facelets application, you can use a very simple template file and `index.xhtml` page. The template page, `template.xhtml`, looks like this:

```
<?xml version='1.0' encoding='UTF-8' ?>
<!DOCTYPE html PUBLIC "-//W3C//DTD XHTML 1.0 Transitional//EN"
        "http://www.w3.org/TR/xhtml1/DTD/xhtml1-transitional.dtd">
<html xmlns="http://www.w3.org/1999/xhtml"
     xmlns:h="http://java.sun.com/jsf/html"
     xmlns:ui="http://java.sun.com/jsf/facelets">
  <h:head>
      <meta http-equiv="Content-Type"
            content="text/html; charset=UTF-8"/>
      <link href="resources/css/default.css"
            rel="stylesheet" type="text/css"/>
      <title>
          <ui:insert name="title">Default Title</ui:insert>
      </title>
  </h:head>

  <body>
      <div id="container">
          <div id="header">
              <h2><ui:insert name="head">Head</ui:insert></h2>
          </div>

          <div id="space">
              <p></p>
          </div>

          <div id="content">
              <ui:insert name="content"/>
          </div>
      </div>
  </body>
</html>
```

To create the Facelets page, you can redefine the title and head, then add a small form to the content:

```
<?xml version='1.0' encoding='UTF-8' ?>
<!DOCTYPE html PUBLIC "-//W3C//DTD XHTML 1.0 Transitional//EN"
          "http://www.w3.org/TR/xhtml1/DTD/xhtml1-transitional.dtd">
<html xmlns="http://www.w3.org/1999/xhtml"
      xmlns:ui="http://java.sun.com/jsf/facelets"
      xmlns:h="http://java.sun.com/jsf/html"
      xmlns:f="http://java.sun.com/jsf/core">
   <ui:composition template="/template.xhtml">

       <ui:define name="title">Simple Greeting</ui:define>
       <ui:define name="head">Simple Greeting</ui:define>
       <ui:define name="content">
           <h:form id="greetme">
               <p><h:outputLabel value="Enter your name: " for="name"/>
                  <h:inputText id="name" value="#{printer.name}"/></p>
               <p><h:commandButton value="Say Hello"
                                    action="#{printer.createSalutation}"/></p>
               <p><h:outputText value="#{printer.salutation}"/> </p>
           </h:form>
       </ui:define>

   </ui:composition>
</html>
```

The form asks the user to type a name. The button is labeled Say Hello, and the action defined for it is to call the `createSalutation` method of the `Printer` managed bean. This method in turn calls the `greet` method of the defined `Greeting` class.

The output text for the form is the value of the greeting returned by the setter method. Depending on whether the default or the `@Informal` version of the greeting is injected, this is one of the following, where *name* is the name typed by the user:

```
Hello, name.
```

```
Hi, name!
```

The Facelets page and template are located in the following directory:

tut-install/examples/cdi/simplegreeting/web

The simple CSS file that is used by the Facelets page is in the following location:

tut-install/examples/cdi/simplegreeting/web/resources/css/default.css

Configuration Files

You must create an empty `beans.xml` file to indicate to GlassFish Server that your application is a CDI application. This file can have content in some situations, but not in simple applications like this one.

Your application also needs the basic web application deployment descriptors web.xml and sun-web.xml. These configuration files are located in the following directory:

tut-install/examples/cdi/simplegreeting/web/WEB-INF

Building, Packaging, Deploying, and Running the simplegreeting CDI Example

You can build, package, deploy, and run the simplegreeting application by using either NetBeans IDE or the Ant tool.

▼ To Build, Package, and Deploy the simplegreeting Example Using NetBeans IDE

This procedure builds the application into the following directory:

tut-install/examples/cdi/simplegreeting/build/web

The contents of this directory are deployed to the GlassFish Server.

1   In NetBeans IDE, select File→Open Project.

2   In the Open Project dialog, navigate to:
    tut-install/examples/cdi/

3   Select the simplegreeting folder.

4   Select the Open as Main Project check box.

5   Click Open Project.

6   (Optional) To modify the Printer.java file, perform these steps:

   a. Expand the Source Packages node.

   b. Expand the greetings node.

   c. Double-click the Printer.java file.

   d. In the edit pane, comment out the @Informal annotation:
       ```
       //@Informal
       @Inject
       Greeting greeting;
       ```

e. Save the file.

7   In the Projects tab, right-click the simplegreeting project and select Deploy.

▼ To Build, Package, and Deploy the simplegreeting Example Using Ant

1   In a terminal window, go to:

tut-install/examples/cdi/simplegreeting/

2   Type the following command:

ant

This command calls the default target, which builds and packages the application into a WAR file, simplegreeting.war, located in the dist directory.

3   Type the following command:

ant deploy

Typing this command deploys simplegreeting.war to the GlassFish Server.

▼ To Run the simplegreeting Example

1   In a web browser, type the following URL:

http://localhost:8080/simplegreeting

The Simple Greeting page opens.

2   Type a name in the text field.

For example, suppose that you type **Duke**.

3   Click the Say Hello button.

If you did not modify the Printer.java file, the following text string appears below the button:

Hi, Duke!

If you commented out the @Informal annotation in the Printer.java file, the following text string appears below the button:

Hello, Duke.

Figure 18–1 shows what the application looks like if you did not modify the Printer.java file.

FIGURE 18–1   Simple Greeting Application

The guessnumber CDI Example

The guessnumber example, somewhat more complex than the simplegreeting example, illustrates the use of producer methods and of session and application scope. The example is a game in which you try to guess a number in fewer than ten attempts. It is similar to the guessnumber example described in Chapter 5, "Introduction to Facelets," except that you can keep guessing until you get the right answer or until you use up your ten attempts.

The example includes four source files, a Facelets page and template, and configuration files. The configuration files and the template are the same as those used for the simplegreeting example.

The guessnumber Source Files

The four source files for the guessnumber example are

- The @MaxNumber qualifier interface
- The @Random qualifier interface
- The Generator managed bean, which defines producer methods
- The UserNumberBean managed bean

The source files are located in the following directory:

tut-install/examples/cdi/guessnumber/src/java/guessnumber

The @MaxNumber and @Random Qualifier Interfaces

The @MaxNumber qualifier interface is defined as follows:

```
package guessnumber;

import static java.lang.annotation.ElementType.FIELD;
import static java.lang.annotation.ElementType.METHOD;
import static java.lang.annotation.ElementType.PARAMETER;
import static java.lang.annotation.ElementType.TYPE;
import static java.lang.annotation.RetentionPolicy.RUNTIME;

import java.lang.annotation.Documented;
import java.lang.annotation.Retention;
import java.lang.annotation.Target;

import javax.inject.Qualifier;

@Target( { TYPE, METHOD, PARAMETER, FIELD })
@Retention(RUNTIME)
@Documented
@Qualifier
public @interface MaxNumber {

}
```

The @Random qualifier interface is defined as follows:

```
package guessnumber;

import static java.lang.annotation.ElementType.FIELD;
import static java.lang.annotation.ElementType.METHOD;
import static java.lang.annotation.ElementType.PARAMETER;
import static java.lang.annotation.ElementType.TYPE;
import static java.lang.annotation.RetentionPolicy.RUNTIME;

import java.lang.annotation.Documented;
import java.lang.annotation.Retention;
import java.lang.annotation.Target;

import javax.inject.Qualifier;

@Target( { TYPE, METHOD, PARAMETER, FIELD })
@Retention(RUNTIME)
@Documented
@Qualifier
public @interface Random {

}
```

The Generator Managed Bean

The Generator managed bean contains the two producer methods for the application. The bean has the @ApplicationScoped annotation to specify that its context extends for the duration of the user's interaction with the application:

```
package guessnumber;

import java.io.Serializable;
```

```
import javax.enterprise.context.ApplicationScoped;
import javax.enterprise.inject.Produces;

@ApplicationScoped
public class Generator implements Serializable {

    private static final long serialVersionUID = -7213673465118041882L;

    private java.util.Random random =
        new java.util.Random( System.currentTimeMillis() );

    private int maxNumber = 100;

    java.util.Random getRandom() {
        return random;
    }

    @Produces @Random int next() {
        return getRandom().nextInt(maxNumber);
    }

    @Produces @MaxNumber int getMaxNumber() {
        return maxNumber;
    }

}
```

The UserNumberBean Managed Bean

The UserNumberBean managed bean, the backing bean for the JavaServer Faces application, provides the basic logic for the game. This bean does the following:

- Implements setter and getter methods for the bean fields

- Injects the two qualifier objects

- Provides a reset method that allows you to begin a new game after you complete one

- Provides a check method that determines whether the user has guessed the number

- Provides a validateNumberRange method that determines whether the user's input is correct

The bean is defined as follows:

```
package guessnumber;

import java.io.Serializable;

import javax.annotation.PostConstruct;
import javax.enterprise.context.SessionScoped;
import javax.enterprise.inject.Instance;
import javax.inject.Inject;
import javax.inject.Named;
import javax.faces.application.FacesMessage;
```

```
import javax.faces.component.UIComponent;
import javax.faces.component.UIInput;
import javax.faces.context.FacesContext;

@Named
@SessionScoped
public class UserNumberBean implements Serializable {

    private static final long serialVersionUID = 1L;
    private int number;
    private Integer userNumber;
    private int minimum;
    private int remainingGuesses;

    @MaxNumber
    @Inject
    private int maxNumber;

    private int maximum;

    @Random
    @Inject
    Instance<Integer> randomInt;

    public UserNumberBean() {
    }

    public int getNumber() {
        return number;
    }

    public void setUserNumber(Integer user_number) {
        userNumber = user_number;
    }

    public Integer getUserNumber() {
        return userNumber;
    }

    public int getMaximum() {
        return (this.maximum);
    }

    public void setMaximum(int maximum) {
        this.maximum = maximum;
    }

    public int getMinimum() {
        return (this.minimum);
    }

    public void setMinimum(int minimum) {
        this.minimum = minimum;
    }

    public int getRemainingGuesses() {
        return remainingGuesses;
    }
```

```
public String check() throws InterruptedException {
    if (userNumber > number) {
        maximum = userNumber - 1;
    }
    if (userNumber < number) {
        minimum = userNumber + 1;
    }
    if (userNumber == number) {
        FacesContext.getCurrentInstance().addMessage(null,
            new FacesMessage("Correct!"));
    }
    remainingGuesses--;
    return null;
}

@PostConstruct
public void reset() {
    this.minimum = 0;
    this.userNumber = 0;
    this.remainingGuesses = 10;
    this.maximum = maxNumber;
    this.number = randomInt.get();
}

public void validateNumberRange(FacesContext context,
                               UIComponent toValidate,
                               Object value) {
    if (remainingGuesses <= 0) {
        FacesMessage message = new FacesMessage("No guesses left!");
        context.addMessage(toValidate.getClientId(context), message);
        ((UIInput) toValidate).setValid(false);
        return;
    }
    int input = (Integer) value;

    if (input < minimum || input > maximum) {
        ((UIInput) toValidate).setValid(false);

        FacesMessage message = new FacesMessage("Invalid guess");
        context.addMessage(toValidate.getClientId(context), message);
    }
}
}
```

The Facelets Page

This example uses the same template that the simplegreeting example uses. The index.xhtml file, however, is more complex.

```xml
<?xml version='1.0' encoding='UTF-8' ?>
<!DOCTYPE html PUBLIC "-//W3C//DTD XHTML 1.0 Transitional//EN"
          "http://www.w3.org/TR/xhtml1/DTD/xhtml1-transitional.dtd">
<html xmlns="http://www.w3.org/1999/xhtml"
      xmlns:ui="http://java.sun.com/jsf/facelets"
      xmlns:h="http://java.sun.com/jsf/html"
      xmlns:f="http://java.sun.com/jsf/core">
    <ui:composition template="/template.xhtml">

        <ui:define name="title">Guess My Number</ui:define>
        <ui:define name="head">Guess My Number</ui:define>
        <ui:define name="content">
            <h:form id="GuessMain">
                <div style="color: black; font-size: 24px;">
                    <p>I'm thinking of a number between
                    <span style="color: blue">#{userNumberBean.minimum}</span> and
                    <span style="color: blue">#{userNumberBean.maximum}</span>. You have
                    <span style="color: blue">#{userNumberBean.remainingGuesses}</span>
                    guesses.</p>
                </div>
                <h:panelGrid border="0" columns="5" style="font-size: 18px;">
                    Number:
                    <h:inputText id="inputGuess"
                        value="#{userNumberBean.userNumber}"
                        required="true" size="3"
                        disabled="#{userNumberBean.number eq userNumberBean.userNumber}"
                        validator="#{userNumberBean.validateNumberRange}">
                    </h:inputText>
                    <h:commandButton id="GuessButton" value="Guess"
                        action="#{userNumberBean.check}"
                        disabled="#{userNumberBean.number eq userNumberBean.userNumber}"/>
                    <h:commandButton id="RestartButton" value="Reset"
                        action="#{userNumberBean.reset}"
                        immediate="true" />
                    <h:outputText id="Higher" value="Higher!"
rendered="#{userNumberBean.number gt userNumberBean.userNumber and userNumberBean.userNumber ne 0}"
                        style="color: red"/>
                    <h:outputText id="Lower" value="Lower!"
rendered="#{userNumberBean.number lt userNumberBean.userNumber and userNumberBean.userNumber ne 0}"
                        style="color: red"/>
                </h:panelGrid>
                <div style="color: red; font-size: 14px;">
                    <h:messages id="messages" globalOnly="false"/>
                </div>
            </h:form>
        </ui:define>

    </ui:composition>
</html>
```

The Facelets page presents the user with the minimum and maximum values and the number of guesses remaining. The user's interaction with the game takes place within the panelGrid table, which contains an input field, Guess and Reset buttons, and a text field that appears if the guess is higher or lower than the correct number. Every time the user clicks the Guess button, the userNumberBean.check method is called to reset the maximum or minimum value or, if the guess is correct, to generate a FacesMessage to that effect. The method that determines whether each guess is valid is userNumberBean.validateNumberRange.

Building, Packaging, Deploying, and Running the guessnumber CDI Example

You can build, package, deploy, and run the guessnumber application by using either NetBeans IDE or the Ant tool.

▼ To Build, Package, and Deploy the guessnumber Example Using NetBeans IDE

This procedure builds the application into the following directory:

tut-install/examples/cdi/guessnumber/build/web

The contents of this directory are deployed to the GlassFish Server.

1 In NetBeans IDE, select File→Open Project.

2 In the Open Project dialog, navigate to:

tut-install/examples/cdi/

3 Select the guessnumber folder.

4 Select the Open as Main Project check box.

5 Click Open Project.

6 In the Projects tab, right-click the guessnumber project and select Deploy.

▼ To Build, Package, and Deploy the guessnumber Example Using Ant

1 In a terminal window, go to:

tut-install/examples/cdi/guessnumber/

2 Type the following command:

ant

This command calls the default target, which builds and packages the application into a WAR file, guessnumber.war, located in the dist directory.

3   Type the following command:

`ant deploy`

The guessnumber.war file will be deployed to the GlassFish Server.

▼ To Run the guessnumber Example

1   In a web browser, type the following URL:

`http://localhost:8080/guessnumber`

The Guess My Number page opens, as shown in Figure 18–2.

FIGURE 18–2   Guess My Number Example

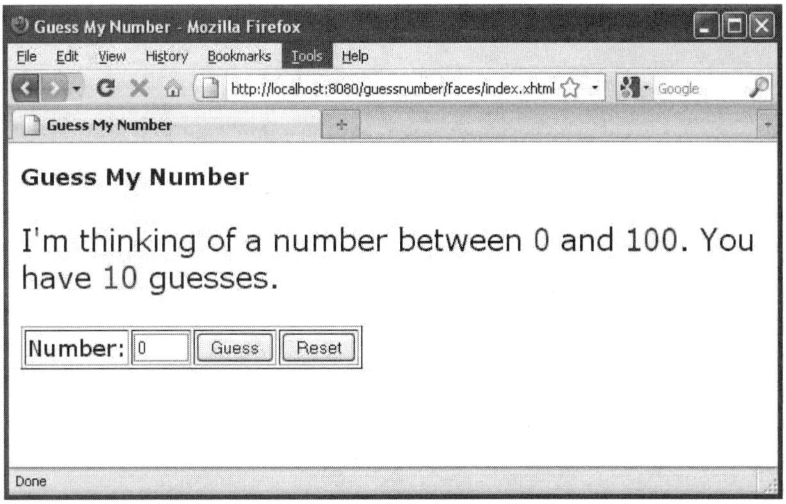

2   Type a number in the Number text field and click Guess.

The minimum and maximum values are modified, along with the remaining number of guesses.

3   Keep guessing numbers until you get the right answer or run out of guesses.

If you get the right answer, the input field and Guess button are grayed out, as shown in Figure 18–3.

FIGURE 18–3 Guess My Number at End of Game

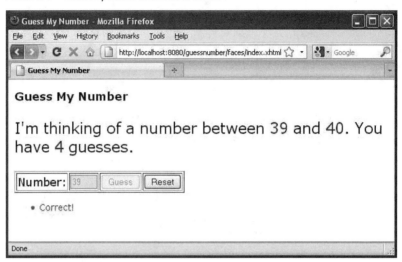

4   Click the Reset button to play the game again with a new random number.

Persistence

Part VI introduces the Java Persistence API. This part contains the following chapters:

Introduction to the Java Persistence API

The Java Persistence API provides Java developers with an object/relational mapping facility for managing relational data in Java applications. Java Persistence consists of four areas:

- The Java Persistence API
- The query language
- The Java Persistence Criteria API
- Object/relational mapping metadata

The following topics are addressed here:

Entities

An entity is a lightweight persistence domain object. Typically, an entity represents a table in a relational database, and each entity instance corresponds to a row in that table. The primary programming artifact of an entity is the entity class, although entities can use helper classes.

The persistent state of an entity is represented through either persistent fields or persistent properties. These fields or properties use object/relational mapping annotations to map the entities and entity relationships to the relational data in the underlying data store.

Requirements for Entity Classes

An entity class must follow these requirements.

- The class must be annotated with the `javax.persistence.Entity` annotation.

- The class must have a public or protected, no-argument constructor. The class may have other constructors.

- The class must not be declared `final`. No methods or persistent instance variables must be declared `final`.

- If an entity instance is passed by value as a detached object, such as through a session bean's remote business interface, the class must implement the `Serializable` interface.

- Entities may extend both entity and non-entity classes, and non-entity classes may extend entity classes.

- Persistent instance variables must be declared private, protected, or package-private and can be accessed directly only by the entity class's methods. Clients must access the entity's state through accessor or business methods.

Persistent Fields and Properties in Entity Classes

The persistent state of an entity can be accessed through either the entity's instance variables or properties. The fields or properties must be of the following Java language types:

- Java primitive types
- `java.lang.String`
- Other serializable types, including:
  - Wrappers of Java primitive types
  - `java.math.BigInteger`
  - `java.math.BigDecimal`
  - `java.util.Date`
  - `java.util.Calendar`
  - `java.sql.Date`
  - `java.sql.Time`
  - `java.sql.TimeStamp`
  - User-defined serializable types
  - `byte[]`
  - `Byte[]`
  - `char[]`
  - `Character[]`
- Enumerated types

- Other entities and/or collections of entities
- Embeddable classes

Entities may use persistent fields, persistent properties, or a combination of both. If the mapping annotations are applied to the entity's instance variables, the entity uses persistent fields. If the mapping annotations are applied to the entity's getter methods for JavaBeans-style properties, the entity uses persistent properties.

Persistent Fields

If the entity class uses persistent fields, the Persistence runtime accesses entity-class instance variables directly. All fields not annotated javax.persistence.Transient or not marked as Java transient will be persisted to the data store. The object/relational mapping annotations must be applied to the instance variables.

Persistent Properties

If the entity uses persistent properties, the entity must follow the method conventions of JavaBeans components. JavaBeans-style properties use getter and setter methods that are typically named after the entity class's instance variable names. For every persistent property *property* of type *Type* of the entity, there is a getter method get*Property* and setter method set*Property*. If the property is a Boolean, you may use is*Property* instead of get*Property*. For example, if a Customer entity uses persistent properties and has a private instance variable called firstName, the class defines a getFirstName and setFirstName method for retrieving and setting the state of the firstName instance variable.

The method signature for single-valued persistent properties are as follows:

```
Type getProperty()
void setProperty(Type type)
```

The object/relational mapping annotations for persistent properties must be applied to the getter methods. Mapping annotations cannot be applied to fields or properties annotated @Transient or marked transient.

Using Collections in Entity Fields and Properties

Collection-valued persistent fields and properties must use the supported Java collection interfaces regardless of whether the entity uses persistent fields or properties. The following collection interfaces may be used:

- java.util.Collection
- java.util.Set

- `java.util.List`
- `java.util.Map`

If the entity class uses persistent fields, the type in the preceding method signatures must be one of these collection types. Generic variants of these collection types may also be used. For example, if it has a persistent property that contains a set of phone numbers, the `Customer` entity would have the following methods:

```
Set<PhoneNumber> getPhoneNumbers() { ... }
void setPhoneNumbers(Set<PhoneNumber>) { ... }
```

If a field or property of an entity consists of a collection of basic types or embeddable classes, use the `javax.persistence.ElementCollection` annotation on the field or property.

The two attributes of `@ElementCollection` are `targetClass` and `fetch`. The `targetClass` attribute specifies the class name of the basic or embeddable class and is optional if the field or property is defined using Java programming language generics. The optional `fetch` attribute is used to specify whether the collection should be retrieved lazily or eagerly, using the `javax.persistence.FetchType` constants of either LAZY or EAGER, respectively. By default, the collection will be fetched lazily.

The following entity, `Person`, has a persistent field, `nicknames`, which is a collection of `String` classes that will be fetched eagerly. The `targetClass` element is not required, because it uses generics to define the field.

```
@Entity
public class Person {
    ...
    @ElementCollection(fetch=EAGER)
    protected Set<String> nickname = new HashSet();
    ...
}
```

Collections of entity elements and relationships may be represented by `java.util.Map` collections. A Map consists of a key and a value.

When using `Map` elements or relationships, the following rules apply.

- The `Map` key or value may be a basic Java programming language type, an embeddable class, or an entity.
- When the `Map` value is an embeddable class or basic type, use the `@ElementCollection` annotation.
- When the `Map` value is an entity, use the `@OneToMany` or `@ManyToMany` annotation.
- Use the `Map` type on only one side of a bidirectional relationship.

If the key type of a `Map` is a Java programming language basic type, use the annotation `javax.persistence.MapKeyColumn` to set the column mapping for the key. By default,

the name attribute of @MapKeyColumn is of the form
*RELATIONSHIP-FIELD/PROPERTY-NAME*_KEY. For example, if the referencing
relationship field name is image, the default name attribute is IMAGE_KEY.

If the key type of a Map is an entity, use the javax.persistence.MapKeyJoinColumn
annotation. If the multiple columns are needed to set the mapping, use the annotation
javax.persistence.MapKeyJoinColumns to include multiple @MapKeyJoinColumn
annotations. If no @MapKeyJoinColumn is present, the mapping column name is by
default set to *RELATIONSHIP-FIELD/PROPERTY-NAME*_KEY. For example, if the
relationship field name is employee, the default name attribute is EMPLOYEE_KEY.

If Java programming language generic types are not used in the relationship field or
property, the key class must be explicitly set using the
javax.persistence.MapKeyClass annotation.

If the Map key is the primary key or a persistent field or property of the entity that is the
Map value, use the javax.persistence.MapKey annotation. The @MapKeyClass and
@MapKey annotations cannot be used on the same field or property.

If the Map value is a Java programming language basic type or an embeddable class, it
will be mapped as a collection table in the underlying database. If generic types are not
used, the @ElementCollection annotation's targetClass attribute must be set to the
type of the Map value.

If the Map value is an entity and part of a many-to-many or one-to-many unidirectional
relationship, it will be mapped as a join table in the underlying database. A
unidirectional one-to-many relationship that uses a Map may also be mapped using the
@JoinColumn annotation.

If the entity is part of a one-to-many/many-to-one bidirectional relationship, it will be
mapped in the table of the entity that represents the value of the Map. If generic types
are not used, the targetEntity attribute of the @OneToMany and @ManyToMany
annotations must be set to the type of the Map value.

Validating Persistent Fields and Properties

The Java API for JavaBeans Validation (Bean Validation) provides a mechanism for
validating application data. Bean Validation is integrated into the Java EE containers,
allowing the same validation logic to be used in any of the tiers of an enterprise
application.

Bean Validation constraints may be applied to persistent entity classes, embeddable
classes, and mapped superclasses. By default, the Persistence provider will
automatically perform validation on entities with persistent fields or properties
annotated with Bean Validation constraints immediately after the PrePersist,
PreUpdate, and PreRemove lifecycle events.

Bean Validation constraints are annotations applied to the fields or properties of Java programming language classes. Bean Validation provides a set of constraints as well as an API for defining custom constraints. Custom constraints can be specific combinations of the default constraints, or new constraints that don't use the default constraints. Each constraint is associated with at least one validator class that validates the value of the constrained field or property. Custom constraint developers must also provide a validator class for the constraint.

Bean Validation constraints are applied to the persistent fields or properties of persistent classes. When adding Bean Validation constraints, use the same access strategy as the persistent class. That is, if the persistent class uses field access, apply the Bean Validation constraint annotations on the class's fields. If the class uses property access, apply the constraints on the getter methods.

Table 9–2 lists Bean Validation's built-in constraints, defined in the `javax.validation.constraints` package.

All the built-in constraints listed in Table 9–2 have a corresponding annotation, *ConstraintName*.`List`, for grouping multiple constraints of the same type on the same field or property. For example, the following persistent field has two `@Pattern` constraints:

```
@Pattern.List({
    @Pattern(regexp="..."),
    @Pattern(regexp="...")
})
```

The following entity class, `Contact`, has Bean Validation constraints applied to its persistent fields.

```
@Entity
public class Contact implements Serializable {
    private static final long serialVersionUID = 1L;
    @Id
    @GeneratedValue(strategy = GenerationType.AUTO)
    private Long id;
    @NotNull
    protected String firstName;
    @NotNull
    protected String lastName;
    @Pattern(regexp="[a-z0-9!#$%&'*+/=?^_'{|}~-]+(?:\\."
        +"[a-z0-9!#$%&'*+/=?^_'{|}~-]+)*@"
        +"(?:[a-z0-9](?:[a-z0-9-]*[a-z0-9])?\\.)+[a-z0-9](?:[a-z0-9-]*[a-z0-9])?)",
            message="{invalid.email}")
    protected String email;
    @Pattern(regexp="^\\(?(\\d{3})\\)?[- ]?(\\d{3})[- ]?(\\d{4})$",
            message="{invalid.phonenumber}")
    protected String mobilePhone;
    @Pattern(regexp="^\\(?(\\d{3})\\)?[- ]?(\\d{3})[- ]?(\\d{4})$",
            message="{invalid.phonenumber}")
    protected String homePhone;
```

```
@Temporal(javax.persistence.TemporalType.DATE)
@Past
protected Date birthday;
...
}
```

The `@NotNull` annotation on the `firstName` and `lastName` fields specifies that those fields are now required. If a new `Contact` instance is created where `firstName` or `lastName` have not been initialized, Bean Validation will throw a validation error. Similarly, if a previously created instance of `Contact` has been modified so that `firstName` or `lastName` are null, a validation error will be thrown.

The `email` field has a `@Pattern` constraint applied to it, with a complicated regular expression that matches most valid email addresses. If the value of `email` doesn't match this regular expression, a validation error will be thrown.

The `homePhone` and `mobilePhone` fields have the same `@Pattern` constraints. The regular expression matches 10 digit telephone numbers in the United States and Canada of the form (*xxx*) *xxx–xxxx*.

The `birthday` field is annotated with the `@Past` constraint, which ensures that the value of `birthday` must be in the past.

Primary Keys in Entities

Each entity has a unique object identifier. A customer entity, for example, might be identified by a customer number. The unique identifier, or *primary key*, enables clients to locate a particular entity instance. Every entity must have a primary key. An entity may have either a simple or a composite primary key.

Simple primary keys use the `javax.persistence.Id` annotation to denote the primary key property or field.

Composite primary keys are used when a primary key consists of more than one attribute, which corresponds to a set of single persistent properties or fields. Composite primary keys must be defined in a primary key class. Composite primary keys are denoted using the `javax.persistence.EmbeddedId` and `javax.persistence.IdClass` annotations.

The primary key, or the property or field of a composite primary key, must be one of the following Java language types:

- Java primitive types
- Java primitive wrapper types
- `java.lang.String`
- `java.util.Date` (the temporal type should be `DATE`)
- `java.sql.Date`

- `java.math.BigDecimal`
- `java.math.BigInteger`

Floating-point types should never be used in primary keys. If you use a generated primary key, only integral types will be portable.

A primary key class must meet these requirements.

- The access control modifier of the class must be `public`.
- The properties of the primary key class must be `public` or `protected` if property-based access is used.
- The class must have a public default constructor.
- The class must implement the `hashCode()` and `equals(Object other)` methods.
- The class must be serializable.
- A composite primary key must be represented and mapped to multiple fields or properties of the entity class or must be represented and mapped as an embeddable class.
- If the class is mapped to multiple fields or properties of the entity class, the names and types of the primary key fields or properties in the primary key class must match those of the entity class.

The following primary key class is a composite key, and the `orderId` and `itemId` fields together uniquely identify an entity:

```
public final class LineItemKey implements Serializable {
    public Integer orderId;
    public int itemId;

    public LineItemKey() {}

    public LineItemKey(Integer orderId, int itemId) {
        this.orderId = orderId;
        this.itemId = itemId;
    }

    public boolean equals(Object otherOb) {
        if (this == otherOb) {
            return true;
        }
        if (!(otherOb instanceof LineItemKey)) {
            return false;
        }
        LineItemKey other = (LineItemKey) otherOb;
        return (
                (orderId==null?other.orderId==null:orderId.equals
                (other.orderId)
                )
                &&
                (itemId == other.itemId)
            );
```

```
    }

    public int hashCode() {
        return (
                (orderId==null?0:orderId.hashCode())
                ^
                ((int) itemId)
            );
    }

    public String toString() {
        return "" + orderId + "-" + itemId;
    }
}
```

Multiplicity in Entity Relationships

Multiplicities are of the following types: one-to-one, one-to-many, many-to-one, and many-to-many:

- **One-to-one**: Each entity instance is related to a single instance of another entity. For example, to model a physical warehouse in which each storage bin contains a single widget, StorageBin and Widget would have a one-to-one relationship. One-to-one relationships use the javax.persistence.OneToOne annotation on the corresponding persistent property or field.

- **One-to-many**: An entity instance can be related to multiple instances of the other entities. A sales order, for example, can have multiple line items. In the order application, Order would have a one-to-many relationship with LineItem. One-to-many relationships use the javax.persistence.OneToMany annotation on the corresponding persistent property or field.

- **Many-to-one**: Multiple instances of an entity can be related to a single instance of the other entity. This multiplicity is the opposite of a one-to-many relationship. In the example just mentioned, the relationship to Order from the perspective of LineItem is many-to-one. Many-to-one relationships use the javax.persistence.ManyToOne annotation on the corresponding persistent property or field.

- **Many-to-many**: The entity instances can be related to multiple instances of each other. For example, each college course has many students, and every student may take several courses. Therefore, in an enrollment application, Course and Student would have a many-to-many relationship. Many-to-many relationships use the javax.persistence.ManyToMany annotation on the corresponding persistent property or field.

Direction in Entity Relationships

The direction of a relationship can be either bidirectional or unidirectional. A bidirectional relationship has both an owning side and an inverse side. A unidirectional relationship has only an owning side. The owning side of a relationship determines how the Persistence runtime makes updates to the relationship in the database.

Bidirectional Relationships

In a *bidirectional* relationship, each entity has a relationship field or property that refers to the other entity. Through the relationship field or property, an entity class's code can access its related object. If an entity has a related field, the entity is said to "know" about its related object. For example, if Order knows what LineItem instances it has and if LineItem knows what Order it belongs to, they have a bidirectional relationship.

Bidirectional relationships must follow these rules.

- The inverse side of a bidirectional relationship must refer to its owning side by using the mappedBy element of the @OneToOne, @OneToMany, or @ManyToMany annotation. The mappedBy element designates the property or field in the entity that is the owner of the relationship.

- The many side of many-to-one bidirectional relationships must not define the mappedBy element. The many side is always the owning side of the relationship.

- For one-to-one bidirectional relationships, the owning side corresponds to the side that contains the corresponding foreign key.

- For many-to-many bidirectional relationships, either side may be the owning side.

Unidirectional Relationships

In a *unidirectional* relationship, only one entity has a relationship field or property that refers to the other. For example, LineItem would have a relationship field that identifies Product, but Product would not have a relationship field or property for LineItem. In other words, LineItem knows about Product, but Product doesn't know which LineItem instances refer to it.

Queries and Relationship Direction

Java Persistence query language and Criteria API queries often navigate across relationships. The direction of a relationship determines whether a query can navigate from one entity to another. For example, a query can navigate from LineItem to Product but cannot navigate in the opposite direction. For Order and LineItem, a query could navigate in both directions because these two entities have a bidirectional relationship.

Cascade Operations and Relationships

Entities that use relationships often have dependencies on the existence of the other entity in the relationship. For example, a line item is part of an order; if the order is deleted, the line item also should be deleted. This is called a cascade delete relationship.

The `javax.persistence.CascadeType` enumerated type defines the cascade operations that are applied in the `cascade` element of the relationship annotations. Table 19–1 lists the cascade operations for entities.

TABLE 19–1 Cascade Operations for Entities

Cascade Operation	Description
ALL	All cascade operations will be applied to the parent entity's related entity. `All` is equivalent to specifying `cascade={DETACH, MERGE, PERSIST, REFRESH, REMOVE}`
DETACH	If the parent entity is detached from the persistence context, the related entity will also be detached.
MERGE	If the parent entity is merged into the persistence context, the related entity will also be merged.
PERSIST	If the parent entity is persisted into the persistence context, the related entity will also be persisted.
REFRESH	If the parent entity is refreshed in the current persistence context, the related entity will also be refreshed.
REMOVE	If the parent entity is removed from the current persistence context, the related entity will also be removed.

Cascade delete relationships are specified using the `cascade=REMOVE` element specification for `@OneToOne` and `@OneToMany` relationships. For example:

```
@OneToMany(cascade=REMOVE, mappedBy="customer")
public Set<Order> getOrders() { return orders; }
```

Orphan Removal in Relationships

When a target entity in one-to-one or one-to-many relationship is removed from the relationship, it is often desirable to cascade the remove operation to the target entity. Such target entities are considered "orphans," and the `orphanRemoval` attribute can be used to specify that orphaned entities should be removed. For example, if an order has many line items and one of them is removed from the order, the removed line item is considered an orphan. If `orphanRemoval` is set to `true`, the line item entity will be deleted when the line item is removed from the order.

The `orphanRemoval` attribute in `@OneToMany` and `@oneToOne` takes a Boolean value and is by default false.

The following example will cascade the remove operation to the orphaned customer entity when it is removed from the relationship:

```
@OneToMany(mappedBy="customer", orphanRemoval="true")
public List<Order> getOrders() { ... }
```

Embeddable Classes in Entities

Embeddable classes are used to represent the state of an entity but don't have a persistent identity of their own, unlike entity classes. Instances of an embeddable class share the identity of the entity that owns it. Embeddable classes exist only as the state of another entity. An entity may have single-valued or collection-valued embeddable class attributes.

Embeddable classes have the same rules as entity classes but are annotated with the `javax.persistence.Embeddable` annotation instead of `@Entity`.

The following embeddable class, `ZipCode`, has the fields `zip` and `plusFour`:

```
@Embeddable
public class ZipCode {
  String zip;
  String plusFour;
...
}
```

This embeddable class is used by the `Address` entity:

```
@Entity
public class Address {
  @Id
  protected long id
  String street1;
  String street2;
  String city;
  String province;
  @Embedded
  ZipCode zipCode;
  String country;
...
}
```

Entities that own embeddable classes as part of their persistent state may annotate the field or property with the `javax.persistence.Embedded` annotation but are not required to do so.

Embeddable classes may themselves use other embeddable classes to represent their state. They may also contain collections of basic Java programming language types or other embeddable classes. Embeddable classes may also contain relationships to other entities or collections of entities. If the embeddable class has such a relationship, the relationship is from the target entity or collection of entities to the entity that owns the embeddable class.

Entity Inheritance

Entities support class inheritance, polymorphic associations, and polymorphic queries. Entity classes can extend non-entity classes, and non-entity classes can extend entity classes. Entity classes can be both abstract and concrete.

The roster example application demonstrates entity inheritance, as described in "Entity Inheritance in the roster Application" on page 370.

Abstract Entities

An abstract class may be declared an entity by decorating the class with @Entity. Abstract entities are like concrete entities but cannot be instantiated.

Abstract entities can be queried just like concrete entities. If an abstract entity is the target of a query, the query operates on all the concrete subclasses of the abstract entity:

```
@Entity
public abstract class Employee {
    @Id
    protected Integer employeeId;
    ...
}
@Entity
public class FullTimeEmployee extends Employee {
    protected Integer salary;
    ...
}
@Entity
public class PartTimeEmployee extends Employee {
    protected Float hourlyWage;
}
```

Mapped Superclasses

Entities may inherit from superclasses that contain persistent state and mapping information but are not entities. That is, the superclass is not decorated with the

@Entity annotation and is not mapped as an entity by the Java Persistence provider. These superclasses are most often used when you have state and mapping information common to multiple entity classes.

Mapped superclasses are specified by decorating the class with the annotation `javax.persistence.MappedSuperclass`:

```
@MappedSuperclass
public class Employee {
    @Id
    protected Integer employeeId;
    ...
}
@Entity
public class FullTimeEmployee extends Employee {
    protected Integer salary;
    ...
}
@Entity
public class PartTimeEmployee extends Employee {
    protected Float hourlyWage;
    ...
}
```

Mapped superclasses cannot be queried and can't be used in `EntityManager` or `Query` operations. You must use entity subclasses of the mapped superclass in `EntityManager` or `Query` operations. Mapped superclasses can't be targets of entity relationships. Mapped superclasses can be abstract or concrete.

Mapped superclasses do not have any corresponding tables in the underlying datastore. Entities that inherit from the mapped superclass define the table mappings. For instance, in the preceding code sample, the underlying tables would be `FULLTIMEEMPLOYEE` and `PARTTIMEEMPLOYEE`, but there is no `EMPLOYEE` table.

Non-Entity Superclasses

Entities may have non-entity superclasses, and these superclasses can be either abstract or concrete. The state of non-entity superclasses is nonpersistent, and any state inherited from the non-entity superclass by an entity class is nonpersistent. Non-entity superclasses may not be used in `EntityManager` or `Query` operations. Any mapping or relationship annotations in non-entity superclasses are ignored.

Entity Inheritance Mapping Strategies

You can configure how the Java Persistence provider maps inherited entities to the underlying datastore by decorating the root class of the hierarchy with the annotation `javax.persistence.Inheritance`. The following mapping strategies are used to map the entity data to the underlying database:

- A single table per class hierarchy
- A table per concrete entity class
- A "join" strategy, whereby fields or properties that are specific to a subclass are mapped to a different table than the fields or properties that are common to the parent class

The strategy is configured by setting the `strategy` element of `@Inheritance` to one of the options defined in the `javax.persistence.InheritanceType` enumerated type:

```
public enum InheritanceType {
    SINGLE_TABLE,
    JOINED,
    TABLE_PER_CLASS
};
```

The default strategy, `InheritanceType.SINGLE_TABLE`, is used if the `@Inheritance` annotation is not specified on the root class of the entity hierarchy.

The Single Table per Class Hierarchy Strategy

With this strategy, which corresponds to the default `InheritanceType.SINGLE_TABLE`, all classes in the hierarchy are mapped to a single table in the database. This table has a *discriminator column* containing a value that identifies the subclass to which the instance represented by the row belongs.

The discriminator column, whose elements are shown in Table 19–2, can be specified by using the `javax.persistence.DiscriminatorColumn` annotation on the root of the entity class hierarchy.

TABLE 19–2 `@DiscriminatorColumn` Elements

Type	Name	Description
`String`	`name`	The name of the column to be used as the discriminator column. The default is `DTYPE`. This element is optional.
`DiscriminatorType`	`discriminatorType`	The type of the column to be used as a discriminator column. The default is `DiscriminatorType.STRING`. This element is optional.

TABLE 19–2 @DiscriminatorColumn Elements   *(Continued)*

Type	Name	Description
String	columnDefinition	The SQL fragment to use when creating the discriminator column. The default is generated by the Persistence provider and is implementation-specific. This element is optional.
String	length	The column length for String-based discriminator types. This element is ignored for non-String discriminator types. The default is 31. This element is optional.

The javax.persistence.DiscriminatorType enumerated type is used to set the type of the discriminator column in the database by setting the discriminatorType element of @DiscriminatorColumn to one of the defined types. DiscriminatorType is defined as:

```
public enum DiscriminatorType {
    STRING,
    CHAR,
    INTEGER
};
```

If @DiscriminatorColumn is not specified on the root of the entity hierarchy and a discriminator column is required, the Persistence provider assumes a default column name of DTYPE and column type of DiscriminatorType.STRING.

The javax.persistence.DiscriminatorValue annotation may be used to set the value entered into the discriminator column for each entity in a class hierarchy. You may decorate only concrete entity classes with @DiscriminatorValue.

If @DiscriminatorValue is not specified on an entity in a class hierarchy that uses a discriminator column, the Persistence provider will provide a default, implementation-specific value. If the discriminatorType element of @DiscriminatorColumn is DiscriminatorType.STRING, the default value is the name of the entity.

This strategy provides good support for polymorphic relationships between entities and queries that cover the entire entity class hierarchy. However, this strategy requires the columns that contain the state of subclasses to be nullable.

The Table per Concrete Class Strategy

In this strategy, which corresponds to InheritanceType.TABLE_PER_CLASS, each concrete class is mapped to a separate table in the database. All fields or properties in the class, including inherited fields or properties, are mapped to columns in the class's table in the database.

This strategy provides poor support for polymorphic relationships and usually requires either SQL UNION queries or separate SQL queries for each subclass for queries that cover the entire entity class hierarchy.

Support for this strategy is optional and may not be supported by all Java Persistence API providers. The default Java Persistence API provider in the GlassFish Server does not support this strategy.

The Joined Subclass Strategy

In this strategy, which corresponds to InheritanceType.JOINED, the root of the class hierarchy is represented by a single table, and each subclass has a separate table that contains only those fields specific to that subclass. That is, the subclass table does not contain columns for inherited fields or properties. The subclass table also has a column or columns that represent its primary key, which is a foreign key to the primary key of the superclass table.

This strategy provides good support for polymorphic relationships but requires one or more join operations to be performed when instantiating entity subclasses. This may result in poor performance for extensive class hierarchies. Similarly, queries that cover the entire class hierarchy require join operations between the subclass tables, resulting in decreased performance.

Some Java Persistence API providers, including the default provider in the GlassFish Server, require a discriminator column that corresponds to the root entity when using the joined subclass strategy. If you are not using automatic table creation in your application, make sure that the database table is set up correctly for the discriminator column defaults, or use the @DiscriminatorColumn annotation to match your database schema. For information on discriminator columns, see "The Single Table per Class Hierarchy Strategy" on page 347.

Managing Entities

Entities are managed by the entity manager, which is represented by javax.persistence.EntityManager instances. Each EntityManager instance is associated with a persistence context: a set of managed entity instances that exist in a particular data store. A persistence context defines the scope under which particular entity instances are created, persisted, and removed. The EntityManager interface defines the methods that are used to interact with the persistence context.

The EntityManager Interface

The EntityManager API creates and removes persistent entity instances, finds entities by the entity's primary key, and allows queries to be run on entities.

Container-Managed Entity Managers

With a *container-managed entity manager*, an `EntityManager` instance's persistence context is automatically propagated by the container to all application components that use the `EntityManager` instance within a single Java Transaction API (JTA) transaction.

JTA transactions usually involve calls across application components. To complete a JTA transaction, these components usually need access to a single persistence context. This occurs when an `EntityManager` is injected into the application components by means of the `javax.persistence.PersistenceContext` annotation. The persistence context is automatically propagated with the current JTA transaction, and `EntityManager` references that are mapped to the same persistence unit provide access to the persistence context within that transaction. By automatically propagating the persistence context, application components don't need to pass references to `EntityManager` instances to each other in order to make changes within a single transaction. The Java EE container manages the lifecycle of container-managed entity managers.

To obtain an `EntityManager` instance, inject the entity manager into the application component:

```
@PersistenceContext
EntityManager em;
```

Application-Managed Entity Managers

With an *application-managed entity manager*, on the other hand, the persistence context is not propagated to application components, and the lifecycle of `EntityManager` instances is managed by the application.

Application-managed entity managers are used when applications need to access a persistence context that is not propagated with the JTA transaction across `EntityManager` instances in a particular persistence unit. In this case, each `EntityManager` creates a new, isolated persistence context. The `EntityManager` and its associated persistence context are created and destroyed explicitly by the application. They are also used when directly injecting `EntityManager` instances can't be done because `EntityManager` instances are not thread-safe. `EntityManagerFactory` instances are thread-safe.

Applications create `EntityManager` instances in this case by using the `createEntityManager` method of `javax.persistence.EntityManagerFactory`.

To obtain an `EntityManager` instance, you first must obtain an `EntityManagerFactory` instance by injecting it into the application component by means of the `javax.persistence.PersistenceUnit` annotation:

```
@PersistenceUnit
EntityManagerFactory emf;
```

Then obtain an `EntityManager` from the `EntityManagerFactory` instance:

```
EntityManager em = emf.createEntityManager();
```

Application-managed entity managers don't automatically propagate the JTA transaction context. Such applications need to manually gain access to the JTA transaction manager and add transaction demarcation information when performing entity operations. The `javax.transaction.UserTransaction` interface defines methods to begin, commit, and roll back transactions. Inject an instance of `UserTransaction` by creating an instance variable annotated with @Resource:

```
@Resource
UserTransaction utx;
```

To begin a transaction, call the `UserTransaction.begin` method. When all the entity operations are complete, call the `UserTransaction.commit` method to commit the transaction. The `UserTransaction.rollback` method is used to roll back the current transaction.

The following example shows how to manage transactions in an application that uses an application-managed entity manager:

```
@PersistenceContext
EntityManagerFactory emf;
EntityManager em;
@Resource
UserTransaction utx;
...
em = emf.createEntityManager();
try {
  utx.begin();
  em.persist(SomeEntity);
  em.merge(AnotherEntity);
  em.remove(ThirdEntity);
  utx.commit();
} catch (Exception e) {
  utx.rollback();
}
```

Finding Entities Using the `EntityManager`

The `EntityManager.find` method is used to look up entities in the data store by the entity's primary key:

```
@PersistenceContext
EntityManager em;
public void enterOrder(int custID, Order newOrder) {
    Customer cust = em.find(Customer.class, custID);
    cust.getOrders().add(newOrder);
```

```
        newOrder.setCustomer(cust);
}
```

Managing an Entity Instance's Lifecycle

You manage entity instances by invoking operations on the entity by means of an
EntityManager instance. Entity instances are in one of four states: new, managed,
detached, or removed.

- New entity instances have no persistent identity and are not yet associated with a
  persistence context.

- Managed entity instances have a persistent identity and are associated with a
  persistence context.

- Detached entity instances have a persistent identity and are not currently
  associated with a persistence context.

- Removed entity instances have a persistent identity, are associated with a persistent
  context, and are scheduled for removal from the data store.

Persisting Entity Instances

New entity instances become managed and persistent either by invoking the persist
method or by a cascading persist operation invoked from related entities that have
the cascade=PERSIST or cascade=ALL elements set in the relationship annotation.
This means that the entity's data is stored to the database when the transaction
associated with the persist operation is completed. If the entity is already managed,
the persist operation is ignored, although the persist operation will cascade to
related entities that have the cascade element set to PERSIST or ALL in the relationship
annotation. If persist is called on a removed entity instance, the entity becomes
managed. If the entity is detached, either persist will throw an
IllegalArgumentException, or the transaction commit will fail.

```
@PersistenceContext
EntityManager em;
...
public LineItem createLineItem(Order order, Product product,
        int quantity) {
    LineItem li = new LineItem(order, product, quantity);
    order.getLineItems().add(li);
    em.persist(li);
    return li;
}
```

The persist operation is propagated to all entities related to the calling entity that
have the cascade element set to ALL or PERSIST in the relationship annotation:

```
@OneToMany(cascade=ALL, mappedBy="order")
public Collection<LineItem> getLineItems() {
    return lineItems;
}
```

Removing Entity Instances

Managed entity instances are removed by invoking the remove method or by a cascading remove operation invoked from related entities that have the cascade=REMOVE or cascade=ALL elements set in the relationship annotation. If the remove method is invoked on a new entity, the remove operation is ignored, although remove will cascade to related entities that have the cascade element set to REMOVE or ALL in the relationship annotation. If remove is invoked on a detached entity, either remove will throw an IllegalArgumentException, or the transaction commit will fail. If invoked on an already removed entity, remove will be ignored. The entity's data will be removed from the data store when the transaction is completed or as a result of the flush operation.

```java
public void removeOrder(Integer orderId) {
    try {
        Order order = em.find(Order.class, orderId);
        em.remove(order);
    }...
```

In this example, all LineItem entities associated with the order are also removed, as Order.getLineItems has cascade=ALL set in the relationship annotation.

Synchronizing Entity Data to the Database

The state of persistent entities is synchronized to the database when the transaction with which the entity is associated commits. If a managed entity is in a bidirectional relationship with another managed entity, the data will be persisted, based on the owning side of the relationship.

To force synchronization of the managed entity to the data store, invoke the flush method of the EntityManager instance. If the entity is related to another entity and the relationship annotation has the cascade element set to PERSIST or ALL, the related entity's data will be synchronized with the data store when flush is called.

If the entity is removed, calling flush will remove the entity data from the data store.

Persistence Units

A persistence unit defines a set of all entity classes that are managed by EntityManager instances in an application. This set of entity classes represents the data contained within a single data store.

Persistence units are defined by the persistence.xml configuration file. The following is an example persistence.xml file:

```xml
<persistence>
    <persistence-unit name="OrderManagement">
        <description>This unit manages orders and customers.
```

```
                    It does not rely on any vendor-specific features and can
                    therefore be deployed to any persistence provider.
            </description>
            <jta-data-source>jdbc/MyOrderDB</jta-data-source>
            <jar-file>MyOrderApp.jar</jar-file>
            <class>com.widgets.Order</class>
            <class>com.widgets.Customer</class>
        </persistence-unit>
</persistence>
```

This file defines a persistence unit named OrderManagement, which uses a JTA-aware data source: jdbc/MyOrderDB. The jar-file and class elements specify managed persistence classes: entity classes, embeddable classes, and mapped superclasses. The jar-file element specifies JAR files that are visible to the packaged persistence unit that contain managed persistence classes, whereas the class element explicitly names managed persistence classes.

The jta-data-source (for JTA-aware data sources) and non-jta-data-source (for non-JTA-aware data sources) elements specify the global JNDI name of the data source to be used by the container.

The JAR file or directory whose META-INF directory contains persistence.xml is called the root of the persistence unit. The scope of the persistence unit is determined by the persistence unit's root. Each persistence unit must be identified with a name that is unique to the persistence unit's scope.

Persistent units can be packaged as part of a WAR or EJB JAR file or can be packaged as a JAR file that can then be included in an WAR or EAR file.

- If you package the persistent unit as a set of classes in an EJB JAR file, persistence.xml should be put in the EJB JAR's META-INF directory.

- If you package the persistence unit as a set of classes in a WAR file, persistence.xml should be located in the WAR file's WEB-INF/classes/META-INF directory.

- If you package the persistence unit in a JAR file that will be included in a WAR or EAR file, the JAR file should be located in either

  - The WEB-INF/lib directory of a WAR

  - The EAR file's library directory

Note – In the Java Persistence API 1.0, JAR files could be located at the root of an EAR file as the root of the persistence unit. This is no longer supported. Portable applications should use the EAR file's library directory as the root of the persistence unit.

Querying Entities

The Java Persistence API provides the following methods for querying entities.

- The Java Persistence query language (JPQL) is a simple, string-based language similar to SQL used to query entities and their relationships. See Chapter 21, "The Java Persistence Query Language," for more information.

- The Criteria API is used to create typesafe queries using Java programming language APIs to query for entities and their relationships. See Chapter 22, "Using the Criteria API to Create Queries," for more information.

Both JPQL and the Criteria API have advantages and disadvantages.

Just a few lines long, JPQL queries are typically more concise and more readable than Criteria queries. Developers familiar with SQL will find it easy to learn the syntax of JPQL. JPQL named queries can be defined in the entity class using a Java programming language annotation or in the application's deployment descriptor. JPQL queries are not typesafe, however, and require a cast when retrieving the query result from the entity manager. This means that type-casting errors may not be caught at compile time. JPQL queries don't support open-ended parameters.

Criteria queries allow you to define the query in the business tier of the application. Although this is also possible using JPQL dynamic queries, Criteria queries provide better performance because JPQL dynamic queries must be parsed each time they are called. Criteria queries are typesafe and therefore don't require casting, as JPQL queries do. The Criteria API is just another Java programming language API and doesn't require developers to learn the syntax of another query language. Criteria queries are typically more verbose than JPQL queries and require the developer to create several objects and perform operations on those objects before submitting the query to the entity manager.

Further Information about Persistence

For more information about the Java Persistence API, see

- Java Persistence 2.0 API specification:

  `http://jcp.org/en/jsr/detail?id=317`

- EclipseLink, the Java Persistence API implementation in the GlassFish Server:

  `http://www.eclipse.org/eclipselink/jpa.php`

- EclipseLink team blog:

  `http://eclipselink.blogspot.com/`

- EclipseLink wiki documentation:

  `http://wiki.eclipse.org/EclipseLink`

20
◆ ◆ ◆   C H A P T E R 2 0

Running the Persistence Examples

This chapter explains how to use the Java Persistence API. The material here focuses on the source code and settings of three examples. The first example, order, is an application that uses a stateful session bean to manage entities related to an ordering system. The second example, roster, is an application that manages a community sports system. The third example, address-book, is a web application that stores contact data. This chapter assumes that you are familiar with the concepts detailed in Chapter 19, "Introduction to the Java Persistence API."

The following topics are addressed here:

- "The order Application" on page 357
- "The roster Application" on page 369
- "The address-book Application" on page 376

The order Application

The order application is a simple inventory and ordering application for maintaining a catalog of parts and placing an itemized order of those parts. The application has entities that represent parts, vendors, orders, and line items. These entities are accessed using a stateful session bean that holds the business logic of the application. A simple singleton session bean creates the initial entities on application deployment. A Facelets web application manipulates the data and displays data from the catalog.

The information contained in an order can be divided into elements. What is the order number? What parts are included in the order? What parts make up that part? Who makes the part? What are the specifications for the part? Are there any schematics for the part? The order application is a simplified version of an ordering system that has all these elements.

The order application consists of a single WAR module that includes the enterprise bean classes, the entities, the support classes, and the Facelets XHTML and class files.

Entity Relationships in the order Application

The order application demonstrates several types of entity relationships: self-referential, one-to-one, one-to-many, many-to-one, and unidirectional relationships.

Self-Referential Relationships

A *self-referential* relationship occurs between relationship fields in the same entity. Part has a field, bomPart, which has a one-to-many relationship with the field parts, which is also in Part. That is, a part can be made up of many parts, and each of those parts has exactly one bill-of-material part.

The primary key for Part is a compound primary key, a combination of the partNumber and revision fields. This key is mapped to the PARTNUMBER and REVISION columns in the EJB_ORDER_PART table:

```
...
@ManyToOne
@JoinColumns({
    @JoinColumn(name="BOMPARTNUMBER",
        referencedColumnName="PARTNUMBER"),
    @JoinColumn(name="BOMREVISION",
        referencedColumnName="REVISION")
})
public Part getBomPart() {
    return bomPart;
}
...
@OneToMany(mappedBy="bomPart")
public Collection<Part> getParts() {
    return parts;
}
...
```

One-to-One Relationships

Part has a field, vendorPart, that has a one-to-one relationship with VendorPart's part field. That is, each part has exactly one vendor part, and vice versa.

Here is the relationship mapping in Part:

```
@OneToOne(mappedBy="part")
public VendorPart getVendorPart() {
    return vendorPart;
}
```

Here is the relationship mapping in VendorPart:

```
@OneToOne
@JoinColumns({
    @JoinColumn(name="PARTNUMBER",
```

```
            referencedColumnName="PARTNUMBER"),
    @JoinColumn(name="PARTREVISION",
        referencedColumnName="REVISION")
})
public Part getPart() {
    return part;
}
```

Note that, because Part uses a compound primary key, the @JoinColumns annotation is used to map the columns in the PERSISTENCE_ORDER_VENDOR_PART table to the columns in PERSISTENCE_ORDER_PART. The PERSISTENCE_ORDER_VENDOR_PART table's PARTREVISION column refers to PERSISTENCE_ORDER_PART's REVISION column.

One-to-Many Relationship Mapped to Overlapping Primary and Foreign Keys

Order has a field, lineItems, that has a one-to-many relationship with LineItem's field order. That is, each order has one or more line item.

LineItem uses a compound primary key that is made up of the orderId and itemId fields. This compound primary key maps to the ORDERID and ITEMID columns in the PERSISTENCE_ORDER_LINEITEM table. ORDERID is a foreign key to the ORDERID column in the PERSISTENCE_ORDER_ORDER table. This means that the ORDERID column is mapped twice: once as a primary key field, orderId; and again as a relationship field, order.

Here's the relationship mapping in Order:

```
@OneToMany(cascade=ALL, mappedBy="order")
    public Collection<LineItem> getLineItems() {
    return lineItems;
}
```

Here is the relationship mapping in LineItem:

```
@ManyToOne
    public Order getOrder() {
    return order;
}
```

Unidirectional Relationships

LineItem has a field, vendorPart, that has a unidirectional many-to-one relationship with VendorPart. That is, there is no field in the target entity in this relationship:

```
@ManyToOne
    public VendorPart getVendorPart() {
    return vendorPart;
}
```

Primary Keys in the order Application

The order application uses several types of primary keys: single-valued primary keys, compound primary keys, and generated primary keys.

Generated Primary Keys

VendorPart uses a generated primary key value. That is, the application does not assign primary key values for the entities but instead relies on the persistence provider to generate the primary key values. The @GeneratedValue annotation is used to specify that an entity will use a generated primary key.

In VendorPart, the following code specifies the settings for generating primary key values:

```
@TableGenerator(
    name="vendorPartGen",
    table="PERSISTENCE_ORDER_SEQUENCE_GENERATOR",
    pkColumnName="GEN_KEY",
    valueColumnName="GEN_VALUE",
    pkColumnValue="VENDOR_PART_ID",
    allocationSize=10)
@Id
@GeneratedValue(strategy=GenerationType.TABLE,
    generator="vendorPartGen")
public Long getVendorPartNumber() {
    return vendorPartNumber;
}
```

The @TableGenerator annotation is used in conjunction with @GeneratedValue's strategy=TABLE element. That is, the strategy used to generate the primary keys is to use a table in the database. The @TableGenerator annotation is used to configure the settings for the generator table. The name element sets the name of the generator, which is vendorPartGen in VendorPart.

The EJB_ORDER_SEQUENCE_GENERATOR table, whose two columns are GEN_KEY and GEN_VALUE, will store the generated primary key values. This table could be used to generate other entity's primary keys, so the pkColumnValue element is set to VENDOR_PART_ID to distinguish this entity's generated primary keys from other entity's generated primary keys. The allocationSize element specifies the amount to increment when allocating primary key values. In this case, each VendorPart's primary key will increment by 10.

The primary key field vendorPartNumber is of type Long, as the generated primary key's field must be an integral type.

Compound Primary Keys

A compound primary key is made up of multiple fields and follows the requirements described in "Primary Keys in Entities" on page 339. To use a compound primary key, you must create a wrapper class.

In order, two entities use compound primary keys: Part and LineItem.

- Part uses the PartKey wrapper class. Part's primary key is a combination of the part number and the revision number. PartKey encapsulates this primary key.

- LineItem uses the LineItemKey class. LineItem's primary key is a combination of the order number and the item number. LineItemKey encapsulates this primary key.

This is the LineItemKey compound primary key wrapper class:

```
package order.entity;

public final class LineItemKey implements
            java.io.Serializable {

    private Integer orderId;
    private int itemId;

    public int hashCode() {
        return ((this.getOrderId()==null
                        ?0:this.getOrderId().hashCode())
                ^ ((int) this.getItemId()));
    }

    public boolean equals(Object otherOb) {
        if (this == otherOb) {
            return true;
        }
        if (!(otherOb instanceof LineItemKey)) {
            return false;
        }
        LineItemKey other = (LineItemKey) otherOb;
        return ((this.getOrderId()==null
                        ?other.orderId==null:this.getOrderId().equals
                (other.orderId)) && (this.getItemId ==
                    other.itemId));
    }

    public String toString() {
        return "" + orderId + "-" + itemId;
    }
}
```

The @IdClass annotation is used to specify the primary key class in the entity class. In LineItem, @IdClass is used as follows:

```
@IdClass(order.entity.LineItemKey.class)
@Entity
...
```

```
public class LineItem {
...
}
```

The two fields in LineItem are tagged with the @Id annotation to mark those fields as part of the compound primary key:

```
@Id
public int getItemId() {
    return itemId;
}
...
@Id
@Column(name="ORDERID", nullable=false,
    insertable=false, updatable=false)
public Integer getOrderId() {
    return orderId;
}
```

For orderId, you also use the @Column annotation to specify the column name in the table and that this column should not be inserted or updated, as it is an overlapping foreign key pointing at the PERSISTENCE_ORDER_ORDER table's ORDERID column (see "One-to-Many Relationship Mapped to Overlapping Primary and Foreign Keys" on page 359). That is, orderId will be set by the Order entity.

In LineItem's constructor, the line item number (LineItem.itemId) is set using the Order.getNextId method:

```
public LineItem(Order order, int quantity, VendorPart
        vendorPart) {
    this.order = order;
    this.itemId = order.getNextId();
    this.orderId = order.getOrderId();
    this.quantity = quantity;
    this.vendorPart = vendorPart;
}
```

Order.getNextId counts the number of current line items, adds 1, and returns that number:

```
public int getNextId() {
    return this.lineItems.size() + 1;
}
```

Part doesn't require the @Column annotation on the two fields that comprise Part's compound primary key, because Part's compound primary key is not an overlapping primary key/foreign key:

```
@IdClass(order.entity.PartKey.class)
@Entity
...
public class Part {
...
```

```
    @Id
    public String getPartNumber() {
        return partNumber;
    }
...
    @Id
    public int getRevision() {
        return revision;
    }
...
}
```

Entity Mapped to More Than One Database Table

Part's fields map to more than one database table: PERSISTENCE_ORDER_PART and PERSISTENCE_ORDER_PART_DETAIL. The PERSISTENCE_ORDER_PART_DETAIL table holds the specification and schematics for the part. The @SecondaryTable annotation is used to specify the secondary table.

```
...
@Entity
@Table(name="PERSISTENCE_ORDER_PART")
@SecondaryTable(name="PERSISTENCE_ORDER_PART_DETAIL", pkJoinColumns={
    @PrimaryKeyJoinColumn(name="PARTNUMBER",
        referencedColumnName="PARTNUMBER"),
    @PrimaryKeyJoinColumn(name="REVISION",
        referencedColumnName="REVISION")
})
public class Part {
...
}
```

PERSISTENCE_ORDER_PART_DETAIL and PERSISTENCE_ORDER_PART share the same primary key values. The pkJoinColumns element of @SecondaryTable is used to specify that PERSISTENCE_ORDER_PART_DETAIL's primary key columns are foreign keys to PERSISTENCE_ORDER_PART. The @PrimaryKeyJoinColumn annotation sets the primary key column names and specifies which column in the primary table the column refers to. In this case, the primary key column names for both PERSISTENCE_ORDER_PART_DETAIL and PERSISTENCE_ORDER_PART are the same: PARTNUMBER and REVISION, respectively.

Cascade Operations in the order Application

Entities that have relationships to other entities often have dependencies on the existence of the other entity in the relationship. For example, a line item is part of an order; if the order is deleted, then the line item also should be deleted. This is called a cascade delete relationship.

In order, there are two cascade delete dependencies in the entity relationships. If the Order to which a LineItem is related is deleted, the LineItem also should be deleted. If the Vendor to which a VendorPart is related is deleted, the VendorPart also should be deleted.

You specify the cascade operations for entity relationships by setting the cascade element in the inverse (nonowning) side of the relationship. The cascade element is set to ALL in the case of Order.lineItems. This means that all persistence operations (deletes, updates, and so on) are cascaded from orders to line items.

Here is the relationship mapping in Order:

```
@OneToMany(cascade=ALL, mappedBy="order")
public Collection<LineItem> getLineItems() {
    return lineItems;
}
```

Here is the relationship mapping in LineItem:

```
@ManyToOne
    public Order getOrder() {
    return order;
}
```

BLOB and CLOB Database Types in the order Application

The PARTDETAIL table in the database has a column, DRAWING, of type BLOB. BLOB stands for binary large objects, which are used for storing binary data, such as an image. The DRAWING column is mapped to the field Part.drawing of type java.io.Serializable. The @Lob annotation is used to denote that the field is large object.

```
@Column(table="PERSISTENCE_ORDER_PART_DETAIL")
@Lob
public Serializable getDrawing() {
    return drawing;
}
```

PERSISTENCE_ORDER_PART_DETAIL also has a column, SPECIFICATION, of type CLOB. CLOB stands for character large objects, which are used to store string data too large to be stored in a VARCHAR column. SPECIFICATION is mapped to the field Part.specification of type java.lang.String. The @Lob annotation is also used here to denote that the field is a large object.

```
@Column(table="PERSISTENCE_ORDER_PART_DETAIL")
@Lob
public String getSpecification() {
```

```
        return specification;
}
```

Both of these fields use the @Column annotation and set the table element to the secondary table.

Temporal Types in the order Application

The Order.lastUpdate persistent property, which is of type java.util.Date, is mapped to the PERSISTENCE_ORDER_ORDER.LASTUPDATE database field, which is of the SQL type TIMESTAMP. To ensure the proper mapping between these types, you must use the @Temporal annotation with the proper temporal type specified in @Temporal's element. @Temporal's elements are of type javax.persistence.TemporalType. The possible values are

- DATE, which maps to java.sql.Date
- TIME, which maps to java.sql.Time
- TIMESTAMP, which maps to java.sql.Timestamp

Here is the relevant section of Order:

```
@Temporal(TIMESTAMP)
public Date getLastUpdate() {
    return lastUpdate;
}
```

Managing the order Application's Entities

The RequestBean stateful session bean contains the business logic and manages the entities of order. RequestBean uses the @PersistenceContext annotation to retrieve an entity manager instance, which is used to manage order's entities in RequestBean's business methods:

```
@PersistenceContext
private EntityManager em;
```

This EntityManager instance is a container-managed entity manager, so the container takes care of all the transactions involved in the managing order's entities.

Creating Entities

The RequestBean.createPart business method creates a new Part entity. The EntityManager.persist method is used to persist the newly created entity to the database.

```
Part part = new Part(partNumber,
    revision,
    description,
```

```
        revisionDate,
        specification,
        drawing);
em.persist(part);
```

The ConfigBean singleton session bean is used to initialize the data in order.
ConfigBean is annotated with @Startup, which indicates that the EJB container
should create ConfigBean when order is deployed. The createData method is
annotated with @PostConstruct and creates the initial entities used by order by
calling RequestsBean's business methods.

Finding Entities

The RequestBean.getOrderPrice business method returns the price of a given order,
based on the orderId. The EntityManager.find method is used to retrieve the entity
from the database.

```
Order order = em.find(Order.class, orderId);
```

The first argument of EntityManager.find is the entity class, and the second is the
primary key.

Setting Entity Relationships

The RequestBean.createVendorPart business method creates a VendorPart
associated with a particular Vendor. The EntityManager.persist method is used to
persist the newly created VendorPart entity to the database, and the
VendorPart.setVendor and Vendor.setVendorPart methods are used to associate
the VendorPart with the Vendor.

```
PartKey pkey = new PartKey();
pkey.partNumber = partNumber;
pkey.revision = revision;

Part part = em.find(Part.class, pkey);
VendorPart vendorPart = new VendorPart(description, price,
    part);
em.persist(vendorPart);

Vendor vendor = em.find(Vendor.class, vendorId);
vendor.addVendorPart(vendorPart);
vendorPart.setVendor(vendor);
```

Using Queries

The RequestBean.adjustOrderDiscount business method updates the discount
applied to all orders. This method uses the findAllOrders named query, defined in
Order:

```
@NamedQuery(
    name="findAllOrders",
    query="SELECT o FROM Order o"
)
```

The `EntityManager.createNamedQuery` method is used to run the query. Because the query returns a `List` of all the orders, the `Query.getResultList` method is used.

```
List orders = em.createNamedQuery(
    "findAllOrders")
    .getResultList();
```

The `RequestBean.getTotalPricePerVendor` business method returns the total price of all the parts for a particular vendor. This method uses a named parameter, `id`, defined in the named query `findTotalVendorPartPricePerVendor` defined in `VendorPart`.

```
@NamedQuery(
    name="findTotalVendorPartPricePerVendor",
    query="SELECT SUM(vp.price) " +
    "FROM VendorPart vp " +
    "WHERE vp.vendor.vendorId = :id"
)
```

When running the query, the `Query.setParameter` method is used to set the named parameter `id` to the value of `vendorId`, the parameter to `RequestBean.getTotalPricePerVendor`:

```
return (Double) em.createNamedQuery(
    "findTotalVendorPartPricePerVendor")
    .setParameter("id", vendorId)
    .getSingleResult();
```

The `Query.getSingleResult` method is used for this query because the query returns a single value.

Removing Entities

The `RequestBean.removeOrder` business method deletes a given order from the database. This method uses the `EntityManager.remove` method to delete the entity from the database.

```
Order order = em.find(Order.class, orderId);
em.remove(order);
```

Building, Packaging, Deploying, and Running the order Application

This section explains how to build, package, deploy, and run the order application. To do this, you will create the database tables in the Java DB server, then build, deploy, and run the example.

▼ To Build, Package, Deploy, and Run order UsingNetBeans IDE

1   In NetBeans IDE, select File→Open Project.

2   In the Open Project dialog, navigate to:

tut-install/examples/persistence/

3   Select the order folder.

4   Select the Open as Main Project check box.

5   Click Open Project.

6   In the Projects tab, right-click the order project and select Run.

NetBeans IDE opens a web browser to http://localhost:8080/order/.

▼ To Build, Package, Deploy, and Run order Using Ant

1   In a terminal window, go to:

tut-install/examples/persistence/order/

2   Type the following command:

ant

This runs the default task, which compiles the source files and packages the application into a WAR file located at
tut-install/examples/persistence/order/dist/order.war.

3   To deploy the WAR, make sure that the GlassFish Server is started, then type the following command:

ant deploy

4   Open a web browser to http://localhost:8080/order/ to create and update the order data.

The all Task

As a convenience, the all task will build, package, deploy, and run the application. To do this, type the following command:

```
ant all
```

The roster Application

The roster application maintains the team rosters for players in recreational sports leagues. The application has four components: Java Persistence API entities (Player, Team, and League), a stateful session bean (RequestBean), an application client (RosterClient), and three helper classes (PlayerDetails, TeamDetails, and LeagueDetails).

Functionally, roster is similar to the order application, with three new features that order does not have: many-to-many relationships, entity inheritance, and automatic table creation at deployment time.

Relationships in the roster Application

A recreational sports system has the following relationships:

- A player can be on many teams.
- A team can have many players.
- A team is in exactly one league.
- A league has many teams.

In roster this system is reflected by the following relationships between the Player, Team, and League entities.

- There is a many-to-many relationship between Player and Team.
- There is a many-to-one relationship between Team and League.

The Many-To-Many Relationship in roster

The many-to-many relationship between Player and Team is specified by using the @ManyToMany annotation. In Team.java, the @ManyToMany annotation decorates the getPlayers method:

```
@ManyToMany
@JoinTable(
    name="EJB_ROSTER_TEAM_PLAYER",
    joinColumns=
        @JoinColumn(name="TEAM_ID", referencedColumnName="ID"),
    inverseJoinColumns=
```

```
            @JoinColumn(name="PLAYER_ID", referencedColumnName="ID")
)
public Collection<Player> getPlayers() {
    return players;
}
```

The @JoinTable annotation is used to specify a database table that will associate player IDs with team IDs. The entity that specifies the @JoinTable is the owner of the relationship, so the Team entity is the owner of the relationship with the Player entity. Because roster uses automatic table creation at deployment time, the container will create a join table named EJB_ROSTER_TEAM_PLAYER.

Player is the inverse, or nonowning, side of the relationship with Team. As one-to-one and many-to-one relationships, the nonowning side is marked by the mappedBy element in the relationship annotation. Because the relationship between Player and Team is bidirectional, the choice of which entity is the owner of the relationship is arbitrary.

In Player.java, the @ManyToMany annotation decorates the getTeams method:

```
@ManyToMany(mappedBy="players")
public Collection<Team> getTeams() {
    return teams;
}
```

Entity Inheritance in the roster Application

The roster application shows how to use entity inheritance, as described in "Entity Inheritance" on page 345.

The League entity in roster is an abstract entity with two concrete subclasses: SummerLeague and WinterLeague. Because League is an abstract class, it cannot be instantiated:

```
...
@Entity
@Table(name = "EJB_ROSTER_LEAGUE")
public abstract class League implements java.io.Serializable {
...
}
```

Instead, when creating a league, clients use SummerLeague or WinterLeague. SummerLeague and WinterLeague inherit the persistent properties defined in League and add only a constructor that verifies that the sport parameter matches the type of sport allowed in that seasonal league. For example, here is the SummerLeague entity:

```
...
@Entity
public class SummerLeague extends League
        implements java.io.Serializable {

    /** Creates a new instance of SummerLeague */
    public SummerLeague() {
    }

    public SummerLeague(String id, String name,
            String sport) throws IncorrectSportException {
        this.id = id;
        this.name = name;
        if (sport.equalsIgnoreCase("swimming") ||
                sport.equalsIgnoreCase("soccer") ||
                sport.equalsIgnoreCase("basketball") ||
                sport.equalsIgnoreCase("baseball")) {
            this.sport = sport;
        } else {
            throw new IncorrectSportException(
                "Sport is not a summer sport.");
        }
    }
}
```

The roster application uses the default mapping strategy of
InheritanceType.SINGLE_TABLE, so the @Inheritance annotation is not required. If
you want to use a different mapping strategy, decorate League with @Inheritance and
specify the mapping strategy in the strategy element:

```
@Entity
@Inheritance(strategy=JOINED)
@Table(name="EJB_ROSTER_LEAGUE")
public abstract class League implements java.io.Serializable {
    ...
}
```

The roster application uses the default discriminator column name, so the
@DiscriminatorColumn annotation is not required. Because you are using automatic
table generation in roster, the Persistence provider will create a discriminator column
called DTYPE in the EJB_ROSTER_LEAGUE table, which will store the name of the
inherited entity used to create the league. If you want to use a different name for the
discriminator column, decorate League with @DiscriminatorColumn and set the name
element:

```
@Entity
@DiscriminatorColumn(name="DISCRIMINATOR")
@Table(name="EJB_ROSTER_LEAGUE")
public abstract class League implements java.io.Serializable {
    ...
}
```

Criteria Queries in the roster Application

The roster application uses Criteria API queries, as opposed to the JPQL queries used in order. Criteria queries are Java programming language, typesafe queries defined in the business tier of roster, in the RequestBean stateless session bean.

Metamodel Classes in the roster Application

Metamodel classes model an entity's attributes and are used by Criteria queries to navigate to an entity's attributes. Each entity class in roster has a corresponding metamodel class, generated at compile time, with the same package name as the entity and appended with an underscore character (_). For example, the roster.entity.Person entity has a corresponding metamodel class, roster.entity.Person_.

Each persistent field or property in the entity class has a corresponding attribute in the entity's metamodel class. For the Person entity, the corresponding metamodel class is:

```
@StaticMetamodel(Person.class)
public class Person_ {
  public static volatile SingularAttribute<Player, String> id;
  public static volatile SingularAttribute<Player, String> name;
  public static volatile SingularAttribute<Player, String> position;
  public static volatile SingularAttribute<Player, Double> salary;
  public static volatile CollectionAttribute<Player, Team> teams;
}
```

Obtaining a CriteriaBuilder Instance in RequestBean

The CrtiteriaBuilder interface defines methods to create criteria query objects and create expressions for modifying those query objects. RequestBean creates an instance of CriteriaBuilder by using a @PostConstruct method, init:

```
@PersistenceContext
private EntityManager em;
private CriteriaBuilder cb;

@PostConstruct
private void init() {
  cb = em.getCriteriaBuilder();
}
```

The EntityManager instance is injected at runtime, and then that EntityManager object is used to create the CriteriaBuilder instance by calling getCriteriaBuilder. The CriteriaBuilder instance is created in a @PostConstruct method to ensure that the EntityManager instance has been injected by the enterprise bean container.

Creating Criteria Queries in RequestBean's Business Methods

Many of the business methods in RequestBean define Criteria queries. One business method, getPlayersByPosition, returns a list of players who play a particular position on a team:

```
public List<PlayerDetails> getPlayersByPosition(String position) {
    logger.info("getPlayersByPosition");
    List<Player> players = null;

    try {
        CriteriaQuery<Player> cq = cb.createQuery(Player.class);
        if (cq != null) {
            Root<Player> player = cq.from(Player.class);

            // set the where clause
            cq.where(cb.equal(player.get(Player_.position), position));
            cq.select(player);
            TypedQuery<Player> q = em.createQuery(cq);
            players = q.getResultList();
        }

        return copyPlayersToDetails(players);
    } catch (Exception ex) {
        throw new EJBException(ex);
    }
}
```

A query object is created by calling the CriteriaBuilder object's createQuery method, with the type set to Player because the query will return a list of players.

The query root, the base entity from which the query will navigate to find the entity's attributes and related entities, is created by calling the from method of the query object. This sets the FROM clause of the query.

The WHERE clause, set by calling the where method on the query object, restricts the results of the query according to the conditions of an expression. The CriteriaBuilder.equal method compares the two expressions. In getPlayersByPosition, the position attribute of the Player_ metamodel class, accessed by calling the get method of the query root, is compared to the position parameter passed to getPlayersByPosition.

The SELECT clause of the query is set by calling the select method of the query object. The query will return Player entities, so the query root object is passed as a parameter to select.

The query object is prepared for execution by calling EntityManager.createQuery, which returns a TypedQuery<T> object with the type of the query, in this case Player. This typed query object is used to execute the query, which occurs when the getResultList method is called, and a List<Player> collection is returned.

Automatic Table Generation in the roster Application

At deployment time, the GlassFish Server will automatically drop and create the database tables used by roster. This is done by setting the eclipselink.ddl-generation property to drop-and-create-tables in persistence.xml:

```
<?xml version="1.0" encoding="UTF-8"?>
<persistence version="2.0"
    xmlns="http://java.sun.com/xml/ns/persistence"
    xmlns:xsi="http://www.w3.org/2001/XMLSchema-instance"
    xsi:schemaLocation="http://java.sun.com/xml/ns/persistence
        http://java.sun.com/xml/ns/persistence/persistence_2_0.xsd">
  <persistence-unit name="em" transaction-type="JTA">
    <jta-data-source>jdbc/__default</jta-data-source>
    <properties>
      <property name="eclipselink.ddl-generation"
                value="drop-and-create-tables"/>
    </properties>
  </persistence-unit>
</persistence>
```

This feature is specific to the Java Persistence API provider used by the GlassFish Server and is nonportable across Java EE servers. Automatic table creation is useful for development purposes, however, and the eclipselink.ddl-generation property may be removed from persistence.xml when preparing the application for production use or when deploying to other Java EE servers.

Building, Packaging, Deploying, and Running the roster Application

This section explains how to build, package, deploy, and run the roster application. You can do this using either NetBeans IDE or Ant.

▼ To Build, Package, Deploy, and Run roster Using NetBeans IDE

1   In NetBeans IDE, select File→Open Project.

2   In the Open Project dialog, navigate to:

    tut-install/examples/persistence/

3   Select the roster folder.

4   Select the Open as Main Project and Open Required Projects check boxes.

5   Click Open Project.

6 **In the Projects tab, right-click the roster project and select Run.**

You will see the following partial output from the application client in the Output tab:

```
List all players in team T2:
P6 Ian Carlyle goalkeeper 555.0
P7 Rebecca Struthers midfielder 777.0
P8 Anne Anderson forward 65.0
P9 Jan Wesley defender 100.0
P10 Terry Smithson midfielder 100.0

List all teams in league L1:
T1 Honey Bees Visalia
T2 Gophers Manteca
T5 Crows Orland

List all defenders:
P2 Alice Smith defender 505.0
P5 Barney Bold defender 100.0
P9 Jan Wesley defender 100.0
P22 Janice Walker defender 857.0
P25 Frank Fletcher defender 399.0
...
```

▼ To Build, Package, Deploy, and Run roster Using Ant

1 **In a terminal window, go to:**

tut-install/examples/persistence/roster/

2 **Type the following command:**

ant

This runs the default task, which compiles the source files and packages the application into an EAR file located at *tut-install*/examples/persistence/roster/dist/roster.ear.

3 **To deploy the EAR, make sure that the GlassFish Server is started; then type the following command:**

ant deploy

The build system will check whether the Java DB database server is running and start it if it is not running, then deploy roster.ear. The GlassFish Server will then drop and create the database tables during deployment, as specified in persistence.xml.

After roster.ear is deployed, a client JAR, rosterClient.jar, is retrieved. This contains the application client.

4 **To run the application client, type the following command:**

ant run

You will see the output, which begins:

```
[echo] running application client container.
[exec] List all players in team T2:
[exec] P6 Ian Carlyle goalkeeper 555.0
[exec] P7 Rebecca Struthers midfielder 777.0
[exec] P8 Anne Anderson forward 65.0
[exec] P9 Jan Wesley defender 100.0
[exec] P10 Terry Smithson midfielder 100.0

[exec] List all teams in league L1:
[exec] T1 Honey Bees Visalia
[exec] T2 Gophers Manteca
[exec] T5 Crows Orland

[exec] List all defenders:
[exec] P2 Alice Smith defender 505.0
[exec] P5 Barney Bold defender 100.0
[exec] P9 Jan Wesley defender 100.0
[exec] P22 Janice Walker defender 857.0
[exec] P25 Frank Fletcher defender 399.0
...
```

The all Task

As a convenience, the all task will build, package, deploy, and run the application. To do this, type the following command:

```
ant all
```

The address-book Application

The address-book example application is a simple web application that stores contact data. It uses a single entity class, Contact, that uses the Java API for JavaBeans Validation (Bean Validation) to validate the data stored in the persistent attributes of the entity, as described in "Validating Persistent Fields and Properties" on page 337.

Bean Validation Constraints in address-book

The Contact entity uses the @NotNull, @Pattern, and @Past constraints on the persistent attributes.

The @NotNull constraint marks the attribute as a required field. The attribute must be set to a non-null value before the entity can be persisted or modified. Bean Validation will throw a validation error if the attribute is null when the entity is persisted or modified.

The @Pattern constraint defines a regular expression that the value of the attribute must match before the entity can be persisted or modified. This constraint has two different uses in address-book.

- The regular expression declared in the @Pattern annotation on the email field matches email addresses of the form *name@domain name.top level domain*, allowing only valid characters for email addresses. For example, username@example.com will pass validation, as will firstname.lastname@mail.example.com. However, firstname,lastname@example.com, which contains an illegal comma character in the local name, will fail validation.

- The mobilePhone and homePhone fields are annotated with a @Pattern constraint that defines a regular expression to match phone numbers of the form (*xxx*) *xxx–xxxx*.

The @Past constraint is applied to the birthday field, which must be a java.util.Date in the past.

Here are the relevant parts of the Contact entity class:

```
@Entity
public class Contact implements Serializable {
    private static final long serialVersionUID = 1L;
    @Id
    @GeneratedValue(strategy = GenerationType.AUTO)
    private Long id;
    @NotNull
    protected String firstName;
    @NotNull
    protected String lastName;
    @Pattern(regexp="[a-z0-9!#$%&'*+/=?^_'{|}~-]+(?:\\."
        +"[a-z0-9!#$%&'*+/=?^_'{|}~-]+)*"
        +"@(?:[a-z0-9](?:[a-z0-9-]*[a-z0-9])?\\.)+[a-z0-9](?:[a-z0-9-]*[a-z0-9])?",
            message="{invalid.email}")
    protected String email;
    @Pattern(regexp="^\\(?(\\d{3})\\)?[- ]?(\\d{3})[- ]?(\\d{4})$",
            message="{invalid.phonenumber}")
    protected String mobilePhone;
    @Pattern(regexp="^\\(?(\\d{3})\\)?[- ]?(\\d{3})[- ]?(\\d{4})$",
            message="{invalid.phonenumber}")
    protected String homePhone;
    @Temporal(javax.persistence.TemporalType.DATE)
    @Past
    protected Date birthday;
    ...
}
```

Specifying Error Messages for Constraints in address-book

Some of the constraints in the Contact entity specify an optional message:

```
@Pattern(regexp="^\\(?(\\d{3})\\)?[- ]?(\\d{3})[- ]?(\\d{4})$",
            message="{invalid.phonenumber}")
    protected String homePhone;
```

The optional message element in the @Pattern constraint overrides the default validation message. The message can be specified directly:

```
@Pattern(regexp="^\\(?(\\d{3})\\)?[- ]?(\\d{3})[- ]?(\\d{4})$",
         message="Invalid phone number!")
   protected String homePhone;
```

The constraints in Contact, however, are strings in the resource bundle *tut-install*/examples/persistence/address-book/src/java/ ValidationMessages.properties. This allows the validation messages to be located in one single properties file and the messages to be easily localized. Overridden Bean Validation messages must be placed in a resource bundle properties file named ValidationMessages.properties in the default package, with localized resource bundles taking the form ValidationMessages_*locale-prefix*.properties. For example, ValidationMessages_es.properties is the resource bundle used in Spanish speaking locales.

Validating Contact Input from a JavaServer Faces Application

The address-book application uses a JavaServer Faces web front end to allow users to enter contacts. While JavaServer Faces has a form input validation mechanism using tags in Facelets XHTML files, address-book doesn't use these validation tags. Bean Validation constraints in JavaServer Faces backing beans, in this case in the Contact entity, automatically trigger validation when the forms are submitted.

The following code snippet from the Create.xhtml Facelets file shows some of the input form for creating new Contact instances:

```
<h:form>
    <h:panelGrid columns="3">
        <h:outputLabel value="#{bundle.CreateContactLabel_firstName}"
                       for="firstName" />
        <h:inputText id="firstName"
                     value="#{contactController.selected.firstName}"
                     title="#{bundle.CreateContactTitle_firstName}" />
        <h:message for="firstName"
                   errorStyle="color: red"
                   infoStyle="color: green" />
        <h:outputLabel value="#{bundle.CreateContactLabel_lastName}"
                       for="lastName" />
        <h:inputText id="lastName"
                     value="#{contactController.selected.lastName}"
                     title="#{bundle.CreateContactTitle_lastName}" />
        <h:message for="lastName"
                   errorStyle="color: red"
                   infoStyle="color: green" />
        ...
    </h:panelGrid>
</h:form>
```

The <h:inputText> tags firstName and lastName are bound to the attributes in the Contact entity instance selected in the ContactController stateless session bean. Each <h:inputText> tag has an associated <h:message> tag that will display validation error messages. The form doesn't require any JavaServer Faces validation tags, however.

Building, Packaging, Deploying, and Running the address-book Application

This section describes how to build, package, deploy, and run the address-book application. You can do this using either NetBeans IDE or Ant.

▼ Building, Packaging, Deploying, and Running the address-book Application in NetBeans IDE

1   In NetBeans IDE, select File→Open Project.

2   In the Open Project dialog, navigate to:

     tut-install/examples/persistence/

3   Select the address-book folder.

4   Select the Open as Main Project and Open Required Projects check boxes.

5   Click Open Project.

6   In the Projects tab, right-click the address-book project and select Run.

     After the application has been deployed, a web browser window appears at the following URL:

     http://localhost:8080/address-book/

7   Click Show All Contact Items, then Create New Contact. Type values in the form fields; then click Save.

     If any of the values entered violate the constraints in Contact, an error message will appear in red beside the form field with the incorrect values.

▼ Building, Packaging, Deploying, and Running the address-book Application Using Ant

1   In a terminal window, go to:

     tut-install/examples/persistence/address-book

2 **Type the following command:**

```
ant
```

This will compile and assemble the address-book application.

3 **Type the following command:**

```
ant deploy
```

This will deploy the application to GlassFish Server.

4 **Open a web browser window and type the following URL:**

```
http://localhost:8080/address-book/
```

Tip – As a convenience, the all task will build, package, deploy, and run the application. To do this, type the following command:

```
ant all
```

---

5 **Click Show All Contact Items, then Create New Contact. Type values in the form fields; then click Save.**

If any of the values entered violate the constraints in Contact, an error message will appear in red beside the form field with the incorrect values.

21

The Java Persistence Query Language

The Java Persistence query language defines queries for entities and their persistent state. The query language allows you to write portable queries that work regardless of the underlying data store.

The query language uses the abstract persistence schemas of entities, including their relationships, for its data model and defines operators and expressions based on this data model. The scope of a query spans the abstract schemas of related entities that are packaged in the same persistence unit. The query language uses an SQL-like syntax to select objects or values based on entity abstract schema types and relationships among them.

This chapter relies on the material presented in earlier chapters. For conceptual information, see Chapter 19, "Introduction to the Java Persistence API." For code examples, see Chapter 20, "Running the Persistence Examples."

The following topics are addressed here:

Query Language Terminology

The following list defines some of the terms referred to in this chapter:

- **Abstract schema**: The persistent schema abstraction (persistent entities, their state, and their relationships) over which queries operate. The query language translates queries over this persistent schema abstraction into queries that are executed over the database schema to which entities are mapped.

- **Abstract schema type**: The type to which the persistent property of an entity evaluates in the abstract schema. That is, each persistent field or property in an entity has a corresponding state field of the same type in the abstract schema. The abstract schema type of an entity is derived from the entity class and the metadata information provided by Java language annotations.

- **Backus-Naur Form (BNF)**: A notation that describes the syntax of high-level languages. The syntax diagrams in this chapter are in BNF notation.

- **Navigation**: The traversal of relationships in a query language expression. The navigation operator is a period.

- **Path expression**: An expression that navigates to a entity's state or relationship field.

- **State field**: A persistent field of an entity.

- **Relationship field**: A persistent relationship field of an entity whose type is the abstract schema type of the related entity.

Creating Queries Using the Java Persistence Query Language

The `EntityManager.createQuery` and `EntityManager.createNamedQuery` methods are used to query the datastore by using Java Persistence query language queries.

The `createQuery` method is used to create *dynamic queries*, which are queries defined directly within an application's business logic:

```
public List findWithName(String name) {
return em.createQuery(
    "SELECT c FROM Customer c WHERE c.name LIKE :custName")
    .setParameter("custName", name)
    .setMaxResults(10)
    .getResultList();
}
```

The `createNamedQuery` method is used to create *static queries*, or queries that are defined in metadata by using the `javax.persistence.NamedQuery` annotation. The name element of @NamedQuery specifies the name of the query that will be used with the `createNamedQuery` method. The query element of @NamedQuery is the query:

```
@NamedQuery(
    name="findAllCustomersWithName",
    query="SELECT c FROM Customer c WHERE c.name LIKE :custName"
)
```

Here's an example of `createNamedQuery`, which uses the `@NamedQuery`:

```
@PersistenceContext
public EntityManager em;
...
customers = em.createNamedQuery("findAllCustomersWithName")
    .setParameter("custName", "Smith")
    .getResultList();
```

Named Parameters in Queries

Named parameters are query parameters that are prefixed with a colon (`:`). Named parameters in a query are bound to an argument by the following method:

```
javax.persistence.Query.setParameter(String name, Object value)
```

In the following example, the `name` argument to the `findWithName` business method is bound to the `:custName` named parameter in the query by calling `Query.setParameter`:

```
public List findWithName(String name) {
    return em.createQuery(
        "SELECT c FROM Customer c WHERE c.name LIKE :custName")
        .setParameter("custName", name)
        .getResultList();
}
```

Named parameters are case-sensitive and may be used by both dynamic and static queries.

Positional Parameters in Queries

You may use positional parameters instead of named parameters in queries. Positional parameters are prefixed with a question mark (`?`) followed the numeric position of the parameter in the query. The `Query.setParameter(integer position, Object value)` method is used to set the parameter values.

In the following example, the `findWithName` business method is rewritten to use input parameters:

```
public List findWithName(String name) {
    return em.createQuery(
        "SELECT c FROM Customer c WHERE c.name LIKE ?1")
```

```
        .setParameter(1, name)
        .getResultList();
}
```

Input parameters are numbered starting from 1. Input parameters are case-sensitive, and may be used by both dynamic and static queries.

Simplified Query Language Syntax

This section briefly describes the syntax of the query language so that you can quickly move on to "Example Queries" on page 385. When you are ready to learn about the syntax in more detail, see "Full Query Language Syntax" on page 390.

Select Statements

A select query has six clauses: SELECT, FROM, WHERE, GROUP BY, HAVING, and ORDER BY. The SELECT and FROM clauses are required, but the WHERE, GROUP BY, HAVING, and ORDER BY clauses are optional. Here is the high-level BNF syntax of a query language select query:

```
QL_statement ::= select_clause from_clause
  [where_clause][groupby_clause][having_clause][orderby_clause]
```

- The SELECT clause defines the types of the objects or values returned by the query.

- The FROM clause defines the scope of the query by declaring one or more identification variables, which can be referenced in the SELECT and WHERE clauses. An identification variable represents one of the following elements:

    - The abstract schema name of an entity

    - An element of a collection relationship

    - An element of a single-valued relationship

    - A member of a collection that is the multiple side of a one-to-many relationship

- The WHERE clause is a conditional expression that restricts the objects or values retrieved by the query. Although the clause is optional, most queries have a WHERE clause.

- The GROUP BY clause groups query results according to a set of properties.

- The HAVING clause is used with the GROUP BY clause to further restrict the query results according to a conditional expression.

- The ORDER BY clause sorts the objects or values returned by the query into a specified order.

Update and Delete Statements

Update and delete statements provide bulk operations over sets of entities. These statements have the following syntax:

```
update_statement :: = update_clause [where_clause]
delete_statement :: = delete_clause [where_clause]
```

The update and delete clauses determine the type of the entities to be updated or deleted. The WHERE clause may be used to restrict the scope of the update or delete operation.

Example Queries

The following queries are from the Player entity of the roster application, which is documented in "The roster Application" on page 369.

Simple Queries

If you are unfamiliar with the query language, these simple queries are a good place to start.

A Basic Select Query

```
SELECT p
FROM Player p
```

- **Data retrieved**: All players.
- **Description**: The FROM clause declares an identification variable named p, omitting the optional keyword AS. If the AS keyword were included, the clause would be written as follows:

```
FROM Player AS
 p
```

The Player element is the abstract schema name of the Player entity.

- **See also**: "Identification Variables" on page 396.

Eliminating Duplicate Values

```
SELECT DISTINCT
 p
FROM Player p
WHERE p.position = ?1
```

- **Data retrieved**: The players with the position specified by the query's parameter.
- **Description**: The DISTINCT keyword eliminates duplicate values.

  The WHERE clause restricts the players retrieved by checking their position, a persistent field of the Player entity. The ?1 element denotes the input parameter of the query.
- **See also**: "Input Parameters" on page 401 and "The DISTINCT Keyword" on page 411.

Using Named Parameters

```
SELECT DISTINCT p
FROM Player p
WHERE p.position = :position AND p.name = :name
```

- **Data retrieved**: The players having the specified positions and names.
- **Description**: The position and name elements are persistent fields of the Player entity. The WHERE clause compares the values of these fields with the named parameters of the query, set using the Query.setNamedParameter method. The query language denotes a named input parameter using a colon (:) followed by an identifier. The first input parameter is :position, the second is :name.

Queries That Navigate to Related Entities

In the query language, an expression can traverse, or navigate, to related entities. These expressions are the primary difference between the Java Persistence query language and SQL. Queries navigates to related entities, whereas SQL joins tables.

A Simple Query with Relationships

```
SELECT DISTINCT p
FROM Player p, IN(p.teams) t
```

- **Data retrieved**: All players who belong to a team.
- **Description**: The FROM clause declares two identification variables: p and t. The p variable represents the Player entity, and the t variable represents the related Team entity. The declaration for t references the previously declared p variable. The IN keyword signifies that teams is a collection of related entities. The p.teams expression navigates from a Player to its related Team. The period in the p.teams expression is the navigation operator.

  You may also use the JOIN statement to write the same query:

```
SELECT DISTINCT p
FROM Player p JOIN p.teams t
```

This query could also be rewritten as:

```
SELECT DISTINCT p
FROM Player p
WHERE p.team IS NOT EMPTY
```

Navigating to Single-Valued Relationship Fields

Use the JOIN clause statement to navigate to a single-valued relationship field:

```
SELECT t
 FROM Team t JOIN t.league l
 WHERE l.sport = 'soccer' OR l.sport ='football'
```

In this example, the query will return all teams that are in either soccer or football leagues.

Traversing Relationships with an Input Parameter

```
SELECT DISTINCT p
FROM Player p, IN (p.teams) AS t
WHERE t.city = :city
```

- **Data retrieved**: The players whose teams belong to the specified city.

- **Description**: This query is similar to the previous example but adds an input parameter. The AS keyword in the FROM clause is optional. In the WHERE clause, the period preceding the persistent variable city is a delimiter, not a navigation operator. Strictly speaking, expressions can navigate to relationship fields (related entities) but not to persistent fields. To access a persistent field, an expression uses the period as a delimiter.

  Expressions cannot navigate beyond (or further qualify) relationship fields that are collections. In the syntax of an expression, a collection-valued field is a terminal symbol. Because the teams field is a collection, the WHERE clause cannot specify p.teams.city (an illegal expression).

- **See also**: "Path Expressions" on page 398.

Traversing Multiple Relationships

```
SELECT DISTINCT p
FROM Player p, IN (p.teams) t
WHERE t.league = :league
```

- **Data retrieved**: The players who belong to the specified league.

- **Description**: The expressions in this query navigate over two relationships. The p.teams expression navigates the Player-Team relationship, and the t.league expression navigates the Team-League relationship.

In the other examples, the input parameters are String objects; in this example, the parameter is an object whose type is a League. This type matches the league relationship field in the comparison expression of the WHERE clause.

Navigating According to Related Fields

```
SELECT DISTINCT p
FROM Player p, IN (p.teams) t
WHERE t.league.sport = :sport
```

- **Data retrieved**: The players who participate in the specified sport.

- **Description**: The sport persistent field belongs to the League entity. To reach the sport field, the query must first navigate from the Player entity to Team (p.teams) and then from Team to the League entity (t.league). Because it is not a collection, the league relationship field can be followed by the sport persistent field.

Queries with Other Conditional Expressions

Every WHERE clause must specify a conditional expression, of which there are several kinds. In the previous examples, the conditional expressions are comparison expressions that test for equality. The following examples demonstrate some of the other kinds of conditional expressions. For descriptions of all conditional expressions, see "WHERE Clause" on page 400.

The LIKE Expression

```
SELECT p
 FROM Player p
 WHERE p.name LIKE 'Mich%'
```

- **Data retrieved**: All players whose names begin with "Mich."

- **Description**: The LIKE expression uses wildcard characters to search for strings that match the wildcard pattern. In this case, the query uses the LIKE expression and the % wildcard to find all players whose names begin with the string "Mich." For example, "Michael" and "Michelle" both match the wildcard pattern.

- **See also**: "LIKE Expressions" on page 403.

The IS NULL Expression

```
SELECT t
 FROM Team t
 WHERE t.league IS NULL
```

- **Data retrieved**: All teams not associated with a league.

- **Description**: The IS NULL expression can be used to check whether a relationship has been set between two entities. In this case, the query checks whether the teams are associated with any leagues and returns the teams that do not have a league.

- **See also**: "NULL Comparison Expressions" on page 403 and "NULL Values" on page 408.

The IS EMPTY Expression

```
SELECT p
FROM Player p
WHERE p.teams IS EMPTY
```

- **Data retrieved**: All players who do not belong to a team.

- **Description**: The teams relationship field of the Player entity is a collection. If a player does not belong to a team, the teams collection is empty, and the conditional expression is TRUE.

- **See also**: "Empty Collection Comparison Expressions" on page 404.

The BETWEEN Expression

```
SELECT DISTINCT p
FROM Player p
WHERE p.salary BETWEEN :lowerSalary AND :higherSalary
```

- **Data retrieved**: The players whose salaries fall within the range of the specified salaries.

- **Description**: This BETWEEN expression has three arithmetic expressions: a persistent field (p.salary) and the two input parameters (:lowerSalary and :higherSalary). The following expression is equivalent to the BETWEEN expression:

  ```
  p.salary >= :lowerSalary AND p.salary <= :higherSalary
  ```

- **See also**: "BETWEEN Expressions" on page 402.

Comparison Operators

```
SELECT DISTINCT p1
FROM Player p1, Player p2
WHERE p1.salary > p2.salary AND p2.name = :name
```

- **Data retrieved**: All players whose salaries are higher than the salary of the player with the specified name.

- **Description**: The FROM clause declares two identification variables (p1 and p2) of the same type (Player). Two identification variables are needed because the WHERE clause compares the salary of one player (p2) with that of the other players (p1).

- **See also**: "Identification Variables" on page 396.

Bulk Updates and Deletes

The following examples show how to use the UPDATE and DELETE expressions in queries. UPDATE and DELETE operate on multiple entities according to the condition or conditions set in the WHERE clause. The WHERE clause in UPDATE and DELETE queries follows the same rules as SELECT queries.

Update Queries

```
UPDATE Player p
SET p.status = 'inactive'
WHERE p.lastPlayed < :inactiveThresholdDate
```

- **Description**: This query sets the status of a set of players to inactive if the player's last game was longer than the date specified in inactiveThresholdDate.

Delete Queries

```
DELETE
FROM Player p
WHERE p.status = 'inactive'
AND p.teams IS EMPTY
```

- **Description**: This query deletes all inactive players who are not on a team.

Full Query Language Syntax

This section discusses the query language syntax, as defined in the Java Persistence API 2.0 specification available at http://jcp.org/en/jsr/detail?id=317. Much of the following material paraphrases or directly quotes the specification.

BNF Symbols

Table 21–1 describes the BNF symbols used in this chapter.

TABLE 21–1 BNF Symbol Summary

Symbol	Description
::=	The element to the left of the symbol is defined by the constructs on the right.
*	The preceding construct may occur zero or more times.
{...}	The constructs within the braces are grouped together.
[...]	The constructs within the brackets are optional.
|	An exclusive OR.
BOLDFACE	A keyword; although capitalized in the BNF diagram, keywords are not case-sensitive.
White space	A whitespace character can be a space, a horizontal tab, or a line feed.

BNF Grammar of the Java Persistence Query Language

Here is the entire BNF diagram for the query language:

```
QL_statement ::= select_statement | update_statement | delete_statement
select_statement ::= select_clause from_clause [where_clause] [groupby_clause]
    [having_clause] [orderby_clause]
update_statement ::= update_clause [where_clause]
delete_statement ::= delete_clause [where_clause]
from_clause ::=
    FROM identification_variable_declaration
        {, {identification_variable_declaration |
            collection_member_declaration}}*
identification_variable_declaration ::=
        range_variable_declaration { join | fetch_join }*
range_variable_declaration ::= abstract_schema_name [AS]
        identification_variable
join ::= join_spec join_association_path_expression [AS]
        identification_variable
fetch_join ::= join_specFETCH join_association_path_expression
association_path_expression ::=
        collection_valued_path_expression |
        single_valued_association_path_expression
join_spec::= [LEFT [OUTER] |INNER] JOIN
join_association_path_expression ::=
        join_collection_valued_path_expression |
        join_single_valued_association_path_expression
join_collection_valued_path_expression::=
    identification_variable.collection_valued_association_field
join_single_valued_association_path_expression::=
        identification_variable.single_valued_association_field
collection_member_declaration ::=
        IN (collection_valued_path_expression) [AS]
        identification_variable
single_valued_path_expression ::=
        state_field_path_expression |
        single_valued_association_path_expression
state_field_path_expression ::=
    {identification_variable |
    single_valued_association_path_expression}.state_field
single_valued_association_path_expression ::=
    identification_variable.{single_valued_association_field.}*
    single_valued_association_field
collection_valued_path_expression ::=
    identification_variable.{single_valued_association_field.}*
    collection_valued_association_field
state_field ::=
    {embedded_class_state_field.}*simple_state_field
update_clause ::=UPDATE abstract_schema_name [[AS]
    identification_variable] SET update_item {, update_item}*
update_item ::= [identification_variable.]{state_field |
    single_valued_association_field} = new_value
new_value ::=
    simple_arithmetic_expression |
    string_primary |
    datetime_primary |
```

```
            boolean_primary |
            enum_primary simple_entity_expression |
            NULL
    delete_clause ::= DELETE FROM abstract_schema_name [[AS]
        identification_variable]
    select_clause ::= SELECT [DISTINCT] select_expression {,
        select_expression}*
    select_expression ::=
        single_valued_path_expression |
        aggregate_expression |
        identification_variable |
        OBJECT(identification_variable) |
        constructor_expression
    constructor_expression ::=
        NEW constructor_name(constructor_item {,
        constructor_item}*)
    constructor_item ::= single_valued_path_expression |
        aggregate_expression
    aggregate_expression ::=
        {AVG |MAX |MIN |SUM} ([DISTINCT]
            state_field_path_expression) |
        COUNT ([DISTINCT] identification_variable |
            state_field_path_expression |
            single_valued_association_path_expression)
    where_clause ::= WHERE conditional_expression
    groupby_clause ::= GROUP BY groupby_item {, groupby_item}*
    groupby_item ::= single_valued_path_expression
    having_clause ::= HAVING conditional_expression
    orderby_clause ::= ORDER BY orderby_item {, orderby_item}*
    orderby_item ::= state_field_path_expression [ASC |DESC]
    subquery ::= simple_select_clause subquery_from_clause
        [where_clause] [groupby_clause] [having_clause]
    subquery_from_clause ::=
        FROM subselect_identification_variable_declaration
            {, subselect_identification_variable_declaration}*
    subselect_identification_variable_declaration ::=
        identification_variable_declaration |
        association_path_expression [AS] identification_variable |
        collection_member_declaration
    simple_select_clause ::= SELECT [DISTINCT]
        simple_select_expression
    simple_select_expression::=
        single_valued_path_expression |
        aggregate_expression |
        identification_variable
    conditional_expression ::= conditional_term |
        conditional_expression OR conditional_term
    conditional_term ::= conditional_factor | conditional_term AND
        conditional_factor
    conditional_factor ::= [NOT] conditional_primary
    conditional_primary ::= simple_cond_expression |(
        conditional_expression)
    simple_cond_expression ::=
        comparison_expression |
        between_expression |
        like_expression |
        in_expression |
        null_comparison_expression |
        empty_collection_comparison_expression |
```

```
        collection_member_expression |
        exists_expression
between_expression ::=
        arithmetic_expression [NOT] BETWEEN
            arithmetic_expressionAND arithmetic_expression |
        string_expression [NOT] BETWEEN string_expression AND
            string_expression |
        datetime_expression [NOT] BETWEEN
            datetime_expression AND datetime_expression
in_expression ::=
        state_field_path_expression [NOT] IN (in_item {, in_item}*
        | subquery)
in_item ::= literal | input_parameter
like_expression ::=
        string_expression [NOT] LIKE pattern_value [ESCAPE
            escape_character]
null_comparison_expression ::=
        {single_valued_path_expression | input_parameter} IS [NOT]
            NULL
empty_collection_comparison_expression ::=
        collection_valued_path_expression IS [NOT] EMPTY
collection_member_expression ::= entity_expression
        [NOT] MEMBER [OF] collection_valued_path_expression
exists_expression::= [NOT] EXISTS (subquery)
all_or_any_expression ::= {ALL |ANY |SOME} (subquery)
comparison_expression ::=
        string_expression comparison_operator {string_expression |
        all_or_any_expression} |
        boolean_expression {= |<> } {boolean_expression |
        all_or_any_expression} |
        enum_expression {= |<> } {enum_expression |
        all_or_any_expression} |
        datetime_expression comparison_operator
            {datetime_expression | all_or_any_expression} |
        entity_expression {= |<> } {entity_expression |
        all_or_any_expression} |
        arithmetic_expression comparison_operator
            {arithmetic_expression | all_or_any_expression}
comparison_operator ::= = |> |>= |< |<= |<>
arithmetic_expression ::= simple_arithmetic_expression |
        (subquery)
simple_arithmetic_expression ::=
        arithmetic_term | simple_arithmetic_expression {+ |- }
            arithmetic_term
arithmetic_term ::= arithmetic_factor | arithmetic_term {* |/ }
        arithmetic_factor
arithmetic_factor ::= [{+ |- }] arithmetic_primary
arithmetic_primary ::=
        state_field_path_expression |
        numeric_literal |
        (simple_arithmetic_expression) |
        input_parameter |
        functions_returning_numerics |
        aggregate_expression
string_expression ::= string_primary | (subquery)
string_primary ::=
        state_field_path_expression |
        string_literal |
        input_parameter |
```

```
        functions_returning_strings |
        aggregate_expression
datetime_expression ::= datetime_primary | (subquery)
datetime_primary ::=
        state_field_path_expression |
        input_parameter |
        functions_returning_datetime |
        aggregate_expression
boolean_expression ::= boolean_primary | (subquery)
boolean_primary ::=
        state_field_path_expression |
        boolean_literal |
        input_parameter
 enum_expression ::= enum_primary | (subquery)
enum_primary ::=
        state_field_path_expression |
        enum_literal |
        input_parameter
entity_expression ::=
        single_valued_association_path_expression |
            simple_entity_expression
simple_entity_expression ::=
        identification_variable |
        input_parameter
functions_returning_numerics::=
        LENGTH(string_primary) |
        LOCATE(string_primary, string_primary[,
            simple_arithmetic_expression]) |
        ABS(simple_arithmetic_expression) |
        SQRT(simple_arithmetic_expression) |
        MOD(simple_arithmetic_expression,
            simple_arithmetic_expression) |
        SIZE(collection_valued_path_expression)
functions_returning_datetime ::=
        CURRENT_DATE |
        CURRENT_TIME |
        CURRENT_TIMESTAMP
functions_returning_strings ::=
        CONCAT(string_primary, string_primary) |
        SUBSTRING(string_primary,
            simple_arithmetic_expression,
            simple_arithmetic_expression)|
        TRIM([[trim_specification] [trim_character] FROM]
            string_primary) |
        LOWER(string_primary) |
        UPPER(string_primary)
trim_specification ::= LEADING | TRAILING | BOTH
```

FROM Clause

The FROM clause defines the domain of the query by declaring identification variables.

Identifiers

An identifier is a sequence of one or more characters. The first character must be a valid first character (letter, $, _) in an identifier of the Java programming language, hereafter in this chapter called simply "Java". Each subsequent character in the sequence must be a valid nonfirst character (letter, digit, $, _) in a Java identifier. (For details, see the Java SE API documentation of the `isJavaIdentifierStart` and `isJavaIdentifierPart` methods of the `Character` class.) The question mark (?) is a reserved character in the query language and cannot be used in an identifier.

A query language identifier is case-sensitive, with two exceptions:

- Keywords
- Identification variables

An identifier cannot be the same as a query language keyword. Here is a list of query language keywords:

ABS	ALL	AND	ANY	AS
ASC	AVG	BETWEEN	BIT_LENGTH	BOTH
BY	CASE	CHAR_LENGTH	CHARACTER_LENGTH	CLASS
COALESCE	CONCAT	COUNT	CURRENT_DATE	CURRENT_TIMESTAMP
DELETE	DESC	DISTINCT	ELSE	EMPTY
END	ENTRY	ESCAPE	EXISTS	FALSE
FETCH	FROM	GROUP	HAVING	IN
INDEX	INNER	IS	JOIN	KEY
LEADING	LEFT	LENGTH	LIKE	LOCATE
LOWER	MAX	MEMBER	MIN	MOD
NEW	NOT	NULL	NULLIF	OBJECT
OF	OR	ORDER	OUTER	POSITION
SELECT	SET	SIZE	SOME	SQRT
SUBSTRING	SUM	THEN	TRAILING	TRIM
TRUE	TYPE	UNKNOWN	UPDATE	UPPER
VALUE	WHEN	WHERE		

It is not recommended that you use an SQL keyword as an identifier, because the list of keywords may expand to include other reserved SQL words in the future.

Identification Variables

An *identification variable* is an identifier declared in the FROM clause. Although they can reference identification variables, the SELECT and WHERE clauses cannot declare them. All identification variables must be declared in the FROM clause.

Because it is an identifier, an identification variable has the same naming conventions and restrictions as an identifier, with the exception that an identification variables is case-insensitive. For example, an identification variable cannot be the same as a query language keyword. (See the preceding section for more naming rules.) Also, within a given persistence unit, an identification variable name must not match the name of any entity or abstract schema.

The FROM clause can contain multiple declarations, separated by commas. A declaration can reference another identification variable that has been previously declared (to the left). In the following FROM clause, the variable t references the previously declared variable p:

```
FROM Player p, IN (p.teams) AS t
```

Even if it is not used in the WHERE clause, an identification variable's declaration can affect the results of the query. For example, compare the next two queries. The following query returns all players, whether or not they belong to a team:

```
SELECT p
FROM Player p
```

In contrast, because it declares the t identification variable, the next query fetches all players who belong to a team:

```
SELECT p
FROM Player p, IN (p.teams) AS t
```

The following query returns the same results as the preceding query, but the WHERE clause makes it easier to read:

```
SELECT p
FROM Player p
WHERE p.teams IS NOT EMPTY
```

An identification variable always designates a reference to a single value whose type is that of the expression used in the declaration. There are two kinds of declarations: range variable and collection member.

Range Variable Declarations

To declare an identification variable as an abstract schema type, you specify a range variable declaration. In other words, an identification variable can range over the abstract schema type of an entity. In the following example, an identification variable named p represents the abstract schema named Player:

```
FROM Player p
```

A range variable declaration can include the optional AS operator:

```
FROM Player AS p
```

To obtain objects, a query usually uses path expressions to navigate through the relationships. But for those objects that cannot be obtained by navigation, you can use a range variable declaration to designate a starting point, or *root*.

If the query compares multiple values of the same abstract schema type, the FROM clause must declare multiple identification variables for the abstract schema:

```
FROM Player p1, Player p2
```

For an example of such a query, see "Comparison Operators" on page 389.

Collection Member Declarations

In a one-to-many relationship, the multiple side consists of a collection of entities. An identification variable can represent a member of this collection. To access a collection member, the path expression in the variable's declaration navigates through the relationships in the abstract schema. (For more information on path expressions, see "Path Expressions" on page 398.) Because a path expression can be based on another path expression, the navigation can traverse several relationships. See "Traversing Multiple Relationships" on page 387.

A collection member declaration must include the IN operator but can omit the optional AS operator.

In the following example, the entity represented by the abstract schema named Player has a relationship field called teams. The identification variable called t represents a single member of the teams collection.

```
FROM Player p, IN (p.tea
ms) t
```

Joins

The JOIN operator is used to traverse over relationships between entities and is functionally similar to the IN operator.

In the following example, the query joins over the relationship between customers and orders:

```
SELECT c
 FROM Customer c JOIN c.orders o
 WHERE c.status = 1 AND o.totalPrice > 10000
```

The INNER keyword is optional:

```
SELECT c
 FROM Customer c INNER JOIN c.orders o
 WHERE c.status = 1 AND o.totalPrice > 10000
```

These examples are equivalent to the following query, which uses the IN operator:

```
SELECT c
 FROM Customer c, IN(c.orders) o
 WHERE c.status = 1 AND o.totalPrice > 10000
```

You can also join a single-valued relationship:

```
SELECT t
 FROM Team t JOIN t.league l
 WHERE l.sport = :sport
```

A LEFT JOIN or LEFT OUTER JOIN retrieves a set of entities where matching values in the join condition may be absent. The OUTER keyword is optional.

```
SELECT c.name, o.totalPrice
FROM Order o LEFT JOIN o.customer c
```

A FETCH JOIN is a join operation that returns associated entities as a side effect of running the query. In the following example, the query returns a set of departments and, as a side effect, the associated employees of the departments, even though the employees were not explicitly retrieved by the SELECT clause.

```
SELECT d
FROM Department d LEFT JOIN FETCH d.employees
WHERE d.deptno = 1
```

Path Expressions

Path expressions are important constructs in the syntax of the query language, for several reasons. First, path expressions define navigation paths through the relationships in the abstract schema. These path definitions affect both the scope and the results of a query. Second, path expressions can appear in any of the main clauses of a query (SELECT, DELETE, HAVING, UPDATE, WHERE, FROM, GROUP BY, ORDER BY). Finally, although much of the query language is a subset of SQL, path expressions are extensions not found in SQL.

Examples of Path Expressions

Here, the WHERE clause contains a single_valued_path_expression; the p is an identification variable, and salary is a persistent field of Player:

```
SELECT DISTINCT p
FROM Player p
 WHERE p.salary BETWEEN :lowerSalary AND :higherSalary
```

Here, the WHERE clause also contains a `single_valued_path_expression`; t is an identification variable, league is a single-valued relationship field, and sport is a persistent field of league:

```
SELECT DISTINCT p
FROM Player p, IN (p.teams) t
 WHERE t.league.sport = :sport
```

Here, the WHERE clause contains a `collection_valued_path_expression`; p is an identification variable, and teams designates a collection-valued relationship field:

```
SELECT DISTINCT p
FROM Player p
 WHERE p.teams IS EMPTY
```

Expression Types

The type of a path expression is the type of the object represented by the ending element, which can be one of the following:

- Persistent field
- Single-valued relationship field
- Collection-valued relationship field

For example, the type of the expression p.salary is double because the terminating persistent field (salary) is a double.

In the expression p.teams, the terminating element is a collection-valued relationship field (teams). This expression's type is a collection of the abstract schema type named Team. Because Team is the abstract schema name for the Team entity, this type maps to the entity. For more information on the type mapping of abstract schemas, see "Return Types" on page 410.

Navigation

A path expression enables the query to navigate to related entities. The terminating elements of an expression determine whether navigation is allowed. If an expression contains a single-valued relationship field, the navigation can continue to an object that is related to the field. However, an expression cannot navigate beyond a persistent field or a collection-valued relationship field. For example, the expression p.teams.league.sport is illegal because teams is a collection-valued relationship field. To reach the sport field, the FROM clause could define an identification variable named t for the teams field:

```
FROM Player AS p, IN (p.teams) t
 WHERE t.league.sport = 'soccer'
```

WHERE **Clause**

The WHERE clause specifies a conditional expression that limits the values returned by the query. The query returns all corresponding values in the data store for which the conditional expression is TRUE. Although usually specified, the WHERE clause is optional. If the WHERE clause is omitted, the query returns all values. The high-level syntax for the WHERE clause follows:

```
where_clause ::= WHERE conditional_expression
```

Literals

There are four kinds of literals: string, numeric, Boolean, and enum.

- **String literals**: A string literal is enclosed in single quotes:

  ```
  'Duke'
  ```

  If a string literal contains a single quote, you indicate the quote by using two single quotes:

  ```
  'Duke''s'
  ```

  Like a Java String, a string literal in the query language uses the Unicode character encoding.

- **Numeric literals**: There are two types of numeric literals: exact and approximate.

  An exact numeric literal is a numeric value without a decimal point, such as 65, –233, and +12. Using the Java integer syntax, exact numeric literals support numbers in the range of a Java long.

  An approximate numeric literal is a numeric value in scientific notation, such as 57., –85.7, and +2.1. Using the syntax of the Java floating-point literal, approximate numeric literals support numbers in the range of a Java double.

- **Boolean literals**: A Boolean literal is either TRUE or FALSE. These keywords are not case-sensitive.

- **Enum literals**: The Java Persistence query language supports the use of enum literals using the Java enum literal syntax. The enum class name must be specified as a fully qualified class name:

  ```
  SELECT e
   FROM Employee e
   WHERE e.status = com.xyz.EmployeeStatus.FULL_TIME
  ```

Input Parameters

An input parameter can be either a named parameter or a positional parameter.

- A named input parameter is designated by a colon (:) followed by a string; for example, :name.
- A positional input parameter is designated by a question mark (?) followed by an integer. For example, the first input parameter is ?1, the second is ?2, and so forth.

The following rules apply to input parameters.

- They can be used only in a WHERE or HAVING clause.
- Positional parameters must be numbered, starting with the integer 1.
- Named parameters and positional parameters may not be mixed in a single query.
- Named parameters are case-sensitive.

Conditional Expressions

A WHERE clause consists of a conditional expression, which is evaluated from left to right within a precedence level. You can change the order of evaluation by using parentheses.

Operators and Their Precedence

Table 21–2 lists the query language operators in order of decreasing precedence.

TABLE 21–2 Query Language Order Precedence

Type	Precedence Order
Navigation	. (a period)
Arithmetic	+ – (unary)
	* / (multiplication and division)
	+ – (addition and subtraction)

TABLE 21–2 Query Language Order Precedence   *(Continued)*

Type	Precedence Order
Comparison	=
	>
	>=
	<
	<=
	<> (not equal)
	[NOT] BETWEEN
	[NOT] LIKE
	[NOT] IN
	IS [NOT] NULL
	IS [NOT] EMPTY
	[NOT] MEMBER OF
Logical	NOT
	AND
	OR

BETWEEN Expressions

A BETWEEN expression determines whether an arithmetic expression falls within a range of values.

These two expressions are equivalent:

```
p.age BETWEEN 15 AND 19
 p.age >= 15 AND p.age <= 19
```

The following two expressions also are equivalent:

```
p.age NOT BETWEEN 15 AND 19
 p.age < 15 OR p.age > 19
```

If an arithmetic expression has a NULL value, the value of the BETWEEN expression is unknown.

IN Expressions

An IN expression determines whether a string belongs to a set of string literals or whether a number belongs to a set of number values.

The path expression must have a string or numeric value. If the path expression has a NULL value, the value of the IN expression is unknown.

In the following example, the expression is TRUE if the country is UK , but FALSE if the country is Peru.

```
o.country IN ('UK', 'US', 'France')
```

You may also use input parameters:

```
o.country IN ('UK', 'US', 'France', :country)
```

LIKE Expressions

A LIKE expression determines whether a wildcard pattern matches a string.

The path expression must have a string or numeric value. If this value is NULL, the value of the LIKE expression is unknown. The pattern value is a string literal that can contain wildcard characters. The underscore (_) wildcard character represents any single character. The percent (%) wildcard character represents zero or more characters. The ESCAPE clause specifies an escape character for the wildcard characters in the pattern value. Table 21–3 shows some sample LIKE expressions.

TABLE 21–3   LIKE Expression Examples

Expression	TRUE	FALSE
address.phone LIKE '12%3'	'123'	'1234'
	'12993'	
asentence.word LIKE 'l_se'	'lose'	'loose'
aword.underscored LIKE '_%' ESCAPE '\'	'_foo'	'bar'
address.phone NOT LIKE '12%3'	'1234'	'123'
		'12993'

NULL Comparison Expressions

A NULL comparison expression tests whether a single-valued path expression or an input parameter has a NULL value. Usually, the NULL comparison expression is used to test whether a single-valued relationship has been set:

```
SELECT t
 FROM Team t
 WHERE t.league IS NULL
```

This query selects all teams where the league relationship is not set. Note that the following query is *not* equivalent:

```
SELECT t
 FROM Team t
 WHERE t.league = NULL
```

The comparison with NULL using the equals operator (=) always returns an unknown value, even if the relationship is not set. The second query will always return an empty result.

Empty Collection Comparison Expressions

The IS [NOT] EMPTY comparison expression tests whether a collection-valued path expression has no elements. In other words, it tests whether a collection-valued relationship has been set.

If the collection-valued path expression is NULL, the empty collection comparison expression has a NULL value.

Here is an example that finds all orders that do not have any line items:

```
SELECT o
FROM Order o
WHERE o.lineItems IS EMPTY
```

Collection Member Expressions

The [NOT] MEMBER [OF] collection member expression determines whether a value is a member of a collection. The value and the collection members must have the same type.

If either the collection-valued or single-valued path expression is unknown, the collection member expression is unknown. If the collection-valued path expression designates an empty collection, the collection member expression is FALSE.

The OF keyword is optional.

The following example tests whether a line item is part of an order:

```
SELECT o
 FROM Order o
 WHERE :lineItem MEMBER OF o.lineItems
```

Subqueries

Subqueries may be used in the WHERE or HAVING clause of a query. Subqueries must be surrounded by parentheses.

The following example finds all customers who have placed more than ten orders:

```
SELECT c
FROM Customer c
WHERE (SELECT COUNT(o) FROM c.orders o) > 10
```

Subqueries may contain EXISTS, ALL, and ANY expressions.

- **EXISTS expressions**: The [NOT] EXISTS expression is used with a subquery and is true only if the result of the subquery consists of one or more values and is false otherwise.

  The following example finds all employees whose spouses are also employees:

  ```
  SELECT DISTINCT emp
  FROM Employee emp
  WHERE EXISTS (
      SELECT spouseEmp
      FROM Employee spouseEmp
      WHERE spouseEmp = emp.spouse)
  ```

- **ALL and ANY expressions**: The ALL expression is used with a subquery and is true if all the values returned by the subquery are true or if the subquery is empty.

  The ANY expression is used with a subquery and is true if some of the values returned by the subquery are true. An ANY expression is false if the subquery result is empty or if all the values returned are false. The SOME keyword is synonymous with ANY.

  The ALL and ANY expressions are used with the =, <, <=, >, >=, and <> comparison operators.

  The following example finds all employees whose salaries are higher than the salaries of the managers in the employee's department:

  ```
  SELECT emp
  FROM Employee emp
  WHERE emp.salary > ALL (
      SELECT m.salary
      FROM Manager m
      WHERE m.department = emp.department)
  ```

Functional Expressions

The query language includes several string, arithmetic, and date/time functions that may be used in the SELECT, WHERE, or HAVING clause of a query. The functions are listed in Table 21–4, Table 21–5, and Table 21–6.

In Table 21–4, the start and length arguments are of type int and designate positions in the String argument. The first position in a string is designated by 1.

TABLE 21–4   String Expressions

Function Syntax	Return Type
CONCAT(String, String)	String
LENGTH(String)	int
LOCATE(String, String [, start])	int
SUBSTRING(String, start, length)	String
TRIM([[LEADING|TRAILING|BOTH] char) FROM] (String)	String
LOWER(String)	String
UPPER(String)	String

The CONCAT function concatenates two strings into one string.

The LENGTH function returns the length of a string in characters as an integer.

The LOCATE function returns the position of a given string within a string. This function returns the first position at which the string was found as an integer. The first argument is the string to be located. The second argument is the string to be searched. The optional third argument is an integer that represents the starting string position. By default, LOCATE starts at the beginning of the string. The starting position of a string is 1. If the string cannot be located, LOCATE returns 0.

The SUBSTRING function returns a string that is a substring of the first argument based on the starting position and length.

The TRIM function trims the specified character from the beginning and/or end of a string. If no character is specified, TRIM removes spaces or blanks from the string. If the optional LEADING specification is used, TRIM removes only the leading characters from the string. If the optional TRAILING specification is used, TRIM removes only the trailing characters from the string. The default is BOTH, which removes the leading and trailing characters from the string.

The LOWER and UPPER functions convert a string to lowercase or uppercase, respectively.

In Table 21–5, the number argument can be an int, a float, or a double.

TABLE 21-5   Arithmetic Expressions

Function Syntax	Return Type
ABS(number)	int, float, or double
MOD(int, int)	int
SQRT(double)	double
SIZE(Collection)	int

The ABS function takes a numeric expression and returns a number of the same type as the argument.

The MOD function returns the remainder of the first argument divided by the second.

The SQRT function returns the square root of a number.

The SIZE function returns an integer of the number of elements in the given collection.

In Table 21-6, the date/time functions return the date, time, or timestamp on the database server.

TABLE 21-6   Date/Time Expressions

Function Syntax	Return Type
CURRENT_DATE	java.sql.Date
CURRENT_TIME	java.sql.Time
CURRENT_TIMESTAMP	java.sql.Timestamp

Case Expressions

Case expressions change based on a condition, similar to the case keyword of the Java programming language. The CASE keyword indicates the start of a case expression, and the expression is terminated by the END keyword. The WHEN and THEN keywords define individual conditions, and the ELSE keyword defines the default condition should none of the other conditions be satisfied.

The following query selects the name of a person and a conditional string, depending on the subtype of the Person entity. If the subtype is Student, the string kid is returned . If the subtype is Guardian or Staff, the string adult is returned. If the entity is some other subtype of Person, the string unknown is returned.

```
SELECT p.name
CASE TYPE(p)
  WHEN Student THEN 'kid'
```

```
        WHEN Guardian THEN 'adult'
        WHEN Staff THEN 'adult'
        ELSE 'unknown'
END
FROM Person p
```

The following query sets a discount for various types of customers. Gold-level customers get a 20% discount, silver-level customers get a 15% discount, bronze-level customers get a 10% discount, and everyone else gets a 5% discount.

```
UPDATE Customer c
SET c.discount =
    CASE c.level
        WHEN 'Gold' THEN 20
        WHEN 'SILVER' THEN 15
        WHEN 'Bronze' THEN 10
        ELSE 5
    END
```

NULL Values

If the target of a reference is not in the persistent store, the target is NULL. For conditional expressions containing NULL, the query language uses the semantics defined by SQL92. Briefly, these semantics are as follows.

- If a comparison or arithmetic operation has an unknown value, it yields a NULL value.

- Two NULL values are not equal. Comparing two NULL values yields an unknown value.

- The IS NULL test converts a NULL persistent field or a single-valued relationship field to TRUE. The IS NOT NULL test converts them to FALSE.

- Boolean operators and conditional tests use the three-valued logic defined by Table 21–7 and Table 21–8. (In these tables, T stands for TRUE, F for FALSE, and U for unknown.)

TABLE 21–7   AND Operator Logic

AND	T	F	U
T	T	F	U
F	F	F	F
U	U	F	U

TABLE 21-8 OR Operator Logic

OR	T	F	U
T	T	T	T
F	T	F	U
U	T	U	U

Equality Semantics

In the query language, only values of the same type can be compared. However, this rule has one exception: Exact and approximate numeric values can be compared. In such a comparison, the required type conversion adheres to the rules of Java numeric promotion.

The query language treats compared values as if they were Java types and not as if they represented types in the underlying data store. For example, a persistent field that could be either an integer or a NULL must be designated as an Integer object and not as an int primitive. This designation is required because a Java object can be NULL, but a primitive cannot.

Two strings are equal only if they contain the same sequence of characters. Trailing blanks are significant; for example, the strings 'abc' and 'abc ' are not equal.

Two entities of the same abstract schema type are equal only if their primary keys have the same value. Table 21–9 shows the operator logic of a negation, and Table 21–10 shows the truth values of conditional tests.

TABLE 21-9 NOT Operator Logic

NOT Value	Value
T	F
F	T
U	U

TABLE 21-10 Conditional Test

Conditional Test	T	F	U
Expression IS TRUE	T	F	F
Expression IS FALSE	F	T	F
Expression is unknown	F	F	T

SELECT **Clause**

The SELECT clause defines the types of the objects or values returned by the query.

Return Types

The return type of the SELECT clause is defined by the result types of the select expressions contained within it. If multiple expressions are used, the result of the query is an Object[], and the elements in the array correspond to the order of the expressions in the SELECT clause and in type to the result types of each expression.

A SELECT clause cannot specify a collection-valued expression. For example, the SELECT clause p.teams is invalid because teams is a collection. However, the clause in the following query is valid because the t is a single element of the teams collection:

```
SELECT t
FROM Player p, IN (p.teams) t
```

The following query is an example of a query with multiple expressions in the SELECT clause:

```
SELECT c.name, c.country.name
 FROM customer c
 WHERE c.lastname = 'Coss' AND c.firstname = 'Roxane'
```

This query returns a list of Object[] elements; the first array element is a string denoting the customer name, and the second array element is a string denoting the name of the customer's country.

The result of a query may be the result of an aggregate function, listed in Table 21–11.

TABLE 21–11   Aggregate Functions in Select Statements

Name	Return Type	Description
AVG	Double	Returns the mean average of the fields
COUNT	Long	Returns the total number of results
MAX	The type of the field	Returns the highest value in the result set
MIN	The type of the field	Returns the lowest value in the result set

TABLE 21-11   Aggregate Functions in Select Statements   *(Continued)*

Name	Return Type	Description
SUM	`Long` (for integral fields) `Double` (for floating-point fields) `BigInteger` (for `BigInteger` fields) `BigDecimal` (for `BigDecimal` fields)	Returns the sum of all the values in the result set

For select method queries with an aggregate function (`AVG`, `COUNT`, `MAX`, `MIN`, or `SUM`) in the `SELECT` clause, the following rules apply:

- The `AVG`, `MAX`, `MIN`, and `SUM` functions return `null` if there are no values to which the function can be applied.

- The `COUNT` function returns 0 if there are no values to which the function can be applied.

The following example returns the average order quantity:

```
SELECT AVG(o.quantity)
 FROM Order o
```

The following example returns the total cost of the items ordered by Roxane Coss:

```
SELECT SUM(l.price)
FROM Order o JOIN o.lineItems l JOIN o.customer c
WHERE c.lastname = 'Coss' AND c.firstname = 'Roxane'
```

The following example returns the total number of orders:

```
SELECT COUNT(o)
FROM Order o
```

The following example returns the total number of items that have prices in Hal Incandenza's order:

```
SELECT COUNT(l.price)
FROM Order o JOIN o.lineItems l JOIN o.customer c
WHERE c.lastname = 'Incandenza' AND c.firstname = 'Hal'
```

The DISTINCT Keyword

The `DISTINCT` keyword eliminates duplicate return values. If a query returns a `java.util.Collection`, which allows duplicates, you must specify the `DISTINCT` keyword to eliminate duplicates.

Constructor Expressions

Constructor expressions allow you to return Java instances that store a query result element instead of an `Object[]`.

The following query creates a `CustomerDetail` instance per `Customer` matching the `WHERE` clause. A `CustomerDetail` stores the customer name and customer's country name. So the query returns a `List` of `CustomerDetail` instances:

```
SELECT NEW com.xyz.CustomerDetail(c.name, c.country.name)
 FROM customer c
WHERE c.lastname = 'Coss' AND c.firstname = 'Roxane'
```

ORDER BY Clause

As its name suggests, the ORDER BY clause orders the values or objects returned by the query.

If the ORDER BY clause contains multiple elements, the left-to-right sequence of the elements determines the high-to-low precedence.

The ASC keyword specifies ascending order, the default, and the DESC keyword indicates descending order.

When using the ORDER BY clause, the SELECT clause must return an orderable set of objects or values. You cannot order the values or objects for values or objects not returned by the SELECT clause. For example, the following query is valid because the ORDER BY clause uses the objects returned by the SELECT clause:

```
SELECT o
FROM Customer c JOIN c.orders o JOIN c.address a
WHERE a.state = 'CA'
ORDER BY o.quantity, o.totalcost
```

The following example is *not* valid, because the ORDER BY clause uses a value not returned by the SELECT clause:

```
SELECT p.product_name
FROM Order o, IN(o.lineItems) l JOIN o.customer c
WHERE c.lastname = 'Faehmel' AND c.firstname = 'Robert'
ORDER BY o.quantity
```

GROUP BY and HAVING Clauses

The GROUP BY clause allows you to group values according to a set of properties.

The following query groups the customers by their country and returns the number of customers per country:

```
SELECT c.country, COUNT(c)
 FROM Customer c GROUP BY c.country
```

The HAVING clause is used with the GROUP BY clause to further restrict the returned result of a query.

The following query groups orders by the status of their customer and returns the customer status plus the average `totalPrice` for all orders where the corresponding customers has the same status. In addition, it considers only customers with status 1, 2, or 3, so orders of other customers are not taken into account:

```
SELECT c.status, AVG(o.totalPrice)
 FROM Order o JOIN o.customer c
GROUP BY c.status HAVING c.status IN (1, 2, 3)
```

22

Using the Criteria API to Create Queries

The Criteria API is used to define queries for entities and their persistent state by creating query-defining objects. Criteria queries are written using Java programming language APIs, are typesafe, and are portable. Such queries work regardless of the underlying data store.

The following topics are addressed here:

- "Overview of the Criteria and Metamodel APIs" on page 415
- "Using the Metamodel API to Model Entity Classes" on page 417
- "Using the Criteria API and Metamodel API to Create Basic Typesafe Queries" on page 418

Overview of the Criteria and Metamodel APIs

Similar to JPQL, the Criteria API is based on the abstract schema of persistent entities, their relationships, and embedded objects. The Criteria API operates on this abstract schema to allow developers to find, modify, and delete persistent entities by invoking Java Persistence API entity operations. The Metamodel API works in concert with the Criteria API to model persistent entity classes for Criteria queries.

The Criteria API and JPQL are closely related and are designed to allow similar operations in their queries. Developers familiar with JPQL syntax will find equivalent object-level operations in the Criteria API.

The following simple Criteria query returns all instances of the Pet entity in the data source:

```
EntityManager em = ...;
CriteriaBuilder cb = em.getCriteriaBuilder();
CriteriaQuery<Pet> cq = cb.createQuery(Pet.class);
Root<Pet> pet = cq.from(Pet.class);
cq.select(pet);
```

```
TypedQuery<Pet> q = em.createQuery(cq);
List<Pet> allPets = q.getResultList();
```

The equivalent JPQL query is:

```
SELECT p
FROM Pet p
```

This query demonstrates the basic steps to create a Criteria query:

1. Use an `EntityManager` instance to create a `CriteriaBuilder` object.

2. Create a query object by creating an instance of the `CriteriaQuery` interface. This query object's attributes will be modified with the details of the query.

3. Set the query root by calling the `from` method on the `CriteriaQuery` object.

4. Specify what the type of the query result will be by calling the `select` method of the `CriteriaQuery` object.

5. Prepare the query for execution by creating a `TypedQuery<T>` instance, specifying the type of the query result.

6. Execute the query by calling the `getResultList` method on the `TypedQuery<T>` object. Because this query returns a collection of entities, the result is stored in a `List`.

The tasks associated with each step are discussed in detail in this chapter.

To create a `CriteriaBuilder` instance, call the `getCriteriaBuilder` method on the `EntityManager` instance:

```
CriteriaBuilder cb = em.getCriteriaBuilder();
```

The query object is created by using the `CriteriaBuilder` instance:

```
CriteriaQuery<Pet> cq = cb.createQuery(Pet.class);
```

The query will return instances of the `Pet` entity, so the type of the query is specified when the `CriteriaQuery` object is created to create a typesafe query.

The `FROM` clause of the query is set, and the root of the query specified, by calling the `from` method of the query object:

```
Root<Pet> pet = cq.from(Pet.class);
```

The `SELECT` clause of the query is set by calling the `select` method of the query object and passing in the query root:

```
cq.select(pet);
```

The query object is now used to create a `TypedQuery<T>` object that can be executed against the data source. The modifications to the query object are captured to create a ready-to-execute query:

```
TypedQuery<Pet> q = em.createQuery(cq);
```

This typed query object is executed by calling its `getResultList` method, because this query will return multiple entity instances. The results are stored in a `List<Pet>` collection-valued object.

```
List<Pet> allPets = q.getResultList();
```

Using the Metamodel API to Model Entity Classes

The Metamodel API is used to create a metamodel of the managed entities in a particular persistence unit. For each entity class in a particular package, a metamodel class is created with a trailing underscore and with attributes that correspond to the persistent fields or properties of the entity class.

The following entity class, `com.example.Pet`, has four persistent fields: `id`, `name`, `color`, and `owners`:

```
package com.example;

...

@Entity
public class Pet {
  @Id
  protected Long id;
  protected String name;
  protected String color;
  @ManyToOne
  protected Set<Person> owners;
  ...
}
```

The corresponding Metamodel class is:

```
package com.example;

...

@Static Metamodel(Pet.class)
public class Pet_ {

  public static volatile SingularAttribute<Pet, Long> id;
  public static volatile SingularAttribute<Pet, String> name;
  public static volatile SingularAttribute<Pet, String> color;
  public static volatile SetAttribute<Pet, Person> owners;
}
```

The metamodel class and its attributes are used in Criteria queries to refer to the managed entity classes and their persistent state and relationships.

Using Metamodel Classes

Metamodel classes that correspond to entity classes are of the following type:

```
javax.persistence.metamodel.EntityType<T>
```

Metamodel classes are typically generated by annotation processors either at development time or at runtime. Developers of applications that use Criteria queries may generate static metamodel classes by using the persistence provider's annotation processor or may obtain the metamodel class by either calling the getModel method on the query root object or first obtaining an instance of the Metamodel interface and then passing the entity type to the instance's entity method.

The following code snippet shows how to obtain the Pet entity's metamodel class by calling Root<T>.getModel:

```
EntityManager em = ...;
CriteriaBuilder cb = em.getCriteriaBuilder();
CriteriaQuery cq = cb.createQuery(Pet.class);
Root<Pet> pet = cq.from(Pet.class);
EntityType<Pet> Pet_ = pet.getModel();
```

The following code snippet shows how to obtain the Pet entity's metamodel class by first obtaining a metamodel instance by using EntityManager.getMetamodel and then calling entity on the metamodel instance:

```
EntityManager em = ...;
Metamodel m = em.getMetamodel();
EntityType<Pet> Pet_ = m.entity(Pet.class);
```

Using the Criteria API and Metamodel API to Create Basic Typesafe Queries

The basic semantics of a Criteria query consists of a SELECT clause, a FROM clause, and an optional WHERE clause, similar to a JPQL query. Criteria queries set these clauses by using Java programming language objects, so the query can be created in a typesafe manner.

Creating a Criteria Query

The javax.persistence.criteria.CriteriaBuilder interface is used to construct

- Criteria queries
- Selections
- Expressions

- Predicates
- Ordering

To obtain an instance of the `CriteriaBuilder` interface, call the `getCriteriaBuilder` method on either an `EntityManager` or an `EntityManagerFactory` instance.

The following code shows how to obtain a `CriteriaBuilder` instance by using the `EntityManager.getCriteriaBuilder` method.

```
EntityManager em = ...;
CriteriaBuilder cb = em.getCriteriaBuilder();
```

Criteria queries are constructed by obtaining an instance of the following interface:

```
javax.persistence.criteria.CriteriaQuery
```

`CriteriaQuery` objects define a particular query that will navigate over one or more entities. Obtain `CriteriaQuery` instances by calling one of the `CriteriaBuilder.createQuery` methods. For creating typesafe queries, call the `CriteriaBuilder.createQuery` method as follows:

```
CriteriaQuery<Pet> cq = cb.createQuery(Pet.class);
```

The `CriteriaQuery` object's type should be set to the expected result type of the query. In the preceding code, the object's type is set to `CriteriaQuery<Pet>` for a query that will find instances of the `Pet` entity.

In the following code snippet, a `CriteriaQuery` object is created for a query that returns a `String`:

```
CriteriaQuery<String> cq = cb.createQuery(String.class);
```

Query Roots

For a particular `CriteriaQuery`object, the root entity of the query, from which all navigation originates, is called the *query root*. It is similar to the FROM clause in a JPQL query.

Create the query root by calling the `from` method on the `CriteriaQuery` instance. The argument to the `from` method is either the entity class or an `EntityType<T>` instance for the entity.

The following code sets the query root to the Pet entity:

```
CriteriaQuery<Pet> cq = cb.createQuery(Pet.class);
Root<Pet> pet = cq.from(Pet.class);
```

The following code sets the query root to the Pet class by using an EntityType<T> instance:

```
EntityManager em = ...;
Metamodel m = em.getMetamodel();
EntityType<Pet> Pet_ = m.entity(Pet.class);
Root<Pet> pet = cq.from(Pet_);
```

Criteria queries may have more than one query root. This usually occurs when the query navigates from several entities.

The following code has two Root instances:

```
CriteriaQuery<Pet> cq = cb.createQuery(Pet.class);
Root<Pet> pet1 = cq.from(Pet.class);
Root<Pet> pet2 = cq.from(Pet.class);
```

Querying Relationships Using Joins

For queries that navigate to related entity classes, the query must define a join to the related entity by calling one of the From.join methods on the query root object or another join object. The join methods are similar to the JOIN keyword in JPQL.

The target of the join uses the Metamodel class of type EntityType<T> to specify the persistent field or property of the joined entity.

The join methods return an object of type Join<X, Y>, where X is the source entity and Y is the target of the join. In the following code snippet, Pet is the source entity, and Owner is the target:

```
CriteriaQuery<Pet> cq = cb.createQuery(Pet.class);
Metamodel m = em.getMetamodel();
EntityType<Pet> Pet_ = m.entity(Pet.class);

Root<Pet> pet = cq.from(Pet.class);
Join<Pet, Owner> owner = pet.join(Pet_.owners);
```

Joins can be chained together to navigate to related entities of the target entity without having to create a Join<X, Y> instance for each join:

```
CriteriaQuery<Pet> cq = cb.createQuery(Pet.class);
Metamodel m = em.getMetamodel();
EntityType<Pet> Pet_ = m.entity(Pet.class);
EntityType<Owner> Owner_ = m.entity(Owner.class);

Root<Pet> pet = cq.from(Pet.class);
Join<Owner, Address> address = cq.join(Pet_.owners).join(Owner_.addresses);
```

Path Navigation in Criteria Queries

Path objects are used in the SELECT and WHERE clauses of a Criteria query and can be query root entities, join entities, or other Path objects. The Path.get method is used to navigate to attributes of the entities of a query.

The argument to the get method is the corresponding attribute of the entity's Metamodel class. The attribute can either be a single-valued attribute, specified by @SingularAttribute in the Metamodel class, or a collection-valued attribute, specified by one of @CollectionAttribute, @SetAttribute, @ListAttribute, or @MapAttribute.

The following query returns the names of all the pets in the data store. The get method is called on the query root, pet, with the name attribute of the Pet entity's Metamodel class, Pet_ as the argument:

```
CriteriaQuery<String> cq = cb.createQuery(String.class);
Metamodel m = em.getMetamodel();
EntityType<Pet> Pet_ = m.entity(Pet.class);

Root<Pet> pet = cq.from(Pet.class);
cq.select(pet.get(Pet_.name));
```

Restricting Criteria Query Results

The results of a query can be restricted on the CriteriaQuery object according to conditions set by calling the CriteriaQuery.where method. Calling the where method is analogous to setting the WHERE clause in a JPQL query.

The where method evaluates instances of the Expression interface to restrict the results according to the conditions of the expressions. Expression instances are created by using methods defined in the Expression and CriteriaBuilder interfaces.

The Expression Interface Methods

An Expression object is used in a query's SELECT, WHERE, or HAVING clause. Table 22–1 shows conditional methods you can use with Expression objects.

TABLE 22–1 Conditional Methods in the Expression Interface

Method	Description
isNull	Tests whether an expression is null
isNotNull	Tests whether an expression is not null
in	Tests whether an expression is within a list of values

The following query uses the `Expression.isNull` method to find all pets where the `color` attribute is null:

```
CriteriaQuery<Pet> cq = cb.createQuery(Pet.class);
Metamodel m = em.getMetamodel();
EntityType<Pet> Pet_ = m.entity(Pet.class);
Root<Pet> pet = cq.from(Pet.class);
cq.where(pet.get(Pet_.color).isNull());
```

The following query uses the `Expression.in` method to find all brown and black pets:

```
CriteriaQuery<Pet> cq = cb.createQuery(Pet.class);
Metamodel m = em.getMetamodel();
EntityType<Pet> Pet_ = m.entity(Pet.class);
Root<Pet> pet = cq.from(Pet.class);
cq.where(pet.get(Pet_.color).in("brown", "black"));
```

The `in` method also can check whether an attribute is a member of a collection.

Expression Methods in the `CriteriaBuilder` Interface

The `CriteriaBuilder` interface defines additional methods for creating expressions. These methods correspond to the arithmetic, string, date, time, and case operators and functions of JPQL. Table 22–2 shows conditional methods you can use with `CriteriaBuilder` objects.

TABLE 22–2 Conditional Methods in the `CriteriaBuilder` Interface

Conditional Method	Description
equal	Tests whether two expressions are equal
notEqual	Tests whether two expressions are not equal
gt	Tests whether the first numeric expression is greater than the second numeric expression
ge	Tests whether the first numeric expression is greater than or equal to the second numeric expression
lt	Tests whether the first numeric expression is less than the second numeric expression
le	Tests whether the first numeric expression is less than or equal to the second numeric expression
between	Tests whether the first expression is between the second and third expression in value
like	Tests whether the expression matches a given pattern

The following code uses the `CriteriaBuilder.equal` method:

```
CriteriaQuery<Pet> cq = cb.createQuery(Pet.class);
Metamodel m = em.getMetamodel();
EntityType<Pet> Pet_ = m.entity(Pet.class);
Root<Pet> pet = cq.from(Pet.class);
cq.where(cb.equal(pet.get(Pet_.name)), "Fido");
...
```

The following code uses the `CriteriaBuilder.gt` method:

```
CriteriaQuery<Pet> cq = cb.createQuery(Pet.class);
Metamodel m = em.getMetamodel();
EntityType<Pet> Pet_ = m.entity(Pet.class);
Root<Pet> pet = cq.from(Pet.class);
Date someDate = new Date(...);
cq.where(cb.gt(pet.get(Pet_.birthday)), date);
```

The following code uses the `CriteriaBuilder.between` method:

```
CriteriaQuery<Pet> cq = cb.createQuery(Pet.class);
Metamodel m = em.getMetamodel();
EntityType<Pet> Pet_ = m.entity(Pet.class);
Root<Pet> pet = cq.from(Pet.class);
Date firstDate = new Date(...);
Date secondDate = new Date(...);
cq.where(cb.between(pet.get(Pet_.birthday)), firstDate, secondDate);
```

The following code uses the `CriteriaBuilder.like` method:

```
CriteriaQuery<Pet> cq = cb.createQuery(Pet.class);
Metamodel m = em.getMetamodel();
EntityType<Pet> Pet_ = m.entity(Pet.class);
Root<Pet> pet = cq.from(Pet.class);
cq.where(cb.like(pet.get(Pet_.name)), "*do");
```

Multiple conditional predicates can be specified by using the compound predicate methods of the `CriteriaBuilder` interface, as shown in Table 22-3.

TABLE 22-3 Compound Predicate Methods in the `CriteriaBuilder` Interface

Method	Description
and	A logical conjunction of two Boolean expressions
or	A logical disjunction of two Boolean expressions
not	A logical negation of the given Boolean expression

The following code shows the use of compound predicates in queries:

```
CriteriaQuery<Pet> cq = cb.createQuery(Pet.class);
Metamodel m = em.getMetamodel();
EntityType<Pet> Pet_ = m.entity(Pet.class);
Root<Pet> pet = cq.from(Pet.class);
cq.where(cb.equal(pet.get(Pet_.name), "Fido")
    .and(cb.equal(pet.get(Pet_.color), "brown"));
```

Managing Criteria Query Results

For queries that return more than one result, it's often helpful to organize those results. The CriteriaQuery interface defines the orderBy method to order query results according to attributes of an entity. The CriteriaQuery interface also defines the groupBy method to group the results of a query together according to attributes of an entity, and the having method to restrict those groups according to a condition.

Ordering Results

The order of the results of a query can be set by calling the CriteriaQuery.orderBy method and passing in an Order object. Order objects are created by calling either the CriteriaBuilder.asc or the CriteriaBuilder.desc method. The asc method is used to order the results by ascending value of the passed expression parameter. The desc method is used to order the results by descending value of the passed expression parameter. The following query shows the use of the desc method:

```
CriteriaQuery<Pet> cq = cb.createQuery(Pet.class);
Root<Pet> pet = cq.from(Pet.class);
cq.select(pet);
cq.orderBy(cb.desc(pet.get(Pet_.birthday)));
```

In this query, the results will be ordered by the pet's birthday from highest to lowest. That is, pets born in December will appear before pets born in May.

The following query shows the use of the asc method:

```
CriteriaQuery<Pet> cq = cb.createQuery(Pet.class);
Root<Pet> pet = cq.from(Pet.class);
Join<Owner, Address> address = cq.join(Pet_.owners).join(Owner_.address);
cq.select(pet);
cq.orderBy(cb.asc(address.get(Address_.postalCode)));
```

In this query, the results will be ordered by the pet owner's postal code from lowest to highest. That is, pets whose owner lives in the 10001 zip code will appear before pets whose owner lives in the 91000 zip code.

If more than one Order object is passed to orderBy, the precedence is determined by the order in which they appear in the argument list of orderBy. The first Order object has precedence.

The following code orders results by multiple criteria:

```
CriteriaQuery<Pet> cq = cb.createQuery(Pet.class);
Root<Pet> pet = cq.from(Pet.class);
Join<Pet, Owner> owner = cq.join(Pet_.owners);
cq.select(pet);
cq.orderBy(cb.asc(owner.get(Owner_.lastName), owner.get(Owner_.firstName)));
```

The results of this query will be ordered alphabetically by the pet owner's last name, then first name.

Grouping Results

The `CriteriaQuery.groupBy` method partitions the query results into groups. These groups are set by passing an expression to `groupBy`:

```
CriteriaQuery<Pet> cq = cb.createQuery(Pet.class);
Root<Pet> pet = cq.from(Pet.class);
cq.groupBy(pet.get(Pet_.color));
```

This query returns all `Pet` entities and groups the results by the pet's color.

The `CriteriaQuery.having` method is used in conjunction with `groupBy` to filter over the groups. The `having` method takes a conditional expression as a parameter. By calling the `having` method, the query result is restricted according to the conditional expression:

```
CriteriaQuery<Pet> cq = cb.createQuery(Pet.class);
Root<Pet> pet = cq.from(Pet.class);
cq.groupBy(pet.get(Pet_.color));
cq.having(cb.in(pet.get(Pet_.color)).value("brown").value("blonde"));
```

In this example, the query groups the returned `Pet` entities by color, as in the preceding example. However, the only returned groups will be `Pet` entities where the `color` attribute is set to `brown` or `blonde`. That is, no gray-colored pets will be returned in this query.

Executing Queries

To prepare a query for execution, create a `TypedQuery<T>` object with the type of the query result by passing the `CriteriaQuery` object to `EntityManager.createQuery`.

Queries are executed by calling either `getSingleResult` or `getResultList` on the `TypedQuery<T>` object.

Single-Valued Query Results

The `TypedQuery<T>.getSingleResult` method is used for executing queries that return a single result:

```
CriteriaQuery<Pet> cq = cb.createQuery(Pet.class);
...
TypedQuery<Pet> q = em.createQuery(cq);
Pet result = q.getSingleResult();
```

Collection-Valued Query Results

The TypedQuery<T>.getResultList method is used for executing queries that return a collection of objects:

```
CriteriaQuery<Pet> cq = cb.createQuery(Pet.class);
...
TypedQuery<Pet> q = em.createQuery(cq);
List<Pet> results = q.getResultList();
```

Security

Part VII introduces basic security concepts and examples. This part contains the following chapters:

- Chapter 23, "Introduction to Security in the Java EE Platform"
- Chapter 24, "Getting Started Securing Web Applications"
- Chapter 25, "Getting Started Securing Enterprise Applications"

Introduction to Security in the Java EE Platform

The chapters in Part VII discuss security requirements in web tier and enterprise tier applications. Every enterprise that has either sensitive resources that can be accessed by many users or resources that traverse unprotected, open, networks, such as the Internet, needs to be protected.

This chapter introduces basic security concepts and security mechanisms. More information on these concepts and mechanisms can be found in the chapter on security in the Java EE 6 specification. This document is available for download online at `http://www.jcp.org/en/jsr/detail?id=316`.

In this tutorial, security requirements are also addressed in the following chapters.

- Chapter 24, "Getting Started Securing Web Applications," explains how to add security to web components, such as servlets.

- Chapter 25, "Getting Started Securing Enterprise Applications," explains how to add security to Java EE components, such as enterprise beans and application clients.

Some of the material in this chapter assumes that you understand basic security concepts. To learn more about these concepts before you begin this chapter, you should explore the Java SE security web site at `http://download.oracle.com/docs/cd/E17409_01/javase/6/docs/technotes/guides/security/`.

The following topics are addressed here:

- "Overview of Java EE Security" on page 430
- "Security Mechanisms" on page 435
- "Securing Containers" on page 439
- "Securing the GlassFish Server" on page 440
- "Working with Realms, Users, Groups, and Roles" on page 441
- "Establishing a Secure Connection Using SSL" on page 449
- "Further Information about Security" on page 454

Overview of Java EE Security

Enterprise tier and web tier applications are made up of components that are deployed into various containers. These components are combined to build a multitier enterprise application. Security for components is provided by their containers. A container provides two kinds of security: declarative and programmatic.

- *Declarative security* expresses an application component's security requirements by using either deployment descriptors or annotations.

  A deployment descriptor is an XML file that is external to the application and that expresses an application's security structure, including security roles, access control, and authentication requirements. For more information about deployment descriptors, read "Using Deployment Descriptors for Declarative Security" on page 439.

  Annotations, also called metadata, are used to specify information about security within a class file. When the application is deployed, this information can be either used by or overridden by the application deployment descriptor. Annotations save you from having to write declarative information inside XML descriptors. Instead, you simply put annotations on the code, and the required information gets generated. For this tutorial, annotations are used for securing applications wherever possible. For more information about annotations, see "Using Annotations to Specify Security Information" on page 439.

- *Programmatic security* is embedded in an application and is used to make security decisions. Programmatic security is useful when declarative security alone is not sufficient to express the security model of an application. For more information about programmatic security, read "Using Programmatic Security" on page 440.

A Simple Security Example

The security behavior of a Java EE environment may be better understood by examining what happens in a simple application with a web client, a user interface, and enterprise bean business logic.

In the following example, which is taken from the Java EE 6 Specification, the web client relies on the web server to act as its authentication proxy by collecting user authentication data from the client and using it to establish an authenticated session.

Step 1: Initial Request

In the first step of this example, the web client requests the main application URL. This action is shown in Figure 23–1.

FIGURE 23–1   Initial Request

FIGURE 23–1   Initial Request

Since the client has not yet authenticated itself to the application environment, the server responsible for delivering the web portion of the application, hereafter referred to as the *web server*, detects this and invokes the appropriate authentication mechanism for this resource. For more information on these mechanisms, see "Security Mechanisms" on page 435.

Step 2: Initial Authentication

The web server returns a form that the web client uses to collect authentication data, such as user name and password, from the user. The web client forwards the authentication data to the web server, where it is validated by the web server, as shown in Figure 23–2. The validation mechanism may be local to a server or may leverage the underlying security services. On the basis of the validation, the web server sets a credential for the user.

FIGURE 23–2   Initial Authentication

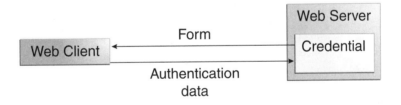

Step 3: URL Authorization

The credential is used for future determinations of whether the user is authorized to access restricted resources it may request. The web server consults the security policy associated with the web resource to determine the security roles that are permitted access to the resource. The security policy is derived from annotations or from the deployment descriptor. The web container then tests the user's credential against each role to determine whether it can map the user to the role. Figure 23–3 shows this process.

FIGURE 23-3   URL Authorization

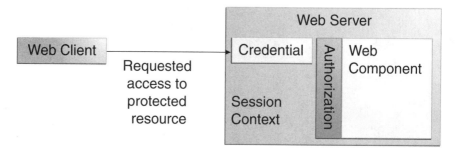

The web server's evaluation stops with an "is authorized" outcome when the web server is able to map the user to a role. A "not authorized" outcome is reached if the web server is unable to map the user to any of the permitted roles.

Step 4: Fulfilling the Original Request

If the user is authorized, the web server returns the result of the original URL request, as shown in Figure 23–4.

FIGURE 23-4   Fulfilling the Original Request

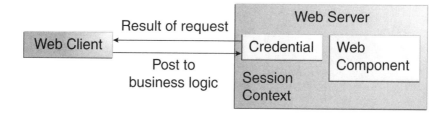

In our example, the response URL of a web page is returned, enabling the user to post form data that needs to be handled by the business-logic component of the application. See Chapter 24, "Getting Started Securing Web Applications," for more information on protecting web applications.

Step 5: Invoking Enterprise Bean Business Methods

The web page performs the remote method call to the enterprise bean, using the user's credential to establish a secure association between the web page and the enterprise bean, as shown in Figure 23–5. The association is implemented as two related security contexts: one in the web server and one in the EJB container.

FIGURE 23-5   Invoking an Enterprise Bean Business Method

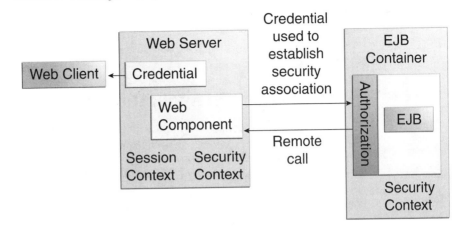

The EJB container is responsible for enforcing access control on the enterprise bean method. The container consults the security policy associated with the enterprise bean to determine the security roles that are permitted access to the method. The security policy is derived from annotations or from the deployment descriptor. For each role, the EJB container determines whether it can map the caller to the role by using the security context associated with the call.

The container's evaluation stops with an "is authorized" outcome when the container is able to map the caller's credential to a role. A "not authorized" outcome is reached if the container is unable to map the caller to any of the permitted roles. A "not authorized" result causes an exception to be thrown by the container and propagated back to the calling web page.

If the call is authorized, the container dispatches control to the enterprise bean method. The result of the bean's execution of the call is returned to the web page and ultimately to the user by the web server and the web client.

Features of a Security Mechanism

A properly implemented security mechanism will provide the following functionality:

- Prevent unauthorized access to application functions and business or personal data (authentication)

- Hold system users accountable for operations they perform (non-repudiation)

- Protect a system from service interruptions and other breaches that affect quality of service

Ideally, properly implemented security mechanisms will also be

- Easy to administer
- Transparent to system users
- Interoperable across application and enterprise boundaries

Characteristics of Application Security

Java EE applications consist of components that can contain both protected and unprotected resources. Often, you need to protect resources to ensure that only authorized users have access. *Authorization* provides controlled access to protected resources. Authorization is based on identification and authentication. *Identification* is a process that enables recognition of an entity by a system, and *authentication* is a process that verifies the identity of a user, device, or other entity in a computer system, usually as a prerequisite to allowing access to resources in a system.

Authorization and authentication are not required for an entity to access unprotected resources. Accessing a resource without authentication is referred to as unauthenticated, or anonymous, access.

The characteristics of application security that, when properly addressed, help to minimize the security threats faced by an enterprise include the following:

- **Authentication**: The means by which communicating entities, such as client and server, prove to each other that they are acting on behalf of specific identities that are authorized for access. This ensures that users are who they say they are.

- **Authorization**, or **access control**: The means by which interactions with resources are limited to collections of users or programs for the purpose of enforcing integrity, confidentiality, or availability constraints. This ensures that users have permission to perform operations or access data.

- **Data integrity**: The means used to prove that information has not been modified by a third party, an entity other than the source of the information. For example, a recipient of data sent over an open network must be able to detect and discard messages that were modified after they were sent. This ensures that only authorized users can modify data.

- **Confidentiality**, or **data privacy**: The means used to ensure that information is made available only to users who are authorized to access it. This ensures that only authorized users can view sensitive data.

- **Non-repudiation**: The means used to prove that a user who performed some action cannot reasonably deny having done so. This ensures that transactions can be proved to have happened.

- **Quality of Service**: The means used to provide better service to selected network traffic over various technologies.

- **Auditing**: The means used to capture a tamper-resistant record of security-related events for the purpose of being able to evaluate the effectiveness of security policies and mechanisms. To enable this, the system maintains a record of transactions and security information.

Security Mechanisms

The characteristics of an application should be considered when deciding the layer and type of security to be provided for applications. The following sections discuss the characteristics of the common mechanisms that can be used to secure Java EE applications. Each of these mechanisms can be used individually or with others to provide protection layers based on the specific needs of your implementation.

Java SE Security Mechanisms

Java SE provides support for a variety of security features and mechanisms:

- **Java Authentication and Authorization Service (JAAS)**: JAAS is a set of APIs that enable services to authenticate and enforce access controls upon users. JAAS provides a pluggable and extensible framework for programmatic user authentication and authorization. JAAS is a core Java SE API and is an underlying technology for Java EE security mechanisms.

- **Java Generic Security Services (Java GSS-API)**: Java GSS-API is a token-based API used to securely exchange messages between communicating applications. The GSS-API offers application programmers uniform access to security services atop a variety of underlying security mechanisms, including Kerberos.

- **Java Cryptography Extension (JCE)**: JCE provides a framework and implementations for encryption, key generation and key agreement, and Message Authentication Code (MAC) algorithms. Support for encryption includes symmetric, asymmetric, block, and stream ciphers. Block ciphers operate on groups of bytes; stream ciphers operate on one byte at a time. The software also supports secure streams and sealed objects.

- **Java Secure Sockets Extension (JSSE)**: JSSE provides a framework and an implementation for a Java version of the Secure Sockets Layer (SSL) and Transport Layer Security (TLS) protocols and includes functionality for data encryption, server authentication, message integrity, and optional client authentication to enable secure Internet communications.

- **Simple Authentication and Security Layer (SASL)**: SASL is an Internet standard (RFC 2222) that specifies a protocol for authentication and optional establishment of a security layer between client and server applications. SASL defines how authentication data is to be exchanged but does not itself specify the contents of that data. SASL is a framework into which specific authentication mechanisms that specify the contents and semantics of the authentication data can fit.

Java SE also provides a set of tools for managing keystores, certificates, and policy files; generating and verifying JAR signatures; and obtaining, listing, and managing Kerberos tickets.

For more information on Java SE security, visit `http://download.oracle.com/docs/cd/E17409_01/javase/6/docs/technotes/guides/security/`.

Java EE Security Mechanisms

Java EE security services are provided by the component container and can be implemented by using declarative or programmatic techniques (see "Securing Containers" on page 439). Java EE security services provide a robust and easily configured security mechanism for authenticating users and authorizing access to application functions and associated data at many different layers. Java EE security services are separate from the security mechanisms of the operating system.

Application-Layer Security

In Java EE, component containers are responsible for providing application-layer security, security services for a specific application type tailored to the needs of the application. At the application layer, application firewalls can be used to enhance application protection by protecting the communication stream and all associated application resources from attacks.

Java EE security is easy to implement and configure and can offer fine-grained access control to application functions and data. However, as is inherent to security applied at the application layer, security properties are not transferable to applications running in other environments and protect data only while it is residing in the application environment. In the context of a traditional enterprise application, this is not necessarily a problem, but when applied to a web services application, in which data often travels across several intermediaries, you would need to use the Java EE security mechanisms along with transport-layer security and message-layer security for a complete security solution.

The advantages of using application-layer security include the following.

- Security is uniquely suited to the needs of the application.
- Security is fine grained, with application-specific settings.

The disadvantages of using application-layer security include the following.

- The application is dependent on security attributes that are not transferable between application types.
- Support for multiple protocols makes this type of security vulnerable.
- Data is close to or contained within the point of vulnerability.

For more information on providing security at the application layer, see "Securing Containers" on page 439.

Transport-Layer Security

Transport-layer security is provided by the transport mechanisms used to transmit information over the wire between clients and providers; thus, transport-layer security relies on secure HTTP transport (HTTPS) using Secure Sockets Layer (SSL). Transport security is a point-to-point security mechanism that can be used for authentication, message integrity, and confidentiality. When running over an SSL-protected session, the server and client can authenticate each other and negotiate an encryption algorithm and cryptographic keys before the application protocol transmits or receives its first byte of data. Security is active from the time the data leaves the client until it arrives at its destination, or vice versa, even across intermediaries. The problem is that the data is not protected once it gets to the destination. One solution is to encrypt the message before sending.

Transport-layer security is performed in a series of phases, as follows.

- The client and server agree on an appropriate algorithm.
- A key is exchanged using public-key encryption and certificate-based authentication.
- A symmetric cipher is used during the information exchange.

Digital certificates are necessary when running HTTPS using SSL. The HTTPS service of most web servers will not run unless a digital certificate has been installed. Digital certificates have already been created for the GlassFish Server.

The advantages of using transport-layer security include the following.

- It is relatively simple, well-understood, standard technology.
- It applies to both a message body and its attachments.

The disadvantages of using transport-layer security include the following.

- It is tightly coupled with the transport-layer protocol.
- It represents an all-or-nothing approach to security. This implies that the security mechanism is unaware of message contents, so that you cannot selectively apply security to portions of the message as you can with message-layer security.

- Protection is transient. The message is protected only while in transit. Protection is removed automatically by the endpoint when it receives the message.

- It is not an end-to-end solution, simply point-to-point.

For more information on transport-layer security, see "Establishing a Secure Connection Using SSL" on page 449.

Message-Layer Security

In message-layer security, security information is contained within the SOAP message and/or SOAP message attachment, which allows security information to travel along with the message or attachment. For example, a portion of the message may be signed by a sender and encrypted for a particular receiver. When sent from the initial sender, the message may pass through intermediate nodes before reaching its intended receiver. In this scenario, the encrypted portions continue to be opaque to any intermediate nodes and can be decrypted only by the intended receiver. For this reason, message-layer security is also sometimes referred to as end-to-end security.

The advantages of message-layer security include the following.

- Security stays with the message over all hops and after the message arrives at its destination.

- Security can be selectively applied to different portions of a message and, if using XML Web Services Security, to attachments.

- Message security can be used with intermediaries over multiple hops.

- Message security is independent of the application environment or transport protocol.

The disadvantage of using message-layer security is that it is relatively complex and adds some overhead to processing.

The GlassFish Server supports message security using Metro, a web services stack that uses Web Services Security (WSS) to secure messages. Because this message security is specific to Metro and is not a part of the Java EE platform, this tutorial does not discuss using WSS to secure messages. See the *Metro User's Guide* at https://metro.dev.java.net/guide/.

Securing Containers

In Java EE, the component containers are responsible for providing application security. A container provides two types of security: declarative and programmatic.

Using Annotations to Specify Security Information

Annotations enable a declarative style of programming and so encompass both the declarative and programmatic security concepts. Users can specify information about security within a class file by using annotations. The GlassFish Server uses this information when the application is deployed. Not all security information can be specified by using annotations, however. Some information must be specified in the application deployment descriptors.

Specific annotations that can be used to specify security information within an enterprise bean class file are described in "Securing an Enterprise Bean Using Declarative Security" on page 489. Chapter 24, "Getting Started Securing Web Applications," describes how to use annotations to secure web applications where possible. Deployment descriptors are described only where necessary.

For more information on annotations, see "Further Information about Security" on page 454.

Using Deployment Descriptors for Declarative Security

Declarative security can express an application component's security requirements by using deployment descriptors. Because deployment descriptor information is declarative, it can be changed without the need to modify the source code. At runtime, the Java EE server reads the deployment descriptor and acts upon the corresponding application, module, or component accordingly. Deployment descriptors must provide certain structural information for each component if this information has not been provided in annotations or is not to be defaulted.

This part of the tutorial does not document how to create deployment descriptors; it describes only the elements of the deployment descriptor relevant to security. NetBeans IDE provides tools for creating and modifying deployment descriptors.

Different types of components use different formats, or schemas, for their deployment descriptors. The security elements of deployment descriptors discussed in this tutorial include the following.

- Web components may use a web application deployment descriptor named web.xml.

  The schema for web component deployment descriptors is provided in Chapter 14 of the Java Servlet 3.0 specification (JSR 315), which can be downloaded from http://jcp.org/en/jsr/detail?id=315.

- Enterprise JavaBeans components may use an EJB deployment descriptor named META-INF/ejb-jar.xml, contained in the EJB JAR file.

  The schema for enterprise bean deployment descriptors is provided in Chapter 19 of the EJB 3.1 specification (JSR 318), which can be downloaded from http://jcp.org/en/jsr/detail?id=318.

Using Programmatic Security

Programmatic security is embedded in an application and is used to make security decisions. Programmatic security is useful when declarative security alone is not sufficient to express the security model of an application. The API for programmatic security consists of methods of the EJBContext interface and the HttpServletRequest interface. These methods allow components to make business-logic decisions based on the security role of the caller or remote user.

Programmatic security is discussed in more detail in the following sections:

- "Using Programmatic Security with Web Applications" on page 469
- "Securing an Enterprise Bean Programmatically" on page 493

Securing the GlassFish Server

This tutorial describes deployment to the GlassFish Server, which provides highly secure, interoperable, and distributed component computing based on the Java EE security model. GlassFish Server supports the Java EE 6 security model. You can configure GlassFish Server for the following purposes:

- Adding, deleting, or modifying authorized users. For more information on this topic, see "Working with Realms, Users, Groups, and Roles" on page 441.

- Configuring secure HTTP and Internet Inter-Orb Protocol (IIOP) listeners.

- Configuring secure Java Management Extensions (JMX) connectors.

- Adding, deleting, or modifying existing or custom realms.

- Defining an interface for pluggable authorization providers using Java Authorization Contract for Containers (JACC). JACC defines security contracts between the GlassFish Server and authorization policy modules. These contracts specify how the authorization providers are installed, configured, and used in access decisions.

- Using pluggable audit modules.

- Customizing authentication mechanisms. All implementations of Java EE 6 compatible Servlet containers are required to support the Servlet Profile of JSR 196, which offers an avenue for customizing the authentication mechanism applied by the web container on behalf of one or more applications.

- Setting and changing policy permissions for an application.

Working with Realms, Users, Groups, and Roles

You often need to protect resources to ensure that only authorized users have access. See "Characteristics of Application Security" on page 434 for an introduction to the concepts of authentication, identification, and authorization.

This section discusses setting up users so that they can be correctly identified and either given access to protected resources or denied access if they are not authorized to access the protected resources. To authenticate a user, you need to follow these basic steps.

1. The application developer writes code to prompt for a user name and password. The various methods of authentication are discussed in "Specifying an Authentication Mechanism in the Deployment Descriptor" on page 467.

2. The application developer communicates how to set up security for the deployed application by use of a metadata annotation or deployment descriptor. This step is discussed in "Setting Up Security Roles" on page 446.

3. The server administrator sets up authorized users and groups on the GlassFish Server. This is discussed in "Managing Users and Groups on the GlassFish Server" on page 444.

4. The application deployer maps the application's security roles to users, groups, and principals defined on the GlassFish Server. This topic is discussed in "Mapping Roles to Users and Groups" on page 447.

What Are Realms, Users, Groups, and Roles?

A *realm* is a security policy domain defined for a web or application server. A realm contains a collection of users, who may or may not be assigned to a group. Managing users on the GlassFish Server is discussed in "Managing Users and Groups on the GlassFish Server" on page 444.

An application will often prompt for a user name and password before allowing access to a protected resource. After the user name and password have been entered, that information is passed to the server, which either authenticates the user and sends the protected resource or does not authenticate the user, in which case access to the protected resource is denied. This type of user authentication is discussed in "Specifying an Authentication Mechanism in the Deployment Descriptor" on page 467.

In some applications, authorized users are assigned to roles. In this situation, the role assigned to the user in the application must be mapped to a principal or group defined on the application server. Figure 23–6 shows this. More information on mapping roles to users and groups can be found in "Setting Up Security Roles" on page 446.

The following sections provide more information on realms, users, groups, and roles.

FIGURE 23–6   Mapping Roles to Users and Groups

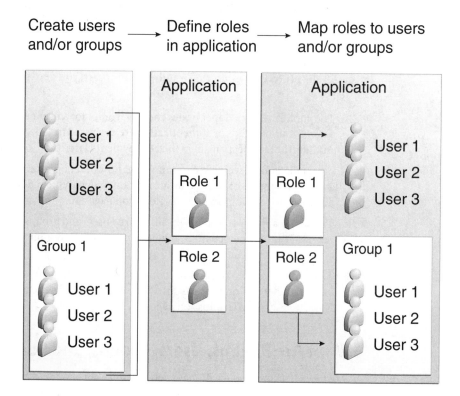

What Is a Realm?

A realm is a security policy domain defined for a web or application server. The protected resources on a server can be partitioned into a set of protection spaces, each with its own authentication scheme and/or authorization database containing a collection of users and groups. For a web application, a realm is a complete database of users and groups identified as valid users of a web application or a set of web applications and controlled by the same authentication policy.

The Java EE server authentication service can govern users in multiple realms. The `file`, `admin-realm`, and `certificate` realms come preconfigured for the GlassFish Server.

In the `file` realm, the server stores user credentials locally in a file named `keyfile`. You can use the Administration Console to manage users in the `file` realm. When using the `file` realm, the server authentication service verifies user identity by checking the `file` realm. This realm is used for the authentication of all clients except for web browser clients that use HTTPS and certificates.

In the `certificate` realm, the server stores user credentials in a certificate database. When using the `certificate` realm, the server uses certificates with HTTPS to authenticate web clients. To verify the identity of a user in the `certificate` realm, the authentication service verifies an X.509 certificate. For step-by-step instructions for creating this type of certificate, see "Working with Digital Certificates" on page 450. The common name field of the X.509 certificate is used as the principal name.

The `admin-realm` is also a `file` realm and stores administrator user credentials locally in a file named `admin-keyfile`. You can use the Administration Console to manage users in this realm in the same way you manage users in the `file` realm. For more information, see "Managing Users and Groups on the GlassFish Server" on page 444.

What Is a User?

A *user* is an individual or application program identity that has been defined in the GlassFish Server. In a web application, a user can have associated with that identify a set of roles that entitle the user to access all resources protected by those roles. Users can be associated with a group.

A Java EE user is similar to an operating system user. Typically, both types of users represent people. However, these two types of users are not the same. The Java EE server authentication service has no knowledge of the user name and password you provide when you log in to the operating system. The Java EE server authentication service is not connected to the security mechanism of the operating system. The two security services manage users that belong to different realms.

What Is a Group?

A *group* is a set of authenticated users, classified by common traits, defined in the GlassFish Server. A Java EE user of the `file` realm can belong to a group on the GlassFish Server. (A user in the `certificate` realm cannot.) A group on the GlassFish Server is a category of users classified by common traits, such as job title or customer profile. For example, most customers of an e-commerce application might belong to the CUSTOMER group, but the big spenders would belong to the PREFERRED group. Categorizing users into groups makes it easier to control the access of large numbers of users.

A group on the GlassFish Server has a different scope from a role. A group is designated for the entire GlassFish Server, whereas a role is associated only with a specific application in the GlassFish Server.

What Is a Role?

A *role* is an abstract name for the permission to access a particular set of resources in an application. A role can be compared to a key that can open a lock. Many people might have a copy of the key. The lock doesn't care who you are, only that you have the right key.

Some Other Terminology

The following terminology is also used to describe the security requirements of the Java EE platform:

- **Principal**: An entity that can be authenticated by an authentication protocol in a security service that is deployed in an enterprise. A principal is identified by using a principal name and authenticated by using authentication data.

- **Security policy domain**, also known as **security domain** or **realm**: A scope over which a common security policy is defined and enforced by the security administrator of the security service.

- **Security attributes**: A set of attributes associated with every principal. The security attributes have many uses: for example, access to protected resources and auditing of users. Security attributes can be associated with a principal by an authentication protocol.

- **Credential**: An object that contains or references security attributes used to authenticate a principal for Java EE services. A principal acquires a credential upon authentication or from another principal that allows its credential to be used.

Managing Users and Groups on the GlassFish Server

Follow these steps for managing users before you run the tutorial examples.

▼ To Add Users to the GlassFish Server

1 **Start the GlassFish Server, if you haven't already done so.**

Information on starting the GlassFish Server is available in "Starting and Stopping the GlassFish Server" on page 41.

2 **Start the Administration Console, if you haven't already done so.**

To start the Administration Console, open a web browser and specify the URL `http://localhost:4848/`. If you changed the default Admin port during installation, type the correct port number in place of 4848.

3 **In the navigation tree, expand the Configuration node.**

4 **Expand the Security node.**

5 **Expand the Realms node.**

6 **Select the realm to which you are adding users.**

- **Select the `file` realm to add users you want to access applications running in this realm.**

  For the example security applications, select the `file` realm.

  The Edit Realm page opens.

- **Select the `admin-realm` to add users you want to enable as system administrators of the GlassFish Server.**

  The Edit Realm page opens.

  You cannot add users to the `certificate` realm by using the Administration Console. In the `certificate` realm, you can add only certificates. For information on adding (importing) certificates to the `certificate` realm, see "Adding Users to the Certificate Realm" on page 446.

7 **On the Edit Realm page, click the Manage Users button.**

The File Users or Admin Users page opens.

8 **On the File Users or Admin Users page, click New to add a new user to the realm.**

The New File Realm User page opens.

9   **Type values in the User ID, Group List, New Password, and Confirm New Password fields.**

For the Admin Realm, the Group List field is read-only, and the group name is asadmin. Restart the GlassFish Server and Administration Console after you add a user to the Admin Realm.

For more information on these properties, see "Working with Realms, Users, Groups, and Roles" on page 441.

For the example security applications, specify a user with any name and password you like, but make sure that the user is assigned to the group TutorialUser. The user name and password are case-sensitive. Keep a record of the user name and password for working with the examples later in this tutorial.

10   **Click OK to add this user to the realm, or click Cancel to quit without saving.**

Adding Users to the Certificate Realm

In the certificate realm, user identity is set up in the GlassFish Server security context and populated with user data obtained from cryptographically verified client certificates. For step-by-step instructions for creating this type of certificate, see "Working with Digital Certificates" on page 450.

Setting Up Security Roles

When you design an enterprise bean or web component, you should always think about the kinds of users who will access the component. For example, a web application for a human resources department might have a different request URL for someone who has been assigned the role of DEPT_ADMIN than for someone who has been assigned the role of DIRECTOR. The DEPT_ADMIN role may let you view employee data, but the DIRECTOR role enables you to modify employee data, including salary data. Each of these security roles is an abstract logical grouping of users that is defined by the person who assembles the application. When an application is deployed, the deployer will map the roles to security identities in the operational environment, as shown in Figure 23–6.

For Java EE components, you define security roles using the @DeclareRoles and @RolesAllowed metadata annotations.

The following is an example of an application in which the role of DEPT-ADMIN is authorized for methods that review employee payroll data, and the role of DIRECTOR is authorized for methods that change employee payroll data.

The enterprise bean would be annotated as shown in the following code:

```
import javax.annotation.security.DeclareRoles;
import javax.annotation.security.RolesAllowed;
...
@DeclareRoles({"DEPT-ADMIN", "DIRECTOR"})
@Stateless public class PayrollBean implements Payroll {
    @Resource SessionContext ctx;

    @RolesAllowed("DEPT-ADMIN")
    public void reviewEmployeeInfo(EmplInfo info) {

        oldInfo = ... read from database;

        // ...
    }

    @RolesAllowed("DIRECTOR")
    public void updateEmployeeInfo(EmplInfo info) {

        newInfo = ... update database;

        // ...
    }
    ...
}
```

For a servlet, you can use the @HttpConstraint annotation within the
@ServletSecurity annotation to specify the roles that are allowed to access the
servlet. For example, a servlet might be annotated as follows:

```
@WebServlet(name = "PayrollServlet", urlPatterns = {"/payroll"})
@ServletSecurity(
@HttpConstraint(transportGuarantee = TransportGuarantee.CONFIDENTIAL,
    rolesAllowed = {"DEPT-ADMIN", "DIRECTOR"}))
public class GreetingServlet extends HttpServlet {
```

These annotations are discussed in more detail in "Specifying Security for Basic
Authentication Using Annotations" on page 476 and "Securing an Enterprise Bean
Using Declarative Security" on page 489.

After users have provided their login information and the application has declared
what roles are authorized to access protected parts of an application, the next step is to
map the security role to the name of a user, or principal.

Mapping Roles to Users and Groups

When you are developing a Java EE application, you don't need to know what
categories of users have been defined for the realm in which the application will be run.
In the Java EE platform, the security architecture provides a mechanism for mapping
the roles defined in the application to the users or groups defined in the runtime realm.

The role names used in the application are often the same as the group names defined on the GlassFish Server. Under these circumstances, you can enable a default principal-to-role mapping on the GlassFish Server by using the Administration Console. The task "To Set Up Your System for Running the Security Examples" on page 474 explains how to do this. All the tutorial security examples use default principal-to-role mapping.

If the role names used in an application are not the same as the group names defined on the server, use the runtime deployment descriptor to specify the mapping. The following example demonstrates how to do this mapping in the sun-web.xml file, which is the file used for web applications:

```
<sun-web-app>
    ...
    <security-role-mapping>
        <role-name>Mascot</role-name>
        <principal-name>Duke</principal-name>
    </security-role-mapping>

    <security-role-mapping>
        <role-name>Admin</role-name>
        <group-name>Director</group-name>
    </security-role-mapping>
    ...
</sun-web-app>
```

A role can be mapped to specific principals, specific groups, or both. The principal or group names must be valid principals or groups in the current default realm or in the realm specified in the login-config element. In this example, the role of Mascot used in the application is mapped to a principal, named Duke, that exists on the application server. Mapping a role to a specific principal is useful when the person occupying that role may change. For this application, you would need to modify only the runtime deployment descriptor rather than search and replace throughout the application for references to this principal.

Also in this example, the role of Admin is mapped to a group of users assigned the group name of Director. This is useful because the group of people authorized to access director-level administrative data has to be maintained only on the GlassFish Server. The application developer does not need to know who these people are, but only needs to define the group of people who will be given access to the information.

The role-name must match the role-name in the security-role element of the corresponding deployment descriptor or the role name defined in a @DeclareRoles annotation.

Establishing a Secure Connection Using SSL

Secure Socket Layer (SSL) technology is security that is implemented at the transport layer (see "Transport-Layer Security" on page 437 for more information about transport-layer security). SSL allows web browsers and web servers to communicate over a secure connection. In this secure connection, the data is encrypted before being sent and then is decrypted upon receipt and before processing. Both the browser and the server encrypt all traffic before sending any data.

SSL addresses the following important security considerations:

- **Authentication**: During your initial attempt to communicate with a web server over a secure connection, that server will present your web browser with a set of credentials in the form of a server certificate. The purpose of the certificate is to verify that the site is who and what it claims to be. In some cases, the server may request a certificate proving that the client is who and what it claims to be; this mechanism is known as client authentication.

- **Confidentiality**: When data is being passed between the client and the server on a network, third parties can view and intercept this data. SSL responses are encrypted so that the data cannot be deciphered by the third party and the data remains confidential.

- **Integrity**: When data is being passed between the client and the server on a network, third parties can view and intercept this data. SSL helps guarantee that the data will not be modified in transit by that third party.

The SSL protocol is designed to be as efficient as securely possible. However, encryption and decryption are computationally expensive processes from a performance standpoint. It is not strictly necessary to run an entire web application over SSL, and it is customary for a developer to decide which pages require a secure connection and which do not. Pages that might require a secure connection include those for login, personal information, shopping cart checkouts, or credit card information transmittal. Any page within an application can be requested over a secure socket by simply prefixing the address with https: instead of http:. Any pages that absolutely require a secure connection should check the protocol type associated with the page request and take the appropriate action if https: is not specified.

Using name-based virtual hosts on a secured connection can be problematic. This is a design limitation of the SSL protocol itself. The *SSL handshake*, whereby the client browser accepts the server certificate, must occur before the HTTP request is accessed. As a result, the request information containing the virtual host name cannot be determined before authentication, and it is therefore not possible to assign multiple certificates to a single IP address. If all virtual hosts on a single IP address need to authenticate against the same certificate, the addition of multiple virtual hosts should not interfere with normal SSL operations on the server. Be aware, however, that most client browsers will compare the server's domain name against the domain name listed in the certificate, if any; this is applicable primarily to official certificates signed by a certificate authority (CA). If the domain names do not match, these browsers will display a warning to the client. In general, only address-based virtual hosts are commonly used with SSL in a production environment.

Verifying and Configuring SSL Support

As a general rule, you must address the following issues to enable SSL for a server:

- There must be a `Connector` element for an SSL connector in the server deployment descriptor.
- There must be valid keystore and certificate files.
- The location of the keystore file and its password must be specified in the server deployment descriptor.

An SSL HTTPS connector is already enabled in the GlassFish Server.

For testing purposes and to verify that SSL support has been correctly installed, load the default introduction page with a URL that connects to the port defined in the server deployment descriptor:

```
https://localhost:8181/
```

The `https` in this URL indicates that the browser should be using the SSL protocol. The `localhost` in this example assumes that you are running the example on your local machine as part of the development process. The `8181` in this example is the secure port that was specified where the SSL connector was created. If you are using a different server or port, modify this value accordingly.

The first time that you load this application, the New Site Certificate or Security Alert dialog box appears. Select Next to move through the series of dialog boxes, and select Finish when you reach the last dialog box. The certificates will display only the first time. When you accept the certificates, subsequent hits to this site assume that you still trust the content.

Working with Digital Certificates

Digital certificates for the GlassFish Server have already been generated and can be found in the directory *as-install*/*domain-dir*/`config`/. These digital certificates are self-signed and are intended for use in a development environment; they are not intended for production purposes. For production purposes, generate your own certificates and have them signed by a CA.

To use SSL, an application or web server must have an associated certificate for each external interface, or IP address, that accepts secure connections. The theory behind this design is that a server should provide some kind of reasonable assurance that its owner is who you think it is, particularly before receiving any sensitive information. It may be useful to think of a certificate as a "digital driver's license" for an Internet address. The certificate states with which company the site is associated, along with some basic contact information about the site owner or administrator.

The digital certificate is cryptographically signed by its owner and is difficult for anyone else to forge. For sites involved in e-commerce or in any other business transaction in which authentication of identity is important, a certificate can be purchased from a well-known CA such as VeriSign or Thawte. If your server certificate is self-signed, you must install it in the GlassFish Server keystore file (`keystore.jks`). If your client certificate is self-signed, you should install it in the GlassFish Server truststore file (`cacerts.jks`).

Sometimes, authentication is not really a concern. For example, an administrator might simply want to ensure that data being transmitted and received by the server is private and cannot be snooped by anyone eavesdropping on the connection. In such cases, you can save the time and expense involved in obtaining a CA certificate and simply use a self-signed certificate.

SSL uses *public-key cryptography*, which is based on *key pairs*. Key pairs contain one public key and one private key. Data encrypted with one key can be decrypted only with the other key of the pair. This property is fundamental to establishing trust and privacy in transactions. For example, using SSL, the server computes a value and encrypts it by using its private key. The encrypted value is called a *digital signature*. The client decrypts the encrypted value by using the server's public key and compares the value to its own computed value. If the two values match, the client can trust that the signature is authentic, because only the private key could have been used to produce such a signature.

Digital certificates are used with HTTPS to authenticate web clients. The HTTPS service of most web servers will not run unless a digital certificate has been installed. Use the procedure outlined in the next section, "Creating a Server Certificate" on page 452, to set up a digital certificate that can be used by your application or web server to enable SSL.

One tool that can be used to set up a digital certificate is `keytool`, a key and certificate management utility that ships with the JDK. This tool enables users to administer their own public/private key pairs and associated certificates for use in self-authentication, whereby the user authenticates himself or herself to other users or services, or data integrity and authentication services, using digital signatures. The tool also allows users to cache the public keys, in the form of certificates, of their communicating peers. For a better understanding of `keytool` and public-key cryptography, see the keytool documentation at `http://download.oracle.com/docs/cd/E17409_01/javase/6/docs/technotes/tools/solaris/keytool.html`.

Creating a Server Certificate

A server certificate has already been created for the GlassFish Server and can be found in the *domain-dir*/`config`/ directory. The server certificate is in `keystore.jks`. The `cacerts.jks` file contains all the trusted certificates, including client certificates.

If necessary, you can use `keytool` to generate certificates. The `keytool` utility stores the keys and certificates in a file termed a *keystore*, a repository of certificates used for identifying a client or a server. Typically, a keystore is a file that contains one client's or one server's identity. The keystore protects private keys by using a password.

If you don't specify a directory when specifying the keystore file name, the keystores are created in the directory from which the `keytool` command is run. This can be the directory where the application resides, or it can be a directory common to many applications.

The general steps for creating a server certificate are as follows.

1. Create the keystore.
2. Export the certificate from the keystore.
3. Sign the certificate.
4. Import the certificate into a *truststore:* a repository of certificates used for verifying the certificates. A truststore typically contains more than one certificate.

"To Use `keytool` to Create a Server Certificate" on page 452 provides specific information on using the `keytool` utility to perform these steps.

▼ To Use `keytool` to Create a Server Certificate

Run `keytool` to generate a new key pair in the default development keystore file, `keystore.jks`. This example uses the alias `server-alias` to generate a new public/private key pair and wrap the public key into a self-signed certificate inside `keystore.jks`. The key pair is generated by using an algorithm of type RSA, with a default password of `changeit`. For more information and other examples of creating and managing keystore files, read the `keytool` online help at `http://download.oracle.com/docs/cd/E17409_01/javase/6/docs/technotes/tools/solaris/keytool.html`.

Note – RSA is public-key encryption technology developed by RSA Data Security, Inc.

From the directory in which you want to create the key pair, run `keytool` as shown in the following steps.

1   **Generate the server certificate.**

Type the keytool command all on one line:

```
java-home/bin/keytool -genkey -alias server-alias -keyalg RSA -keypass changeit
-storepass changeit -keystore keystore.jks
```

When you press Enter, keytool prompts you to enter the server name, organizational unit, organization, locality, state, and country code.

You must type the server name in response to keytool's first prompt, in which it asks for first and last names. For testing purposes, this can be localhost.

When you run the example applications, the host (server name) specified in the keystore must match the host identified in the javaee.server.name property specified in the file *tut-install*/examples/bp-project/build.properties.

2   **Export the generated server certificate in keystore.jks into the file server.cer.**

Type the keytool command all on one line:

```
java-home/bin/keytool -export -alias server-alias -storepass changeit
-file server.cer -keystore keystore.jks
```

3   **If you want to have the certificate signed by a CA, read the example at http://download.oracle.com/ docs/cd/E17409_01/javase/6/docs/technotes/tools/solaris/keytool.html.**

4   **To add the server certificate to the truststore file, cacerts.jks, run keytool from the directory where you created the keystore and server certificate.**

Use the following parameters:

```
java-home/bin/keytool -import -v -trustcacerts -alias server-alias
-file server.cer -keystore cacerts.jks -keypass changeit -storepass changeit
```

Information on the certificate, such as that shown next, will appear:

```
Owner: CN=localhost, OU=Sun Micro, O=Docs, L=Santa Clara, ST=CA,
C=USIssuer: CN=localhost, OU=Sun Micro, O=Docs, L=Santa Clara, ST=CA,
C=USSerial number: 3e932169Valid from: Tue Apr 08Certificate
fingerprints:MD5: 52:9F:49:68:ED:78:6F:39:87:F3:98:B3:6A:6B:0F:90 SHA1:
EE:2E:2A:A6:9E:03:9A:3A:1C:17:4A:28:5E:97:20:78:3F:
Trust this certificate? [no]:
```

5   **Type yes, then press the Enter or Return key.**

The following information appears:

```
Certificate was added to keystore[Saving cacerts.jks]
```

Further Information about Security

For more information about security in Java EE applications, see

- Java EE 6 specification:

  `http://jcp.org/en/jsr/detail?id=316`

- The *Oracle GlassFish Server 3.0.1 Application Development Guide*, which includes security information for application developers, such as information on security settings in the deployment descriptors specific to the GlassFish Server

- The *Oracle GlassFish Server 3.0.1 Administration Guide*, which includes information on setting security settings for the GlassFish Server

- Enterprise JavaBeans 3.1 specification:

  `http://jcp.org/en/jsr/detail?id=318`

- Implementing Enterprise Web Services 1.3 specification:

  `http://jcp.org/en/jsr/detail?id=109`

- Java SE security information:

  `http://download.oracle.com/`
  `docs/cd/E17409_01/javase/6/docs/technotes/guides/security/`

- Java Servlet 3.0 specification:

  `http://jcp.org/en/jsr/detail?id=315`

- Java Authorization Contract for Containers 1.3 specification:

  `http://jcp.org/en/jsr/detail?id=115`

- *Java Authentication and Authorization Service (JAAS) Reference Guide:*

  `http://download.oracle.com/`
  `docs/cd/E17409_01/javase/6/docs/technotes/guides/security/jaas/`
  `JAASRefGuide.html`

- *Java Authentication and Authorization Service (JAAS): LoginModule Developer's Guide:*

  `http://download.oracle.com/`
  `docs/cd/E17409_01/javase/6/docs/technotes/guides/security/jaas/`
  `JAASLMDevGuide.html`

24

Getting Started Securing Web Applications

A web application is accessed using a web browser over a network, such as the Internet or a company's intranet. As discussed in "Distributed Multitiered Applications" on page 6, the Java EE platform uses a distributed multitiered application model, and web applications run in the web tier.

Web applications contain resources that can be accessed by many users. These resources often traverse unprotected, open networks, such as the Internet. In such an environment, a substantial number of web applications will require some type of security. The ways to implement security for Java EE web applications are discussed in a general way in "Securing Containers" on page 439. This chapter provides more detail and a few examples that explore these security services as they relate to web components.

Securing applications and their clients in the business tier and the EIS tier is discussed in Chapter 25, "Getting Started Securing Enterprise Applications."

The following topics are addressed here:

- "Overview of Web Application Security" on page 455
- "Securing Web Applications" on page 457
- "Using Programmatic Security with Web Applications" on page 469
- "Examples: Securing Web Applications" on page 474

Overview of Web Application Security

In the Java EE platform, web components provide the dynamic extension capabilities for a web server. Web components can be Java servlets or JavaServer Faces pages. The interaction between a web client and a web application is illustrated in Figure 24–1.

FIGURE 24–1   Java Web Application Request Handling

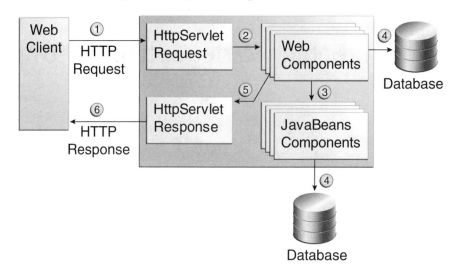

Certain aspects of web application security can be configured when the application is installed, or deployed, to the web container. Annotations and/or deployment descriptors are used to relay information to the deployer about security and other aspects of the application. Specifying this information in annotations or in the deployment descriptor helps the deployer set up the appropriate security policy for the web application. Any values explicitly specified in the deployment descriptor override any values specified in annotations.

Security for Java EE web applications can be implemented in the following ways.

- **Declarative security**: Can be implemented using either metadata annotations or an application's deployment descriptor. See "Overview of Java EE Security" on page 430 for more information.

  Declarative security for web applications is described in "Securing Web Applications" on page 457.

- **Programmatic security**: Is embedded in an application and can be used to make security decisions when declarative security alone is not sufficient to express the security model of an application. Declarative security alone may not be sufficient when conditional login in a particular work flow, instead of for all cases, is required in the middle of an application. See "Overview of Java EE Security" on page 430 for more information.

  Servlet 3.0 provides the `authenticate`, `login`, and `logout` methods of the `HttpServletRequest` interface. With the addition of the `authenticate`, `login`, and `logout` methods to the Servlet specification, an application deployment descriptor is no longer required for web applications but may still be used to further specify security requirements beyond the basic default values.

Programmatic security is discussed in "Using Programmatic Security with Web Applications" on page 469

- **Message Security**: Works with web services and incorporates security features, such as digital signatures and encryption, into the header of a SOAP message, working in the application layer, ensuring end-to-end security. Message security is not a component of Java EE 6 and is mentioned here for informational purposes only.

Some of the material in this chapter builds on material presented earlier in this tutorial. In particular, this chapter assumes that you are familiar with the information in the following chapters:

- Chapter 3, "Getting Started with Web Applications"
- Chapter 4, "JavaServer Faces Technology"
- Chapter 10, "Java Servlet Technology"
- Chapter 23, "Introduction to Security in the Java EE Platform"

Securing Web Applications

Web applications are created by application developers who give, sell, or otherwise transfer the application to an application deployer for installation into a runtime environment. Application developers communicate how to set up security for the deployed application by using annotations or deployment descriptors. This information is passed on to the deployer, who uses it to define method permissions for security roles, set up user authentication, and set up the appropriate transport mechanism. If the application developer doesn't define security requirements, the deployer will have to determine the security requirements independently.

Some elements necessary for security in a web application cannot be specified as annotations for all types of web applications. This chapter explains how to secure web applications using annotations wherever possible. It explains how to use deployment descriptors where annotations cannot be used.

Specifying Security Constraints

A *security constraint* is used to define the access privileges to a collection of resources using their URL mapping.

If your web application uses a servlet, you can express the security constraint information by using annotations. Specifically, you use the @HttpConstraint and, optionally, the @HttpMethodConstraint annotations within the @ServletSecurity annotation to specify a security constraint.

If your web application does not use a servlet, however, you must specify a security-constraint element in the deployment descriptor file. The authentication mechanism cannot be expressed using annotations, so if you use any authentication method other than BASIC (the default), a deployment descriptor is required.

The following subelements can be part of a security-constraint:

- **Web resource collection** (web-resource-collection): A list of URL patterns (the part of a URL *after* the host name and port you want to constrain) and HTTP operations (the methods within the files that match the URL pattern you want to constrain) that describe a set of resources to be protected. Web resource collections are discussed in "Specifying a Web Resource Collection" on page 458.

- **Authorization constraint** (auth-constraint): Specifies whether authentication is to be used and names the roles authorized to perform the constrained requests. For more information about authorization constraints, see "Specifying an Authentication Mechanism in the Deployment Descriptor" on page 467.

- **User data constraint** (user-data-constraint): Specifies how data is protected when transported between a client and a server. User data constraints are discussed in "Specifying a Secure Connection" on page 459.

Specifying a Web Resource Collection

A web resource collection consists of the following subelements:

- web-resource-name is the name you use for this resource. Its use is optional.

- url-pattern is used to list the request URI to be protected. Many applications have both unprotected and protected resources. To provide unrestricted access to a resource, do not configure a security constraint for that particular request URI.

  The request URI is the part of a URL *after* the host name and port. For example, let's say that you have an e-commerce site with a catalog that you would want anyone to be able to access and browse, and a shopping cart area for customers only. You could set up the paths for your web application so that the pattern /cart/* is protected but nothing else is protected. Assuming that the application is installed at context path /myapp, the following are true:

  - http://localhost:8080/myapp/index.xhtml is *not* protected.
  - http://localhost:8080/myapp/cart/index.xhtml *is* protected.

  A user will be prompted to log in the first time he or she accesses a resource in the cart/ subdirectory.

- http-method or http-method-omission is used to specify which methods should be protected or which methods should be omitted from protection. An HTTP method is protected by a web-resource-collection under any of the following circumstances:

- If no HTTP methods are named in the collection (which means that all are protected)

- If the collection specifically names the HTTP method in an `http-method` subelement

- If the collection contains one or more `http-method-omission` elements, none of which names the HTTP method

Specifying an Authorization Constraint

An authorization constraint (`auth-constraint`) contains the `role-name` element. You can use as many `role-name` elements as needed here.

An authorization constraint establishes a requirement for authentication and names the roles authorized to access the URL patterns and HTTP methods declared by this security constraint. If there is no authorization constraint, the container must accept the request without requiring user authentication. If there is an authorization constraint but no roles are specified within it, the container will not allow access to constrained requests under any circumstances. Each role name specified here must either correspond to the role name of one of the `security-role` elements defined for this web application or be the specially reserved role name *, which indicates all roles in the web application. Role names are case sensitive. The roles defined for the application must be mapped to users and groups defined on the server, except when default principal-to-role mapping is used.

For more information about security roles, see "Declaring Security Roles" on page 468. For information on mapping security roles, see "Mapping Roles to Users and Groups" on page 447.

For a servlet, the `@HttpConstraint` and `@HttpMethodConstraint` annotations accept a `rolesAllowed` element that specifies the authorized roles.

Specifying a Secure Connection

A user data constraint (`user-data-constraint` in the deployment descriptor) contains the `transport-guarantee` subelement. A user data constraint can be used to require that a protected transport-layer connection, such as HTTPS, be used for all constrained URL patterns and HTTP methods specified in the security constraint. The choices for transport guarantee are `CONFIDENTIAL`, `INTEGRAL`, or `NONE`. If you specify `CONFIDENTIAL` or `INTEGRAL` as a security constraint, it generally means that the use of SSL is required and applies to all requests that match the URL patterns in the web resource collection, not just to the login dialog box.

The strength of the required protection is defined by the value of the transport guarantee.

- Specify CONFIDENTIAL when the application requires that data be transmitted so as to prevent other entities from observing the contents of the transmission.

- Specify INTEGRAL when the application requires that the data be sent between client and server in such a way that it cannot be changed in transit.

- Specify NONE to indicate that the container must accept the constrained requests on any connection, including an unprotected one.

Note – In practice, Java EE servers treat the CONFIDENTIAL and INTEGRAL transport guarantee values identically.

The user data constraint is handy to use in conjunction with basic and form-based user authentication. When the login authentication method is set to BASIC or FORM, passwords are not protected, meaning that passwords sent between a client and a server on an unprotected session can be viewed and intercepted by third parties. Using a user data constraint with the user authentication mechanism can alleviate this concern. Configuring a user authentication mechanism is described in "Specifying an Authentication Mechanism in the Deployment Descriptor" on page 467.

To guarantee that data is transported over a secure connection, ensure that SSL support is configured for your server. SSL support is already configured for the GlassFish Server.

Note – After you switch to SSL for a session, you should never accept any non-SSL requests for the rest of that session. For example, a shopping site might not use SSL until the checkout page, and then it might switch to using SSL to accept your card number. After switching to SSL, you should stop listening to non-SSL requests for this session. The reason for this practice is that the session ID itself was not encrypted on the earlier communications. This is not so bad when you're only doing your shopping, but after the credit card information is stored in the session, you don't want anyone to use that information to fake the purchase transaction against your credit card. This practice could be easily implemented by using a filter.

Specifying Separate Security Constraints for Various Resources

You can create a separate security constraint for various resources within your application. For example, you could allow users with the role of PARTNER access to the GET and POST methods of all resources with the URL pattern /acme/wholesale/* and allow users with the role of CLIENT access to the GET and POST methods of all resources with the URL pattern /acme/retail/*. An example of a deployment descriptor that would demonstrate this functionality is the following:

```
<!-- SECURITY CONSTRAINT #1 -->
<security-constraint>
    <web-resource-collection>
        <web-resource-name>wholesale</web-resource-name>
        <url-pattern>/acme/wholesale/*</url-pattern>
        <http-method>GET</http-method>
        <http-method>POST</http-method>
    </web-resource-collection>
    <auth-constraint>
        <role-name>PARTNER</role-name>
    </auth-constraint>
    <user-data-constraint>
        <transport-guarantee>CONFIDENTIAL</transport-guarantee>
    </user-data-constraint>
</security-constraint>

<!-- SECURITY CONSTRAINT #2 -->
<security-constraint>
    <web-resource-collection>
        <web-resource-name>retail</web-resource-name>
        <url-pattern>/acme/retail/*</url-pattern>
        <http-method>GET</http-method>
        <http-method>POST</http-method>
    </web-resource-collection>
    <auth-constraint>
        <role-name>CLIENT</role-name>
    </auth-constraint>
    <user-data-constraint>
        <transport-guarantee>CONFIDENTIAL</transport-guarantee>
    </user-data-constraint>
</security-constraint>
```

When the same url-pattern and http-method occur in multiple security constraints, the constraints on the pattern and method are defined by combining the individual constraints, which could result in unintentional denial of access.

Specifying Authentication Mechanisms

A user authentication mechanism specifies

- The way a user gains access to web content
- With basic authentication, the realm in which the user will be authenticated
- With form-based authentication, additional attributes

When an authentication mechanism is specified, the user must be authenticated before access is granted to any resource that is constrained by a security constraint. There can be multiple security constraints applying to multiple resources, but the same authentication method will apply to all constrained resources in an application.

Before you can authenticate a user, you must have a database of user names, passwords, and roles configured on your web or application server. For information on setting up the user database, see "Managing Users and Groups on the GlassFish Server" on page 444.

HTTP basic authentication and form-based authentication are not very secure authentication mechanisms. Basic authentication sends user names and passwords over the Internet as Base64-encoded text; form-based authentication sends this data as plain text. In both cases, the target server is not authenticated. Therefore, these forms of authentication leave user data exposed and vulnerable. If someone can intercept the transmission, the user name and password information can easily be decoded. However, when a secure transport mechanism, such as SSL, or security at the network level, such as the Internet Protocol Security (IPsec) protocol or virtual private network (VPN) strategies, is used in conjunction with basic or form-based authentication, some of these concerns can be alleviated. To specify a secure transport mechanism, use the elements described in "Specifying a Secure Connection" on page 459.

HTTP Basic Authentication

Specifying *HTTP basic authentication* requires that the server request a user name and password from the web client and verify that the user name and password are valid by comparing them against a database of authorized users in the specified or default realm.

Basic authentication is the default when you do not specify an authentication mechanism.

When basic authentication is used, the following actions occur:

1. A client requests access to a protected resource.

2. The web server returns a dialog box that requests the user name and password.

3. The client submits the user name and password to the server.

4. The server authenticates the user in the specified realm and, if successful, returns the requested resource.

Figure 24–2 shows what happens when you specify HTTP basic authentication.

FIGURE 24–2   HTTP Basic Authentication

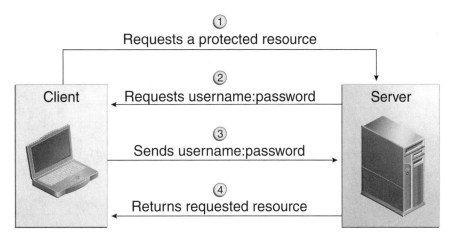

Form-Based Authentication

Form-based authentication allows the developer to control the look and feel of the login authentication screens by customizing the login screen and error pages that an HTTP browser presents to the end user. When form-based authentication is declared, the following actions occur.

1. A client requests access to a protected resource.

2. If the client is unauthenticated, the server redirects the client to a login page.

3. The client submits the login form to the server.

4. The server attempts to authenticate the user.

    a. If authentication succeeds, the authenticated user's principal is checked to ensure that it is in a role that is authorized to access the resource. If the user is authorized, the server redirects the client to the resource by using the stored URL path.

    b. If authentication fails, the client is forwarded or redirected to an error page.

Figure 24–3 shows what happens when you specify form-based authentication.

FIGURE 24–3 Form-Based Authentication

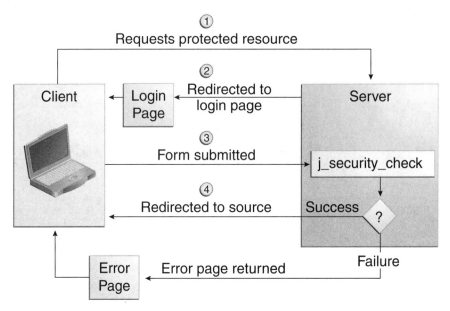

The section "Example: Form-Based Authentication with a JavaServer Faces Application" on page 479 is an example application that uses form-based authentication.

When you create a form-based login, be sure to maintain sessions using cookies or SSL session information.

For authentication to proceed appropriately, the action of the login form must always be j_security_check. This restriction is made so that the login form will work no matter which resource it is for and to avoid requiring the server to specify the action field of the outbound form. The following code snippet shows how the form should be coded into the HTML page:

```
<form method="POST" action="j_security_check">
<input type="text" name="j_username">
<input type="password" name="j_password">
</form>
```

Digest Authentication

Like basic authentication, *digest authentication* authenticates a user based on a user name and a password. However, unlike basic authentication, digest authentication does not send user passwords over the network. Instead, the client sends a one-way cryptographic hash of the password and additional data. Although passwords are not sent on the wire, digest authentication requires that clear-text password equivalents be available to the authenticating container so that it can validate received authenticators by calculating the expected digest.

Client Authentication

With *client authentication*, the web server authenticates the client by using the client's public key certificate. Client authentication is a more secure method of authentication than either basic or form-based authentication. It uses HTTP over SSL (HTTPS), in which the server authenticates the client using the client's public key certificate. SSL technology provides data encryption, server authentication, message integrity, and optional client authentication for a TCP/IP connection. You can think of a public key certificate as the digital equivalent of a passport. The certificate is issued by a trusted organization, a certificate authority (CA), and provides identification for the bearer.

Before using client authentication, make sure the client has a valid public key certificate. For more information on creating and using public key certificates, read "Working with Digital Certificates" on page 450.

Mutual Authentication

With *mutual authentication*, the server and the client authenticate each other. Mutual authentication is of two types:

- Certificate-based (see Figure 24–4)
- User name/password-based (see Figure 24–5)

When using certificate-based mutual authentication, the following actions occur.

1. A client requests access to a protected resource.

2. The web server presents its certificate to the client.

3. The client verifies the server's certificate.

4. If successful, the client sends its certificate to the server.

5. The server verifies the client's credentials.

6. If successful, the server grants access to the protected resource requested by the client.

Figure 24–4 shows what occurs during certificate-based mutual authentication.

FIGURE 24–4 Certificate-Based Mutual Authentication

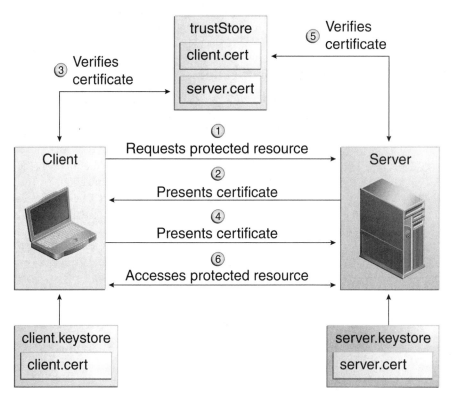

In user name/password-based mutual authentication, the following actions occur.

1. A client requests access to a protected resource.

2. The web server presents its certificate to the client.

3. The client verifies the server's certificate.

4. If successful, the client sends its user name and password to the server, which verifies the client's credentials.

5. If the verification is successful, the server grants access to the protected resource requested by the client.

Figure 24–5 shows what occurs during user name/password-based mutual authentication.

FIGURE 24–5 User Name/Password-Based Mutual Authentication

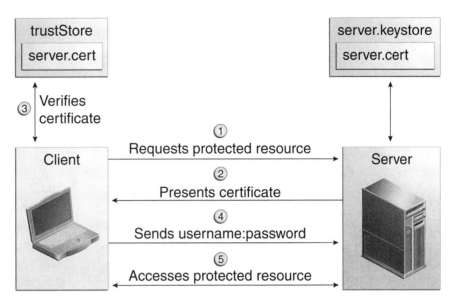

Specifying an Authentication Mechanism in the Deployment Descriptor

To specify an authentication mechanism, use the login-config element. It can contain the following subelements.

- The auth-method subelement configures the authentication mechanism for the web application. The element content must be either NONE, BASIC, DIGEST, FORM, or CLIENT-CERT.

- The realm-name subelement indicates the realm name to use when the basic authentication scheme is chosen for the web application.

- The form-login-config subelement specifies the login and error pages that should be used when form-based login is specified.

Note – Another way to specify form-based authentication is to use the authenticate, login, and logout methods of HttpServletRequest, as discussed in "Authenticating Users Programmatically" on page 469.

When you try to access a web resource that is constrained by a security-constraint element, the web container activates the authentication mechanism that has been configured for that resource. The authentication mechanism specifies how the user will be prompted to log in. If the login-config element is present and the auth-method element contains a value other than NONE, the user must be authenticated to access the resource. If you do not specify an authentication mechanism, authentication of the user is not required.

The following example shows how to declare form-based authentication in your deployment descriptor:

```
<login-config>
    <auth-method>FORM</auth-method>
    <realm-name>file</realm-name>
    <form-login-config>
        <form-login-page>/login.xhtml</form-login-page>
        <form-error-page>/error.xhtml</form-error-page>
    </form-login-config>
</login-config>
```

The login and error page locations are specified relative to the location of the deployment descriptor. Examples of login and error pages are shown in "Creating the Login Form and the Error Page" on page 480.

The following example shows how to declare digest authentication in your deployment descriptor:

```
<login-config>
    <auth-method>DIGEST</auth-method>
</login-config>
```

The following example shows how to declare client authentication in your deployment descriptor:

```
<login-config>
    <auth-method>CLIENT-CERT</auth-method>
</login-config>
```

Declaring Security Roles

You can declare security role names used in web applications by using the security-role element of the deployment descriptor. Use this element to list all the security roles that you have referenced in your application.

The following snippet of a deployment descriptor declares the roles that will be used in an application using the security-role element and specifies which of these roles is authorized to access protected resources using the auth-constraint element:

```
<security-constraint>
    <web-resource-collection>
        <web-resource-name>Protected Area</web-resource-name>
        <url-pattern>/security/protected/*</url-pattern>
        <http-method>PUT</http-method>
```

```
            <http-method>DELETE</http-method>
            <http-method>GET</http-method>
            <http-method>POST</http-method>
      </web-resource-collection>
      <auth-constraint>
            <role-name>manager</role-name>
      </auth-constraint>
</security-constraint>

 <!-- Security roles used by this web application -->
<security-role>
      <role-name>manager</role-name>
</security-role>
<security-role>
      <role-name>employee</role-name>
</security-role>
```

In this example, the security-role element lists all the security roles used in the application: manager and employee. This enables the deployer to map all the roles defined in the application to users and groups defined on the GlassFish Server.

The auth-constraint element specifies the role, manager, that can access the HTTP methods PUT, DELETE, GET, POST located in the directory specified by the url-pattern element (/jsp/security/protected/*).

The @ServletSecurity annotation cannot be used in this situation because its constraints apply to all URL patterns specified by the @WebServlet annotation.

Using Programmatic Security with Web Applications

Programmatic security is used by security-aware applications when declarative security alone is not sufficient to express the security model of the application.

Authenticating Users Programmatically

Servlet 3.0 specifies the following methods of the HttpServletRequest interface that enable you to authenticate users for a web application programmatically:

- authenticate, which allows an application to instigate authentication of the request caller by the container from within an unconstrained request context. A login dialog box displays and collects the user name and password for authentication purposes.

- login, which allows an application to collect username and password information as an alternative to specifying form-based authentication in an application deployment descriptor.

- logout, which allows an application to reset the caller identity of a request.

The following example code shows how to use the `login` and `logout` methods:

```
package test;

import java.io.IOException;
import java.io.PrintWriter;
import java.math.BigDecimal;
import javax.ejb.EJB;
import javax.servlet.ServletException;
import javax.servlet.annotation.WebServlet;
import javax.servlet.http.HttpServlet;
import javax.servlet.http.HttpServletRequest;
import javax.servlet.http.HttpServletResponse;

@WebServlet(name="TutorialServlet", urlPatterns={"/TutorialServlet"})
public class TutorialServlet extends HttpServlet {
    @EJB
    private ConverterBean converterBean;

    /**
     * Processes requests for both HTTP <code>GET</code>
     *     and <code>POST</code> methods.
     * @param request servlet request
     * @param response servlet response
     * @throws ServletException if a servlet-specific error occurs
     * @throws IOException if an I/O error occurs
     */
    protected void processRequest(HttpServletRequest request,
            HttpServletResponse response)
    throws ServletException, IOException {
        response.setContentType("text/html;charset=UTF-8");
        PrintWriter out = response.getWriter();
        try {

            out.println("<html>");
            out.println("<head>");
            out.println("<title>Servlet TutorialServlet</title>");
            out.println("</head>");
            out.println("<body>");
            request.login("TutorialUser", "TutorialUser");
            BigDecimal result =
                converterBean.dollarToYen(new BigDecimal("1.0"));
            out.println("<h1>Servlet TutorialServlet result of dollarToYen= "
                + result + "</h1>");
            out.println("</body>");
            out.println("</html>");
        } catch (Exception e) {
            throw new ServletException(e);
        } finally {
            request.logout();
            out.close();
        }
    }
}
```

The following example code shows how to use the `authenticate` method:

```
package com.sam.test;

import java.io.*;
import javax.servlet.*;
import javax.servlet.http.*;

public class TestServlet extends HttpServlet {

    protected void processRequest(HttpServletRequest request,
            HttpServletResponse response)
            throws ServletException, IOException {
        response.setContentType("text/html;charset=UTF-8");
        PrintWriter out = response.getWriter();
        try {
            request.authenticate(response);
            out.println("Authenticate Successful");
        } finally {
            out.close();
        }
    }
}
```

Checking Caller Identity Programmatically

In general, security management should be enforced by the container in a manner that is transparent to the web component. The security API described in this section should be used only in the less frequent situations in which web component methods need to access the security context information.

Servlet 3.0 specifies the following methods that enable you to access security information about the component's caller:

- getRemoteUser, which determines the user name with which the client authenticated. The getRemoteUser method returns the name of the remote user (the caller) associated by the container with the request. If no user has been authenticated, this method returns null.

- isUserInRole, which determines whether a remote user is in a specific security role. If no user has been authenticated, this method returns false. This method expects a String user role-name parameter.

   The security-role-ref element should be declared in the deployment descriptor with a role-name subelement containing the role name to be passed to the method. Using security role references is discussed in "Declaring and Linking Role References" on page 473.

- getUserPrincipal, which determines the principal name of the current user and returns a java.security.Principal object. If no user has been authenticated, this method returns null. Calling the getName method on the Principal returned by getUserPrincipal returns the name of the remote user.

Your application can make business-logic decisions based on the information obtained using these APIs.

Example Code for Programmatic Security

The following code demonstrates the use of programmatic security for the purposes of
programmatic login. This servlet does the following:

1. It displays information about the current user.

2. It prompts the user to log in.

3. It prints out the information again to demonstrate the effect of the `login` method.

4. It logs the user out.

5. It prints out the information again to demonstrate the effect of the `logout` method.

```
package enterprise.programmatic_login;

import java.io.*;
import java.net.*;
import javax.annotation.security.DeclareRoles;
import javax.servlet.*;
import javax.servlet.http.*;

@DeclareRoles("javaee6user")
public class LoginServlet extends HttpServlet {

    /**
     * Processes requests for both HTTP GET and POST methods.
     * @param request servlet request
     * @param response servlet response
     */
    protected void processRequest(HttpServletRequest request,
                HttpServletResponse response)
            throws ServletException, IOException {
        response.setContentType("text/html;charset=UTF-8");
        PrintWriter out = response.getWriter();
        try {
            String userName = request.getParameter("txtUserName");
            String password = request.getParameter("txtPassword");

            out.println("Before Login" + "<br><br>");
            out.println("IsUserInRole?.."
                        + request.isUserInRole("javaee6user")+"<br>");
            out.println("getRemoteUser?.." + request.getRemoteUser()+"<br>");
            out.println("getUserPrincipal?.."
                        + request.getUserPrincipal()+"<br>");
            out.println("getAuthType?.." + request.getAuthType()+"<br><br>");

            try {
                request.login(userName, password);
            } catch(ServletException ex) {
                out.println("Login Failed with a ServletException.."
                    + ex.getMessage());
                return;
            }
            out.println("After Login..."+"<br><br>");
            out.println("IsUserInRole?.."
                        + request.isUserInRole("javaee6user")+"<br>");
```

```
                        out.println("getRemoteUser?.." + request.getRemoteUser()+"<br>");
                        out.println("getUserPrincipal?.."
                                    + request.getUserPrincipal()+"<br>");
                        out.println("getAuthType?.." + request.getAuthType()+"<br><br>");

                        request.logout();
                        out.println("After Logout..."+"<br><br>");
                        out.println("IsUserInRole?.."
                                    + request.isUserInRole("javaee6user")+"<br>");
                        out.println("getRemoteUser?.." + request.getRemoteUser()+"<br>");
                        out.println("getUserPrincipal?.."
                                    + request.getUserPrincipal()+"<br>");
                        out.println("getAuthType?.." + request.getAuthType()+"<br>");
                } finally {
                        out.close();
                }
        }
        ...
}
```

Declaring and Linking Role References

A *security role reference* defines a mapping between the name of a role that is called
from a web component using isUserInRole(String role) and the name of a security
role that has been defined for the application. If no security-role-ref element is
declared in a deployment descriptor and the isUserInRole method is called, the
container defaults to checking the provided role name against the list of all security
roles defined for the web application. Using the default method instead of using the
security-role-ref element limits your flexibility to change role names in an
application without also recompiling the servlet making the call.

The security-role-ref element is used when an application uses the
HttpServletRequest.isUserInRole(String role). The value passed to the
isUserInRole method is a String representing the role name of the user. The value of
the role-name element must be the String used as the parameter to the
HttpServletRequest.isUserInRole(String role). The role-link must contain
the name of one of the security roles defined in the security-role elements. The
container uses the mapping of security-role-ref to security-role when
determining the return value of the call.

For example, to map the security role reference cust to the security role with role
name bankCustomer, the syntax would be:

```
<servlet>
...
    <security-role-ref>
        <role-name>cust</role-name>
        <role-link>bankCustomer</role-link>
    </security-role-ref>
...
</servlet>
```

If the servlet method is called by a user in the `bankCustomer` security role, `isUserInRole("cust")` returns `true`.

The `role-link` element in the `security-role-ref` element must match a `role-name` defined in the `security-role` element of the same `web.xml` deployment descriptor, as shown here:

```
<security-role>
    <role-name>bankCustomer</role-name>
</security-role>
```

A security role reference, including the name defined by the reference, is scoped to the component whose deployment descriptor contains the `security-role-ref` deployment descriptor element.

Examples: Securing Web Applications

Some basic setup is required before any of the example applications will run correctly. The examples use annotations, programmatic security, and/or declarative security to demonstrate adding security to existing web applications.

Here are some other locations where you will find examples of securing various types of applications:

- "Example: Securing an Enterprise Bean with Declarative Security" on page 497
- "Example: Securing an Enterprise Bean with Programmatic Security" on page 501
- GlassFish samples: `https://glassfish-samples.dev.java.net/`

▼ To Set Up Your System for Running the Security Examples

To set up your system for running the security examples, you need to configure a user database that the application can use for authenticating users. Before continuing, follow these steps.

1 **Add an authorized user to the GlassFish Server. For the examples in this chapter and in Chapter 25, "Getting Started Securing Enterprise Applications," add a user to the `file` realm of the GlassFish Server, and assign the user to the group `TutorialUser`:**

   a. From the Administration Console, expand the Configuration node.

   b. Expand the Security node.

   c. Expand the Realms node.

d. Select the File node.

e. On the Edit Realm page, click Manage Users.

f. On the File Users page, click New.

g. In the User ID field, type a User ID.

h. In the Group List field, type TutorialUser.

i. In the New Password and Confirm New Password fields, type a password.

j. Click OK.

Be sure to write down the user name and password for the user you create so that you can use it for testing the example applications. Authentication is case sensitive for both the user name and password, so write down the user name and password exactly. This topic is discussed more in "Managing Users and Groups on the GlassFish Server" on page 444.

2 Set up Default Principal to Role Mapping on the GlassFish Server:

a. From the Administration Console, expand the Configuration node.

b. Select the Security node.

c. Select the Default Principal to Role Mapping Enabled check box.

d. Click Save.

Example: Basic Authentication with a Servlet

This example explains how to use basic authentication with a servlet. With basic authentication of a servlet, the web browser presents a standard login dialog that is not customizable. When a user submits his or her name and password, the server determines whether the user name and password are those of an authorized user and sends the requested web resource if the user is authorized to view it.

In general, the following steps are necessary for adding basic authentication to an unsecured servlet, such as the ones described in Chapter 3, "Getting Started with Web Applications." In the example application included with this tutorial, many of these steps have been completed for you and are listed here simply to show what needs to be done should you wish to create a similar application. The completed version of this example application can be found in the directory *tut-install*/examples/security/hello2_basicauth/.

1. Follow the steps in "To Set Up Your System for Running the Security Examples" on page 474.

2. Create a web module as described in Chapter 3, "Getting Started with Web Applications," for the servlet example, hello2.

3. Add the appropriate security annotations to the servlet. The security annotations are described in "Specifying Security for Basic Authentication Using Annotations" on page 476.

4. Build, package, and deploy the web application by following the steps in "To Build, Package, and Deploy the Servlet Basic Authentication Example Using NetBeans IDE" on page 477 or "To Build, Package, and Deploy the Servlet Basic Authentication Example Using Ant" on page 478.

5. Run the web application by following the steps described in "To Run the Basic Authentication Servlet" on page 478.

Specifying Security for Basic Authentication Using Annotations

The default authentication mechanism used by the GlassFish Server is basic authentication. With basic authentication, the GlassFish Server spawns a standard login dialog to collect user name and password data for a protected resource. Once the user is authenticated, access to the protected resource is permitted.

To specify security for a servlet, use the @ServletSecurity annotation. This annotation allows you to specify both specific constraints on HTTP methods and more general constraints that apply to all HTTP methods for which no specific constraint is specified. Within the @ServletSecurity annotation, you can specify the following annotations:

- The @HttpMethodConstraint annotation, which applies to a specific HTTP method

- The more general @HttpConstraint annotation, which applies to all HTTP methods for which there is no corresponding @HttpMethodConstraint annotation

Both the @HttpMethodConstraint and @HttpConstraint annotations within the @ServletSecurity annotation can specify the following:

- A transportGuarantee element that specifies the data protection requirements (that is, whether or not SSL/TLS is required) that must be satisfied by the connections on which requests arrive. Valid values for this element are NONE and CONFIDENTIAL.

- A rolesAllowed element that specifies the names of the authorized roles.

For the hello2_basicauth application, the GreetingServlet has the following annotations:

```
@WebServlet(name = "GreetingServlet", urlPatterns = {"/greeting"})
@ServletSecurity(
@HttpConstraint(transportGuarantee = TransportGuarantee.CONFIDENTIAL,
    rolesAllowed = {"TutorialUser"}))
```

These annotations specify that the request URI /greeting can be accessed only by users who have been authorized to access this URL because they have been verified to be in the role TutorialUser. The data will be sent over a protected transport in order to keep the user name and password data from being read in transit.

▼ To Build, Package, and Deploy the Servlet Basic Authentication Example Using NetBeans IDE

1   Follow the steps in "To Set Up Your System for Running the Security Examples" on page 474.

2   In NetBeans IDE, select File→Open Project.

3   In the Open Project dialog, navigate to:

    tut-install/examples/security

4   Select the hello2_basicauth folder.

5   Select the Open as Main Project check box.

6   Click Open Project.

7   Right-click hello2_basicauth in the Projects pane and select Deploy.

    This option builds and deploys the example application to your GlassFish Server instance.

▼ **To Build, Package, and Deploy the Servlet Basic Authentication Example Using Ant**

1 Follow the steps in "To Set Up Your System for Running the Security Examples" on page 474.

2 In a terminal window, go to:

tut-install/examples/security/hello2_basicauth/

3 Type the following command:

ant

This command calls the default target, which builds and packages the application into a WAR file, hello2_basicauth.war, that is located in the dist directory.

4 Make sure that the GlassFish Server is started.

5 To deploy the application, type the following command:

ant deploy

▼ **To Run the Basic Authentication Servlet**

1 In a web browser, navigate to the following URL:

https://localhost:8181/hello2_basicauth/greeting

You may be prompted to accept the security certificate for the server. If so, accept the security certificate. If the browser warns that the certificate is invalid because it is self-signed, add a security exception for the application.

An Authentication Required dialog box appears. Its appearance varies, depending on the browser you use. Figure 24–6 shows an example.

FIGURE 24–6   Sample Basic Authentication Dialog Box

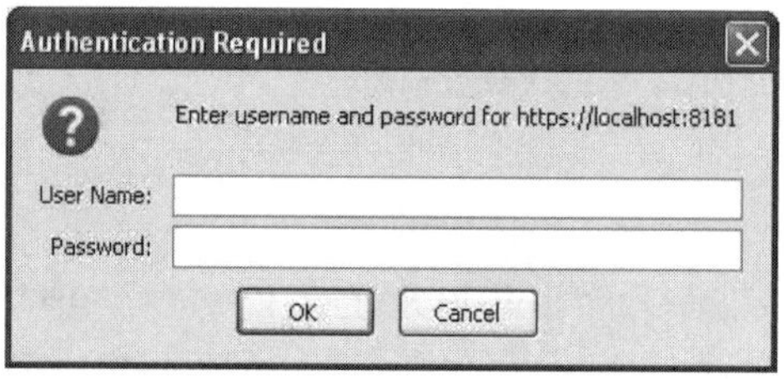

2   Type a user name and password combination that corresponds to a user who has already been created in the `file` realm of the GlassFish Server and has been assigned to the group of `TutorialUser`; then click OK.

Basic authentication is case sensitive for both the user name and password, so type the user name and password exactly as defined for the GlassFish Server.

The server returns the requested resource if all the following conditions are met.

- A user with the user name you entered is defined for the GlassFish Server.

- The user with the user name you entered has the password you entered.

- The user name and password combination you entered is assigned to the group `TutorialUser` on the GlassFish Server.

- The role of `TutorialUser`, as defined for the application, is mapped to the group `TutorialUser`, as defined for the GlassFish Server.

When these conditions are met and the server has authenticated the user, the application will appear as shown in Figure 3–2 but with a different URL.

3   Type a name in the text field and click the Submit button.

Because you have already been authorized, the name you enter in this step does not have any limitations. You have unlimited access to the application now.

The application responds by saying "Hello" to you, as shown in Figure 3–3 but with a different URL.

Next Steps   For repetitive testing of this example, you may need to close and reopen your browser. You should also run the ant `undeploy` and ant `clean` targets or the NetBeans IDE Clean and Build option to get a fresh start.

Example: Form-Based Authentication with a JavaServer Faces Application

This example explains how to use form-based authentication with a JavaServer Faces application. With form-based authentication, you can customize the login screen and error pages that are presented to the web client for authentication of the user name and password. When a user submits his or her name and password, the server determines whether the user name and password are those of an authorized user and, if authorized, sends the requested web resource.

This example, `hello1_formauth`, adds security to the basic JavaServer Faces application shown in "Web Modules: The `hello1` Example" on page 53.

In general, the steps necessary for adding form-based authentication to an unsecured JavaServer Faces application are similar to those described in "Example: Basic Authentication with a Servlet" on page 475. The major difference is that you must use a deployment descriptor to specify the use of form-based authentication, as described in "Specifying Security for the Form-Based Authentication Example" on page 481. In addition, you must create a login form page and a login error page, as described in "Creating the Login Form and the Error Page" on page 480.

The completed version of this example application can be found in the directory *tut-install*/examples/security/hello1_formauth/.

Creating the Login Form and the Error Page

When using form-based login mechanisms, you must specify a page that contains the form you want to use to obtain the user name and password, as well as a page to display if login authentication fails. This section discusses the login form and the error page used in this example. "Specifying Security for the Form-Based Authentication Example" on page 481 shows how you specify these pages in the deployment descriptor.

The login page can be an HTML page, a JavaServer Faces or JSP page, or a servlet, and it must return an HTML page containing a form that conforms to specific naming conventions (see the Java Servlet 3.0 specification for more information on these requirements). To do this, include the elements that accept user name and password information between <form></form> tags in your login page. The content of an HTML page, JavaServer Faces or JSP page, or servlet for a login page should be coded as follows:

```
<form method=post action="j_security_check">
    <input type="text" name="j_username">
    <input type="password" name= "j_password">
</form>
```

The full code for the login page used in this example can be found at *tut-install*/examples/security/hello1_formauth/web/login.xhtml. An example of the running login form page is shown later, in Figure 24–7. Here is the code for this page:

```
<html xmlns="http://www.w3.org/1999/xhtml"
    xmlns:h="http://java.sun.com/jsf/html">
    <h:head>
        <title>Login Form</title>
    </h:head>
    <h:body>
        <h2>Hello, please log in:</h2>
        <form name="loginForm" method="POST" action="j_security_check">
            <p><strong>Please type your user name: </strong>
                <input type="text" name="j_username" size="25"></p>
            <p><strong>Please type your password: </strong>
                <input type="password" size="15" name="j_password"></p>
            <p>
                <input type="submit" value="Submit"/>
                <input type="reset" value="Reset"/></p>
```

```
        </form>
    </h:body>
</html>
```

The login error page is displayed if the user enters a user name and password combination that is not authorized to access the protected URI. For this example, the login error page can be found at *tut-install*/examples/security/hello1_formauth/web/error.xhtml. For this example, the login error page explains the reason for receiving the error page and provides a link that will allow the user to try again. Here is the code for this page:

```
<html xmlns="http://www.w3.org/1999/xhtml"
    xmlns:h="http://java.sun.com/jsf/html">
    <h:head>
        <title>Login Error</title>
    </h:head>
    <h:body>
    <h2>Invalid user name or password.</h2>

    <p>Please enter a user name or password that is authorized to access this
        application. For this application, this means a user that has been
        created in the <code>file</code> realm and has been assigned to the
        <em>group</em> of <code>TutorialUser</code>.</p>
    <h:link outcome="login">Return to login page</h:link>

    </h:body>
</html>
```

Specifying Security for the Form-Based Authentication Example

This example takes a very simple servlet-based web application and adds form-based security. To specify form-based instead of basic authentication for a JavaServer Faces example, you must use the deployment descriptor.

The following sample code shows the security elements added to the deployment descriptor for this example, which can be found in *tut-install*/examples/security/hello1_formauth/web/WEB-INF/web.xml.

```
<security-constraint>
    <display-name>Constraint1</display-name>
    <web-resource-collection>
        <web-resource-name>wrcoll</web-resource-name>
        <description/>
        <url-pattern>/*</url-pattern>
    </web-resource-collection>
    <auth-constraint>
        <description/>
        <role-name>TutorialUser</role-name>
    </auth-constraint>
</security-constraint>

<login-config>
    <auth-method>FORM</auth-method>
```

```
            <realm-name>file</realm-name>
            <form-login-config>
                <form-login-page>/login.xhtml</form-login-page>
                <form-error-page>/error.xhtml</form-error-page>
            </form-login-config>
        </login-config>

        <security-role>
            <description/>
            <role-name>TutorialUser</role-name>
        </security-role>
```

▼ To Build, Package, and Deploy the Form-Based Authentication Example Using NetBeans IDE

1   Follow the steps in "To Set Up Your System for Running the Security Examples" on page 474.

2   Open the project in NetBeans IDE by selecting File→Open Project.

3   In the Open Project dialog, navigate to:

    tut-install/examples/security

4   Select the hello1_formauth folder.

5   Select the Open as Main Project check box.

6   Click Open Project.

7   Right-click hello1_formauth in the Projects pane and select Deploy.

▼ To Build, Package, and Deploy the Form-Based Authentication Example Using Ant

1   Follow the steps in "To Set Up Your System for Running the Security Examples" on page 474.

2   In a terminal window, go to:

    tut-install/examples/security/hello2_formauth/

3   Type the following command at the terminal window or command prompt:

    ant

This target will spawn any necessary compilations, copy files to the *tut-install*/examples/security/hello2_formauth/build/ directory, create the WAR file, and copy it to the *tut-install*/examples/security/hello2_formauth/dist/ directory.

4   To deploy `hello2_formauth.war` to the GlassFish Server, type the following command:

`ant deploy`

▼ To Run the Form-Based Authentication Example

To run the web client for `hello1_formauth`, follow these steps.

1   **Open a web browser to the following URL:**

`https://localhost:8181/hello1_formauth/`

The login form displays in the browser, as shown in Figure 24–7.

FIGURE 24–7   Form-Based Login Page

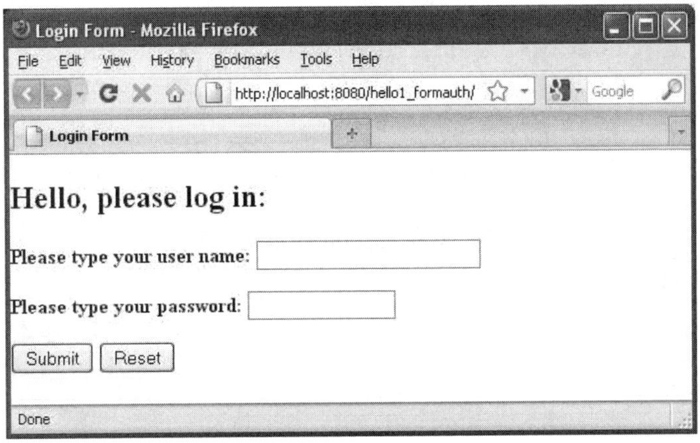

2   **Type a user name and password combination that corresponds to a user who has already been created in the `file` realm of the GlassFish Server and has been assigned to the group of `TutorialUser`.**

Form-based authentication is case sensitive for both the user name and password, so type the user name and password exactly as defined for the GlassFish Server.

3   **Click the Submit button.**

If you entered My_Name as the name and My_Pwd for the password, the server returns the requested resource if all the following conditions are met.

- A user with the user name My_Name is defined for the GlassFish Server.

- The user with the user name My_Name has a password My_Pwd defined for the GlassFish Server.

- The user My_Name with the password My_Pwd is assigned to the group TutorialUser on the GlassFish Server.

- The role TutorialUser, as defined for the application, is mapped to the group TutorialUser, as defined for the GlassFish Server.

When these conditions are met and the server has authenticated the user, the application appears.

4   Type your name and click the Submit button.

Because you have already been authorized, the name you enter in this step does not have any limitations. You have unlimited access to the application now.

The application responds by saying "Hello" to you.

Next Steps   For additional testing and to see the login error page generated, close and reopen your browser, type the application URL, and type a user name and password that are not authorized.

Note – For repetitive testing of this example, you may need to close and reopen your browser. You should also run the ant clean and ant undeploy commands to ensure a fresh build if using the Ant tool, or select Clean and Build then Deploy if using NetBeans IDE.

Getting Started Securing Enterprise Applications

The following parties are responsible for administering security for enterprise applications:

- **System administrator**: Responsible for setting up a database of users and assigning them to the proper group. The system administrator is also responsible for setting GlassFish Serverproperties that enable the applications to run properly. Some security-related examples set up a default principal-to-role mapping, anonymous users, default users, and propagated identities. When needed for this tutorial, the steps for performing specific tasks are provided.

- **Application developer/bean provider**: Responsible for annotating the classes and methods of the enterprise application in order to provide information to the deployer about which methods need to have restricted access. This tutorial describes the steps necessary to complete this task.

- **Deployer**: Responsible for taking the security view provided by the application developer and implementing that security upon deployment. This document provides the information needed to accomplish this task for the tutorial example applications.

The following topics are addressed here:

Securing Enterprise Beans

Enterprise beans are Java EE components that implement EJB technology. Enterprise beans run in the EJB container, a runtime environment within the GlassFish Server. Although transparent to the application developer, the EJB container provides system-level services, such as transactions and security to its enterprise beans, which form the core of transactional Java EE applications.

Enterprise bean methods can be secured in either of the following ways:

- **Declarative security** (preferred): Expresses an application component's security requirements using either deployment descriptors or annotations. The presence of an annotation in the business method of an enterprise bean class that specifies method permissions is all that is needed for method protection and authentication in some situations. This section discusses this simple and efficient method of securing enterprise beans.

  Because of some limitations to the simplified method of securing enterprise beans, you would want to continue to use the deployment descriptor to specify security information in some instances. An authentication mechanism must be configured on the server for the simple solution to work. Basic authentication is the GlassFish Server's default authentication method.

  This tutorial explains how to invoke user name/password authentication of authorized users by decorating the enterprise application's business methods with annotations that specify method permissions.

  To make the deployer's task easier, the application developer can define security roles. A security role is a grouping of permissions that a given type of application users must have in order to successfully use the application. For example, in a payroll application, some users will want to view their own payroll information (*employee*), some will need to view others' payroll information (*manager*), and some will need to be able to change others' payroll information (*payrollDept*). The application developer would determine the potential users of the application and which methods would be accessible to which users. The application developer would then decorate classes or methods of the enterprise bean with annotations that specify the types of users authorized to access those methods. Using annotations to specify authorized users is described in "Specifying Authorized Users by Declaring Security Roles" on page 490.

  When one of the annotations is used to define method permissions, the deployment system will automatically require user name/password authentication. In this type of authentication, a user is prompted to enter a user name and password, which will be compared against a database of known users. If the user is found and the password matches, the roles that the user is assigned will be compared against the roles that are authorized to access the method. If the user is authenticated and found to have a role that is authorized to access that method, the data will be returned to the user.

Using declarative security is discussed in "Securing an Enterprise Bean Using Declarative Security" on page 489.

- **Programmatic security**: For an enterprise bean, code embedded in a business method that is used to access a caller's identity programmatically and that uses this information to make security decisions. Programmatic security is useful when declarative security alone is not sufficient to express the security model of an application.

  In general, security management should be enforced by the container in a manner that is transparent to the enterprise beans' business methods. The programmatic security APIs described in this chapter should be used only in the less frequent situations in which the enterprise bean business methods need to access the security-context information, such as when you want to grant access based on the time of day or other nontrivial condition checks for a particular role.

  Programmatic security is discussed in "Securing an Enterprise Bean Programmatically" on page 493.

Some of the material in this chapter assumes that you have already read Chapter 14, "Enterprise Beans," Chapter 15, "Getting Started with Enterprise Beans," and Chapter 23, "Introduction to Security in the Java EE Platform."

As mentioned earlier, enterprise beans run in the EJB container, a runtime environment within the GlassFish Server, as shown in Figure 25–1.

FIGURE 25–1   Java EE Server and Containers

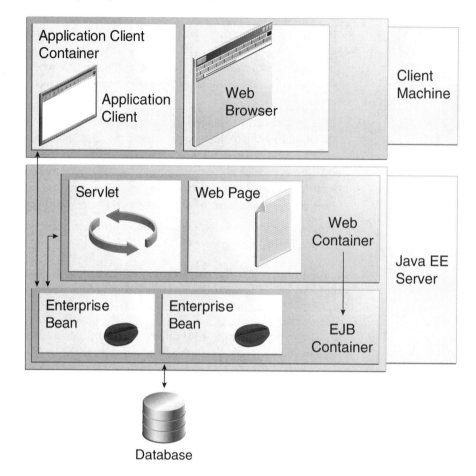

This section discusses securing a Java EE application where one or more modules, such as EJB JAR files, are packaged into an EAR file, the archive file that holds the application. Security annotations will be used in the Java programming class files to specify authorized users and basic, or user name/password, authentication.

Enterprise beans often provide the business logic of a web application. In these cases, packaging the enterprise bean within the web application's WAR module simplifies deployment and application organization. Enterprise beans may be packaged within a WAR module as Java class files or within a JAR file that is bundled within the WAR module. When a servlet or JavaServer Faces page handles the web front end and the application is packaged into a WAR module as a Java class file, security for the application can be handled in the application's web.xml file. The EJB in the WAR file can have its own deployment descriptor, `ejb-jar.xml`, if required. Securing web applications using `web.xml` is discussed in Chapter 24, "Getting Started Securing Web Applications."

The following sections describe declarative and programmatic security mechanisms that can be used to protect enterprise bean resources. The protected resources include enterprise bean methods that are called from application clients, web components, or other enterprise beans.

For more information on this topic, read the Enterprise JavaBeans 3.1 specification. This document can be downloaded from `http://jcp.org/en/jsr/detail?id=318`. Chapter 17 of this specification, "Security Management," discusses security management for enterprise beans.

Securing an Enterprise Bean Using Declarative Security

Declarative security enables the application developer to specify which users are authorized to access which methods of the enterprise beans and to authenticate these users with basic, or username-password, authentication. Frequently, the person who is developing an enterprise application is not the same person who is responsible for deploying the application. An application developer who uses declarative security to define method permissions and authentications mechanisms is passing along to the deployer a *security view* of the enterprise beans contained in the EJB JAR. When a security view is passed on to the deployer, he or she uses this information to define method permissions for security roles. If you don't define a security view, the deployer will have to determine what each business method does to determine which users are authorized to call each method.

A security view consists of a set of security roles, a semantic grouping of permissions that a given type of users of an application must have to successfully access the application. Security roles are meant to be logical roles, representing a type of user. You can define method permissions for each security role. A method permission is a permission to invoke a specified group of methods of an enterprise bean's business interface, home interface, component interface, and/or web service endpoints. After method permissions are defined, user name/password authentication will be used to verify the identity of the user.

It is important to keep in mind that security roles are used to define the logical security view of an application. They should not be confused with the user groups, users, principals, and other concepts that exist in the GlassFish Server. An additional step is required to map the roles defined in the application to users, groups, and principals that are the components of the user database in the file realm of the GlassFish Server. These steps are outlined in "Mapping Roles to Users and Groups" on page 447.

The following sections show how an application developer uses declarative security to either secure an application or to create a security view to pass along to the deployer.

Specifying Authorized Users by Declaring Security Roles

This section discusses how to use annotations to specify the method permissions for the methods of a bean class. For more information on these annotations, refer to the Common Annotations for the Java Platform specification at `http://jcp.org/en/jsr/detail?id=250`.

Method permissions can be specified on the class, the business methods of the class, or both. Method permissions can be specified on a method of the bean class to override the method permissions value specified on the entire bean class. The following annotations are used to specify method permissions:

- `@DeclareRoles`: Specifies all the roles that the application will use, including roles not specifically named in a `@RolesAllowed` annotation. The set of security roles the application uses is the total of the security roles defined in the `@DeclareRoles` and `@RolesAllowed` annotations.

  The `@DeclareRoles` annotation is specified on a bean class, where it serves to declare roles that can be tested (for example, by calling `isCallerInRole`) from within the methods of the annotated class. When declaring the name of a role used as a parameter to the `isCallerInRole(String roleName)` method, the declared name must be the same as the parameter value.

  The following example code demonstrates the use of the `@DeclareRoles` annotation:

  ```
  @DeclareRoles("BusinessAdmin")
  public class Calculator {
      ...
  }
  ```

  The syntax for declaring more than one role is as shown in the following example:

  ```
  @DeclareRoles({"Administrator", "Manager", "Employee"})
  ```

- `@RolesAllowed("`*list-of-roles*`")`: Specifies the security roles permitted to access methods in an application. This annotation can be specified on a class or on one or more methods. When specified at the class level, the annotation applies to all methods in the class. When specified on a method, the annotation applies to that method only and overrides any values specified at the class level.

  To specify that no roles are authorized to access methods in an application, use the `@DenyAll` annotation. To specify that a user in any role is authorized to access the application, use the `@PermitAll` annotation.

  When used in conjunction with the `@DeclareRoles` annotation, the combined set of security roles is used by the application.

The following example code demonstrates the use of the @RolesAllowed annotation:

```
@DeclareRoles({"Administrator", "Manager", "Employee"})
public class Calculator {

    @RolesAllowed("Administrator")
    public void setNewRate(int rate) {
        ...
    }
}
```

- @PermitAll: Specifies that *all* security roles are permitted to execute the specified method or methods. The user is not checked against a database to ensure that he or she is authorized to access this application.

This annotation can be specified on a class or on one or more methods. Specifying this annotation on the class means that it applies to all methods of the class. Specifying it at the method level means that it applies to only that method.

The following example code demonstrates the use of the @PermitAll annotation:

```
import javax.annotation.security.*;
@RolesAllowed("RestrictedUsers")
public class Calculator {

    @RolesAllowed("Administrator")
    public void setNewRate(int rate) {
        //...
    }
    @PermitAll
    public long convertCurrency(long amount) {
        //...
    }
}
```

- @DenyAll: Specifies that *no* security roles are permitted to execute the specified method or methods. This means that these methods are excluded from execution in the Java EE container.

The following example code demonstrates the use of the @DenyAll annotation:

```
import javax.annotation.security.*;
@RolesAllowed("Users")
public class Calculator {
    @RolesAllowed("Administrator")
    public void setNewRate(int rate) {
        //...
    }
    @DenyAll
    public long convertCurrency(long amount) {
        //...
    }
}
```

The following code snippet demonstrates the use of the @DeclareRoles annotation with the isCallerInRole method. In this example, the @DeclareRoles annotation declares a role that the enterprise bean PayrollBean uses to make the security check by using isCallerInRole("payroll") to verify that the caller is authorized to change salary data:

```
@DeclareRoles("payroll")
@Stateless public class PayrollBean implements Payroll {
    @Resource SessionContext ctx;

    public void updateEmployeeInfo(EmplInfo info) {

        oldInfo = ... read from database;

        // The salary field can be changed only by callers
        // who have the security role "payroll"
        Principal callerPrincipal = ctx.getCallerPrincipal();
        if (info.salary != oldInfo.salary && !ctx.isCallerInRole("payroll")) {
            throw new SecurityException(...);
        }
        ...
    }
    ...
}
```

The following example code illustrates the use of the @RolesAllowed annotation:

```
@RolesAllowed("admin")
public class SomeClass {
    public void aMethod () {...}
    public void bMethod () {...}
    ...
}

@Stateless public class MyBean extends SomeClass implements A  {

    @RolesAllowed("HR")
    public void aMethod () {...}

    public void cMethod () {...}
    ...
}
```

In this example, assuming that aMethod, bMethod, and cMethod are methods of business interface A, the method permissions values of methods aMethod and bMethod are @RolesAllowed("HR") and @RolesAllowed("admin"), respectively. The method permissions for method cMethod have not been specified.

To clarify, the annotations are not inherited by the subclass itself. Instead, the annotations apply to methods of the superclass that are inherited by the subclass.

Specifying an Authentication Mechanism and Secure Connection

When method permissions are specified, basic user name/password authentication will be invoked by the GlassFish Server.

To use a different type of authentication or to require a secure connection using SSL, specify this information in an application deployment descriptor.

Securing an Enterprise Bean Programmatically

Programmatic security, code that is embedded in a business method, is used to access a caller's identity programmatically and uses this information to make security decisions within the method itself.

Accessing an Enterprise Bean Caller's Security Context

In general, security management should be enforced by the container in a manner that is transparent to the enterprise bean's business methods. The security API described in this section should be used only in the less frequent situations in which the enterprise bean business methods need to access the security context information, such as when you want to restrict access to a particular time of day.

The javax.ejb.EJBContext interface provides two methods that allow the bean provider to access security information about the enterprise bean's caller:

- getCallerPrincipal, which allows the enterprise bean methods to obtain the current caller principal's name. The methods might, for example, use the name as a key to information in a database.

  The following code sample illustrates the use of the getCallerPrincipal method:

```
@Stateless public class EmployeeServiceBean implements EmployeeService {
    @Resource SessionContext ctx;
    @PersistenceContext EntityManager em;

    public void changePhoneNumber(...) {
        ...
        // obtain the caller principal.
        callerPrincipal = ctx.getCallerPrincipal();

        // obtain the caller principal's name.
        callerKey = callerPrincipal.getName();

        // use callerKey as primary key to find EmployeeRecord
        EmployeeRecord myEmployeeRecord =
            em.find(EmployeeRecord.class, callerKey);

        // update phone number
        myEmployeeRecord.setPhoneNumber(...);

        ...
    }
}
```

In this example, the enterprise bean obtains the principal name of the current caller and uses it as the primary key to locate an `EmployeeRecord` entity. This example assumes that application has been deployed such that the current caller principal contains the primary key used for the identification of employees (for example, employee number).

- `isCallerInRole`, which the enterprise bean code can use to allow the bean provider/application developer to code the security checks that cannot be easily defined using method permissions. Such a check might impose a role-based limit on a request, or it might depend on information stored in the database.

The enterprise bean code can use the `isCallerInRole` method to test whether the current caller has been assigned to a given security role. Security roles are defined by the bean provider or the application assembler and are assigned by the deployer to principals or principal groups that exist in the operational environment.

The following code sample illustrates the use of the `isCallerInRole` method:

```
@Stateless public class PayrollBean implements Payroll {
    @Resource SessionContext ctx;

    public void updateEmployeeInfo(EmplInfo info) {

        oldInfo = ... read from database;

        // The salary field can be changed only by callers
        // who have the security role "payroll"
        if (info.salary != oldInfo.salary &&
            !ctx.isCallerInRole("payroll")) {
                throw new SecurityException(...);
        }
        ...
    }
    ...
}
```

You would use programmatic security in this way to dynamically control access to a method, for example, when you want to deny access except during a particular time of day. An example application that uses the `getCallerPrincipal` and `isCallerInRole` methods is described in "Example: Securing an Enterprise Bean with Programmatic Security" on page 501.

Propagating a Security Identity (Run-As)

You can specify whether a caller's security identity should be used for the execution of specified methods of an enterprise bean or whether a specific run-as identity should be used. Figure 25–2 illustrates this concept.

FIGURE 25–2 Security Identity Propagation

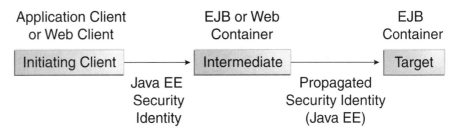

In this illustration, an application client is making a call to an enterprise bean method in one EJB container. This enterprise bean method, in turn, makes a call to an enterprise bean method in another container. The security identity during the first call is the identity of the caller. The security identity during the second call can be any of the following options.

- By default, the identity of the caller of the intermediate component is propagated to the target enterprise bean. This technique is used when the target container trusts the intermediate container.

- A *specific* identity is propagated to the target enterprise bean. This technique is used when the target container expects access using a specific identity.

  To propagate an identity to the target enterprise bean, configure a run-as identity for the bean, as described in "Configuring a Component's Propagated Security Identity" on page 495. Establishing a run-as identity for an enterprise bean does not affect the identities of its callers, which are the identities tested for permission to access the methods of the enterprise bean. The run-as identity establishes the identity that the enterprise bean will use when it makes calls.

  The run-as identity applies to the enterprise bean as a whole, including all the methods of the enterprise bean's business interface, local and remote interfaces, component interface, and web service endpoint interfaces, the message listener methods of a message-driven bean, the timeout method of an enterprise bean, and all internal methods of the bean that might be called in turn.

Configuring a Component's Propagated Security Identity

You can configure an enterprise bean's run-as, or propagated, security identity by using the @RunAs annotation, which defines the role of the application during execution in a Java EE container. The annotation can be specified on a class, allowing developers to execute an application under a particular role. The role must map to the user/group information in the container's security realm. The @RunAs annotation specifies the name of a security role as its parameter.

Here is some example code that demonstrates the use of the @RunAs annotation.

```
@RunAs("Admin")
public class Calculator {
    //....
}
```

You will have to map the run-as role name to a given principal defined on the GlassFish Server if the given roles are associated with more than one user principal.

Trust between Containers

When an enterprise bean is designed so that either the original caller identity or a designated identity is used to call a target bean, the target bean will receive the propagated identity only. The target bean will not receive any authentication data.

There is no way for the target container to authenticate the propagated security identity. However, because the security identity is used in authorization checks (for example, method permissions or with the isCallerInRole method), it is vitally important that the security identity be authentic. Because no authentication data is available to authenticate the propagated identity, the target must trust that the calling container has propagated an authenticated security identity.

By default, the GlassFish Server is configured to trust identities that are propagated from different containers. Therefore, you do not need to take any special steps to set up a trust relationship.

Deploying Secure Enterprise Beans

The deployer is responsible for ensuring that an assembled application is secure after it has been deployed in the target operational environment. If a security view has been provided to the deployer through the use of security annotations and/or a deployment descriptor, the security view is mapped to the mechanisms and policies used by the security domain in the target operational environment, which in this case is the GlassFish Server. If no security view is provided, the deployer must set up the appropriate security policy for the enterprise bean application.

Deployment information is specific to a web or application server.

Examples: Securing Enterprise Beans

The following examples show how to secure enterprise beans using declarative and programmatic security.

Example: Securing an Enterprise Bean with Declarative Security

This section discusses how to configure an enterprise bean for basic user name/password authentication. When a bean that is constrained in this way is requested, the server requests a user name and password from the client and verifies that the user name and password are valid by comparing them against a database of authorized users on the GlassFish Server.

If the topic of authentication is new to you, see "Specifying an Authentication Mechanism in the Deployment Descriptor" on page 467.

This example demonstrates security by starting with the unsecured enterprise bean application, cart, which is found in the directory *tut-install*/examples/ejb/cart/ and is discussed in "The cart Example" on page 271.

In general, the following steps are necessary to add user name/password authentication to an existing application that contains an enterprise bean. In the example application included with this tutorial, these steps have been completed for you and are listed here simply to show what needs to be done should you wish to create a similar application.

1. Create an application like the one in "The cart Example" on page 271. The example in this tutorial starts with this example and demonstrates adding basic authentication of the client to this application. The example application discussed in this section can be found at *tut-install*/examples/security/cart-secure/.

2. If you have not already done so, complete the steps in "To Set Up Your System for Running the Security Examples" on page 474 to configure your system for running the tutorial applications.

3. Modify the source code for the enterprise bean, CartBean.java, to specify which roles are authorized to access which protected methods. This step is discussed in "Annotating the Bean" on page 497.

4. Build, package, and deploy the enterprise bean; then build and run the client application by following the steps in "To Build, Package, Deploy, and Run the Secure Cart Example Using NetBeans IDE" on page 499 or "To Build, Package, Deploy, and Run the Secure Cart Example Using Ant" on page 500.

Annotating the Bean

The source code for the original cart application was modified as shown in the following code snippet (modifications in **bold**). The resulting file can be found in the following location:

```
tut-install/examples/security/cart-secure/cart-secure-ejb/src/java/cart/
ejb/CartBean.java
```

The code snippet is as follows:

```java
package cart.ejb;

import cart.util.BookException;
import cart.util.IdVerifier;
import java.util.ArrayList;
import java.util.List;
import javax.ejb.Remove;
import javax.ejb.Stateful;
import javax.annotation.security.DeclareRoles;
import javax.annotation.security.RolesAllowed;

@Stateful
@DeclareRoles("TutorialUser")
public class CartBean implements Cart {
    List<String> contents;
    String customerId;
    String customerName;

    public void initialize(String person) throws BookException {
        if (person == null) {
            throw new BookException("Null person not allowed.");
        } else {
            customerName = person;
        }

        customerId = "0";
        contents = new ArrayList<String>();
    }

    public void initialize(
        String person,
        String id) throws BookException {
        if (person == null) {
            throw new BookException("Null person not allowed.");
        } else {
            customerName = person;
        }

        IdVerifier idChecker = new IdVerifier();

        if (idChecker.validate(id)) {
            customerId = id;
        } else {
            throw new BookException("Invalid id: " + id);
        }

        contents = new ArrayList<String>();
    }

    @RolesAllowed("TutorialUser")
    public void addBook(String title) {
        contents.add(title);
    }

    @RolesAllowed("TutorialUser")
    public void removeBook(String title) throws BookException {
```

```
        boolean result = contents.remove(title);

        if (result == false) {
            throw new BookException("\"" + title + "\" not in cart.");
        }
    }

    @RolesAllowed("TutorialUser")
    public List<String> getContents() {
        return contents;
    }

    @Remove()
    @RolesAllowed("TutorialUser")
    public void remove() {
        contents = null;
    }
}
```

The @RolesAllowed annotation is specified on methods for which you want to restrict access. In this example, only users in the role of TutorialUser will be allowed to add and remove books from the cart and to list the contents of the cart. A @RolesAllowed annotation implicitly declares a role that will be referenced in the application; therefore, no @DeclareRoles annotation is required. The presence of the @RolesAllowed annotation also implicitly declares that authentication will be required for a user to access these methods. If no authentication method is specified in the deployment descriptor, the type of authentication will be user name/password authentication.

▼ To Build, Package, Deploy, and Run the Secure Cart Example Using NetBeans IDE

1   Follow the steps in "To Set Up Your System for Running the Security Examples" on page 474.

2   In NetBeans IDE, select File→Open Project.

3   In the Open Project dialog, navigate to:

    tut-install/examples/security/

4   Select the cart-secure folder.

5   Select the Open as Main Project and Open Required Projects check boxes.

6   Click Open Project.

7   In the Projects tab, right-click the cart-secure project and select Build.

8   In the Projects tab, right-click the `cart-secure` project and select Deploy.

This step builds and packages the application into `cart-secure.ear`, located in the directory *tut-install*`/examples/security/cart-secure/dist/`, and deploys this EAR file to your GlassFish Server instance.

9   To run the application client, right-click the `cart-secure` project and select Run.

A `Login for user:` dialog box appears.

10   In the dialog box, type the user name and password of a file realm user created on the GlassFish Server and assigned to the group `TutorialUser`; then click OK.

If the user name and password you enter are authenticated, the output of the application client appears in the Output pane:

```
...
Retrieving book title from cart: Infinite Jest
Retrieving book title from cart: Bel Canto
Retrieving book title from cart: Kafka on the Shore
Removing "Gravity's Rainbow" from cart.
Caught a BookException: "Gravity's Rainbow" not in cart.
Java Result: 1
...
```

If the user name and password are not authenticated, the dialog box reappears until you type correct values.

▼ To Build, Package, Deploy, and Run the Secure Cart Example Using Ant

1   Follow the steps in "To Set Up Your System for Running the Security Examples" on page 474.

2   In a terminal window, go to:

tut-install`/examples/security/cart-secure/`

3   To build the application and package it into an EAR file, type the following command at the terminal window or command prompt:

`ant`

4   To deploy the application to the GlassFish Server, type the following command:

`ant deploy`

5   To run the application client, type the following command:

`ant run`

This task retrieves the application client JAR and runs the application client.

A `Login for user:` dialog box appears.

6 **In the dialog box, type the user name and password of a file realm user created on the GlassFish Server and assigned to the group `TutorialUser`; then click OK.**

If the user name and password are authenticated, the client displays the following output:

```
[echo] running application client container.
[exec] Retrieving book title from cart: Infinite Jest
[exec] Retrieving book title from cart: Bel Canto
[exec] Retrieving book title from cart: Kafka on the Shore
[exec] Removing "Gravity's Rainbow" from cart.
[exec] Caught a BookException: "Gravity's Rainbow" not in cart.
[exec] Result: 1
```

If the username and password are not authenticated, the dialog box reappears until you type correct values.

Example: Securing an Enterprise Bean with Programmatic Security

This example demonstrates how to use the `getCallerPrincipal` and `isCallerInRole` methods with an enterprise bean. This example starts with a very simple EJB application, `converter`, and modifies the methods of the `ConverterBean` so that currency conversion will occur only when the requester is in the role of `TutorialUser`.

The completed version of this example can be found in the directory *tut-install/*`examples/security/converter-secure`. This example is based on the unsecured enterprise bean application, `converter`, which is discussed in Chapter 15, "Getting Started with Enterprise Beans," and is found in the directory *tut-install*/`examples/ejb/converter/`. This section builds on the example by adding the necessary elements to secure the application by using the `getCallerPrincipal` and `isCallerInRole` methods, which are discussed in more detail in "Accessing an Enterprise Bean Caller's Security Context" on page 493.

In general, the following steps are necessary when using the `getCallerPrincipal` and `isCallerInRole` methods with an enterprise bean. In the example application included with this tutorial, many of these steps have been completed for you and are listed here simply to show what needs to be done should you wish to create a similar application.

1. Create a simple enterprise bean application.

2. Set up a user on the GlassFish Server in the `file` realm, in the group `TutorialUser`, and set up default principal to role mapping. To do this, follow the steps in "To Set Up Your System for Running the Security Examples" on page 474.

3. Modify the bean to add the `getCallerPrincipal` and `isCallerInRole` methods.

4. If the application contains a web client that is a servlet, specify security for the servlet, as described in "Specifying Security for Basic Authentication Using Annotations" on page 476.

5. Build, package, deploy, and run the application.

Modifying ConverterBean

The source code for the original ConverterBean class was modified to add the if..else clause that tests whether the caller is in the role of TutorialUser.. If the user is in the correct role, the currency conversion is computed and displayed. If the user is not in the correct role, the computation is not performed, and the application displays the result as 0. The code example can be found in the following file:

tut-install/examples/ejb/converter-secure/converter-secure-ejb/src/java/
converter/ejb/ConverterBean.java

The code snippet (with modifications shown in **bold**) is as follows:

```
package converter.ejb;

import java.math.BigDecimal;
import javax.ejb.Stateless;
import java.security.Principal;
import javax.annotation.Resource;
import javax.ejb.SessionContext;
import javax.annotation.security.DeclareRoles;
import javax.annotation.security.RolesAllowed;

@Stateless()
@DeclareRoles("TutorialUser")
public class ConverterBean{

    @Resource SessionContext ctx;
    private BigDecimal yenRate = new BigDecimal("89.5094");
    private BigDecimal euroRate = new BigDecimal("0.0081");

    @RolesAllowed("TutorialUser")
     public BigDecimal dollarToYen(BigDecimal dollars) {
        BigDecimal result = new BigDecimal("0.0");
        Principal callerPrincipal = ctx.getCallerPrincipal();
        if (ctx.isCallerInRole("TutorialUser")) {
            result = dollars.multiply(yenRate);
            return result.setScale(2, BigDecimal.ROUND_UP);
        } else {
            return result.setScale(2, BigDecimal.ROUND_UP);
        }
    }

    @RolesAllowed("TutorialUser")
    public BigDecimal yenToEuro(BigDecimal yen) {
        BigDecimal result = new BigDecimal("0.0");
        Principal callerPrincipal = ctx.getCallerPrincipal();
        if (ctx.isCallerInRole("TutorialUser")) {
            result = yen.multiply(euroRate);
```

```
            return result.setScale(2, BigDecimal.ROUND_UP);
        } else {
            return result.setScale(2, BigDecimal.ROUND_UP);
        }
    }
}
```

Modifying `ConverterServlet`

The following annotations specify security for the converter web client, `ConverterServlet`:

```
@WebServlet(name = "ConverterServlet", urlPatterns = {"/"})
@ServletSecurity(
@HttpConstraint(transportGuarantee = TransportGuarantee.CONFIDENTIAL,
    rolesAllowed = {"TutorialUser"}))
```

▼ To Build, Package, and Deploy the Secure Converter Example Using NetBeans IDE

1   Follow the steps in "To Set Up Your System for Running the Security Examples" on page 474.

2   In NetBeans IDE, select File→Open Project.

3   In the Open Project dialog, navigate to:

    tut-install/examples/security/

4   Select the `converter-secure` folder.

5   Select the Open as Main Project check box.

6   Click Open Project.

7   Right-click the `converter-secure` project and select Build.

8   Right-click the `converter-secure` project and select Deploy.

▼ To Build, Package, and Deploy the Secure Converter Example Using Ant

1   Follow the steps in "To Set Up Your System for Running the Security Examples" on page 474.

2   In a terminal window, go to:

    tut-install/examples/security/converter-secure/

3 **Type the following command:**

`ant all`

This command both builds and deploys the example.

▼ To Run the Secure Converter Example

1 **Open a web browser to the following URL:**

`http://localhost:8080/converter`

An Authentication Required dialog box appears.

2 **Type a user name and password combination that corresponds to a user who has already been created in the `file` realm of the GlassFish Server and has been assigned to the group of `TutorialUser`; then click OK.**

The screen shown in Figure 15–1 appears.

3 **Type `100` in the input field and click Submit.**

A second page appears, showing the converted values.

Securing Application Clients

The Java EE authentication requirements for application clients are the same as for other Java EE components, and the same authentication techniques can be used as for other Java EE application components. No authentication is necessary when accessing unprotected web resources.

When accessing protected web resources, the usual varieties of authentication can be used: HTTP basic authentication, SSL client authentication, or HTTP login-form authentication. These authentication methods are discussed in "Specifying an Authentication Mechanism in the Deployment Descriptor" on page 467.

Authentication is required when accessing protected enterprise beans. The authentication mechanisms for enterprise beans are discussed in "Securing Enterprise Beans" on page 486.

An application client makes use of an authentication service provided by the application client container for authenticating its users. The container's service can be integrated with the native platform's authentication system, so that a single sign-on capability is used. The container can authenticate the user either when the application is started or when a protected resource is accessed.

An application client can provide a class, called a login module, to gather authentication data. If so, the `javax.security.auth.callback.CallbackHandler` interface must be implemented, and the class name must be specified in its deployment descriptor. The application's callback handler must fully support Callback objects specified in the javax.security.auth.callback package.

Using Login Modules

An application client can use the Java Authentication and Authorization Service (JAAS) to create *login modules* for authentication. A JAAS-based application implements the javax.security.auth.callback.CallbackHandler interface so that it can interact with users to enter specific authentication data, such as user names or passwords, or to display error and warning messages.

Applications implement the CallbackHandler interface and pass it to the login context, which forwards it directly to the underlying login modules. A login module uses the callback handler both to gather input, such as a password or smart card PIN, from users and to supply information, such as status information, to users. Because the application specifies the callback handler, an underlying login module can remain independent of the various ways that applications interact with users.

For example, the implementation of a callback handler for a GUI application might display a window to solicit user input. Or the implementation of a callback handler for a command-line tool might simply prompt the user for input directly from the command line.

The login module passes an array of appropriate callbacks to the callback handler's handle method, such as a NameCallback for the user name and a PasswordCallback for the password; the callback handler performs the requested user interaction and sets appropriate values in the callbacks. For example, to process a NameCallback, the CallbackHandler might prompt for a name, retrieve the value from the user, and call the setName method of the NameCallback to store the name.

For more information on using JAAS for login modules for authentication, refer to the following sources (see "Further Information about Security" on page 454 for the URLs):

- *Java Authentication and Authorization Service (JAAS) Reference Guide*
- *Java Authentication and Authorization Service (JAAS): LoginModule Developer's Guide*

Using Programmatic Login

Programmatic login enables the client code to supply user credentials. If you are using an EJB client, you can use the com.sun.appserv.security.ProgrammaticLogin class with its convenient login and logout methods. Programmatic login is specific to a server.

Securing Enterprise Information Systems Applications

In EIS applications, components request a connection to an EIS resource. As part of this connection, the EIS can require a sign-on for the requester to access the resource. The application component provider has two choices for the design of the EIS sign-on:

- **Container-managed sign-on**: The application component lets the container take the responsibility of configuring and managing the EIS sign-on. The container determines the user name and password for establishing a connection to an EIS instance. For more information, see "Container-Managed Sign-On" on page 506.

- **Component-managed sign-on**: The application component code manages EIS sign-on by including code that performs the sign-on process to an EIS. For more information, see "Component-Managed Sign-On" on page 506.

You can also configure security for resource adapters. See "Configuring Resource Adapter Security" on page 507 for more information.

Container-Managed Sign-On

In container-managed sign-on, an application component does not have to pass any sign-on security information to the getConnection() method. The security information is supplied by the container, as shown in the following example:

```
// Business method in an application component
Context initctx = new InitialContext();
// Perform JNDI lookup to obtain a connection factory
javax.resource.cci.ConnectionFactory cxf =
    (javax.resource.cci.ConnectionFactory)initctx.lookup(
    "java:comp/env/eis/MainframeCxFactory");
// Invoke factory to obtain a connection. The security
// information is not passed in the getConnection method
javax.resource.cci.Connection cx = cxf.getConnection();
...
```

Component-Managed Sign-On

In component-managed sign-on, an application component is responsible for passing the needed sign-on security information to the resource to the getConnection method. For example, security information might be a user name and password, as shown here:

```
// Method in an application component
Context initctx = new InitialContext();

// Perform JNDI lookup to obtain a connection factory
javax.resource.cci.ConnectionFactory cxf =
```

```
(javax.resource.cci.ConnectionFactory)initctx.lookup(
"java:comp/env/eis/MainframeCxFactory");

// Get a new ConnectionSpec
com.myeis.ConnectionSpecImpl properties = //..

// Invoke factory to obtain a connection
properties.setUserName("...");
properties.setPassword("...");
javax.resource.cci.Connection cx =
    cxf.getConnection(properties);
...
```

Configuring Resource Adapter Security

A resource adapter is a system-level software component that typically implements network connectivity to an external resource manager. A resource adapter can extend the functionality of the Java EE platform either by implementing one of the Java EE standard service APIs, such as a JDBC driver, or by defining and implementing a resource adapter for a connector to an external application system. Resource adapters can also provide services that are entirely local, perhaps interacting with native resources. Resource adapters interface with the Java EE platform through the Java EE service provider interfaces (Java EE SPI). A resource adapter that uses the Java EE SPIs to attach to the Java EE platform will be able to work with all Java EE products.

To configure the security settings for a resource adapter, you need to edit the resource adapter descriptor file, ra.xml. Here is an example of the part of an ra.xml file that configures the following security properties for a resource adapter:

```
<authentication-mechanism>
    <authentication-mechanism-type>
        BasicPassword
    </authentication-mechanism-type>
    <credential-interface>
        javax.resource.spi.security.PasswordCredential
    </credential-interface>
</authentication-mechanism>
<reauthentication-support>false</reauthentication-support>
```

You can find out more about the options for configuring resource adapter security by reviewing *as-install*/lib/dtds/connector_1_0.dtd. You can configure the following elements in the resource adapter deployment descriptor file:

- **Authentication mechanisms**: Use the authentication-mechanism element to specify an authentication mechanism supported by the resource adapter. This support is for the resource adapter, not for the underlying EIS instance.

  There are two supported mechanism types:

  - BasicPassword, which supports the following interface:

    javax.resource.spi.security.PasswordCredential

- **Kerbv5**, which supports the following interface:

  `javax.resource.spi.security.GenericCredential`

  The GlassFish Server does not currently support this mechanism type.

- **Reauthentication support**: Use the `reauthentication-support` element to specify whether the resource adapter implementation supports reauthentication of existing `Managed-Connection` instances. Options are `true` or `false`.

- **Security permissions**: Use the `security-permission` element to specify a security permission that is required by the resource adapter code. Support for security permissions is optional and is not supported in the current release of the GlassFish Server. You can, however, manually update the `server.policy` file to add the relevant permissions for the resource adapter.

  The security permissions listed in the deployment descriptor are different from those required by the default permission set as specified in the connector specification.

  For more information on the implementation of the security permission specification, visit `http://download.oracle.com/docs/cd/E17409_01/javase/6/docs/technotes/guides/security/PolicyFiles.html#FileSyntax`.

In addition to specifying resource adapter security in the `ra.xml` file, you can create a security map for a connector connection pool to map an application principal or a user group to a back-end EIS principal. The security map is usually used if one or more EIS back-end principals are used to execute operations (on the EIS) initiated by various principals or user groups in the application.

▼ To Map an Application Principal to EIS Principals

When using the GlassFish Server, you can use security maps to map the caller identity of the application (principal or user group) to a suitable EIS principal in container-managed transaction-based scenarios. When an application principal initiates a request to an EIS, the GlassFish Server first checks for an exact principal by using the security map defined for the connector connection pool to determine the mapped back-end EIS principal. If there is no exact match, the GlassFish Server uses the wildcard character specification, if any, to determine the mapped back-end EIS principal. Security maps are used when an application user needs to execute EIS operations that require to be executed as a specific identity in the EIS.

To work with security maps, use the Administration Console. From the Administration Console, follow these steps to get to the security maps page.

1   In the navigation tree, expand the Resources node.

2 Expand the Connectors node.

3 Select the Connector Connection Pools node.

4 On the Connector Connection Pools page, click the name of the connection pool for which you want to create a security map.

5 Click the Security Maps tab.

6 Click New to create a new security map for the connection pool.

7 Type a name by which you will refer to the security map, as well as the other required information.

Click the Help button for more information on the individual options.

Java EE Supporting Technologies

Part VIII introduces several technologies that support the Java EE platform. This part contains the following chapters:

26

Introduction to Java EE Supporting Technologies

The Java EE platform includes several technologies and APIs that extend its functionality. These technologies allow applications to access a wide range of services in a uniform manner. These technologies are explained in greater in Chapter 27, "Transactions," and Chapter 28, "Resource Connections."

The following topics are addressed here:

- "Transactions" on page 513
- "Resources" on page 514

Transactions

In a Java EE application, a transaction is a series of actions that must all complete successfully, or else all the changes in each action are backed out. Transactions end in either a commit or a rollback.

The Java Transaction API (JTA) allows applications to access transactions in a manner that is independent of specific implementations. JTA specifies standard Java interfaces between a transaction manager and the parties involved in a distributed transaction system: the transactional application, the Java EE server, and the manager that controls access to the shared resources affected by the transactions.

The JTA defines the `UserTransaction` interface that applications use to start, commit, or abort transactions. Application components get a `UserTransaction` object through a JNDI lookup by using the name `java:comp/UserTransaction` or by requesting injection of a `UserTransaction` object. An application server uses a number of JTA-defined interfaces to communicate with a transaction manager; a transaction manager uses JTA-defined interfaces to interact with a resource manager.

See Chapter 27, "Transactions," for a more detailed explanation. The JTA 1.1 specification is available at `http://www.oracle.com/technetwork/java/javaee/tech/jta-138684.html`.

Resources

A resource is a program object that provides connections to such systems as database servers and messaging systems.

The Java EE Connector Architecture and Resource Adapters

The Java EE Connector Architecture enables Java EE components to interact with enterprise information systems (EISs) and EISs to interact with Java EE components. EIS software includes such kinds of systems as enterprise resource planning (ERP), mainframe transaction processing, and nonrelational databases. Connector architecture simplifies the integration of diverse EISs. Each EIS requires only one implementation of the Connector architecture. Because it adheres to the Connector specification, an implementation is portable across all compliant Java EE servers.

The specification defines the contracts for an application server as well as for resource adapters, which are system-level software drivers for specific EIS resources. These standard contracts provide pluggability between application servers and EISs. The Java EE Connector Architecture 1.6 specification defines new system contracts such as Generic Work Context and Security Inflow. The Java EE Connector Architecture 1.6 specification is available at `http://jcp.org/en/jsr/detail?id=322`.

A resource adapter is a Java EE component that implements the Connector architecture for a specific EIS. A resource adapter can choose to support the following levels of transactions:

- `NoTransaction`: No transaction support is provided.
- `LocalTransaction`: Resource manager local transactions are supported.
- `XATransaction`: The resource adapter supports the XA distributed transaction processing model and the JTA `XATransaction` interface.

See Chapter 28, "Resource Connections," for a more detailed explanation of resource adapters.

Java Message Service

Messaging is a method of communication between software components or applications. A messaging system is a peer-to-peer facility: A messaging client can send messages to, and receive messages from, any other client. Each client connects to a messaging agent that provides facilities for creating, sending, receiving, and reading messages.

The Java Message Service (JMS) API allows applications to create, send, receive, and read messages. It defines a common set of interfaces and associated semantics that allow programs written in the Java programming language to communicate with other messaging implementations.

The JMS API minimizes the set of concepts a programmer must learn in order to use messaging products but provides enough features to support sophisticated messaging applications. It also strives to maximize the portability of JMS applications across JMS providers in the same messaging domain.

Java Database Connectivity Software

To store, organize, and retrieve data, most applications use relational databases. Java EE applications access relational databases through the JDBC API.

A JDBC resource, or data source, provides applications with a means of connecting to a database. Typically, a JDBC resource is created for each database accessed by the applications deployed in a domain. Transactional access to JDBC resources is available from servlets, JavaServer Faces pages, and enterprise beans. The connection pooling and distributed transaction features are intended for use by JDBC drivers to coordinate with an application server. For more information, see "`DataSource` Objects and Connection Pools" on page 530.

CHAPTER 27

Transactions

A typical enterprise application accesses and stores information in one or more databases. Because this information is critical for business operations, it must be accurate, current, and reliable. Data integrity would be lost if multiple programs were allowed to update the same information simultaneously or if a system that failed while processing a business transaction were to leave the affected data only partially updated. By preventing both of these scenarios, software transactions ensure data integrity. Transactions control the concurrent access of data by multiple programs. In the event of a system failure, transactions make sure that after recovery, the data will be in a consistent state.

The following topics are addressed here:

What Is a Transaction?

To emulate a business transaction, a program may need to perform several steps. A financial program, for example, might transfer funds from a checking account to a savings account by using the steps listed in the following pseudocode:

```
begin transaction
    debit checking account
    credit savings account
    update history log
commit transaction
```

Either all or none of the three steps must complete. Otherwise, data integrity is lost. Because the steps within a transaction are a unified whole, a *transaction* is often defined as an indivisible unit of work.

A transaction can end in two ways: with a commit or with a rollback. When a transaction commits, the data modifications made by its statements are saved. If a statement within a transaction fails, the transaction rolls back, undoing the effects of all statements in the transaction. In the pseudocode, for example, if a disk drive were to crash during the `credit` step, the transaction would roll back and undo the data modifications made by the `debit` statement. Although the transaction fails, data integrity would be intact because the accounts still balance.

In the preceding pseudocode, the `begin` and `commit` statements mark the boundaries of the transaction. When designing an enterprise bean, you determine how the boundaries are set by specifying either container-managed or bean-managed transactions.

Container-Managed Transactions

In an enterprise bean with *container-managed transaction demarcation*, the EJB container sets the boundaries of the transactions. You can use container-managed transactions with any type of enterprise bean: session or message-driven. Container-managed transactions simplify development because the enterprise bean code does not explicitly mark the transaction's boundaries. The code does not include statements that begin and end the transaction. By default, if no transaction demarcation is specified, enterprise beans use container-managed transaction demarcation.

Typically, the container begins a transaction immediately before an enterprise bean method starts and commits the transaction just before the method exits. Each method can be associated with a single transaction. Nested or multiple transactions are not allowed within a method.

Container-managed transactions do not require all methods to be associated with transactions. When developing a bean, you can set the transaction attributes to specify which of the bean's methods are associated with transactions.

Enterprise beans that use container-managed transaction demarcation must not use any transaction-management methods that interfere with the container's transaction demarcation boundaries. Examples of such methods are the `commit`, `setAutoCommit`, and `rollback` methods of `java.sql.Connection` or the `commit` and `rollback` methods of `javax.jms.Session`. If you require control over the transaction demarcation, you must use application-managed transaction demarcation.

Enterprise beans that use container-managed transaction demarcation also must not use the `javax.transaction.UserTransaction` interface.

Transaction Attributes

A *transaction attribute* controls the scope of a transaction. Figure 27–1 illustrates why controlling the scope is important. In the diagram, method-A begins a transaction and then invokes method-B of Bean-2. When method-B executes, does it run within the scope of the transaction started by method-A, or does it execute with a new transaction? The answer depends on the transaction attribute of method-B.

FIGURE 27–1 Transaction Scope

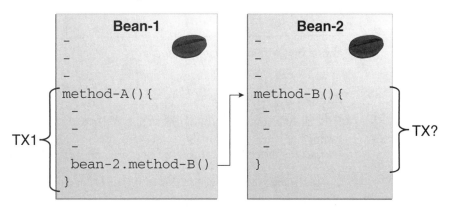

A transaction attribute can have one of the following values:

- Required
- RequiresNew
- Mandatory
- NotSupported
- Supports
- Never

Required **Attribute**

If the client is running within a transaction and invokes the enterprise bean's method, the method executes within the client's transaction. If the client is not associated with a transaction, the container starts a new transaction before running the method.

The Required attribute is the implicit transaction attribute for all enterprise bean methods running with container-managed transaction demarcation. You typically do not set the Required attribute unless you need to override another transaction attribute. Because transaction attributes are declarative, you can easily change them later.

RequiresNew **Attribute**

If the client is running within a transaction and invokes the enterprise bean's method, the container takes the following steps:

1. Suspends the client's transaction
2. Starts a new transaction
3. Delegates the call to the method
4. Resumes the client's transaction after the method completes

If the client is not associated with a transaction, the container starts a new transaction before running the method.

You should use the RequiresNew attribute when you want to ensure that the method always runs within a new transaction.

Mandatory **Attribute**

If the client is running within a transaction and invokes the enterprise bean's method, the method executes within the client's transaction. If the client is not associated with a transaction, the container throws a TransactionRequiredException.

Use the Mandatory attribute if the enterprise bean's method must use the transaction of the client.

NotSupported **Attribute**

If the client is running within a transaction and invokes the enterprise bean's method, the container suspends the client's transaction before invoking the method. After the method has completed, the container resumes the client's transaction.

If the client is not associated with a transaction, the container does not start a new transaction before running the method.

Use the NotSupported attribute for methods that don't need transactions. Because transactions involve overhead, this attribute may improve performance.

Supports **Attribute**

If the client is running within a transaction and invokes the enterprise bean's method, the method executes within the client's transaction. If the client is not associated with a transaction, the container does not start a new transaction before running the method.

Because the transactional behavior of the method may vary, you should use the Supports attribute with caution.

Never **Attribute**

If the client is running within a transaction and invokes the enterprise bean's method, the container throws a RemoteException. If the client is not associated with a transaction, the container does not start a new transaction before running the method.

Summary of Transaction Attributes

Table 27–1 summarizes the effects of the transaction attributes. Both the T1 and the T2 transactions are controlled by the container. A T1 transaction is associated with the client that calls a method in the enterprise bean. In most cases, the client is another enterprise bean. A T2 transaction is started by the container just before the method executes.

In the last column of Table 27–1, the word "None" means that the business method does not execute within a transaction controlled by the container. However, the database calls in such a business method might be controlled by the transaction manager of the database management system.

TABLE 27–1 Transaction Attributes and Scope

Transaction Attribute	Client's Transaction	Business Method's Transaction
Required	None	T2
	T1	T1
RequiresNew	None	T2
	T1	T2
Mandatory	None	Error
	T1	T1
NotSupported	None	None
	T1	None
Supports	None	None
	T1	T1
Never	None	None
	T1	Error

Setting Transaction Attributes

Transaction attributes are specified by decorating the enterprise bean class or method with a javax.ejb.TransactionAttribute annotation and setting it to one of the javax.ejb.TransactionAttributeType constants.

If you decorate the enterprise bean class with @TransactionAttribute, the specified TransactionAttributeType is applied to all the business methods in the class. Decorating a business method with @TransactionAttribute applies the TransactionAttributeType only to that method. If a @TransactionAttribute annotation decorates both the class and the method, the method TransactionAttributeType overrides the class TransactionAttributeType.

The TransactionAttributeType constants shown in Table 27–2 encapsulate the transaction attributes described earlier in this section.

TABLE 27–2 TransactionAttributeType Constants

Transaction Attribute	TransactionAttributeType Constant
Required	TransactionAttributeType.REQUIRED
RequiresNew	TransactionAttributeType.REQUIRES_NEW
Mandatory	TransactionAttributeType.MANDATORY
NotSupported	TransactionAttributeType.NOT_SUPPORTED
Supports	TransactionAttributeType.SUPPORTS
Never	TransactionAttributeType.NEVER

The following code snippet demonstrates how to use the @TransactionAttribute annotation:

```
@TransactionAttribute(NOT_SUPPORTED)
@Stateful
public class TransactionBean implements Transaction {
...
    @TransactionAttribute(REQUIRES_NEW)
    public void firstMethod() {...}

    @TransactionAttribute(REQUIRED)
    public void secondMethod() {...}

    public void thirdMethod() {...}

    public void fourthMethod() {...}
}
```

In this example, the TransactionBean class's transaction attribute has been set to NotSupported, firstMethod has been set to RequiresNew, and secondMethod has been set to Required. Because a @TransactionAttribute set on a method overrides the class @TransactionAttribute, calls to firstMethod will create a new transaction, and calls to secondMethod will either run in the current transaction or start a new transaction. Calls to thirdMethod or fourthMethod do not take place within a transaction.

Rolling Back a Container-Managed Transaction

There are two ways to roll back a container-managed transaction. First, if a system exception is thrown, the container will automatically roll back the transaction. Second, by invoking the setRollbackOnly method of the EJBContext interface, the bean method instructs the container to roll back the transaction. If the bean throws an application exception, the rollback is not automatic but can be initiated by a call to setRollbackOnly.

Synchronizing a Session Bean's Instance Variables

The SessionSynchronization interface, which is optional, allows stateful session bean instances to receive transaction synchronization notifications. For example, you could synchronize the instance variables of an enterprise bean with their corresponding values in the database. The container invokes the SessionSynchronization methods (afterBegin, beforeCompletion, and afterCompletion) at each of the main stages of a transaction.

The afterBegin method informs the instance that a new transaction has begun. The container invokes afterBegin immediately before it invokes the business method.

The container invokes the beforeCompletion method after the business method has finished but just before the transaction commits. The beforeCompletion method is the last opportunity for the session bean to roll back the transaction (by calling setRollbackOnly).

The afterCompletion method indicates that the transaction has completed. This method has a single boolean parameter whose value is true if the transaction was committed and false if it was rolled back.

Methods Not Allowed in Container-Managed Transactions

You should not invoke any method that might interfere with the transaction boundaries set by the container. The list of prohibited methods follows:

- The commit, setAutoCommit, and rollback methods of java.sql.Connection
- The getUserTransaction method of javax.ejb.EJBContext
- Any method of javax.transaction.UserTransaction

You can, however, use these methods to set boundaries in application-managed transactions.

Bean-Managed Transactions

In *bean-managed transaction demarcation*, the code in the session or message-driven bean explicitly marks the boundaries of the transaction. Although beans with container-managed transactions require less coding, they have one limitation: When a method is executing, it can be associated with either a single transaction or no transaction at all. If this limitation will make coding your bean difficult, you should consider using bean-managed transactions.

The following pseudocode illustrates the kind of fine-grained control you can obtain with application-managed transactions. By checking various conditions, the pseudocode decides whether to start or stop certain transactions within the business method:

```
begin transaction
...
    update table-a
...
    if (condition-x)
    commit transaction
    else if (condition-y)
    update table-b
    commit transaction
    else
    rollback transaction
    begin transaction
    update table-c
    commit transaction
```

When coding an application-managed transaction for session or message-driven beans, you must decide whether to use Java Database Connectivity or JTA transactions. The sections that follow discuss both types of transactions.

JTA Transactions

JTA, or the Java Transaction API, allows you to demarcate transactions in a manner that is independent of the transaction manager implementation. GlassFish Server implements the transaction manager with the Java Transaction Service (JTS). However, your code doesn't call the JTS methods directly but instead invokes the JTA methods, which then call the lower-level JTS routines.

A *JTA transaction* is controlled by the Java EE transaction manager. You may want to use a JTA transaction because it can span updates to multiple databases from different vendors. A particular DBMS's transaction manager may not work with heterogeneous databases. However, the Java EE transaction manager does have one limitation: It does not support nested transactions. In other words, it cannot start a transaction for an instance until the preceding transaction has ended.

To demarcate a JTA transaction, you invoke the `begin`, `commit`, and `rollback` methods of the `javax.transaction.UserTransaction` interface.

Returning without Committing

In a stateless session bean with bean-managed transactions, a business method must commit or roll back a transaction before returning. However, a stateful session bean does not have this restriction.

In a stateful session bean with a JTA transaction, the association between the bean instance and the transaction is retained across multiple client calls. Even if each business method called by the client opens and closes the database connection, the association is retained until the instance completes the transaction.

In a stateful session bean with a JDBC transaction, the JDBC connection retains the association between the bean instance and the transaction across multiple calls. If the connection is closed, the association is not retained.

Methods Not Allowed in Bean-Managed Transactions

Do not invoke the `getRollbackOnly` and `setRollbackOnly` methods of the `EJBContext` interface in bean-managed transactions. These methods should be used only in container-managed transactions. For bean-managed transactions, invoke the `getStatus` and `rollback` methods of the `UserTransaction` interface.

Transaction Timeouts

For container-managed transactions, you can use the Administration Console to configure the transaction timeout interval. See "Starting the Administration Console" on page 42.

For enterprise beans with bean-managed JTA transactions, you invoke the `setTransactionTimeout` method of the `UserTransaction` interface.

▼ To Set a Transaction Timeout

1   In the Administration Console, expand the Configuration node and select Transaction Service.

2   On the Transaction Service page, set the value of the Transaction Timeout field to the value of your choice (for example, 5).

With this setting, if the transaction has not completed within 5 seconds, the EJB container rolls it back.

The default value is 0, meaning that the transaction will not time out.

3   Click Save.

Updating Multiple Databases

The Java EE transaction manager controls all enterprise bean transactions except for bean-managed JDBC transactions. The Java EE transaction manager allows an enterprise bean to update multiple databases within a transaction. Figure 27–2 and Figure 27–3 show two scenarios for updating multiple databases in a single transaction.

In Figure 27–2, the client invokes a business method in Bean-A. The business method begins a transaction, updates Database X, updates Database Y, and invokes a business method in Bean-B. The second business method updates Database Z and returns control to the business method in Bean-A, which commits the transaction. All three database updates occur in the same transaction.

In Figure 27–3, the client calls a business method in Bean-A, which begins a transaction and updates Database X. Then Bean-A invokes a method in Bean-B, which resides in a remote Java EE server. The method in Bean-B updates Database Y. The transaction managers of the Java EE servers ensure that both databases are updated in the same transaction.

FIGURE 27–2   Updating Multiple Databases

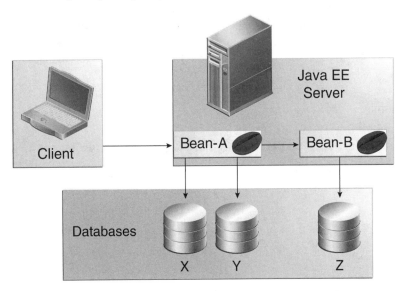

FIGURE 27–3   Updating Multiple Databases across Java EE Servers

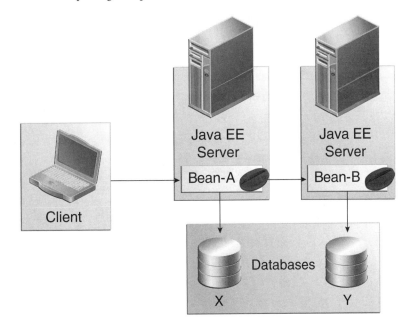

Transactions in Web Components

You can demarcate a transaction in a web component by using either the `java.sql.Connection` or the `javax.transaction.UserTransaction` interface. These are the same interfaces that a session bean with bean-managed transactions can use. Transactions demarcated with the `UserTransaction` interface are discussed in "JTA Transactions" on page 524.

Further Information about Transactions

For more information about transactions, see

- Java Transaction API 1.1 specification:

  `http://www.oracle.com/technetwork/java/javaee/tech/jta-138684.html`

28

Resource Connections

Java EE components can access a wide variety of resources, including databases, mail sessions, Java Message Service objects, and URLs. The Java EE 6 platform provides mechanisms that allow you to access all these resources in a similar manner. This chapter explains how to get connections to several types of resources.

The following topics are addressed here:

- "Resources and JNDI Naming" on page 529
- "DataSource Objects and Connection Pools" on page 530
- "Resource Injection" on page 531
- "Resource Adapters and Contracts" on page 534
- "Metadata Annotations" on page 538
- "Common Client Interface" on page 540
- "Further Information about Resources" on page 541

Resources and JNDI Naming

In a distributed application, components need to access other components and resources, such as databases. For example, a servlet might invoke remote methods on an enterprise bean that retrieves information from a database. In the Java EE platform, the Java Naming and Directory Interface (JNDI) naming service enables components to locate other components and resources.

A *resource* is a program object that provides connections to systems, such as database servers and messaging systems. (A Java Database Connectivity resource is sometimes referred to as a data source.) Each resource object is identified by a unique, people-friendly name, called the JNDI name. For example, the JNDI name of the JDBC resource for the Java DB database that is shipped with the GlassFish Server is jdbc/__default.

An administrator creates resources in a JNDI namespace. In the GlassFish Server, you can use either the Administration Console or the `asadmin` command to create resources. Applications then use annotations to inject the resources. If an application uses resource injection, the GlassFish Server invokes the JNDI API, and the application is not required to do so. However, it is also possible for an application to locate resources by making direct calls to the JNDI API.

A resource object and its JNDI name are bound together by the naming and directory service. To create a new resource, a new name/object binding is entered into the JNDI namespace. You inject resources by using the `@Resource` annotation in an application.

You can use a deployment descriptor to override the resource mapping that you specify in an annotation. Using a deployment descriptor allows you to change an application by repackaging it rather than by both recompiling the source files and repackaging. However, for most applications, a deployment descriptor is not necessary.

DataSource **Objects and Connection Pools**

To store, organize, and retrieve data, most applications use a relational database. Java EE 6 components may access relational databases through the JDBC API. For information on this API, see `http://www.oracle.com/technetwork/java/javase/tech/index-jsp-136101.html`.

In the JDBC API, databases are accessed by using `DataSource` objects. A `DataSource` has a set of properties that identify and describe the real-world data source that it represents. These properties include such information as the location of the database server, the name of the database, the network protocol to use to communicate with the server, and so on. In the GlassFish Server, a data source is called a JDBC resource.

Applications access a data source by using a connection, and a `DataSource` object can be thought of as a factory for connections to the particular data source that the `DataSource` instance represents. In a basic `DataSource` implementation, a call to the `getConnection` method returns a connection object that is a physical connection to the data source.

A `DataSource` object may be registered with a JNDI naming service. If so, an application can use the JNDI API to access that `DataSource` object, which can then be used to connect to the data source it represents.

`DataSource` objects that implement connection pooling also produce a connection to the particular data source that the `DataSource` class represents. The connection object that the `getConnection` method returns is a handle to a `PooledConnection` object rather than being a physical connection. An application uses the connection object in the same way that it uses a connection. Connection pooling has no effect on application code except that a pooled connection, like all connections, should always be explicitly closed. When an application closes a connection that is pooled, the connection is returned to a pool of reusable connections. The next time getConnection is called, a handle to one of these pooled connections will be returned if one is available. Because connection pooling avoids creating a new physical connection every time one is requested, applications can run significantly faster.

A JDBC connection pool is a group of reusable connections for a particular database. Because creating each new physical connection is time consuming, the server maintains a pool of available connections to increase performance. When it requests a connection, an application obtains one from the pool. When an application closes a connection, the connection is returned to the pool.

Applications that use the Persistence API specify the DataSource object they are using in the jta-data-source element of the persistence.xml file:

```
<jta-data-source>jdbc/MyOrderDB</jta-data-source>
```

This is typically the only reference to a JDBC object for a persistence unit. The application code does not refer to any JDBC objects.

Resource Injection

The javax.annotation.Resource annotation is used to declare a reference to a resource; @Resource can decorate a class, a field, or a method. The container will inject the resource referred to by @Resource into the component either at runtime or when the component is initialized, depending on whether field/method injection or class injection is used. With field-based and method-based injection, the container will inject the resource when the application is initialized. For class-based injection, the resource is looked up by the application at runtime.

The @Resource annotation has the following elements:

- name: The JNDI name of the resource
- type: The Java language type of the resource
- authenticationType: The authentication type to use for the resource
- shareable: Indicates whether the resource can be shared
- mappedName: A nonportable, implementation-specific name to which the resource should be mapped
- description: The description of the resource

The name element is the JNDI name of the resource and is optional for field-based and method-based injection. For field-based injection, the default name is the field name qualified by the class name. For method-based injection, the default name is the JavaBeans property name, based on the method qualified by the class name. The name element must be specified for class-based injection.

The type of resource is determined by one of the following:

- The type of the field the @Resource annotation is decorating for field-based injection
- The type of the JavaBeans property the @Resource annotation is decorating for method-based injection
- The type element of @Resource

For class-based injection, the type element is required.

The authenticationType element is used only for connection factory resources, such as the resources of a connector, also called the resource adapter, or data source. This element can be set to one of the javax.annotation.Resource.AuthenticationType enumerated type values: CONTAINER, the default, and APPLICATION.

The shareable element is used only for Object Resource Broker (ORB) instance resources or connection factory resource. This element indicates whether the resource can be shared between this component and other components and may be set to true, the default, or false.

The mappedName element is a nonportable, implementation-specific name to which the resource should be mapped. Because the name element, when specified or defaulted, is local only to the application, many Java EE servers provide a way of referring to resources across the application server. This is done by setting the mappedName element. Use of the mappedName element is nonportable across Java EE server implementations.

The description element is the description of the resource, typically in the default language of the system on which the application is deployed. This element is used to help identify resources and to help application developers choose the correct resource.

Field-Based Injection

To use field-based resource injection, declare a field and decorate it with the @Resource annotation. The container will infer the name and type of the resource if the name and type elements are not specified. If you do specify the type element, it must match the field's type declaration.

In the following code, the container infers the name of the resource, based on the class name and the field name: com.example.SomeClass/myDB. The inferred type is javax.sql.DataSource.class:

```
package com.example;

public class SomeClass {
    @Resource
    private javax.sql.DataSource myDB;
...
}
```

In the following code, the JNDI name is `customerDB`, and the inferred type is `javax.sql.DataSource.class`:

```
package com.example;

public class SomeClass {
    @Resource(name="customerDB")
    private javax.sql.DataSource myDB;
...
}
```

Method-Based Injection

To use method-based injection, declare a setter method and decorate it with the `@Resource` annotation. The container will infer the name and type of the resource if the name and type elements are not specified. The setter method must follow the JavaBeans conventions for property names: The method name must begin with `set`, have a void return type, and only one parameter. If you do specify the type element, it must match the field's type declaration.

In the following code, the container infers the name of the resource based on the class name and the field name: `com.example.SomeClass/myDB`. The inferred type is `javax.sql.DataSource.class`:

```
package com.example;

public class SomeClass {

    private javax.sql.DataSource myDB;
...
    @Resource
    private void setMyDB(javax.sql.DataSource ds) {
        myDB = ds;
    }
...
}
```

In the following code, the JNDI name is `customerDB`, and the inferred type is `javax.sql.DataSource.class`:

```
package com.example;

public class SomeClass {
```

```
        private javax.sql.DataSource myDB;
    ...
        @Resource(name="customerDB")
        private void setMyDB(javax.sql.DataSource ds) {
            myDB = ds;
        }
    ...
    }
```

Class-Based Injection

To use class-based injection, decorate the class with a @Resource annotation, and set the required name and type elements:

```
@Resource(name="myMessageQueue",
                type="javax.jms.ConnectionFactory")
public class SomeMessageBean {
...
}
```

The @Resources annotation is used to group together multiple @Resource declarations for class-based injection. The following code shows the @Resources annotation containing two @Resource declarations. One is a Java Message Service message queue, and the other is a JavaMail session:

```
@Resources({
    @Resource(name="myMessageQueue",
                    type="javax.jms.ConnectionFactory"),
    @Resource(name="myMailSession",
                    type="javax.mail.Session")
})
public class SomeMessageBean {
...
}
```

Resource Adapters and Contracts

A resource adapter is a Java EE component that implements the Java EE Connector Architecture for a specific EIS. Examples of EISs include enterprise resource planning, mainframe transaction processing, and database systems. As illustrated in Figure 28–1, the resource adapter facilitates communication between a Java EE application and an EIS.

FIGURE 28–1 Resource Adapters

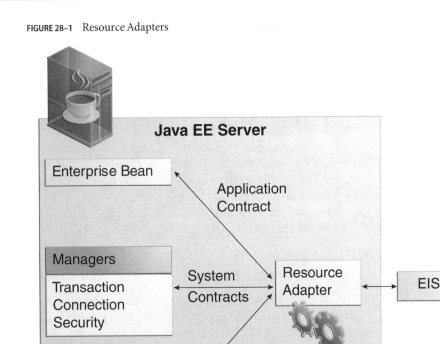

Stored in a Resource Adapter Archive (RAR) file, a resource adapter can be deployed on any Java EE server, much like a Java EE application. A RAR file may be contained in an Enterprise Archive (EAR) file, or it may exist as a separate file.

A resource adapter is analogous to a JDBC driver. Both provide a standard API through which an application can access a resource that is outside the Java EE server. For a resource adapter, the target system is an EIS; for a JDBC driver, it is a DBMS. Resource adapters and JDBC drivers are rarely created by application developers. In most cases, both types of software are built by vendors that sell tools, servers, or integration software.

The resource adapter mediates communication between the Java EE server and the EIS by means of contracts. The application contract defines the API through which a Java EE component, such as an enterprise bean, accesses the EIS. This API is the only view that the component has of the EIS. The system contracts link the resource adapter to important services that are managed by the Java EE server. The resource adapter itself and its system contracts are transparent to the Java EE component.

Management Contracts

The Java EE Connector Architecture defines system contracts that enable resource adapter lifecycle and thread management.

Lifecycle Management

The Connector Architecture specifies a lifecycle management contract that allows an application server to manage the lifecycle of a resource adapter. This contract provides a mechanism for the application server to bootstrap a resource adapter instance during the deployment or application server startup. This contract also provides a means for the application server to notify the resource adapter instance when it is undeployed or when an orderly shutdown of the application server takes place.

Work Management Contract

The Connector Architecture work management contract ensures that resource adapters use threads in the proper, recommended manner. This contract also enables an application server to manage threads for resource adapters.

Resource adapters that improperly use threads can jeopardize the entire application server environment. For example, a resource adapter might create too many threads or might not properly release threads it has created. Poor thread handling inhibits application server shutdown and impacts the application server's performance because creating and destroying threads are expensive operations.

The work management contract establishes a means for the application server to pool and reuse threads, similar to pooling and reusing connections. By adhering to this contract, the resource adapter does not have to manage threads itself. Instead, the resource adapter has the application server create and provide needed threads. When it is finished with a given thread, the resource adapter returns the thread to the application server. The application server manages the thread, either returning it to a pool for later reuse or destroying it. Handling threads in this manner results in increased application server performance and more efficient use of resources.

In addition to moving thread management to the application server, the Connector Architecture provides a flexible model for a resource adapter that uses threads.

- The requesting thread can choose to block (stop its own execution) until the work thread completes.

- The requesting thread can block while it waits to get the work thread. When the application server provides a work thread, the requesting thread and the work thread execute in parallel.

- The resource adapter can opt to submit the work for the thread to a queue. The thread executes the work from the queue at some later point. The resource adapter continues its own execution from the point it submitted the work to the queue, no matter when the thread executes it.

With the latter two approaches, the submitting thread and the work thread may execute simultaneously or independently. For these approaches, the contract specifies a listener mechanism to notify the resource adapter that the thread has completed its operation. The resource adapter can also specify the execution context for the thread, and the work management contract controls the context in which the thread executes.

Generic Work Context Contract

The work management contract between the application server and a resource adapter enables a resource adapter to do a task, such as communicating with the EIS or delivering messages, by delivering Work instances for execution.

A generic work context contract enables a resource adapter to control the contexts in which the Work instances that it submits are executed by the application server's WorkManager. A generic work context mechanism also enables an application server to support new message inflow and delivery schemes. It also provides a richer contextual Work execution environment to the resource adapter while still maintaining control over concurrent behavior in a managed environment.

The generic work context contract standardizes the transaction context and the security context.

Outbound and Inbound Contracts

The Connector Architecture defines the following outbound contracts, system-level contracts between an application server and an EIS that enable outbound connectivity to an EIS.

- The connection management contract supports connection pooling, a technique that enhances application performance and scalability. Connection pooling is transparent to the application, which simply obtains a connection to the EIS.

- The transaction management contract extends the connection management contract and provides support for management of both local and XA transactions.

  A local transaction is limited in scope to a single EIS system, and the EIS resource manager itself manages such transaction. An XA transaction or global transaction can span multiple resource managers. This form of transaction requires transaction coordination by an external transaction manager, typically bundled with an application server. A transaction manager uses a two-phase commit protocol to manage a transaction that spans multiple resource managers or EISs, and uses one-phase commit optimization if only one resource manager is participating in an XA transaction.

- The security management contract provides mechanisms for authentication, authorization, and secure communication between a Java EE server and an EIS to protect the information in the EIS.

    A work security map matches EIS identities to the application server domain's identities.

Inbound contracts are system contracts between a Java EE server and an EIS that enable inbound connectivity from the EIS: pluggability contracts for message providers and contracts for importing transactions.

Metadata Annotations

Java EE Connector Architecture 1.6 introduces a set of annotations to minimize the need for deployment descriptors.

- The @Connector annotation can be used by the resource adapter developer to specify that the JavaBeans component is a resource adapter JavaBeans component. This annotation is used for providing metadata about the capabilities of the resource adapter. Optionally, you can provide a JavaBeans component implementing the ResourceAdapter interface, as in the following example:

```
@Connector(
    description = "Sample adapter using the JavaMail API",
    displayName = "InboundResourceAdapter",
    vendorName = "My Company, Inc.",
    eisType = "MAIL",
    version = "1.0"
)
public class ResourceAdapterImpl
        implements ResourceAdapter, java.io.Serializable {
    ...
    ...
}
```

- The @ConnectionDefinition annotation defines a set of connection interfaces and classes pertaining to a particular connection type, as in the following example:

```
@ConnectionDefinition(
    connectionFactory =
        samples.mailra..api.JavaMailConnectionFactory.class,
    connectionFactoryImpl =
        samples.mailra.ra.outbound.JavaMailConnectionFactoryImpl.class,
    connection =
        samples.connectors.mailconnector.api.JavaMailConnection.class,
    connectionImpl =
        samples.mailra..ra.outbound.JavaMailConnectionImpl.class
)
```

```
public class ManagedConnectionFactoryImpl implements
        ManagedConnectionFactory, Serializable {
    ...
    ...
    @ConfigProperty(defaultValue = "UnknownHostName")
    public void setServerName(String serverName) {
        ...
    }
}
```

- The @AdministeredObject annotation designates a JavaBeans component as an administered object.

- The @Activation annotation contains configuration information pertaining to inbound connectivity from an EIS instance, as in the following example:

```
@Activation(
        messageListeners = {
                samples.mailra.api.JavaMailMessageListener.class
        }
)
public class ActivationSpecImpl
        implements javax.resource.spi.ActivationSpec,
                    java.io.Serializable {
    ...
    @ConfigProperty()
    // serverName property value
    private String serverName = new String("");

    @ConfigProperty()
    // userName property value
    private String userName = new String("");

    @ConfigProperty()
    // password property value
    private String password = new String("");

    @ConfigProperty()
    // folderName property value
    private String folderName = new String("Inbox");

    // protocol property value
    // Normally imap or pop3
    @ConfigProperty(
            description = "Normally imap or pop3"
    )
    private String protocol = new String("imap");
    ...
    ...
}
```

- The @ConfigProperty annotation can be used on JavaBeans components to provide additional configuration information that may be used by the deployer and resource adapter provider. The preceding example code shows several @ConfigProperty annotations.

The specification allows a resource adapter to be developed in mixed-mode form, that is the ability for a resource adapter developer to use both metadata annotations and deployment descriptors in applications. An application assembler or deployer may use the deployment descriptor to override the metadata annotations specified by the resource adapter developer.

The deployment descriptor for a resource adapter is named `ra.xml`. The `metadata-complete` attribute defines whether the deployment descriptor for the resource adapter module is complete or whether the class files available to the module and packaged with the resource adapter need to be examined for annotations that specify deployment information.

For the complete list of annotations and JavaBeans components introduced in the Java EE 6 platform, see the Java EE Connector Architecture 1.6 specification.

Common Client Interface

This section explains how components use the Connector Architecture Common Client Interface (CCI) API and a resource adapter to access data from an EIS. The CCI API defines a set of interfaces and classes whose methods allow a client to perform typical data access operations. The CCI interfaces and classes are as follows:

- `ConnectionFactory`: Provides an application component with a `Connection` instance to an EIS.

- `Connection`: Represents the connection to the underlying EIS.

- `ConnectionSpec`: Provides a means for an application component to pass connection-request-specific properties to the `ConnectionFactory` when making a connection request.

- `Interaction`: Provides a means for an application component to execute EIS functions, such as database stored procedures.

- `InteractionSpec`: Holds properties pertaining to an application component's interaction with an EIS.

- `Record`: The superinterface for the various kinds of record instances. Record instances can be `MappedRecord`, `IndexedRecord`, or `ResultSet` instances, all of which inherit from the `Record` interface.

- `RecordFactory`: Provides an application component with a `Record` instance.

- `IndexedRecord`: Represents an ordered collection of `Record` instances based on the `java.util.List` interface.

A client or application component that uses the CCI to interact with an underlying EIS does so in a prescribed manner. The component must establish a connection to the EIS's resource manager, and it does so using the `ConnectionFactory`. The `Connection` object represents the connection to the EIS and is used for subsequent interactions with the EIS.

The component performs its interactions with the EIS, such as accessing data from a specific table, using an `Interaction` object. The application component defines the Interaction object by using an `InteractionSpec` object. When it reads data from the EIS, such as from database tables, or writes to those tables, the application component does so by using a particular type of `Record` instance: a `MappedRecord`, an `IndexedRecord`, or a `ResultSet` instance.

Note, too, that a client application that relies on a CCI resource adapter is very much like any other Java EE client that uses enterprise bean methods.

Further Information about Resources

For more information about resources and annotations, see

- Java EE 6 Platform Specification (JSR 316):

  `http://jcp.org/en/jsr/detail?id=316`

- Java EE Connector Architecture 1.6 specification:

  `http://jcp.org/en/jsr/detail?id=322`

- EJB 3.1 specification:

  `http://jcp.org/en/jsr/detail?id=318`

- Common Annotations for the Java Platform:

  `http://www.jcp.org/en/jsr/detail?id=250`

Index

getConnection method, 530
getRemoteUser method, 471
getRequestDispatcher method, 191
getRollbackOnly method, 525
getServletContext method, 193
getSession method, 193
getStatus method, 525
getUserPrincipal method, 471
GlassFish Server
    adding users to, 445–446
    downloading, 38
    enabling debugging, 46
    installation tips, 38
    securing, 440–441
    server log, 45–46
    SSL connectors, 450
    starting, 41
    stopping, 42
    tools, 34–35
groups, 444
    managing, 444–446

H

hashCode method, 340
header parameters, 234
helper classes, 258
    session bean example, 276
HTTP, 207
    basic authentication, 462
    over SSL, 465
HTTP methods, 226–229
HTTP request URLs, 185
    query strings, 186
    request paths, 185
HTTP requests, 185
    See also requests
HTTP responses, 186
    See also responses
    status codes, 67–68
HTTPS, 437, 450, 451, 459–460
HttpServlet interface, 180
HttpServletRequest interface, 185, 471
HttpServletResponse interface, 186

HttpSession interface, 193

I

identification, 434–435
implicit navigation, 76
include method, 192
init method, 184
InitialContext interface, 32
initParams attribute, 184
injectable objects, 308
integrity, 449
    of data, 434
internationalizing JavaServer Faces applications,
    FacesContext.getLocale method, 148
invalidate method, 194
isCallerInRole method, 493–494
isUserInRole method, 471

J

JAAS, 33, 435, 505
    login modules, 505
JACC, 30, 441
JAF, 32
JAR files, 17
    query language, 396
JAR signatures, 436
JASPIC, 30–31
Java API for JavaBeans Validation, *See* Bean
    Validation
Java API for XML Binding, 33
Java API for XML Processing, 32
Java API for XML Web Services, *See* JAX-WS
Java Authentication and Authorization
    Service, 435
    See also JAAS
Java Authentication Service Provider Interface for
    Containers, 30–31
Java Authorization Contract for Containers, 30
    See also JACC
Java BluePrints, 44
Java Cryptography Extension (JCE), 435

FREE Online Edition

Your purchase of *The Java EE 6 Tutorial* includes access to a free online edition for 45 days through the Safari Books Online subscription service. Nearly every Addison-Wesley Professional book is available online through Safari Books Online, along with more than 5,000 other technical books and videos from publishers such as Cisco Press, Exam Cram, IBM Press, O'Reilly, Prentice Hall, Que, and Sams.

SAFARI BOOKS ONLINE allows you to search for a specific answer, cut and paste code, download chapters, and stay current with emerging technologies.

Activate your FREE Online Edition at
www.informit.com/safarifree

> **STEP 1:**   Enter the coupon code: JYSIQVH.

> **STEP 2:**   New Safari users, complete the brief registration form.
>   Safari subscribers, just log in.

If you have difficulty registering on Safari or accessing the online edition, please e-mail customer-service@safaribooksonline.com